Workshop Manual

BMW 2000 & 2002 1966-1976

A Floyd CLYMER Publication by:
www.VelocePress.com
Copyright 2017 Veloce Enterprises

INTRODUCTION

Welcome to the world of digital publishing ~ the book you now hold in your hand, was printed using the latest state of the art digital technology. The advent of print-on-demand has forever changed the publishing process, never has information been so accessible and it is our hope that this book serves your informational needs for years to come. If this is your first exposure to digital publishing, we hope that you are pleased with the results. Many more titles of interest to the classic automobile and motorcycle enthusiast, collector and restorer are available via our website at www.VelocePress.com. We hope that you find this title as interesting as we do.

NOTE FROM THE PUBLISHER

The information presented is true and complete to the best of our knowledge. All recommendations are made without any guarantees on the part of the author or the publisher, who also disclaim all liability incurred with the use of this information.

TRADEMARKS

We recognize that some words, model names and designations, for example, mentioned herein are the property of the trademark holder. We use them for identification purposes only. This is not an official publication.

INFORMATION ON THE USE OF THIS PUBLICATION

This manual is an invaluable resource for those interested in performing their own maintenance. However, in today's information age we are constantly subject to changes in common practice, new technology, availability of improved materials and increased awareness of chemical toxicity. As such, it is advised that the user consult with an experienced professional prior to undertaking any procedure described herein. While every care has been taken to ensure correctness of information, it is obviously not possible to guarantee complete freedom from errors or omissions or to accept liability arising from such errors or omissions. Therefore, any individual that uses the information contained within, or elects to perform or participate in do-it-yourself repairs or modifications acknowledges that there is a risk factor involved and that the publisher or its associates cannot be held responsible for personal injury or property damage resulting from the use of the information or the outcome of such procedures.

WARNING!

One final word of advice, this publication is intended to be used as a reference guide, and when in doubt the reader should consult with a qualified technician.

INDEX

ENGINE - Page 1

1 : 1 Description
1 : 2 Engine removing & refitting
1 : 3 Cylinder head removing & refitting
1 : 4 Camshaft removing & refitting
1 : 5 Cylinder head dismantling & reassembly
1 : 6 Cylinder head overhaul
1 : 7 Timing chain & timing gear
1 : 8 Pistons, rings & connecting rods
1 : 9 Flywheel removing & refitting
1 : 10 Crankshaft removing & refitting
1 : 11 Cylinder block & crankcase
1 : 12 Oil pump removing & refitting
1 : 13 Oil pump overhaul
1 : 14 Fullflow filter
1 : 15 Factory exchange engine installation
1 : 16 Exhaust emission control system
1 : 17 Evaporative control system
1 : 18 Fault diagnosis
1 : 19 Technical data

FUEL SYSTEM - Page 25

2 : 1 Description
2 : 2 Fuel pump operating principle
2 : 3 Fuel system maintenance
2 : 4 Fuel pump removing & dismantling
2 : 5 Fuel pump reassembly, refitting & adjustment

Solex 40.PDSI & 40.PDSIT carburetter
2 : 6 Removing & refitting
2 : 7 Operation & adjustment

Solex 40.PHH dual carburetters
2 : 8 Removing & refitting
2 : 9 Operation & adjustment

Solex 40.PDSIT automatic choke carburetter
2 : 10 Operation & adjustment
2 : 11 Air cleaner
2 : 12 Automatic air intake preheat flap
2 : 13 Fuel tank
2 : 14 Fuel injection system

Solex 32/32 DIDTA carburetter
2 : 15 Operation & adjustment
2 : 16 Fault diagnosis
2 : 17 Technical data

IGNITION SYSTEM - Page 39

3 : 1 Description
3 : 2 Maintaining the ignition system
3 : 3 Troubleshooting the ignition system
3 : 4 Distributor removing, overhaul & refitting
3 : 5 Timing the ignition
3 : 6 Spark plugs & H.T. leads
3 : 7 Fault diagnosis
3 : 8 Technical data

COOLING SYSTEM - Page 43

4 : 1 Description
4 : 2 Maintaining the cooling system
4 : 3 Troubleshooting the cooling system
4 : 4 Radiator removing & refitting
4 : 5 Fan belt adjusting & replacing
4 : 6 Water pump removing & refitting
4 : 7 Water pump overhaul
4 : 8 Thermostat removing & refitting
4 : 9 Cold weather precautions
4 : 10 Fault Diagnosis
4 : 11 Technical data

CLUTCH - Page 49

5 : 1 Description
5 : 2 Removing & refitting the clutch
5 : 3 Servicing the clutch components
5 : 4 Servicing the hydraulic system
5 : 5 Bleeding the hydraulic system
5 : 6 Clutch pedal removing & refitting
5 : 7 Self-adjusting diaphragm clutch
5 : 8 Fault diagnosis
5 : 9 Technical data

MANUAL GEARBOX - Page 57

6 : 1 Description
6 : 2 Gearbox removing & refitting
6 : 3 Gearbox disassembly
6 : 4 Synchromesh components
6 : 5 Output shaft & speedometer drive
6 : 6 Layshaft
6 : 7 Third & fourth speed pinion sets
6 : 8 Output shaft grooved bearing
6 : 9 Selector shafts & forks
6 : 10 Refitting input shaft
6 : 11 Fault diagnosis
6 : 12 Technical data

AUTOMATIC GEARBOX - Page 69

6A : 1 Description
6A : 2 Mechanical power flow
6A : 3 Troubleshooting & testing procedure
6A : 4 Throttle linkage adjustment
6A : 5 Gearchange point adjustment
6A : 6 Selector lever adjustment
6A : 7 Removing & refitting gearbox
6A : 8 Fault diagnosis
6A : 9 Technical data

PROPELLER SHAFT - Page 79
REAR AXLE & REAR SUSPENSION

7 : 1 Propeller shaft overhaul
7 : 2 Rear axle removing & refitting
7 : 3 Rear axle carrier removing & refitting
7 : 4 Trailing arm overhaul
7 : 5 Halfshaft overhaul
7 : 6 Shock absorber removing & refitting
7 : 7 Universal joint overhaul
7 : 8 Final drive unit removing & refitting
7 : 9 Differential housing removing & refitting
7 : 10 Differential overhaul
7 : 11 Crownwheel & pinion removing & refitting
7 : 12 Crownwheel & pinion set-up
7 : 13 Fault diagnosis
7 : 14 Technical data

FRONT SUSPENSION & HUBS - Page 91

8 : 1 Description
8 : 2 Front axle carrier removing & refitting
8 : 3 Front axle carrier traction strut bearing
8 : 4 Wheel hub & bearing overhaul
8 : 5 Tie rod lever removing & refitting
8 : 6 Guide joint overhaul
8 : 7 Transverse swinging arm bearing
8 : 8 Anti roll bar removing & refitting
8 : 9 Shock absorber removing & refitting
8 : 10 Shock absorber support bearing overhaul
8 : 11 Shock absorber coil spring removing & refitting
8 : 12 Shock absorber removing & refitting
8 : 13 Fault diagnosis
8 : 14 Technical data

STEERING - Page 99

9 : 1 Description
9 : 2 Steering box removing & refitting
9 : 3 Steering box overhaul
9 : 4 Steering mechanism adjustment
9 : 5 Steering spindle bearing replacement
9 : 6 Steering guide lever removing & refitting
9 : 7 Checking & adjusting tracking
9 : 8 Lubrication
9 : 9 Fault diagnosis
9 : 10 Technical data

BRAKES (WHEELS & TYRES) - Page 105

10 : 1 Description
10 : 2 General & preventative maintenance
10 : 3 Brake pads removing & refitting
10 : 4 Brake calipers removing & refitting
10 : 5 Disc brake overhaul
10 : 6 Drum brake overhaul
10 : 7 Bleeding the hydraulic system
10 : 8 Master cylinder overhaul
10 : 9 Wheel cylinder overhaul
10 : 10 Flexible hose removal
10 : 11 Handbrake cable removing & refitting
10 : 12 Servo unit overhaul
10 : 13 Fault diagnosis
10 : 14 Technical data (including wheels & tyres)

ELECTRICAL SYSTEM - Page 117

11 : 1 Description
11 : 2 Battery maintenance
11 : 3 Alternator
11 : 4 Starter motor overhaul
11 : 5 Windscreen wiper motor removing & refitting
11 : 6 Fuel tank sender unit removing & refitting
11 : 7 Heated rear windshield
11 : 8 Headlamps maintenance
11 : 9 Lighting circuits troubleshooting
11 : 10 External electronic tuning system
11 : 11 Instrument panel
11 : 12 Fault diagnosis
11 : 13 Technical data
11 : 14 Wiring diagrams

BODYWORK - Page 147

12 : 1 Bodywork & accident repairs
12 : 2 Front door removing & refitting
12 : 3 Rear door removing & refitting
12 : 4 Front & rear windshield removing & refitting
12 : 5 Bonnet removing & refitting
12 : 6 Boot lid removing & refitting
12 : 7 Heated rear windshield
12 : 8 Sun roof removing & refitting
12 : 9 Heater removing & refitting

MAINTENANCE & LUBRICATION - Page 167

13 : 1 Routine maintenance
13 : 2 Approved lubricants
13 : 3 Weekly maintenance
13 : 4 Initial 600 mile or first month service
13 : 5 5,000 mile or 6 month maintenance schedule
13 : 6 10,000 mile or annual maintenance schedule
13 : 7 Every 2nd & 4th year maintenance schedule

CAPACITIES - Page 169
DIMENSIONS & TORQUE SETTINGS

14 : 1 Capacities
14 : 2 Dimensions
14 : 3 Torque settings

HISTORY & EVOLUTION OF THE 2000 & 2002 SERIES

The BMW 1500-2002 Series was initially introduced as a 1500 version in September 1961.

During 1964, the cylinder block bore diameter was increased by 2mm; the body and interior trim was restyled and, in April of that same year, 13 inch wheels were added. All of these modifications resulted in the 'new' 1600 4-door saloon with a 2-door version being released in 1966.

Interestingly, many of the mechanical components used in the 1500/1600 Series are shared with the 1800 and ultimately the 2000 & 2002. However, there were a number of technological advancements made over the period of the production run. Some of the more significant were:

March 1969: Self adjusting clutch, dual braking system and wider pedals.

August 1969: Servo assisted brakes became standard equipment.

October 1970: External electronic tuning system added.

The 2002 version of the series was introduced in March 1968. While the 2002 is comparable in many respects, the increased performance of the larger engine makes the 2002 model the most collectible of a 15-year evolution of this series of BMW's.

Location of the Major Identification Numbers

Automatic Gearbox ID Number

Manufacturer's Plate & Chassis Number (Circled) - Located on RH outer edge of front wheel inner fender

Engine Number (Circled) - located on LH side of crankcase directly above starter motor

CHAPTER 1

ENGINE

1 : 1 Description
1 : 2 Engine removing & refitting
1 : 3 Cylinder head removing & refitting
1 : 4 Camshaft removing & refitting
1 : 5 Cylinder head dismantling & reassembly
1 : 6 Cylinder head overhaul
1 : 7 Timing chain & timing gear
1 : 8 Pistons, rings & connecting rods
1 : 9 Flywheel removing & refitting
1 : 10 Crankshaft removing & refitting
1 : 11 Cylinder block & crankcase
1 : 12 Oil pump removing & refitting
1 : 13 Oil pump overhaul
1 : 14 Fullflow filter
1 : 15 Factory exchange engine installation
1 : 16 Exhaust emission control system
1 : 17 Evaporative control system
1 : 18 Fault diagnosis
1 : 19 Technical data

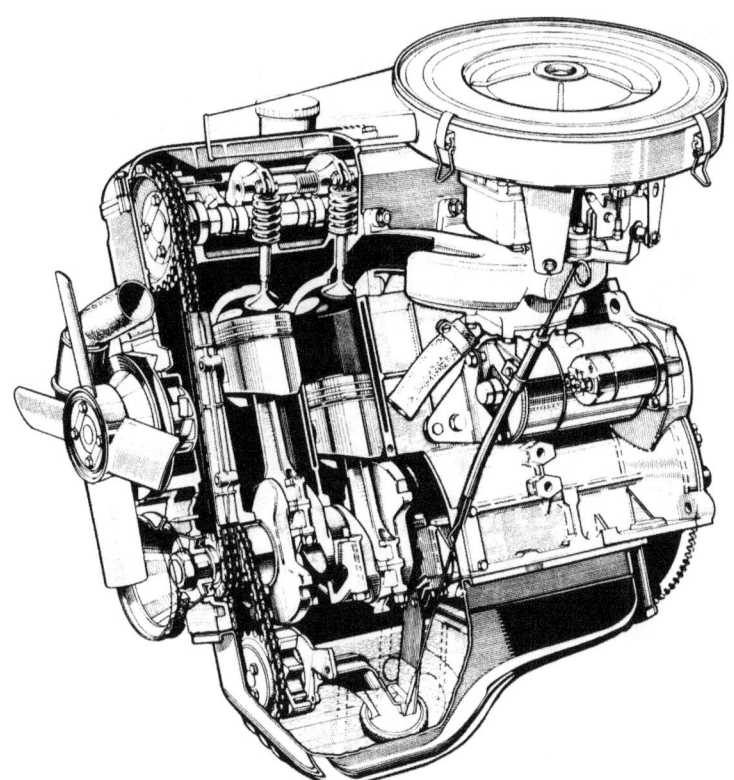

FIG 1:1 BMW 2000 engine

1 : 1 Description

The overhead camshaft engine as shown in **FIG 1:1** is of traditional BMW design and is located at the front of the car in unit with the gearbox. It is tilted to the right in the engine compartment at an angle of 30 deg. to allow for a better position enabling a lower body line to be styled, giving good visibility to the driver. The combustion chamber is of hemispherical swirl action design, with specially shaped piston crowns to give intensive swirl action and thorough ignition of the charge at all engine speeds giving greater engine flexibility.

A five main bearing crankshaft drives the overhead camshaft by a tensioned double tracked chain moving around the crankshaft and camshaft sprocket gears. The inlet and exhaust valves are set in line along the cylinder head and are of the inverted 'V' arrangement adding to the efficiency of the specially designed combustion chambers.

The offset gudgeon pins are retained in the piston using wire circlips. The pistons have two compression rings and one oil control ring, all three located above the gudgeon pin. The connecting rods are fitted with renewable bearing shells lined with a special alloy. The crankshaft runs in similar bearings but end thrust is taken by the centre main bearing which has flanges on either side.

Lubrication is effected using a rotor or gear driven pump located beneath the crankshaft and driven from the front end of the crankshaft by means of a single track chain. A micronic fullflow oil filter is used and the oil pressure controlled by a pressure relief valve located in the pump body.

1 : 2 Engine removing & refitting

The usual operations of decarbonizing and top overhaul can be done without removing the power unit.

It must be stressed that any supports used are firmly based and not likely to collapse during the operation or serious injury could result. To remove the engine proceed as follows:

1 Open the bonnet and cover both the wing surfaces with wing covers. Detach the earth cable from the battery. Mark the relative bonnet and hinge positions using a pencil and then remove the bonnet after releasing the hinge bolts.

2 Remove the radiator cap and open both the water drain cock at the base of the radiator and the drain cock located on the side of the cylinder block. Remove the air filter fastening bolts located on the inside wheel arch panel. Release the rubber manifold hose clamp using a screwdriver. Ease the breather tube away from the cylinder head cover. Lift away the air filter housing together with its hose from the preheated air regulation housing. Release the hose clamp on the front panel and remove the preheating air regulation housing together with its hose.

3 Release the radiator hose on the thermostat housing and also the radiator hose from the water pump. Unscrew the radiator mounting bolts from the front panel and carefully lift away the radiator. Carefully unscrew the thermostat contact from the housing and release it from the retaining clamps.

4 Disconnect the throttle linkage. Release the vacuum line from the check valve on the induction manifold. Carefully pull the fuel line from the fuel pump and

FIG 1:2 Cylinder head bolt tightening sequence

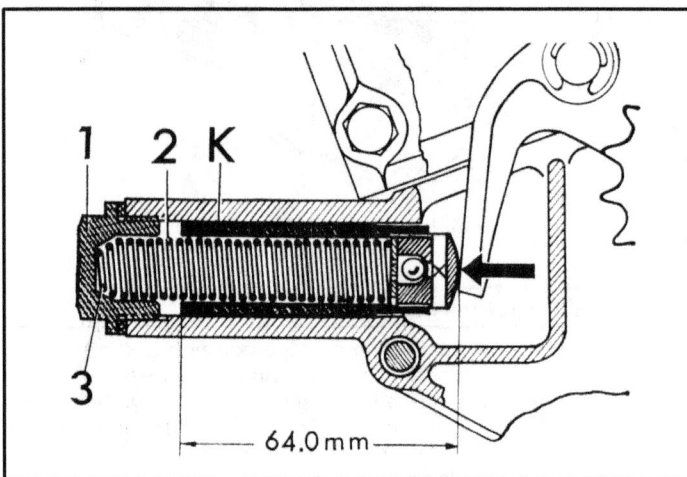

FIG 1:3 Tensioner piston assembly

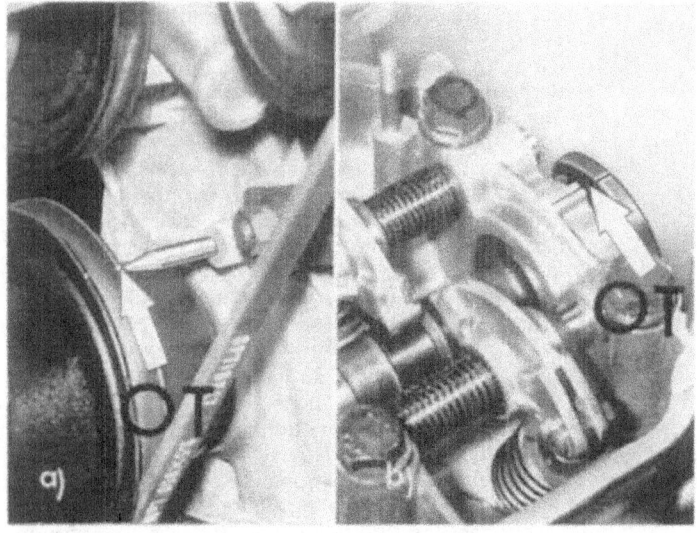

FIG 1:4 Camshaft timing marks

release it from its retaining support. Detach the Bowden cable from the lever at the side of the automatic choke using a pair of engineers pliers. Detach the Bowden cable sleeve from its holder and carefully pull out. Disconnect the auto-choke wire.

5 Carefully lift out the wiring from the cable clamping strap and disconnect the four wires from the alternator. Very carefully disconnect the plug connector from the solenoid switch, pull back the rubber cap and unscrew the fastening nut from the starter cable.

6 Detach the heater hose at the return flow union and from the cylinder head. Remove the earth strap on the engine/gearbox flange. Disconnect the low-tension cable at the side of the distributor and also the connector from the oil pressure warning switch. Carefully remove the high-tension cable from the centre of the ignition coil also release and remove the distributor cap and rotor arm.

7 Very carefully slide the outer rubber gaiter up the gear change lever, together with the foam rubber ring and inner gaiter. Lift the leaf spring out of the selector head and gently push the bolt and leaf spring out of the selector head.

8 Using a garage hydraulic jack, raise the vehicle and support on firmly based stands. Release the exhaust downpipe from the exhaust manifold flange and also the central silentbloc exhaust mounting. Remove the three exhaust silencer mounting bolts and lift away the silencer box.

9 Detach the propeller shaft from the rear of the gearbox by releasing the four self-locking nuts and bolts. It should be noted that the driven shaft within the gearbox is not secured and should be prevented from slipping out by tying it securely to the gearbox housing using a piece of wire. Locate and disconnect the reversing lamps switch terminals and also slacken the retaining screw holding the speedometer cable to the gearbox casing and gently pull out the speedometer cable. Release the fastening bolt for the retaining plate that holds the clutch hydraulic pipe to the gearbox. Release the return spring from the withdrawal arm. Carefully ease back the rubber cap from the clutch hydraulic slave cylinder and using a pair of circlip pliers remove the circlip from the slave cylinder. Carefully pull the slave cylinder forward and lift away the pushrod.

10 Using a garage crane or lifting tackle support the weight of the engine and remove the nuts from the lefthand engine mounting. Also remove the bolts from the righthand engine mounting. Using a garage hydraulic jack support the weight of the gearbox and remove the retaining bolt from the cap bearing from the rear gearbox mounting. Remove the two fastening bolts from the gearbox rear crossmember. Carefully lower the gearbox and lift away the engine.

Refitting the unit to the car:

Refitting is the reverse procedure to dismantling but the following points should be noted:

1 When reassembling the threaded pins of the exhaust manifold system always coat with Molykote paste to ensure ease of dismantling at a later time.

2 When assembling the selector head the bolt should be fitted from the righthand side. Check that the plastic

bushes in the selector head are not worn which, if evident, the bushes must be renewed.

3 When reconnecting the choke control lever, the signal contactor located on the dashboard must be pushed to its lowest position and the choke lever must lie up against the limit.

4 When refilling the cooling system the heater control lever should be set to the position 'hot'. Fill with water and replace the radiator cap and rotate until it engages in the second retaining notch. The water should then be allowed to heat up to its normal operating temperature of approximately 80°C. Once the thermostat has opened, place a large rag over the radiator cap and relieve the pressure by turning it back so that the cap engages in the first retaining notch. Finally check the water level and tighten down the radiator cap to its fully closed position.

1 : 3 Cylinder head removing & refitting

To remove the cylinder head proceed as follows:

1 Open the bonnet and using protective aprons cover the wing surfaces. Detach the earth cable from the battery. Open the radiator drain tap.

2 Carefully ease the breather tube away from the cylinder head cover. Remove the radiator hose from the thermostat housing. Remove the vacuum hose from the check valve. Release and remove the fuel supply hose from the fuel pump.

3 Carefully unscrew the thermostat contact from its location in the thermostat housing. Disconnect the throttle linkage and also the bowden cable from the automatic choke control lever using a pair of engineers pliers to hold the lever securely. Remove the bowden cable sleeve from the bowden cable pivot mounting and gently pull away.

4 Remove the water hose from the induction manifold. Release the dipstick holder fastening nut. Release the heater hose from the cylinder head.

5 Carefully remove the low-tension cable connector from the side of the distributor and also the connection to the oil pressure warning switch. Release and lift away the distributor cap and also the high-tension cable from the ignition coil. Note the position of the spark plug leads and remove these leads from the spark plugs.

6 Release the exhaust downpipe connection from the exhaust manifold flange. Remove the cylinder head cover retaining nuts and carefully lift away the cover together with its gasket.

7 Rotate the engine so that No. 1 cylinder is at top dead centre which is indicated by the pointer being opposite the second notch in the drive pulley. The notch in the camshaft flange must also coincide with the notch marked at the top of the cylinder head. See **FIG 1 : 8**.

8 Release the eight bolts retaining the top camshaft sprocket cover and lift away. Loosen the camshaft drive chain tensioner closure plug and unscrew by hand with extreme caution as this is under the influence of heavy pressure. With the plug removed take out the spring and the piston (see **FIG 1 : 3**).

9 To remove the camshaft drive sprocket bend back the lockplate corners away from the retaining bolts and remove the fastening bolts. Carefully lift away the sprocket and using a piece of wire tie up the chain

FIG 1:5 Top gear cover

FIG 1:6 Camshaft sprocket removal

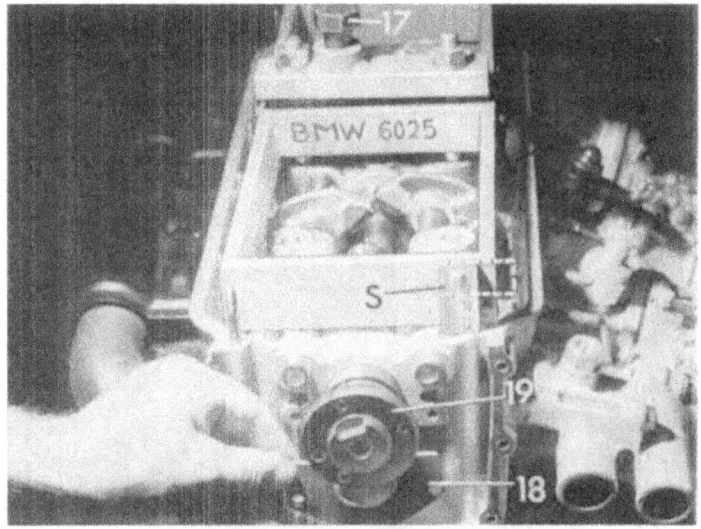

FIG 1:7 Compression frame in position on head

FIG 1:8 Camshaft timing marks

FIG 1:9 Valve clearance adjustment

FIG 1:10 Eccentric adjustment

onto the side of the alternator to ensure that it does not drop and become disengaged from the crankshaft.

10 Remove the cylinder head retaining bolts in the reverse order shown in **FIG 1:2** and carefully lift away the cylinder head. Also lift away the cylinder head gasket taking care not to damage it so that it can be inspected if necessary.

Reassembly:

Reassembly is the reverse procedure to dismantling. The following points however should be noted:

1 Before reassembling the cylinder head to the cylinder block, all the mating surfaces must be perfectly clean. Ensure that the cylinder head bolt threads are free from dirt.

2 Only BMW cylinder head gaskets are to be used and must be checked to ensure that all cooling waterways holes match up with those on the cylinder block. The TI cylinder head gasket may be fitted to the single carburetter engines but under no circumstances fit the single carburetter engine gasket to the TI.

3 The cylinder head bolts must be tightened in the sequence shown in **FIG 1:2** in three stages as follows:

1st .. 25 to 32 lb ft   2nd .. 43 to 47 lb ft
3rd .. 53 to 55 lb ft

Run the engine up to operating temperature, allow it to cool down to 35°C (95°F) and then tighten finally to the torque specified for stage 3.

After running the car for about 600 miles the bolts should be retightened after first slackening them slightly.

4 When refitting the camshaft drive sprocket to the camshaft the work will be made easier if the chain tensioner is relieved by inserting a screwdriver between the tensioning arm and the timing chain gearbox cover. It should be noted that if the timing chain tensioner is of the sprocket type only pistons of 2.519 inch (64 mm) in length should be installed otherwise the timing chain could be very noisy in operation or it could slip (see **FIG 1:3**). Piston size for tensioning strip should be 2.441 inch (62 mm). Upon reassembly the chain tensioner should be bled preferably before the camshaft sprocket is replaced. To do this lay the piston with its recess against the tensioning arm in its housing, carefully slide in the spring with the taper wound end resting inside the closure plug and using an oil can completely fill the housing with oil. Lightly screw home the closure plug. Using a screwdriver move the tensioning arm to and fro until oil starts to issue from the closure plug. Then hold the tensioning lever breast forward and tighten the closure plug.

If a timing chain tensioner of the tensioning rail type is fitted, bleed the piston by moving the rail backwards and forwards until oil emerges from the closure plug. In both cases tighten the closure plug to a torque wrench setting of between 22 to 29 lb ft. Once the tensioner has been reassembled correctly, the camshaft should be rotated until the notch marked in the camshaft flange is opposite to the notch marked on the top of the cylinder head (see **FIG 1:4**). Then mount the sprocket with the chain fitted onto the camshaft flange and reassemble the four retaining bolts together with their lockplates.

5 The gearbox top cover and mating surfaces should be thoroughly clean and dry and then coated with a fine

layer of Atmosit and fitted into place. Locate the two bolts holding the upper and lower gearbox casing together and just tighten. Follow by replacing the remaining six bolts checking on the final tightness of the first two bolts that were inserted. This will ensure that no oil leaks occur when the engine is back in service.
6 Upon reassembling the threaded pins of the exhaust manifold system always coat with Molykote paste to ensure ease of dismantling at a later time.
7 When reassembling the bowden cable to the choke lever always ensure that the choke lever is up against its limit stop and that the signal contact on the dashboard is pressed down into its lowest position. This will ensure correct control.

1 : 4 Camshaft removing & refitting

To remove the camshaft proceed as follows:
1 Open the bonnet and cover the wing surfaces with wing covers. Detach the earth cable from the battery. Remove the air filter, cylinder head cover hose connection and manifold hose connection, electrical cable connections to the distributor and oil pressure switch. Disconnect the accelerator linkage, the choke control cable and the fuel supply line to the fuel pump. Remove the fuel pump, the distributor and the thermometer connection.
2 Disconnect the exhaust downpipe at the exhaust manifold flange. Remove the cylinder head cover and the upper timing chain cover, releasing the bolts in the order shown in **FIG 1 : 5**.
3 Release the lockplates of the camshaft sprocket retaining bolts and remove the four bolts. Inspect the chain tensioner and if it is of the sprocket type insert a screwdriver between the tensioner sprocket and the timing case cover and then carefully lift away the camshaft sprocket as shown in **FIG 1 : 6**.
4 Unscrew the cylinder head retaining bolts as shown in **FIG 1 : 2** and detach the splash oil pipe running the length of the cylinder head.
5 It is recommended that BMW tool 6025 is used for the dismantling of the cylinder head otherwise unnecessary damage could be caused to the various components. Place the cylinder head onto the rocker clamp and locate the compression frame in position as shown in **FIG 1 : 7**. On all 2000 engines the cams E for the No. 2 cylinder inlet and exhaust valves must be adjusted to maximum valve operating clearance before the compression frame is fitted into position. Secure it and swing down the two supports **S**. Screw up the bolt 17 until the camshaft can be withdrawn after first removing the guide plate.

Reassembly:

Reassembly is the reverse procedure to dismantling but the following points should be noted:
1 Upon reassembling the camshaft to the engine ensure that No. 1 cylinder is at TDC and that the notch on the camshaft flange is correctly aligned, with the mark on the top of the cylinder head (see **FIG 1 : 8**).
2 Ensure that the mating surfaces on the upper and lower timing case covers and the cylinder head are thoroughly clean and then coat with a thin layer of Atmosit, then screw up the two bolts clamping the upper and lower

FIG 1:11 Tensioner sprocket retaining clip

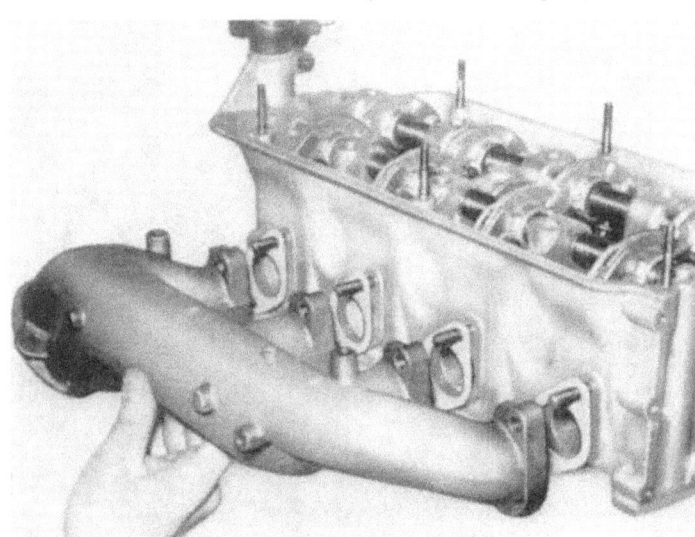

FIG 1:12 Exhaust manifold removal

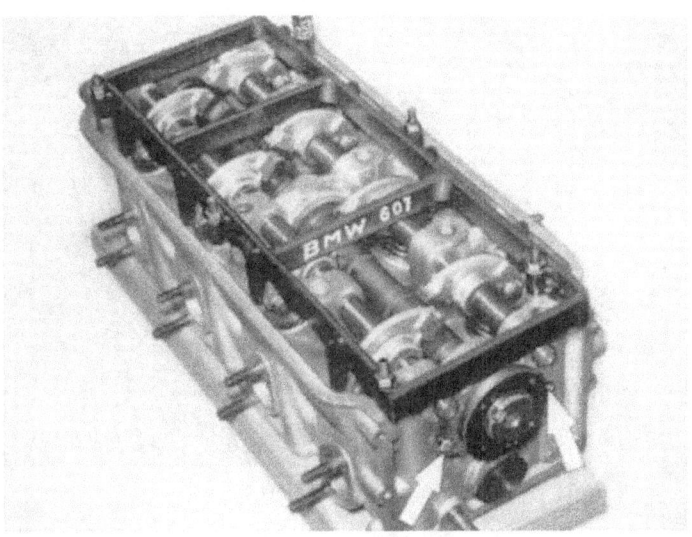

FIG 1:13 Rocker arm holder in position

FIG 1:14 Camshaft guide plate

FIG 1:15 Rocker shaft removal

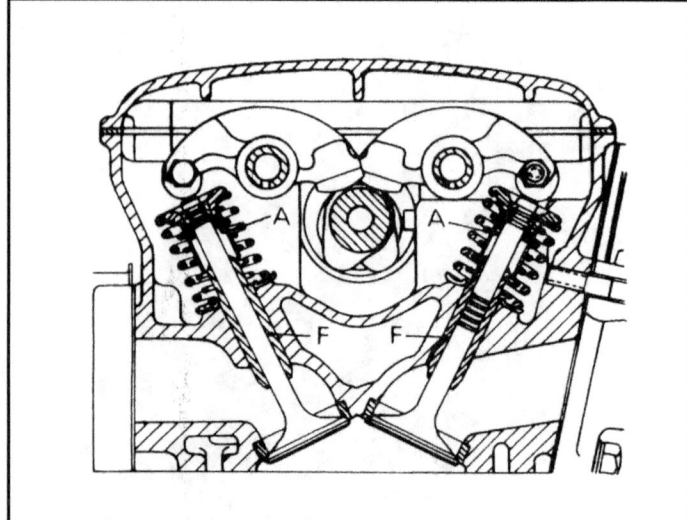

FIG 1:16 Overhead valve layout

case covers together and replace the six retaining bolts to the front of the cylinder head. Finally check the tightness of the first two bolts inserted. This will ensure that there are no oil leaks in service.

3 When reassembling the exhaust downpipe to the manifold coat the threads with Molykote G paste to ensure ease of dismantling at a later time.

Valve clearance adjustment:

The overhead valve clearance must be adjusted whilst the engine is at operating temperature. To complete the adjustment proceed as follows:

1 Turn the engine until both valves on No. 1 cylinder are closed. In this position the timing marks will be at TDC (see **FIGS 1:47** and **1:49**). There will be a clearance between the rocker arms and the tops of the valve stems and the two valves on No. 4 will be overlapping. Overlapping means that they are both open by an equal amount; one just opening and the other just closing.

2 Use a feeler gauge as shown in **FIG 1:10** to measure the clearance on No.1 valves. This should be between .15 and .20 mm (.0059 and .0079 inch).

3 To adjust the clearance use a ring spanner and loosen the locknut as shown in **FIG 1:9**. Turn the eccentric slightly using a piece of strong wire, as shown in **FIG 1:10** and recheck clearance with feeler gauge. Continue adjustment until clearance is correct.

4 To lock the eccentric, hold in place at its correct position and tighten the locknut.

5 When No. 1 cylinder valves are correct, proceed to turn the engine to Nos. 3, 4 and 2 in that order and measure, and adjust if necessary, the remaining valve clearances. When all clearances are correct refit the cylinder head cover, run the engine and check for oil leaks.

1:5 Cylinder head dismantling & reassembly

To dismantle the cylinder head it should first be removed from the engine as detailed in **Section 1:3** and then proceed as follows:

1 Remove the retaining spring clip from the tensioning lever of the sprocket type timing chain tensioner if fitted, and pull off the tensioning lever together with the wheel (see **FIG 1:11**).

2 Carefully place the cylinder head on a soft wood base on the work bench and remove the guide jacket bolts and lift away the guide jacket. Release the exhaust manifold nuts and lift away the manifold.

3 Remove the two nuts holding the fuel pump to the cylinder head and lift away the fuel pump. Release the fastening nuts from the thermostat housing and the induction manifold and lift away the thermostat housing together with the induction manifold.

4 Remove the distributor clamp bolt and lift out the distributor. Release the four retaining bolts holding the distributor flange casting to the front of the cylinder head and lift away.

5 Remove the spark plugs and release the fastening bolts from the guide plates. Attach the rocker arm holder BMW tool 601 as shown in **FIG 1:13** and tighten the nuts evenly until the camshaft is free. Carefully lift away the camshaft and remove the guide plate. Remove the rocker arm holding tool BMW.601 and push the rocker arms and thrust rings on the rocker shaft far enough to one side to permit removal of the retaining

circlips. Using a suitably sized drift drive the rocker shafts out towards the front of the cylinder head as shown in **FIG 1:15**.

6 Using BMW valve lifter 602 remove the valves and valve springs.

Reassembly:

Reassembly is the reverse procedure to dismantling but the following points should be noted:

1 The rocker shafts should be correctly aligned enabling the cylinder head bolts to be correctly refitted (see **FIG 1:15**).

2 Upon reassembling the camshaft, the guide plate F (see **FIG 1:14**), also serves to retain the rocker shafts 'K'. The groove must be aligned to be in contact with the cylinder head and the inner edges of guide plate F must be clean and free from bruising. Once the guide plate has been assembled the camshaft must still be able to revolve freely. Position the camshaft so ensuring the notch in the camshaft flange is opposite to the notch made in the cylinder head as shown in **FIG 1:4**.

3 The mating faces of the distributor flange and the cylinder head front face must be coated with a non-hardening sealing compound. The distributor must be replaced so that the vacuum chamber is facing away from the engine and to the right of the car. Finally reset the ignition timing as detailed in **Chapter 3**.

4 Before refitting the fuel pump ensure that the companion flange is not damaged and that the insulation flange thickness with gaskets and plunger length are correct to specification. Refer to **Section 2:5** for full information.

1:6 Cylinder head overhaul

1 Remove the cylinder head and camshaft as detailed in the previous Section. If decarbonizing is intended, plug all the waterways in the top face of the cylinder block with pieces of rag. Scrape the carbon from the combustion spaces in the head before removing the valves to avoid damage to the seats.

2 **FIG 1:16** shows the valve assembly as assembled into the cylinder head. To remove the valves use BMW valve lifter 602. Remove the valve after marking it to ensure correct reassembly. Clean the ports free from carbon and examine the valve seats and stems.

3 The valve stems must not show any signs of 'picking up' or wear, neither should they be bent. If satisfactory, but the valve seats show pitting too deep for removal by grinding paste, have the seats reground at a garage. If the seat is too far gone or has been burnt, fit new valves. Cylinder head seatings may also be badly worn or pitted and these may be recut once the glass—hard glaze has been removed. If the seats are then too wide they can be reduced by using a special facing cutter. Seatings which are beyond recutting can be restored by having special inserts fitted.

4 To grind-in valves put a light spring under the head of the valve and use a medium-grey carborundum paste unless the seats are in very good condition, when fine-grade paste may be used at once. Use a suction cup tool and grind with a semi-rotary movement, letting the valve rise off the seat occasionally by pressure of the spring under the head. Use grinding paste sparingly. When both seats have a smooth grey matt finish clean away every trace of the grinding paste from both the port and valve.

FIG 1:17 Timing gear front cover retaining bolts

FIG 1:18 Fan pulley assembly

FIG 1:19 Water pump pulley removal

FIG 1:20 Timing gear tensioner and crankshaft oil seal

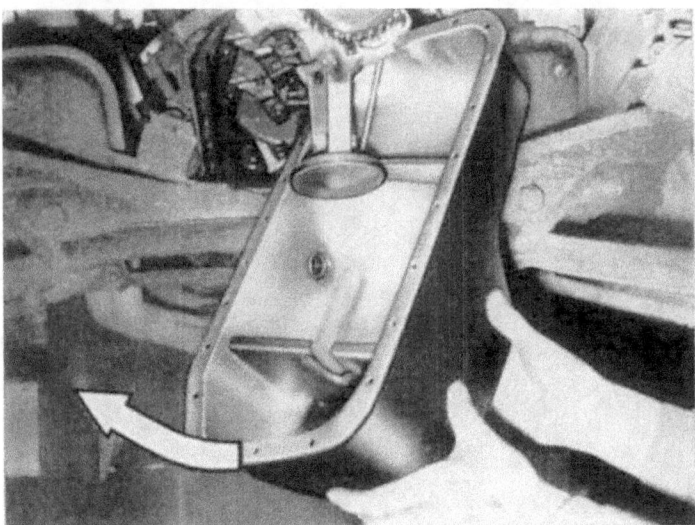

FIG 1:21 Oil sump removal

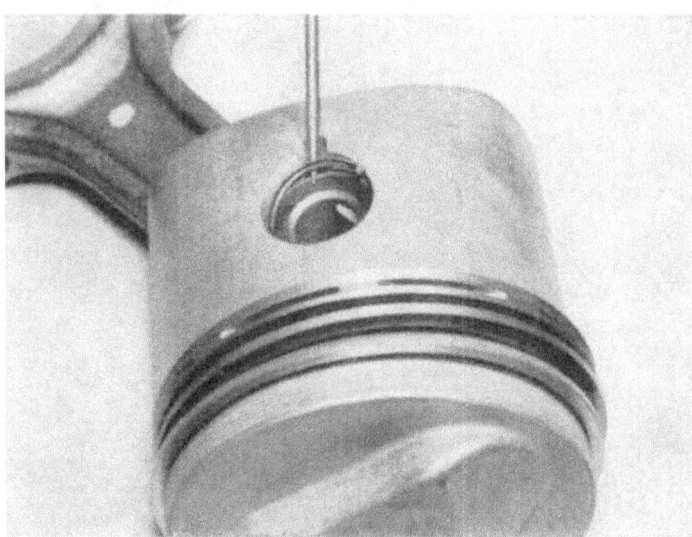

FIG 1:22 Gudgeon pin retaining circlip removal

5 If, on inspection, the valve guides are found to be worn they may be removed. To remove the valve guides, heat the cylinder head in an oven to approximately 180°C. Using a suitably sized drift press out the valve guides into the combustion chamber. The new valve guides may be fitted into the combustion chamber from the rocker shaft side of the cylinder head. Finally reface the valve guides using a .316 inch diameter reamer.

6 Inspect the valve springs for weakness or signs of hairline cracks and that they conform to the specification as detailed in Technical Data.

7 Finish decarbonizing by cleaning carbon from the piston crowns. Spring an old piston ring into the bore on top of the piston and scrape with a blunt tool so that a ring of carbon is left around the periphery to prevent excessive oil consumption. Clean off thoroughly and make sure that the faces of the head and the block are free from any oil or dirt.

Reassembly:

Reassembly is the reverse procedure to dismantling. Ensure that the valve stems are well lubricated before insertion in their guides. The oil seal rings **A** (see **FIG 1:16**), must always be renewed. A damaged oil seal ring will result in an increase in oil consumption. The oil seal ring should be located in the spring washer as shown in the diagram.

1:7 Timing chain & timing gear

To remove the timing chain proceed as follows:
1 Remove the engine as detailed in **Section 1:2**.
2 Remove the engine oil sump drain plug and drain the oil.
3 Remove the supporting yoke with the silentbloc on the righthand side and if available fasten the engine to receiving plate BMW.6001 fitted into the assembly support No. BMW.6000.
4 Carefully remove the oil sump retaining bolts and lift away the sump.
5 Remove the six cylinder head cover retaining bolts and lift away the cover. Carefully rotate the crankshaft so that No. 1 cylinder is set to the TDC position. This is indicated by the tip of the pointer needle pointing to the notch in the pulley (see **FIG 1:4**). In this position the notch marked in the crankshaft flange must be opposite to the notch in the cylinder head.
6 Release the eight bolts from the top timing gear cover in the order shown in **FIG 1:17** and lift away the cover. Loosen the camshaft drive chain tensioner closure plug and unscrew by hand with extreme caution as this is under the influence of heavy spring pressure. With the plug removed, take out the spring and the piston.
7 Carefully unscrew the pulley fastening nut 1 (see **FIG 1:18**), open the hub washers 2 and 3 for the fan fastening bolts, unscrew the bolts and carefully lift away the fan.
8 Loosen the generator clamping bolts, ease back the adjustment and lift off the fan belt. Using a universal two leg puller with suitably threaded legs extract the pulley as shown in **FIG 1:19**.
9 Unscrew the generator mounting bracket and lift away. Release the hose clamp on the righthand end of the rubber return hose, release the water pump retaining bolts and carefully lift away the water pump.

10 Remove the timing chain tensioner as previously described, open the tab washer on the sprocket fastening bolts and remove together with the sprocket and timing chain.
11 Carefully loosen the nut securing the crankshaft pulley, having first locked the crankshaft against movement by wedging a piece of wood between a crankshaft crank web and the crankcase.
12 Remove the six fastening bolts from the lower timing gear cover and lift away the timing gear cover, taking care not to damage the packing ring oil seal. Lift away the chain. The seal may be removed by carefully pressing it inwards. To refit a new seal, heat the timing gearbox cover to approximately 100°C in an oven and insert the seal from behind.
13 Using a screwdriver and a pair of circlip pliers release the tensioning wheel retainer S and lift away the tensioning wheel. This is only applicable if the sprocket type tensioner is fitted (see **FIG 1 : 11**).
14 Remove the three retaining bolts securing the sprocket to the oil pump. Ease forward the sprocket and lift away together with the driving chain.
15 Release the two oil pump housing retaining bolts and carefully ease downwards the oil pump housing so releasing it from the locating dowel sleeves. Remove the sliding rail retainers and lift away the slide rails.
16 Lift away the key from the front of the crankshaft and remove the O-ring. Using a universal puller remove the sprocket wheel from the end of the crankshaft.

Reassembly:

Reassembly is the reverse procedure to dismantling but the following points should be noted:
1 The little O-ring fitted at the front of the crankshaft must always be renewed.
2 When refitting the retainers the machined surface must always face towards the retainer as shown in **FIG 1 : 20.**
3 Adjust the chain tension by fitting the appropriate packing plate as shown in **FIG 1 : 39**. Care must be taken to ensure that the position of the oil bore in the packing plate is correctly located otherwise a failure in lubrication will occur. The correct chain tension should be so adjusted as to permit slight depression of the chain under light thumb pressure.
4 When refitting the crankshaft pulley retaining nut tighten to a torque wrench setting of 101.3 lb ft.
5 When reassembling the camshaft sprocket chain and tensioner the tensioner must be bled before the sprocket is assembled. The piston should be placed with its recess against the tensioning arm. Fit the spring with the taper wound end resting against the closure plug. Screw in the closure plug lightly. Using an oil can fill the oil space with oil. Ensure that the camshaft flange notch is correctly aligned with the notch marked in the cylinder head. Mount the sprocket and chain onto the camshaft flange and refit the four retaining bolts using new tabwashers.
6 When reassembling the water pump it is imperative that new copper gaskets are fitted.
7 When refitting the fan pulley retaining nut tighten to a torque wrench setting of 28.9 lb ft. It is essential that the fan blades are not held for additional leverage to enable the nut to be tightened but increase the fan belt tension and hold the water pump pulley.

FIG 1 : 23 Piston ring gap measurement

FIG 1 : 24 Piston ring side clearance

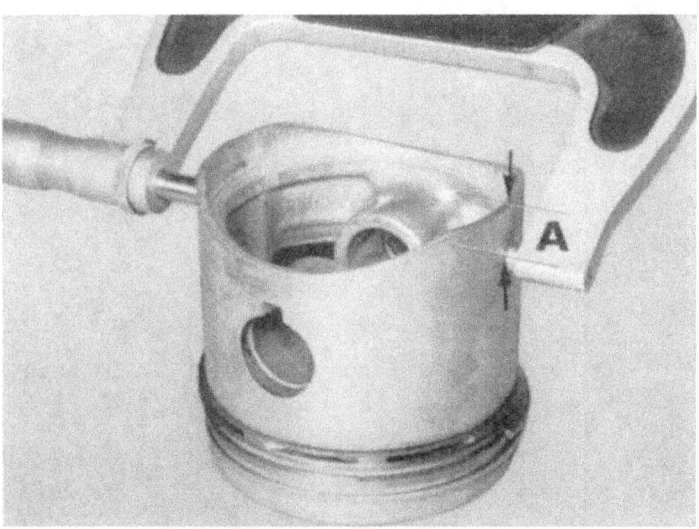

FIG 1 : 25 Piston diameter measurement

FIG 1:26 Piston ring location

FIG 1:27 Piston and gudgeon pin identification

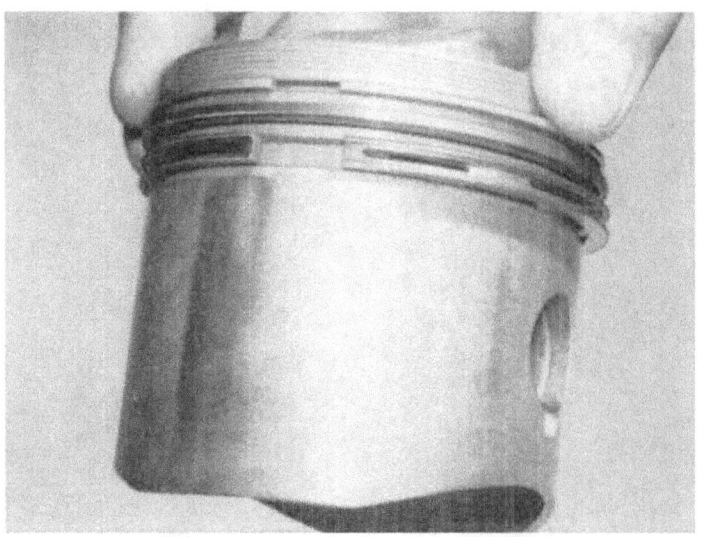

FIG 1:28 Piston ring gap location

8 When assembling the upper timing gearbox cover to the lower timing gearbox cover coat the mating surfaces with a suitable sealing compound. Fit the two cover retaining bolts but do not tighten fully and follow with the remaining six bolts as shown in **FIG 1:17**. Finally tighten the first two bolts.

9 Whenever the cylinder head cover gasket has been disturbed it must be renewed, otherwise this could cause an oil leak.

1:8 Pistons, rings & connecting rods

The piston assemblies may be removed from the engine whilst it is in location in the vehicle. The operation is very straightforward and presents no difficulties. To remove the piston assemblies proceed as follows:

1 Remove the cylinder head as detailed in **Section 1:5**.
2 Drain the oil from the engine sump into a container of suitable capacity. Release the oil sump retaining bolts and carefully ease forward until contact is made with the oil suction baffle plate. Gently turn the sump to the right as shown in **FIG 1:21** and remove.
3 Ensure that the connecting rods and end caps are suitably marked for correct reassembly. Rotate the engine until No. 1 piston is at BDC, release the connecting rod bolts, separate the end cap from the connecting rod and carefully push the piston and connecting rod upwards. Repeat for the remaining three piston assemblies.
4 Using a small screwdriver or suitably pointed tool release one of the gudgeon pin retaining wire clips as shown in **FIG 1:22** and push out the gudgeon pin. This operation may be done whilst the piston is cold. Mark all components for correct reassembly.

Piston rings:

To remove the rings slide a piece of steel like a disused .020 inch feeler gauge under one end and pass it round under the ring, at the same time gently pressing the raised part over onto the piston land above. Always remove and refit rings over the top of the piston. Clean carbon deposit from the ring groove with a piece of broken ring but do not remove metal, otherwise oil consumption will increase.

Before fitting new rings always remove the cylinder bore glaze with special garage equipment and check the ring gap in the bore. Place a piston about 1 inch down the bore and press the new ring down onto it. Measure the gap between the ring ends with a feeler gauge as shown in **FIG 1:23** and file the ends if necessary until the gap is .0118 to .0177 inch for No. 1 and 2 rings. No. 3 ring should be set to have a gap of .0098 to .0157 inch. Check the piston ring side clearance using a feeler gauge as shown in **FIG 1:24**. The clearance should be .0024 to .0034 inch for No. 1 ring, .0014 to .0024 inch for No. 2 ring and .0098 to .0157 inch for No. 3 ring. Finally check the piston fitting clearance using an internal and external micrometer. The piston should be measured as shown in **FIG 1:25** with dimension 'A' .433 inch. The correct piston clearance is .0016 inch.

Reassembly:

This is the reverse procedure to dismantling but the following points should be noted:

1. Only pistons of the same weight classification and the same manufacture should be fitted to an engine otherwise out of balance could occur. The piston crowns are marked with a + or − which denotes the weight group (see **FIG 1 : 27**) and the manufacturers name is marked on the inner side at the piston skirt, which could be Mahle, KS, or Nüral. See Technical Data for oversizes.
2. The piston rings are of the following type, rectangular ring, stepped ring, and equal chamfer oil scraper ring. Each ring has a top and bottom and must not be fitted the wrong way round.
3. The gudgeon pins are specially colour coded and must not be intermixed.
   W stamped on piston crown—white mark on inside of pin.
   S Stamped on piston crown—black mark on inside of pin.
   See Technical Data for further information.
4. Before refitting the pistons to the engine set the ring gaps at 180 deg. to each other thus ensuring the best ring seal (see **FIG 1 : 28**).

Connecting rods:

Big-end bearing liners are renewable. Ensure that the running clearances compare with the information in Technical Data.

Inspection:

Examine the internal face of the rod bearing inserts and if light scratches are noticed carefully remove them by using a hand scraper. Should however deep notches or signs of wear be evident the bearings must be renewed.

The clearance between the connecting rod bearing and journal must be checked by using 'Plastigage' type PG1 calibrated wire as follows:

1. Thoroughly wipe all components with a non-fluffy rag.
2. The piston connecting rod assemblies should be prepared ready for assembly to the crankshaft. Place a piece of calibrated wire on the journal. Fit the connecting rod bearing end caps and tighten to a torque wrench setting of between 37.6 to 41.2 lb ft. Do **not** rotate the connecting rod.
3. Remove the end caps and determine the amount of clearance by comparing the width of the flattened 'Plastigage' with the graduations on the envelope as shown in **FIG 1 : 34**. Compare their result with the specification in Technical Data.
4. Should the clearance be greater than the figures stated, the connecting rod bearings must be replaced by undersize bearings and the crankshaft specially reground at BMW. On no account file either the rod or the cap to take up wear.

Reassembly:

Reassembly is the reverse procedure to dismantling but the following points should be noted:

1. Ensure that the numbers stamped on the connecting rod and end cap match. Also check that connecting rods of the same weight classification are being fitted. This classification is coded using coloured spots.

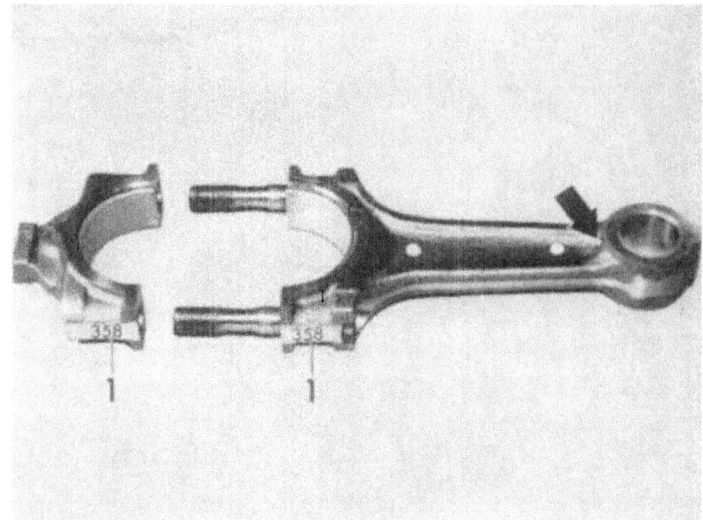

FIG 1 : 29 Connecting rod identification

FIG 1 : 30 Checking flywheel runout

FIG 1 : 31 Flywheel retaining bolt backplate

FIG 1:32 Checking crankshaft end float

FIG 1:33 Crankshaft master bearing

FIG 1:34 Bearing clearance measurement

2 The oil drilling supplying the gudgeon pin lubrication should be assembled to face forwards in the direction of the timing chain and the arrow on the piston crown should also point towards the timing chain.
3 Check that the piston ring slots are 180 deg. to each other and thoroughly lubricate piston and bearing upon fitting (see **FIG 1:28**).
4 The connecting rod end bolts are special 12.K expansion bolts and must not be reused. Always fit new bolts on reassembly and tighten to a torque wrench setting of between 37 to 41.2 lb ft.

1:9 Flywheel removing & refitting

The flywheel may be removed with the engine in situ but with gearbox removed. To complete this operation proceed as follows:
1 Before the flywheel is removed from the engine it is advisable to check for any distortion due to heat from excessive clutch use. Attach a dial gauge to the cylinder block and position so that the probe is in contact with the friction face as shown in **FIG 1:30**. At a diameter of 15.8 inches the maximum runout allowed is .0003 inch. The flywheel face is specially hardened and the maximum allowable skimming thickness is .012 ± .0039 inch. Care must be taken to ensure that the inside wall thickness of the friction face is not less than .531 inch.
2 Lever off the locking plate for the six flywheel to crankshaft retaining bolts as shown in **FIG 1:31** and release the retaining bolts, having first locked the flywheel using BMW tool 6013 or using other suitable means. Carefully lift away the flywheel.
3 Check the condition of the starter ring gear teeth and if chips or serious damage is evident the ring gear must be renewed. Remove the worn starter ring gear from the flywheel by splitting it with a cold chisel. Take care not to damage the flywheel. Ensure that the mating surfaces of the new gear and flywheel are clean and free from burrs. Heat the new ring gear to a temperature of 80°C in an oil bath and install on flywheel using a press.
4 Reassembly is the reverse procedure to dismantling. A new locking plate must be fitted taking care it is pushed squarely onto the bolt heads and the bolts tightened to a torque of 73 lb ft.

1:10 Crankshaft removing & refitting

Drain the engine oil sump and remove the engine as detailed in **Section 1:2**. Thoroughly clean the outside of the engine and then proceed as follows:
1 Remove the lower half of timing gear cover and oil pump and accessories as detailed in **Section 1:7**.
2 Check the crankshaft end float with a dial gauge located on the flywheel as shown in **FIG 1:32** by levering the crankshaft endwise using screwdrivers. This should be between .0024 to .0064 inch. If the clearance is excessive a new centre main bearing incorporating thrust washers must be fitted (see **FIG 1:33**).

3 Remove the flywheel as described in **Section 1:9** and release the crankshaft end cover by releasing the six retaining bolts.
4 Using a dial gauge suitably positioned check the crankshaft sealing ring which if worn or distorted must be renewed.
5 Inspect the gearbox first motion shaft grooved ballbearing for signs of wear or overheating and fit new if necessary.
6 Ensure the connecting rods and end caps are marked for correct reassembly and remove the end cap bolts.
7 Ensure the main bearing caps are suitably marked for correct reassembly and remove the retaining bolts. It should be noted the centre main bearing is the master bearing and it is this which determines the crankshaft end float. This bearing is colour coded according to crankshaft journal diameter and end float.
8 Carefully lift out the crankshaft.

Cleaning crankshaft and oil passages:

To thoroughly clean the crankshaft and oil drillings wash in paraffin ensuring penetration of paraffin into the oil drillings and use a compressed air-line to pass air through the drillings. Wipe dry with a non-fluffy rag.

Main bearings:

Minor scratches on the main bearing inserts can be smoothed out by carefully using a hand scraper. Should there be signs of seizure, excess wear or grooves, fit new bearing inserts.

If on inspection the bearing inserts prove to be satisfactory, to check their clearance to the crankshaft journals proceed as follows:

1 Place a piece of 'Plastigage' calibrated strip on the journal and install the main bearing caps and shell bearings. Tighten the main bearing cap bolts to a torque wrench setting of between 42 and 45.6 lb ft. Do not rotate the crankshaft.
2 Remove the caps and compare the width of the flattened 'Plastigage' with the graduation scale on the envelope (see **FIG 1:34**). The number within the graduation on the envelope indicates the actual bearing clearances. The correct clearance of main bearing to journal is between .0019 and .0027 inch. Should the clearance not be within the wear limit replace bearings. If this still gives an oversize reading the crankshaft will have to be specially reground at BMW. This is because the processing of the crankshaft, which is soft nitriding, requires special treatment. Two sizes of undersize bearings are available. Full dimension details are given in Technical Data. Never file the bearing caps in an attempt to take up wear.

A colour coding is used for reground crankshaft (see **FIG 1:35**).

Main bearing journal (B):

One coloured stripe—1st undersize
Two coloured stripes—2nd undersize
Three coloured stripes—3rd undersize

Big-end bearing journal (A):

One coloured stripe—1st undersize—red or blue
Two coloured stripes—2nd undersize—red or blue
Three coloured stripes— 3rd undersize—red or blue

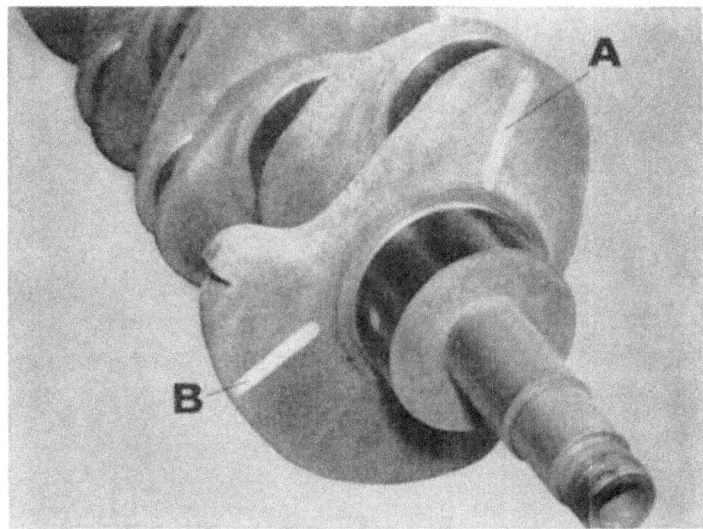

FIG 1:35 Crankshaft journal size identification

FIG 1:36 Crankshaft journal size identification

1 Bearing 2 Cover plate 3 Felt ring 4 End cap
FIG 1:37 Gearbox drive shaft ballbearing assembly

FIG 1:38 Oil pump mounting location

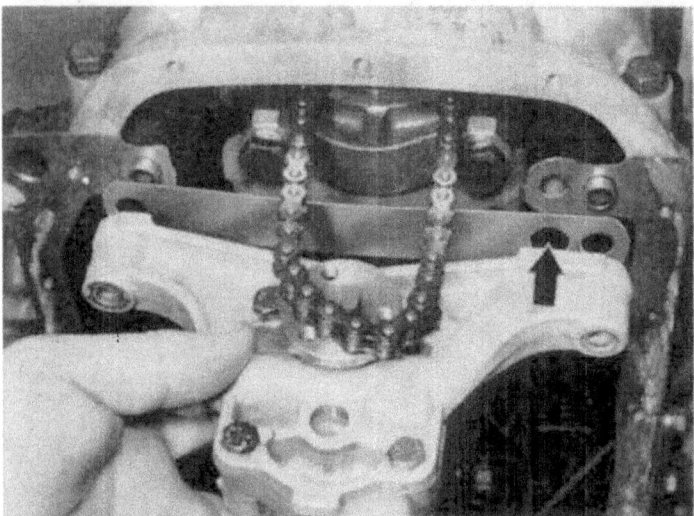

FIG 1:39 Oil pump removal. Note packing shim location

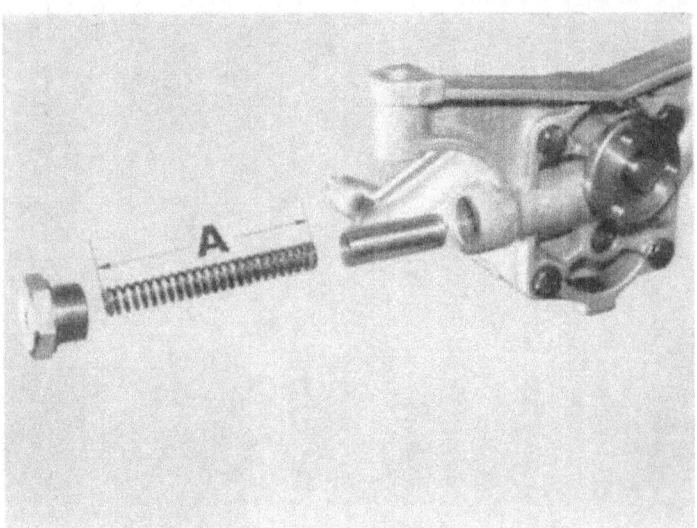

FIG 1:40 Oil pressure relief valve

For an original diameter crankshaft a red or blue colour spot is marked on the counterweight as shown in **FIG 1:36**.

General inspection:

The crankshaft must be thoroughly inspected for signs of cracking at the crankpin and journals as well as the webs. If there are any signs of failure the crankshaft must be renewed.

Should there be any deep notches or the journals found to be oval in excess of .002 inch then the journals should be reground.

Before refitting the crankshaft to the engine always ensure that the oil passages are thoroughly clean and there are no signs of metal dust from the grinding process.

Crankpin and journal alignment:

1 Support the ends of the crankshaft on V-blocks on a surface plate and using a dial indicator gauge check the centre main bearing for runout. The maximum permissible runout is .0008 inch at the centre main bearing.
2 Check for alignment of crankpins.
3 Check for crankpin and journal ovality.
4 Check for crankpin end and journal taper.
5 Flywheel mounting flange. Fit the flywheel, turn the crankshaft and set the dial indicator to edge of flange. Maximum axial runout should not exceed .004 inch.

Refitting crankshaft:

Reassembly of the crankshaft is the reverse procedure to dismantling. The following points should however be noted:

1 If an undersize crankshaft is being used it is essential that the corresponding bearing shells are used.
2 Ensure that the main bearing end caps are correctly located and it is best policy to fit new bolts. Tighten to a torque wrench setting of between 42 and 45.6 lb ft. The oil filter bracket is secured with No. 2 main bearing end cap.
3 Check that the connecting rods are installed in the same positions as noted on removal from engine. Always use new end cap bolts and tighten to a torque wrench setting of between 37.6 and 41.2 lb ft.
4 When reassembling the gearbox drive shaft ballbearing in the end of the crankshaft, always pad the ballbearing race with a high melting point grease. Fit the coverplate with its projection facing outwards. It is recommended that the felt washer be soaked in hot grease and finally drive on the end cap as far as it will go (see **FIG 1:37**).
5 Before reassembling the crankshaft rear cover smear with Atmosit at the contact face with the oil sump.

1:11 Cylinder block & crankcase

Cleaning:

Immerse the complete crankcase in a wash tank containing a water and soda solution and thoroughly wash using a pressure jet. Ensure that all oilways are thoroughly cleaned. Using a compressed air jet blow away traces of moisture and finally wipe internally and externally with a non-fluffy rag.

Cylinder bores:

Examine the cylinder bores and if light scoring marks are detected it is suggested that the block is taken to a garage and refaced using fine emerycloth wrapped around a hone.

Check the cylinder bore dimensions at the top and bottom of the bore to check for taper as well as ovality. Full dimensional details are given in Technical Data.

Cylinder head mating face

The cylinder block may show distortions on the head mating face and may be checked by using a straight edge and feeler gauge placed diagonally across the face and also longitudinally. If distortion is detected a surface grinder should be used, care being taken to remove as little metal as possible.

1 : 12 Oil pump removing & refitting

The oil pump may be removed with the engine in situ. Raise the front of the vehicle, place on firmly based stands and proceed as follows:

1. Release the oil sump retaining bolts and carefully pull forward until contact is made between the oil filter and the baffle plate. Gently turn the oil sump towards the right and ease down forwards and lift away from the underside of the car.
2. Remove the three bolts holding the chain sprocket to the pump and remove the sprockets. Remove the two oil pump retaining bolts, the retaining plate mounting nuts and carefully remove the oil pump assembly downwards making note of any chain tension shims that may be in position between the pump and the underside of the crankcase (see **FIG 1:38** and **FIG 1:39**).

Reassembly:

Reassembly is the reverse procedure to removal but the following points should be noted:

1. Adjust the chain tension with the specially-shaped shims placed between the oil pump and the crankcase. The correct adjustment is obtained when the chain can be depressed under light thumb pressure. Always ensure that the oil hole in the shim mates up with the oil hole in the crankcase otherwise failure of the lubrication system will result.
2. To ensure that no oil leaks occur between the oil sump flange and the underside of the crankcase always check the alignment of the bolt holes and realign as necessary.

1 : 13 Oil pump overhaul

Before dismantling the oil pump thoroughly clean the outside using an oil solvent and blow dry carefully, using a compressed air jet. To dismantle the pump proceed as follows:

1. Unscrew the pressure relief valve spring retaining plug as shown in **FIG 1:40**. Carefully lift away the spring and plunger. Check the length of the spring which should be 2.68 inches. It is very important that the length of the spring is not altered and should the original one fitted to the oil pump differ from the specified length, then a new spring must be fitted.

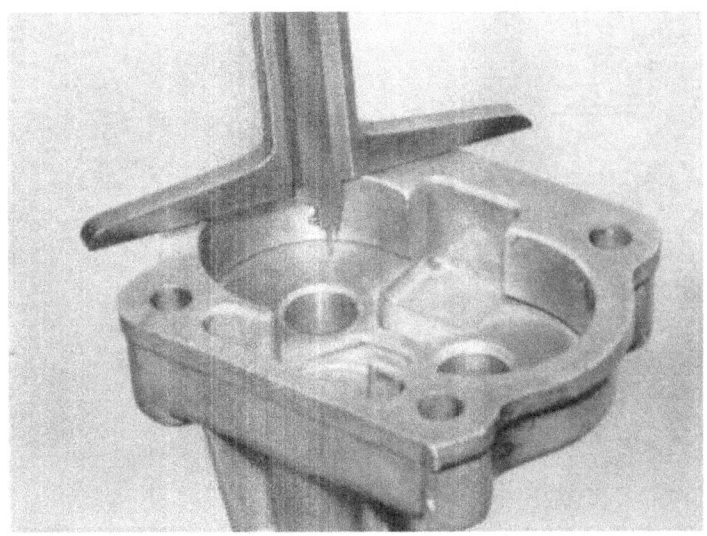

FIG 1:41   Oil pump body wear

FIG 1:42   Oil pump gear backlash

FIG 1:43   Oil pump gear location

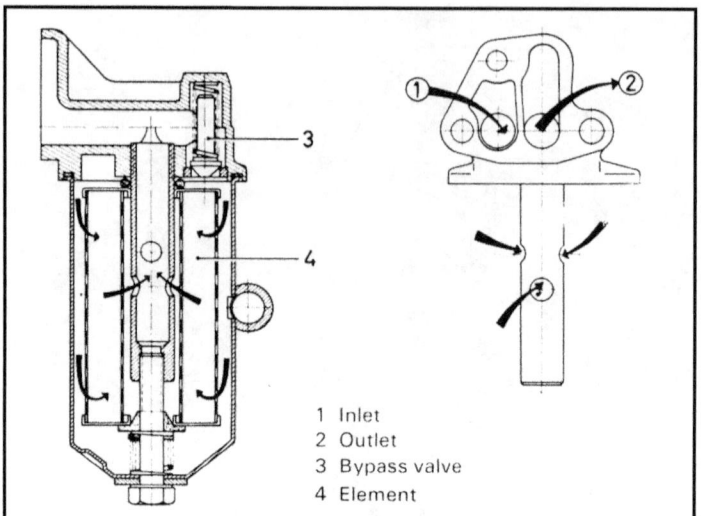

FIG 1:44 Fullflow filter

1 Inlet
2 Outlet
3 Bypass valve
4 Element

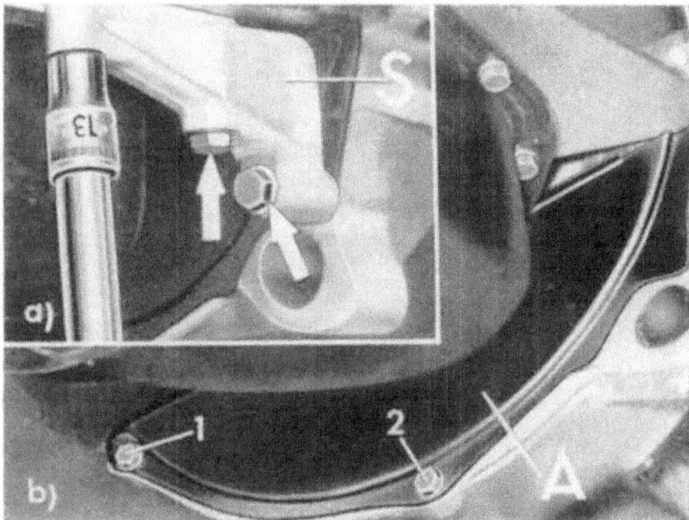

FIG 1:45 Support bracket location

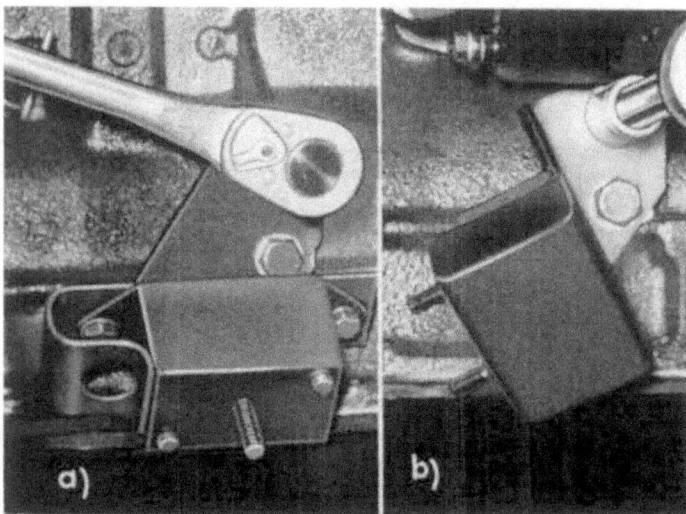

FIG 1:46 Engine mountings

2 Release the four body retaining bolts and separate the two halves of the pump body. Thoroughly clean the mating flange of the body and using a depth gauge as shown in **FIG 1:41**, check the amount of wear at the position shown. The maximum amount of wear permissible is .002 inch.

3 Using a set of feeler gauges check the backlash between the two gears as shown in **FIG 1:42**. The clearance when new should be between .001 and .002 inch. The maximum permissible backlash is .003 inch.

4 Using a vernier or other suitable measuring instrument, check the hub-to-pinion contact face dimension (A) (see **FIG 1:43**). This dimension should be 1.358± .004 inch.

5 Thoroughly check all gear teeth for signs of excessive wear or pitting, and also the main pump body for hairline cracks or signs of distortion. New parts should be fitted as required.

Reassembly:

Reassembly is the reverse procedure to dismantling. It is considered advisable that whilst attention is being given to the oil pump, the oil filter located on the underside of the crankcase should be removed and thoroughly cleaned. Check the filter medium for damage or clogging and either clean or fit a new filter as necessary.

1:14 Fullflow filter

A fullflow oil filter of the renewable element type is located on the side of the engine underneath the alternator. Later cars have a screw-on cartridge filter.

It is recommended that the filter or element be renewed every 4000 miles, and to remove the old element proceed as follows:

1 Disconnect the battery before starting work on the filter. Unscrew the centre bolt, the head of which is located at the base of the filter bowl. Carefully remove the bowl holding upright as it will be full of oil.

2 Discard the old oil into a suitable container and remove the element and clean the inside of the bowl with fuel. Do not attempt to clean the element as nothing useful can be gained by doing so.

3 Remove the old oil seals and fit new as supplied with the new filter element. Place the element in the bowl and fill the bowl with clean engine oil. Tighten the filter bowl retaining bolt.

4 The cartridge type should be unscrewed and a new filter fitted.

5 Reconnect the battery and start the engine. Immediately check for signs of oil leaks between the filter bowl and its main body as it essential that there are no leaks from the filter as this could lead to complete failure of the engine lubrication system.

1:15 Factory exchange engine installation

Should it be necessary to fit a factory reconditioned engine it is recommended that the replacement engine be prepared before the unit is assembled to the vehicle.

1 Remove the original power unit as fully described in **Section 1:2**.

2 Remove the two fastening bolts for the support bracket S (see **FIG 1:45**). Detach the fastening bolts detailed 1 and 2 for the coverplate A from the gearbox and lift away the plate.

3 Remove the starter motor fastening bolts and lift away the starter motor.
4 Remove the fastening bolts holding the engine and gearbox together.
5 Release the righthand silentbloc with limit stop from the crankcase. Also release the lefthand silentbloc from the crankcase (see **FIG 1 : 46**).

Reassembly of units to replacement engine:

1 Replace the two silentbloc mountings with limit stops to the crankcase.
2 Fit the gearbox to the engine and tighten the fastening bolts to a torque wrench setting of 18.1 lb ft.
3 Fit the starter and tighten the retaining bolts to a torque wrench setting of 34 lb ft.
4 Refit the gearbox coverplate ensuring that it is located the correct way round.
5 Refit the two fastening bolts for the support bracket.
6 Refit the engine as described in **Section 1 : 2**.

1 : 16 Exhaust emission control system

Description:

To ensure that the exhaust emission control unit is operating satisfactorily the carburetter requires to be correctly adjusted using an exhaust gas analyzer. Also to ensure effective operation the ignition timing has to be accurately set using a stroboscope. Normally this equipment is not available to car owners and it is therefore suggested that this work be entrusted to the local garage. For reference purposes full details of the two adjustments are given.

Carburetter adjustment:

1 Refer to **FIG 1 : 48** and detach the air hose 1 from the non-return valve and connect the exhaust gas analyser to the exhaust tail pipe.
2 Run the engine at a fast idle speed to allow it to come up to normal operating temperature and then using an electric tachometer set the engine idle speed to 1000 rev/min.
3 Use the slow-running mixture adjustment screw, refer to **Chapter 2**, set the CO content to .8 to 1.2 per cent.
4 Reset the engine idling speed to 1000 rev/min if necessary and repeat the operation until the required value is obtained. Finally reset the normal idling speed.

Ignition timing:

1 Using electronic engine tuning equipment check that the distributor dwell angle is correct.
2 Detach the vacuum advance pipe from the distributor.
3 Set the engine speed to a fast idle and allow to come up to normal operating temperature. Reset the engine idle speed with the assistance of an electric tachometer to 2000 rev/min.
4 Connect the stroboscope into the ignition system and point towards the aperture in the gearbox bellhousing so that the steel ball located in the flywheel can be seen.
5 Adjust the ignition timing as necessary so that the centre of the steel ball is visible at the datum location as shown in **FIG 1 : 47**.

FIG 1:47 Flywheel engine timing steel ball and datum mark

FIG 1:48 Non-return valve and idling adjustment screw

FIG 1:49 Front timing marks

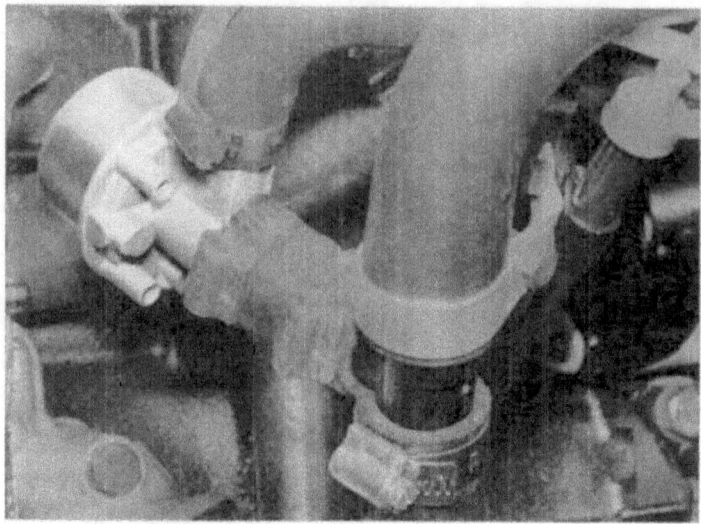

FIG 1:50 Exhaust gas control valve

FIG 1:51 Pressure regulator unit

FIG 1:52 Air pump mountings

Should the engine flywheel not be fitted with a steel ball or there is no inspection opening in the gearbox housing the static ignition timing must be set using the marks on the V-belt pulley. Refer to **FIG 1:49** where it will be seen that the top notch 1 in the pulley is the TDC timing notch, number 2 notch is the static ignition timing notch and number 3 (bottom) notch is for ignition timing using a strobe light at 2000 rev/min.

For 1974 2002 models the correct engine speed is 1400 rev/min and for 2002 tii models it is 2400 rev/min.

After either of the above two methods of checking and adjusting the ignition timing reset the engine idle speed.

Exhaust gas control valve:

This component is very reliable in operation and only needs renewing should difficulty be experienced in the setting of the carburetter to give correct exhaust gas compensation or to cure persistent backfiring in the exhaust system whilst the throttle control is closed. The location is shown in **FIG 1:50**.

Air pump:

To check the operation of the air pump, carefully remove the blow-off pipe from the air pump and lightly press the hand on the pressure relief valve. With the assistance of a second operator allow the engine speed to increase slowly. Normally the pressure release valve will open between 1700 to 2000 rev/min. If the release valve should open earlier the pressure regulator unit should be renewed by first releasing the hose and extracting the pressure regulator unit with the assistance of two screwdrivers. A new pressure regulator unit should be pushed into position (see **FIG 1:51**). Should the pressure release valve only open at an engine speed in excess of 2000 rev/min then the air pump must be renewed. This operation is very straightforward only requiring the removal of the hoses and retaining bolts together with the mounting bushes. These should be checked for wear and renewed as necessary. Tighten the retaining bolts to a torque wrench setting of 33 lb ft (see **FIG 1:52**).

The lower mounting bolt locates in an elongated hole on the mounting bracket and the V-belt tension should be adjusted by easing the air pump away from the engine oil sump using hand pressure only. When correctly adjusted it should be possible to depress the belt between .2 and .4 inch.

Non-return valve:

The non-return valve is located in the manifold as shown in **FIG 1:53**. To remove the valve first detach the heat deflection shield, release the hose and pipe clip on the underside of the manifold and unscrew the non-return valve from the pipe manifold.

Injection pipes:

The injection pipes are located in the exhaust system inside the exhaust manifold. If new pipes are being inserted they should be screwed into the manifold to the length marked on the injection pipe as shown in **FIG 1:54**.

1 : 17 Evaporative control system

This is a further method of preventing the escape to atmosphere of fumes from the fuel system.

The operation of the system centres around the canister 17 in **FIG 1:55**, which is filled with activated carbon and is mounted on the front righthand wheel arch.

Key to Fig 1:55   15 Air cleaner   16 Primary crankcase vent   17 Carbon canister   18 Vapour purge line   19 Vapour storage tank   20 Sealed filler cap   21 Fuel tank   22 Excess fuel return pipe   23 OHC cover   24 Fuel pump   25 Fuel return control valve   26 Vacuum hose   27 Secondary crankcase vacuum control

The method of operation is as follows:

Since the fuel tank is fitted with a sealed filler cap, any fumes arising from the fuel stored in the tank are passed through a small bore hose to a vapour storage tank 19, located under the rear parcel shelf. This tank is coupled by the vapour purge line 18 to the carbon canister where the fumes are absorbed by the carbon. This pipework also provides any venting required by the fuel tank as the fuel level falls.

The carbon canister is also connected by a hose to the carburetter intake so that, when the engine is running, there is a suction applied to the canister which draws out the fuel fumes absorbed by the carbon and consumes them in the engine.

The system requires no maintenance beyond checking that the pipes and hoses are in good condition and securely connected.

1 : 18 Fault diagnosis

(a) Engine will not start

1. Defective coil
2. Faulty distributor capacitor (condenser)
3. Dirty, pitted or incorrectly set contact breaker points
4. Ignition wires loose or insulation faulty
5. Water on sparking plug leads
6. Corrosion of battery terminals or battery discharged
7. Faulty or jammed starter
8. Sparking plug leads wrongly connected
9. Vapour lock in fuel pipes
10. Defective fuel pump
11. Overchoking
12. Underchoking
13. Blocked petrol filter or carburetter jets
14. Leaking valves
15. Sticking valves
16. Valve timing incorrect
17. Ignition timing incorrect

(b) Engine stalls

1. Check 1, 2, 3, 4, 10, 11, 12, 13, 14 and 15 in (a)
2. Sparking plugs defective or gaps incorrect
3. Retarded ignition
4. Mixture too weak
5. Water in fuel system
6. Petrol tank vent blocked
7. Incorrect valve clearance

FIG 1:53   Non-return valve location

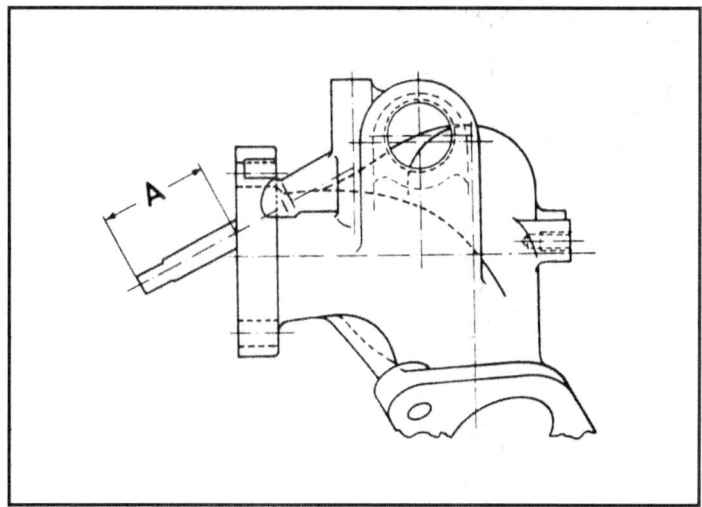

FIG 1:54   Exhaust manifold injection pipe

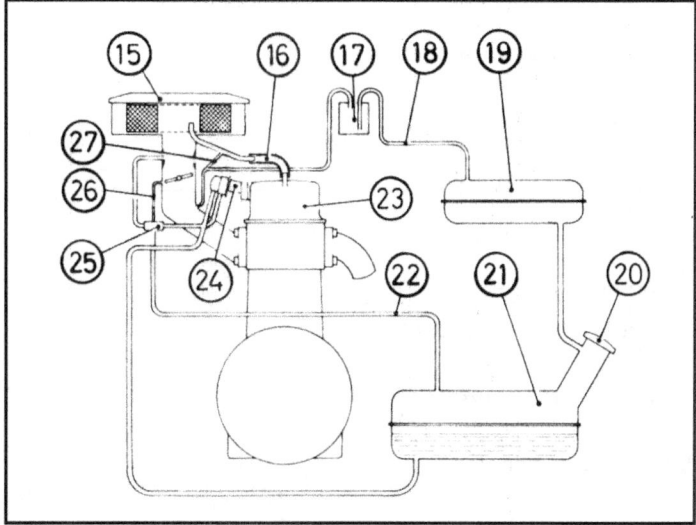

FIG 1:55   The evaporative control system

(c) Engine idles badly

1. Check 2 and 7 in (b)
2. Air leak at manifold joints
3. Slow-running jet blocked or out of adjustment
4. Air leak in carburetter
5. Over-rich mixture
6. Worn piston rings
7. Worn valve stems or guides
8. Weak exhaust valve springs
9. Exhaust emission control valve failure

(d) Engine misfires

1. Check 1, 2, 3, 4, 5, 8, 10, 13, 14, 15, 16, 17 in (a) 2, 3, 4 and 7 in (b)
2. Weak or broken valve springs
3. Exhaust emission control valve failure

(e) Engine overheats

See Chapter 4

(f) Compression low

1. Check 14 and 15 in (a) 6 and 7 in (c) and 2 in (d)
2. Worn piston ring grooves
3. Scored or worn cylinder bores

(g) Engine lacks power

1. Check 3, 10, 11, 13, 14, 15, 16 and 17 in (a) 2, 3, 4 and 7 in (b)
2. Check 6 and 7 in (c) and 2 in (d). Also check (e) and (f)
3. Leaking joint washers
4. Fouled sparking plugs
5. Automatic advance not operating

(h) Burnt valves or seats

1. Check 14 and 15 in (a) 7 in (b) and 2 in (d). Also check (e)
2. Excessive carbon around valve seat and head

(j) Sticking valves

1. Check 2 in (d)
2. Bent valve stem
3. Scored valve stem or guide
4. Incorrect valve clearance

(k) Excessive cylinder wear

1. Check 11 in (a) and see Chapter 4
2. Lack of oil
3. Dirty oil
4. Piston rings gummed up or broken
5. Badly fitting piston rings
6. Connecting rods bent

(l) Excessive oil consumption

1. Check 6 and 7 in (c) and check (k)
2. Ring gaps too wide
3. Oil return holes in piston choked with carbon
4. Scored cylinders
5. Oil level too high
6. External oil leaks
7. Ineffective valve stem oil seals

(m) Crankshaft and connecting rod bearing failure

1. Check 2 in (k)
2. Restricted oilways
3. Worn journals or crankpins
4. Loose bearing caps
5. Extremely low oil pressure
6. Bent connecting rod

(n) Internal water leakage

1. See Chapter 4

(o) Poor circulation

1. See Chapter 4

(p) Corrosion

1. See Chapter 4

(q) High fuel consumption

1. See Chapter 4

(r) Engine vibration

1. Loose alternator bolts
2. Fan blades out of balance
3. Incorrect clearance for front engine mounting rubbers
4. Exhaust pipe mountings too tight
5. Incorrect adjustment of power unit stabilizer

1 : 19 Technical data

Bore and stroke	3.504 x 3.150 (89 x 80)
Capacity	120.66 cu inch (1990 cm^3)
Compression ratio :	
2002, 2000, 2000A, 2000CA	8.5:1
2000TI, 2000 TI Lux, 2000CA	9.3:1
2002, 2002A	8.3:1
2002Tii	10:1 or 9.5:1
Compression pressure :	
Normal	135 to 150 lb/inch
Poor	Below 128 lb/inch
Engine lubrication :	
System	Pressure oil circulation
Oil filter	Full flow
Oil pump	Gear or rotor type
Warning light operation	2.84 to 7.11 lb/sq inch

Valve operating clearances:
  Inlet and exhaust, at operating temperature .. .008 to .010 (20 to 25)
Valve clearance adjustment .. .. Eccentrics on rockers
Valve adjustment sequence:

TDC on cylinder No.	Valve overlap on cylinder No.
1	4
3	2
4	1
2	3

Valve timing (with .002 inch clearance between cam base circle and rocker pad):
  Inlet opens .. .. 4 deg. BTDC
  Inlet closes .. .. 52 deg. ABDC
  Exhaust opens .. .. 52 deg. BBDC
  Exhaust closes .. .. 4 deg. ATDC
Valves:
  Overall length:
    Inlet .. .. 4.087 ± .008
    Exhaust .. .. 4.106 ± .008
  Valve head diameter:
    Inlet 1.732
    Exhaust 1.496
  Valve stem diameter:
    Inlet .. .. .315 − .00098 − .00157
    Exhaust .. .. .315 − .00157 − .00217
  Minimum head thickness at edge:
    Inlet .. .. .039 ± .004
    Exhaust .. .. .059 ± .006
  Maximum head runout:
    Inlet .. .. .0008
    Exhaust .. .. .0008
Valve seats:
  External diameter:
    Inlet .. .. 1.856 − .00035 − .00098
    Exhaust .. .. 1.581 − .00035 − .00098
  Diameter of cylinder head bore for valve seat:
    Inlet .. .. 1.85 + .00098
    Exhaust .. .. 1.575 + .00098
  Interference fit in cylinder head .. .. .. .00394 to .0059
  Valve seat angle .. .. 45 deg.
  Outer correction angle .. .. 15 deg.
  Inner correction angle .. .. 75 deg.
  Valve seat width:

	2000	2002
Inlet	.063 to .079	.059 to .083
Exhaust	.079 to .095	.061 to .081

  Valve seat oversizes .. .. .0079 diameter larger
Valve guides:
  Overall length 2.047
  External diameter .. .. .5512 + .00173 + .0013
  Internal diameter .. .. .3150 + .00059
  Projection into cylinder head .. .. .. .591 ± .02
  Interference fit in cylinder head .. .. .. .0013 to .0027
  Temperature of head when fitting new guides 220 to 240°C
  Oversize diameters .. .. .5551, .559, .563
Valve running clearances:
  Inlet .. .. .00098 to .00216
  Exhaust .. .. .00157 to .00275
  Maximum wear tolerance .. .. .0059
  Valve springs:
    Wire thickness .. .. .167
    External coil diameter 1.260
    Free length 1.811
    Spring force and test length .. .. .. 66 lb at 1.496 inch
  Rockers:
    Bore for rocker shaft .. .. .6103 + .00071
    Bore in cylinder head .. .. .6103 + .00106
    Rocker shaft diameter .. .. .6103 − .00063 − .00134
    Rocker shaft running clearance .. .. .00063 to .00303
    Rocker running clearance .. .. .. .00063 to .00205
  Camshaft:
    Diameters 1.3780, 1.6536, 1.6929
    Tolerance .. .. − .00098, − .00161
    Bore in cylinder head 1.3780, 1.6536, 1.6929
    Tolerance .. .. + .00134, + .00035
    Running clearance .. .. .00063 to .00303
    Axial play .. .. .00063 to .00205
    Cam base circle diameter 1.054
    Cam lift .. .. .2756

Valve gear:
  Operation .. .. Single overhead camshaft and rockers
  Camshaft drive .. .. $\frac{3}{8}$ x duplex roller chain
  Number of links fitted:
    With tensioning rail 94
    With tensioning pinion 96

Chain tensioner:
  Piston length:
    With tensioning rail 2.441
    With tensioning pinion 2.520
  Tensioning rail coil spring free length 6.122
  Wire thickness .. .. .0394 ± .00059
  Tensioning pinion coil spring free length 6.575
  Wire thickness .. .. .0492 ± .00059
  Bore in tensioning pinion .. .. .669 + .0011
  Tensioning pinion bush .. .. .669 – .00063 – .00134
  Running clearance .. .. .00063 to .00240
  Tensioning lever bore .. .. .394 + .00059
  Tensioning lever shaft .. .. .394 – .00051 – .00110
  Running clearance .. .. .00051 to .00169

Crankshaft:
  Main bearing bore in crankcase:
    Red .. .. 2.362 + .00039
    Blue .. .. 2.362 + .00075 + .00039
  Bearing shell thickness:
    Red:
      Original .. .. .0984 – .00039 – .00079
      Stage 1 .. .. .1033 – .00039 – .00079
      Stage 2 .. .. .1082 – .00039 – .00079
      Stage 3 .. .. .1131 – .00039 – .00079
    Blue:
      Original .. .. .0988 – .00039 – .00079
      Stage 1 .. .. .1037 – .00039 – .00079
      Stage 2 .. .. .1087 – .00039 – .00079
      Stage 3 .. .. .1135 – .00039 – .00079
  Bearing play (radial) .. .. .0012 to .0027
  Main bearing journal diameter:
    Red:
      Original .. .. 2.165 – .00039 – .00079
      Stage 1 .. .. 2.155 – .00039 – .00079
      Stage 2 .. .. 2.1457 – .00039 – .00079
      Stage 3 .. .. 2.135 – .00039 – .00079
    Blue:
      Original .. .. 2.165 – .00079 – .00114
      Stage 1 .. .. 2.155 – .00079 – .00114
      Stage 2 .. .. 2.1457 – .00079 – .00114
      Stage 3 .. .. 2.135 – .00039 – .00079
  Big-end bearing journal diameter:
    Original .. .. 1.8898 – .00035 – .00098
    Stage 1 .. .. 1.8799 – .0004 – .0010
    Stage 2 .. .. 1.8701 – .0004 – .0010
    Stage 3 .. .. 1.8602 – .0004 – .0010
  Guide bearing thickness:
    Original .. .. 1.1811 + .0025 + .0010
    Stage 1 .. .. 1.1890 + .0025 + .0010
    Stage 2 .. .. 1.1969 + .0025 + .0010
  Crankshaft axial play .. .. .0024 to .0064
  Maximum runout centre main .. .. .0039 (8 bolts), .00078 (6 bolts)

Connecting rod:
  Overall length 5.315
  Small-end bore in rod .. .. .945 + .00083
  External diameter of small-end bush .. .. .94777 to .94860
  Manufacturer .. .. Messrs. Vandervell
  Big-end bearing bore diameter .. .. 2.047 + .00039
  Bearing shell thickness .. .. .0787 – .00039 – .00075
  Manufacturer .. .. Messrs. Glyco
  Bearing play (radial) .. .. .00114 to .00287

Cylinders:
  Bore:
    Standard .. .. 3.5039 + .00087
    First rebore 3.5137
    Second rebore 3.5236
  Maximum ovality .. .. .00039
  Maximum taper .. .. .00039
  Total wear tolerance on piston and cylinder .. .. .. .0039 to .0059

Pistons:
Design	Conical recessed oval centre
Diameter:	
Standard	3.5024
First oversize	3.5122
Second oversize	3.5220
Piston installed clearance	.0016 to .0039

Piston rings:
First (rectangular ring):	
Height	.0698 (1.75)
End gap	.0118 to .0197 (.3 to .5)
Side clearance	.00059 (.015)
Second (stepped ring):	
Height	.0787 (2.0)
End gap:	
Early cars	.0118 to .0177 (.30 to .45)
Later cars	.0079 to .0157 (.2 to .4)
Side clearance:	
Mahle pistons	.0012 to .0024 (.030 to .062)
KS pistons	.0016 to .0028 (.040 to .072)
Third (double chamfer):	
Height	.1575 (4.0)
End gap	.0098 to .0157 (.25 to .40)
Side clearance:	
Mahle pistons	.0008 to .0020 (.020 to .052)
KS pistons	.0012 to .0024 (.030 to .062)

Gudgeon pins:
Offset from centre line	.0591 (1.5)
Diameter:	
White	.8662 − .00012
Black	.8662 − .00024 − .00012
Clearance in piston	.00004 to .0002
2002, 2002Tii (inteference)	.00012 to .00035
Clearance in small-end bush:	
White	.00012 to .00039
Black	.0002 to .00047

Oil pump:
Type	Gear or rotor
Oil pressure at idle:	
Gear	7.1 to 21.3 lb/sq inch
Rotor	11.4 to 17.1 lb/sq inch
Oil pressure at 4000 rev/min:	
All models	57 lb/sq inch approx.
Relief valve opening pressure:	
Gear	57 to 71 lb/sq inch
Rotor	58 to 64 lb/sq inch
Relief valve spring free length	2.68
Geartooth backlash:	
Normal	.0012 to .0019
Maximum	.0028
Axial play:	
Normal	.0019
Maximum	.0035
Maximum depth in cover	.0019
Distance between housing bulkhead and gearwheel bearing surface at hub	1.358 = .0039

Rotor type pump:
Outer rotor to body clearance	.0039 = .002
Inner rotor to body clearance	.0047 to .0079
Rotor axial play	.0013 to .0037
Maximum depth difference in pump cover	.00197
Distance between hub outer flange and inner rotor	1.6811 = .0039

NOTES

CHAPTER 2

FUEL SYSTEM

2:1 Description
2:2 Fuel pump operating principle
2:3 Fuel system maintenance
2:4 Fuel pump removing & dismantling
2:5 Fuel pump reassembly, refitting & adjustment
Solex 40.PDSI & 40.PDSIT carburetter
2:6 Removing & refitting
2:7 Operation & adjustment
Solex 40.PHH dual carburetters
2:8 Removing & refitting
2:9 Operation & adjustment
Solex 40.PDSIT automatic choke carburetter
2:10 Operation & adjustment
2:11 Air cleaner
2:12 Automatic air intake preheat flap
2:13 Fuel tank
2:14 Fuel injection system
Solex 32/32 DIDTA carburetter
2:15 Operation & adjustment
2:16 Fault diagnosis
2:17 Technical data

2:1 Description

Of the various models covered in this manual only one, the 2002 tii, does not use a mechanical fuel feed pump and one or two Solex carburetters. Single carburetter versions have a Solex 40 PDSI, PDSIT or DIDTA, while dual carburetter engines have two Solex 40 PHH. Information for such servicing and adjustment as the owner/driver might wish to carry out for himself is given in this chapter, details of jet sizes etc. will be found in Technical Data at the end of this chapter.

2002 tii models are equipped with a Kugelfischer system of fuel injection instead of a carburetter and this is not suitable for unskilled attention. A brief description of the system is given at the end of the chapter, together with any adjustments which may be carried out without specialised testing equipment.

2:2 Fuel pump operating principle

Refer to **FIG 2:1**. An eccentric on the rotating camshaft actuates the operating lever 13 via a pushrod which depresses the diaphragm 14 and so creates a depression in the pumping chamber located in the upper body 7. Under atmospheric pressure, petrol passes through the pipeline connection from the fuel tank to the inlet valve into the pumping chamber. The return spring located under the diaphragm then raises the diaphragm, expelling the petrol through the outlet valve and pipeline to the float chamber of the carburetter.

When the float chamber is full of petrol, the pressure in the pipeline and the pump chamber holds the diaphragm depressed against the tension of the return spring.

2:3 Fuel system maintenance

A poor delivery of fuel to the carburetter may be due to a fault in the fuel pump or related lines. Periodically the pump body screws 6 (see **FIG 2:1**) and upper cover screw 1 should be checked for tightness. The fuel pump lines should be disconnected and checked for freedom of restrictions, chafing and loose connections. The fuel pump filter located underneath the top dome should be removed and cleaned periodically. A further filter is located at the base of the fuel tank sender unit in the petrol tank. For removal see **Chapter 12**.

2:4 Fuel pump removing & dismantling

The petrol pump is located on the lefthand side of the engine between the induction manifold and thermostat housing. Remove the fuel pump by first disconnecting the fuel inlet and outlet pipes and releasing the two retaining nuts from the studs in the cylinder head. Carefully lift away the pump from the cylinder head.

Dismantling:

1 Refer to **FIGS 2:1** and **2:2**. Remove the top dome mounting screw 1 and washer 3. Lift off the dome 2, washer 4 and filter 5. Remove the pump body's interlocking screws 6 and separate the upper half from the lower half of the body.
2 Remove the screws 7 and 6 fastening the sealing plate 9 to the lower body. Lift the retaining plate 10 from the pivot 11 and drive out the pivot using a parallel punch and hammer. Lift out spring 12 and pump drive lever 13. Carefully lift out the diaphragm 14.
3 Depress the diaphragm spring 15 (see **FIG 2:3**) and compression collar 16. Thoroughly wash all components in petrol and blow them dry using a compressed air jet or foot pump. Inspect the valves for evidence of damage and valve springs for weakness or cracks. Check to see that the diaphragm reaction spring 15 and operating lever spring 12 are not distorted or unserviceable. Generally inspect all parts for cracks, distortion of the diaphragm for stiffness and also the pump drive lever for distortion, and pivot pin for wear.

2:5 Pump reassembly, refitting & adjustment

Ensure all parts are clean and dry. Assembling is the reverse procedure to dismantling. Lubricate the pump drive lever 13 and pivot pin 11 before placing them in the lower body.

Reassembly is the reverse procedure to dismantling but the following points should be noted:

1 It is recommended that upon reassembling the diaphragm to the body it is brought to its correct position by BMW gauge 5125. The length of the diaphragm return spring 15 must not under any circumstances be altered.
2 The small inlet and outlet butterfly valves located in the upper body of the pump are not interchangeable and it is recommended that they are renewed in pairs.

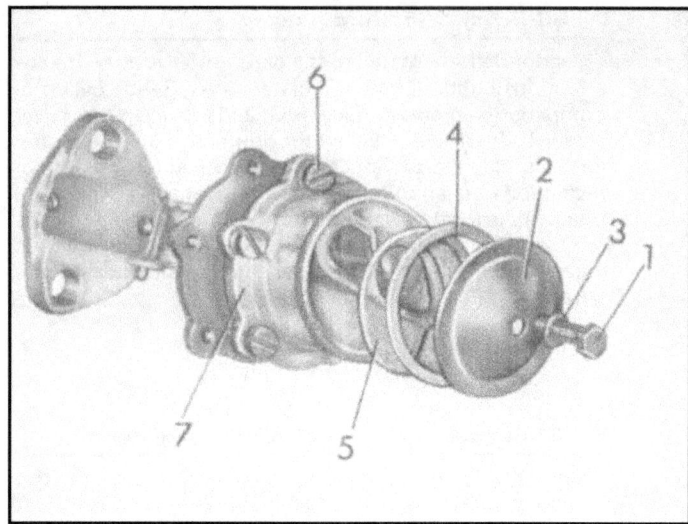

FIG 2:1 Fuel pump upper body

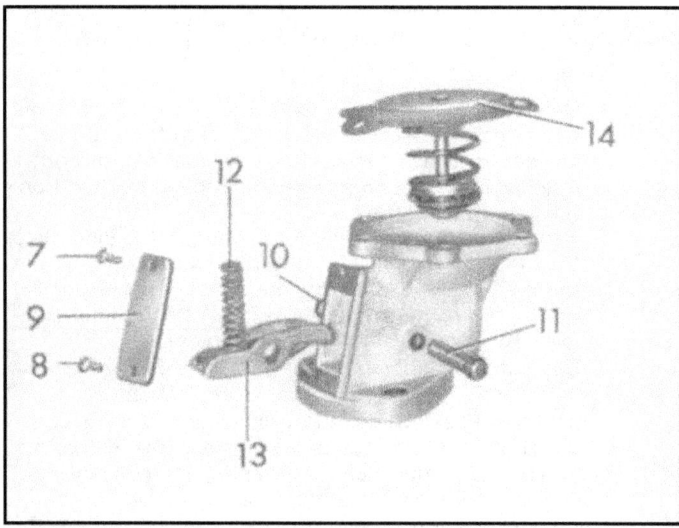

FIG 2:2 Fuel pump lower body

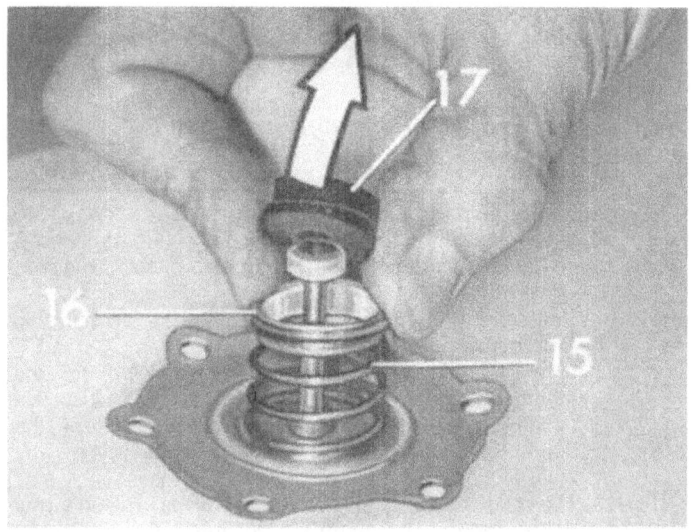

FIG 2:3 Diaphragm assembly

Installation and adjustment:

Refer to **FIG 2:4** where it will be seen that the pump is operated by a pushrod which is operated from the camshaft. A special insulating flange is located between the pump body and the cylinder head and the thickness S must be checked against original specification. Should either the plunger length or insulating flange thickness not be to specification then the operating pressure of the pump will be affected.

Pump plunger and flange specification:

Up to Chassis No. 917583.
Insulating flange thickness S with gaskets .19685 inch thick.
Plunger length L 3.59456 inch.
Pump pressure 2.13 to 2.84 psi.

From Chassis No. 917584.
Insulating flange thickness S with gaskets .78742 inch.
Plunger length L 4.19299 inch.
Pump pressure 3.0 to 3.6 psi.

Solex 40.PDSI & 40.PDSIT carburetter
2:6 Removing & refitting

To remove the carburetter proceed as follows:
1 Slacken the air inlet hose 1 (see **FIG 2:5**), open the air filter cover clips and ease the rubber connection hose 3 from the cylinder headed cover 4 and lift away together with the rubber supply hose 5.
2 Release and remove the petrol supply hose 6 and vacuum hose 7.
3 Using a screwdriver carefully lift away the intermediate throttle control linkage. Disconnect the automatic choke cable 17 (see **FIG 2:6**), from the lever 18 holding firmly with engineers pliers.
4 Carefully disconnect the bowden cable sleeve 19 from the pivot lever 20 and carefully pull away.
5 Remove the two carburetter retaining nuts and lift away the carburetter.

Reassembly:

Reassembly is the reverse procedure to dismantling but the following points should be noted:
1 Once the carburetter has been refitted and all controls connected, the engine should be allowed to run to normal operating temperature and then the idling speed adjusted using the spring-loaded adjustment screw until normal idling speed is obtained.
2 Ensure that the lever 18 (see **FIG 2:6**), lies against its limit stop 21. Also the signal contact located on the dashboard must be pushed down to its lowest position.

Solex 40.PDSI & 40.PDSIT carburetter
2:7 Operation & adjustment

Description and operation:

The Solex 40.PDSI and 40.PDSIT carburetters are of the downdraught design and may be considered to comprise three main parts. The throttle chamber together with the throttle butterfly, the throttle lever and pump intermediate lever and volume control adjustment screw.

The main body of the carburetter consists of a mixing chamber and float chamber, both parts incorporating all the required drillings and jets for the mixing of petrol with air as well as the float chamber with the float which keeps the petrol level constant. An accelerator pump is mounted on the top of the float chamber and is operated by a control rod and intermediate operating lever. The float chamber cover is secured onto the float chamber by means of retaining bolts. It contains the connection tube for the fuel pipe and located from the underside of the needle valve. An air vent tube for the float chamber is positioned in the float chamber cover. The strangler assembly is located in the main venturi tube. On the lower face of the float chamber cover, a special control device is fitted with an enrichment valve for enrichment of the charge under full load conditions. Gaskets are placed between the throttle chamber, the main body and float chamber cover.

The main jet, air correction jet and choke tube are specially matched so as to give the engine maximum performance with a minimum of fuel consumption. It is not recommended that individual carburetter settings are changed but should any adjustment become necessary due to unusual operating conditions or a different type of petrol is being used it is recommended that the manufacturers be contacted and requested for further information.

If a flat spot is noticed when the accelerator pedal is depressed the cause of the trouble is usually in the fuel pump system in the form of a dirty filter or partially blocked fuel pipe.

Dismantling:

1 Refer to **FIG 2:7** and unscrew the fastening screw on the carburetter top cover 11 and lift away together with gasket 12. Remove the float location plate 13 and carefully lift away the float together with its pivoting shaft.
2 Unscrew the seal plug 15 and remove together with its packing ring. Using a screwdriver of suitable blade width carefully remove the main jet.
3 Unscrew the float needle valve assembly 16 and lift out together with its packing ring 17.
4 Using a screwdriver of suitable blade width, carefully remove the air correction jet 19 and the mixture regulating screw G together with its spring.
5 Using a suitably sized spanner remove the idling jet 20. Unscrew the enrichment valve A and lift away together with its packing ring. The enrichment valve is controlled by a vacuum piston K (see **FIG 2:8**). Disconnect the clamp ring from the pump connection linkage and using a screwdriver unscrew the pump cover retaining screws. Lift away the pump cover 21 together with its connection linkage. Gently lift out the diaphragm 22 together with its spring 23.
6 Thoroughly clean all parts of the carburetter using petrol and dry carefully using a gentle compressed air jet.

Reassembly:

Reassembly is the reverse procedure to dismantling. Wherever gaskets are used they must always be renewed.

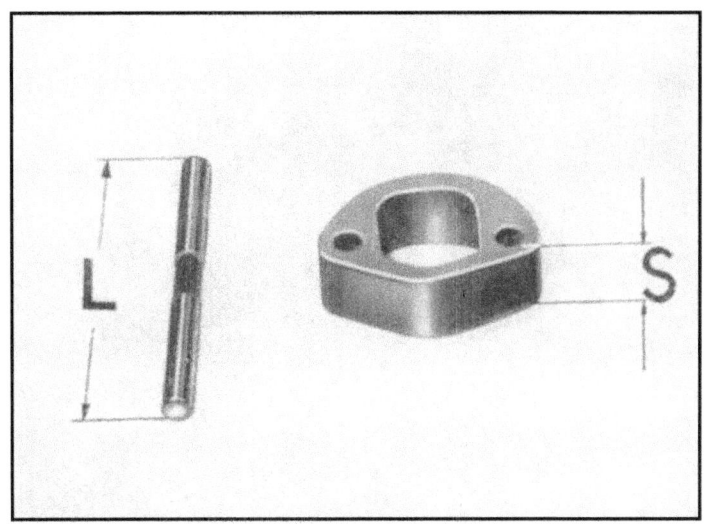

FIG 2:4 Pushrod and spacer

FIG 2:5 Carburetter removal

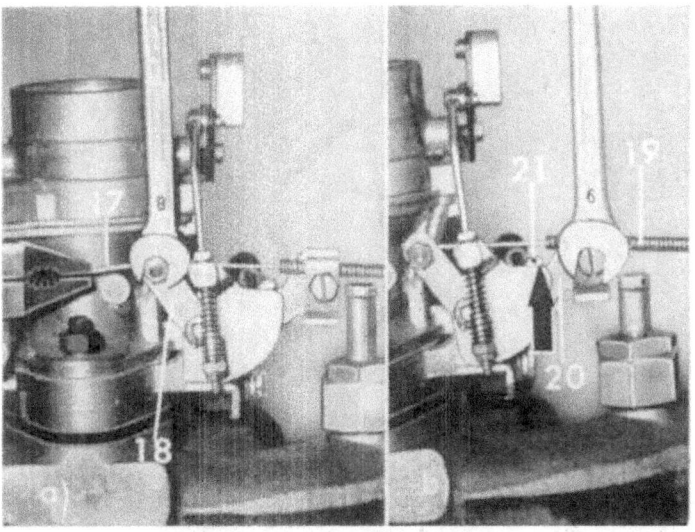

FIG 2:6 Bowden cable release

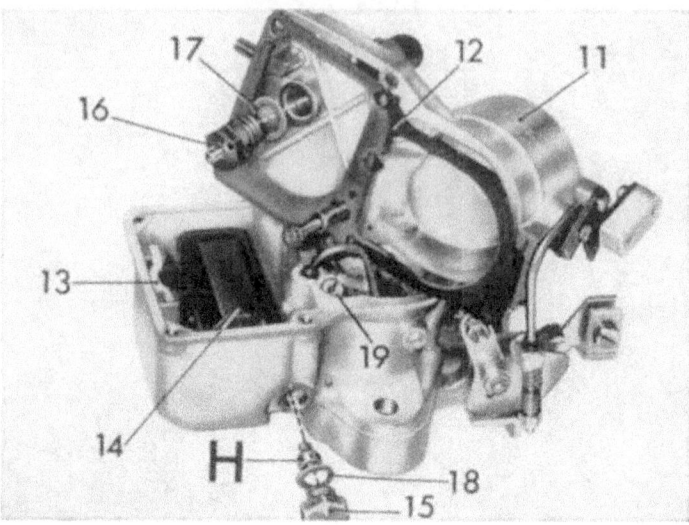

FIG 2:7 Carburetter top cover removed

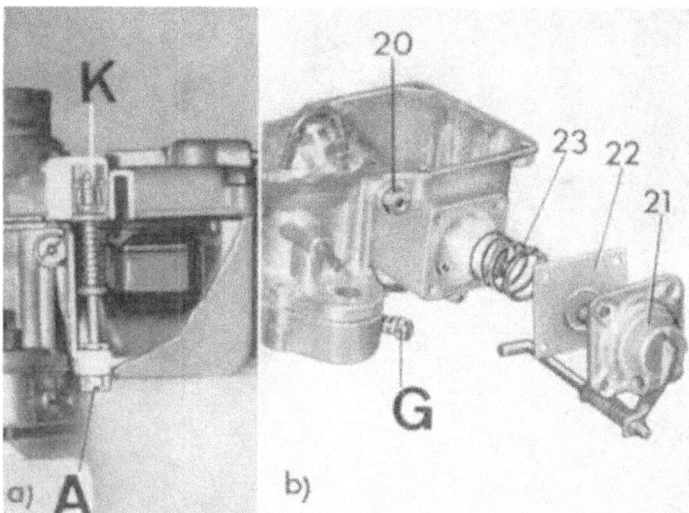

FIG 2:8 Enrichment valve

FIG 2:9 Carburetter adjustment screws

Resetting carburetter:

Once the carburetter has been reassembled to the engine, allow the engine to warm up to normal operating temperature and then adjust the idling screw 24 (see **FIG 2:9**) until the engine is at normal idling speed. The idling mixture should be adjusted by rotating the screw 25 together with idling screw 24 so that when the idling mixture is correct the engine is running smoothly at maximum idling speed.

Fuel level check:

To enable the carburetter to act at maximum efficiency the fuel level in the float chamber must be set and to complete this operation proceed as follows:
1 Allow the engine to run until normal operating temperature is reached. Switch off the engine.
2 Remove the fuel hose and immediately plug the end to ensure that no fuel is allowed to drip onto the hot engine. Remove the carburetter cover retaining screws and very carefully lift off the cover together with its gasket.
3 The fuel level shown as dimension N in **FIG 2:10** should be .669 to .748 inch at normal atmospheric pressure. It is recommended that a vernier depth gauge be used for this operation. Allowance should be made for the thickness of the special packing ring 17 (see **FIG 2:7**) located below the float needle valve.
4 Reassemble the carburetter top cover and reconnect the fuel hose.

Solex 40.PHH dual carburetters
2 : 8 Removing & refitting

To remove the carburetter installation proceed as follows:
1 Remove the air filter housing from the inner wheel arch panel gently release the breather hose from the top of the cylinder head cover and lift away the air filter housing.
2 Carefully pull away the main fuel feed lines (1 and 2) (see **FIG 2:11**), from the two carburetter covers.
3 Release the two fastening nuts (3 and 4) from the bearing support, and disconnect the pushrod (5) and the two tension springs 6. Release the eight carburetter to manifold fastening nuts (arrowed) and carefully lift away the carburetter assemblies.

Reassembly:

Reassembly is the reverse procedure to dismantling but the following points should be noted:
Once the carburetters have been refitted and all controls connected, the engine should be allowed to run to normal operating temperature and then the idling speed adjusted until normal idling speed is obtained

Solex 40.PHH dual carburetters
2 : 9 Operation & adjustment

Initial setting:

If the carburetters have been removed from the engine or their adjustment is suspect then the initial setting should be checked and reset as follows:
1 With the engine stationary remove the air filter housing from the inner wheel arch panel, and carefully pull off the breather hose from the top of the cylinder head cover and lower it so that the end is facing the distributor.

2 Carefully tighten the idling mixture regulation screws (1 to 4) (see **FIG 2:12**), until they are fully but gently screwed to their seating. Turn back each mixture regulation screw exactly one half of a turn.

3 Carefully loosen the synchronization screw (5) and unscrew until it is no longer bearing upon the throttle control lever (7). Unscrew the idling stop screw as far as it will go and screw inwards the synchronization screw 5 until it just comes into contact with the throttle control lever (7). Carefully screw in the idling stop screw (6) until the throttle butterfly lever is just touching. Finally screw in the idling stop screw (6) an extra two turns inwards.

Dual carburetter installation synchronization:

Before the carburetters may be synchronized it is essential that the ignition timing and the valve clearances are checked for correct adjustment and then proceed as follows:

1 Start the engine and allow to run until it reaches its normal operating temperature. Once this has been attained set the idling speed to 1200 rev/min. It should be noted at this point that all four carburetters must be adjusted to allow equal volume of air passage with the aid of a synchrotester.

2 Adjust the second carburetter, 2 in **FIG 2:13**, to coincide with carburetter 3 by means of the synchronizing screw 5.

3 Adjust the first carburetter to coincide with the second carburetter by means of the synchronizing screw 8 in **FIG 2:14**.

4 Adjust the fourth carburetter to coincide with the third carburetter 3 using the synchronizing screw 9 in **FIG 2:15**.

5 With the engine still running and at a fast idle speed adjust the idling mixture by turning the regulation screw inwards or outwards. This setting is correct when the engine reaches the maximum idling speed.

6 Reset the engine idling speed to 800 rev/min and readjust the idling mixture.

Fuel level check and adjustment:

For this test an accurate carburetter fuel level test rig is required as found in many service stations. The information in this section is given for reference purposes so that this operation may be completed with, if necessary, a little improvisation of standard workshop equipment. To complete the check proceed as follows:

1 A fuel container fitted with a hose as shown in **FIG 2:16** must be set to a height (A) of 8 ft—which should be measured from the centre of the carburetter venturi tube to the centre of the fuel container. **FIG 2:16** shows the BMW.6023 test rig and it is necessary when using this particular rig for the expansion chamber (W) to be sealed off with a correctly fitting plug.

2 Remove both carburetters from the engine and referring to **FIG 2:17** release the main jet mounting (H) from the carburetter and replace by adaptor (1).

3 Carefully unscrew the ball valve brackets 2 and attach the level testing adaptor by brackets 4 to the carburetter by means of the special hexagonal bolt brackets 3. Connect the adaptor to the level testing equipment using the transparent plastic tube.

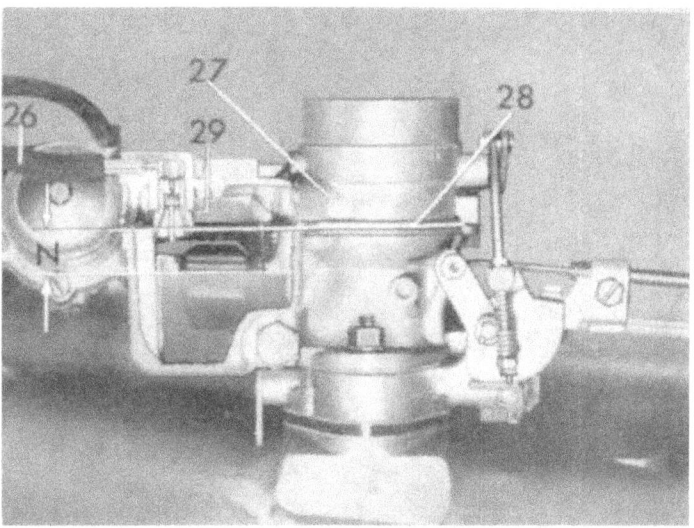

FIG 2:10 Float chamber level

FIG 2:11 Carburetter removal identification

FIG 2:12 Carburetter setting identification

FIG 2:13 Carburetter synchronization

FIG 2:14 Carburetter synchronization

FIG 2:15 Carburetter synchronization

4 Attach the carburetter to the test rig and adjust so that it is exactly in the horizontal position indicated by a spirit level or other suitable means.
5 Bleed the entire fuel system by opening and closing the knurled bleed screw (12) until no air bubbles are visible in the transparent hose (S) (see **FIG 2:18**). This procedure must be repeated before each measurement is taken. It should be noted that the fuel level in the gauge glass must be exactly opposite the marking R on the carburetter housing. Should this not be evident, loosen the locknut (13) and turn the level regulation screw (14) either in or out until the fuel level in the gauge glass (4) coincides with the carburetter marking (R).
6 This operation must be repeated on both carburetter installations.

Injection volume check and adjustment:

To check and adjust the injection volume proceed as follows:

1 Screw the ball valve and main jet carrier into the carburetter and operate the throttle butterfly shaft approximately ten times to its maximum limit. The pressure stroke must be performed quickly and smoothly with sufficient pause in between each individual stroke to allow a supply of fuel to be drawn in.
2 From the measuring glass on the test rig read off the injected volume of petrol which has been used and divide the result by ten. When the injection volume has been correctly regulated between .7 and .9 cc of premium grade fuel should be injected per stroke.
3 To adjust the injection volume by loosening the locknut (15) on the connection linkage (16) as shown in **FIG 2:19**. Should the injection quantity be too great unscrew the nut (17), conversely if the quantity is too small nut should be screwed inwards.
4 Refit the carburetters and synchronize as previously described. If necessary adjust the air fuel mixture.

Choke butterfly adjustment:

Refer to **FIG 2:20** where it will be seen that a set gap A of .0079 inch must be evident between the threaded rod and the choke operating lever. Adjust the threaded rod until the required gap is obtained. Finally adjust the pullrod B (see **FIG 2:21**), until it is a length of 1.614 inch.

Solex 40.PDSIT automatic choke carburetter
2:10 Operation & adjustment

Idling speed adjustment:

To adjust the idling speed start the engine and allow it to run until it reaches normal operating temperature and then proceed as follows:

1 Connect an electric tachometer to the ignition system and screw in the idling mixture adjusting screw 25 (see **FIG 2:9**), as far as it will go.
2 Unscrew the idling mixture adjustment screw approximately 1 to 1½ turns and then screw either in or out slightly until the engine idling speed increases to a maximum as shown on the electric tachometer.
3 Adjust the throttle stop screw 24 so that the idling speed is approximately 800 rev/min. Repeat the idling mixture adjustment screw procedure as previously described whereupon the correct setting should have been obtained.

Cold start setting adjustment:

1 Slowly but firmly depress the accelerator pedal as far as it will go and then release it. This will bring the special stepped disc to 'choke' position.
2 Start the engine but do not under any circumstances operate the accelerator pedal. The engine speed should rise to approximately 2500 to 3000 rev/min and if the outside temperature is below −20°C the engine should be allowed to run for a short while at this determined speed. Should the temperature be above −20°C run the engine at between 2500 to 3000 rev/min as previously described and operate the accelerator pedal once, this will enable the stop lever to engage with the next step on the selector disc and the engine speed should fall to between 1200 to 1600 rev/min. It is in this position that the vehicle may be driven.

As the operating temperature of the engine increases a special bi-metallic spring turns the specially shaped stepped disc further and the engine idling speed will be adjusted accordingly (see **FIG 2:22**) and showing the stepped disc in the choke position.

Cooling water circulation:

When the engine reaches an operating temperature of between 50 to 60°C the choke butterfly must be opened fully. It is in this position that the stepped disc as previously described will be disengaged. Should the choke butterfly appear to operate too slowly the water circulation and the special heating coil should be checked for correct operation.

Choke butterfly setting:

During normal carburetter servicing it is necessary to ensure that the choke butterfly pivot shaft rotates easily in the carburetter body. Lubricate with a thin oil as necessary.

If the temperature outside is below 20°C the choke butterfly should remain in the shut position. Also ensure that the notch on the spring casing as shown in **FIG 2:23** is correctly aligned with the projection on the choke valve housing. Using a voltmeter and ammeter it is recommended that periodically the current consumption of the heating coil be checked. This should be 12 volts requiring a current of 1 amp. Check that the bi-metallic spring is correctly positioned on the driving peg. As the bi-metallic spring is set at the factory it should not be modified in any way. Should either the bi-metallic spring or heating coil require renewal, the spring casing assembly must be renewed as a complete unit.

Depress the choke rod as far as its stop and using a drill shank or similar shaped gauge determine the width of gap A (see **FIG 2:24**). The gap should be set at .2598 ± .0079 inch and can be done after loosening the locknut 1 (see **FIG 2:25**).

Throttle butterfly adjustment setting:

1 Remove the choke mechanism cover by releasing the three retaining bolts and lift away. It is not necessary to release the two water hoses.
2 Carefully pull away the fuel and vacuum hoses and lift away the connection link and remove carburetter as previously described.
3 Raise the stop lever from the stepped disc by operating the throttle lever and close the throttle butterfly fully by hand. Using a drill shank or similar shaped gauge

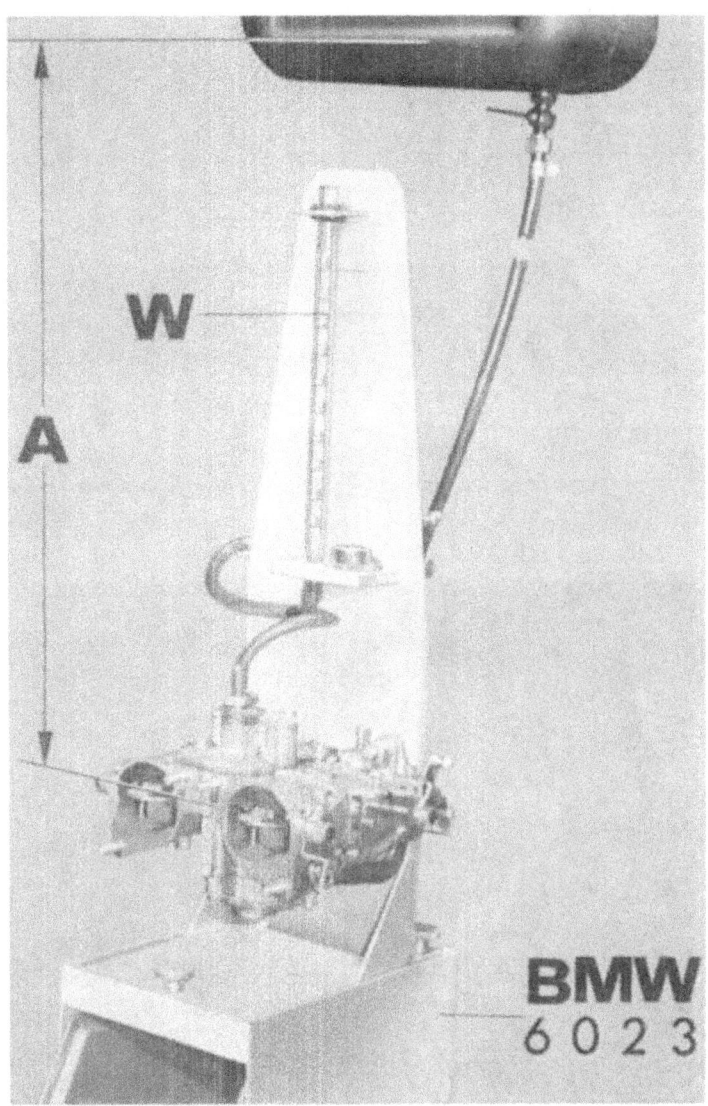

FIG 2:16 Carburetter test rig

FIG 2:17 Fuel level check

FIG 2:18 Fuel level adjustment

FIG 2:19 Injection volume adjustment

FIG 2:20 Choke butterfly adjustment

measure the throttle butterfly gap B as shown in **FIG 2:26**. The gap should be .0591±.0039 inch. Reset the throttle butterfly gap having first removed the locknut 1 (see **FIG 2:25**).

4 Start the engine and allow to come up to normal operating temperature and adjust the engine idling speed as previously described.

5 Should a new carburetter be fitted the throttle butterfly must be opened fully by hand and then the accelerator rod moved once up to the stop so that the automatic choke mechanism is disengaged. Adjust the throttle linkage so that the throttle butterfly is fully closed.

2:11 Air cleaner

Fit a new element periodically, depending on operating conditions. Do not unnecessarily disturb the air cleaner cover at any other time or dirt may find its way to the clean side of the intake.

To remove the element open the air filter cover snap retainers and lift off the air cleaner cover, withdraw and discard the old element, wipe the inside of the body with a non-fluffy rag and reassemble fitting a new element.

2:12 Automatic air intake preheat flap

The automatic air intake preheat flap is located in a housing on the right of the radiator. It is recommended that at 10,000 miles intervals a check be made to ensure that the lever moves freely in the Winter (W) position. Lightly oil all pivot points.

In the 'W' position air drawn in at the front of the vehicle is mixed with hot air from the exhaust manifold until a temperature of approximately 30°C is maintained. Above this temperature the preheat passage closes and fresh air only is supplied to the engine.

In the summer the external lever should be operated to fix the flap in the closed 'S' position. The cover is retained by two spring clips and can be removed to inspect the flap valve.

2:13 Fuel tank

The petrol tank is located in the rear section of the car under the floor panel. It has a capacity of approximately 12.1 Imp. gallons.

Removal:

To remove the petrol tank proceed as follows:

1 Disconnect the positive terminal of the battery and the two leads from the petrol tank unit.

2 Carefully ease away the rubber connection connecting the fuel tank supply pipe to the main supply line. Slacken the filler hose clamp S (see **FIG 2:27**), on the filler union and slide the hose 6 upwards.

3 Release the fuel tank fastening bolts as shown arrowed in **FIG 2:27** and carefully lift away the fuel tank.

4 To replace the petrol tank is the reverse procedure to removal.

Cleaning:

The tank must be thoroughly checked for leaks especially at the joint seams. Should a leak be found, it is advisable for a garage to attend to this as it is very dangerous to apply heat to a petrol tank without first taking strict precautions, and the garage will be in a better position to do this.

To clean the tank interior, remove the drain pipe and spray in a jet of petrol so that all sediment and dirt deposits can be loosened. Then vigorously shake the tank. Flush the tank with petrol and blow the tank dry. Repeat this procedure until the tank is clean. Refit the drain plug.

Whilst the petrol tank is away from the car it is advisable to disconnect the fuel feed pipes at the pump and carburetter installation and ensure that these are clear by using an air jet to one end of the pipe.

2 : 14 Fuel injection system

From the fuel storage tank at the rear end of the car, the fuel is drawn through filters to the Bosch electric fuel pump, which pumps it through a further very fine filter and water trap to the injector pump.

The injector pump, which also includes additional straining for the fuel, is responsible for the delivery of a timed and metered quantity of fuel to each of the four cylinders in the engine in the correct order. There are a number of control devices to ensure the correct timing and metering of this fuel injection charge, according to the ambient or engine temperature and the engine operating conditions at any moment. These components should on no account be adjusted by other than fully qualified personnel, using special equipment and in almost surgically clean surroundings.

Filter renewal:

The fuel filter located on the engine bulkhead should be discarded and renewed every 40,000 miles (60,000 km). This is simply a matter of disconnecting the fuel hoses and undoing the retaining bolts. Make sure that the direction of fuel flow is observed when refitting.

At the same intervals the strainers in the ring piece on the injection pump, at the suction side of the electric fuel feed pump and in the immersed tube level sensor must be taken out and cleaned. Be very careful not to use a cloth for drying these strainers, as the smallest amount of fluff may clog the mesh or interfere with the operation of the injector pump.

Slow-running adjustment:

The engine must be first brought up to normal operating temperature and then the following settings should be checked.

Refer to **FIG 2:28**. Check dimension A. This is the projection of the air regulating cone of the warm-up runner and it should be between .35 and .39 inch (9-10 mm).

Dimension B from the enrichment lever to the collar nut should be .157 inch (4 mm).

The threaded pin 1 must be in full contact with the stop screw 2.

If these specifications are not satisfied, it is likely that the thermo-element is defective or the warm-up sensor requires adjustment or renewal and the car should be taken to the BMW agent.

If these checks are satisfactory, refer to **FIG 2:29** and set an idle speed of 900 ± 50 rev/min by means of the adjusting screw 3.

Now use the slotted screw 4 to adjust the CO emissions to 2-3%. Turning this screw inwards decreases the CO percentage and vice versa.

If this last adjustment alters the idling speed, the correct speed can be regained by using screw 3 as necessary.

FIG 2:21 Pullrod adjustment

FIG 2:22 Cold start setting

FIG 2:23 Spring casing alignment

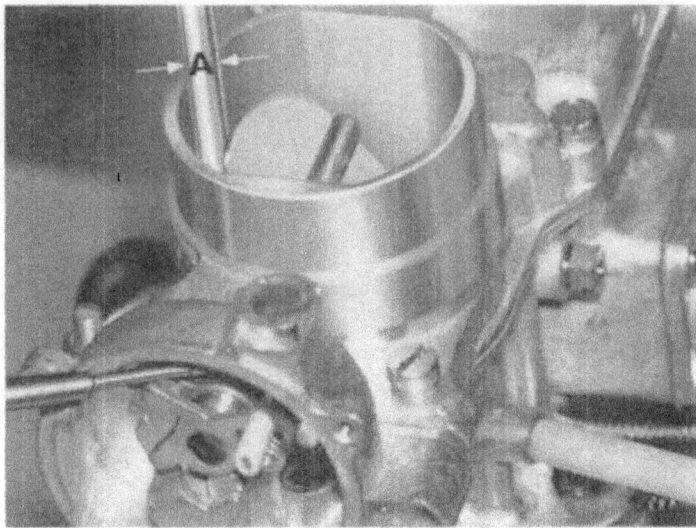

FIG 2:24 Choke butterfly setting

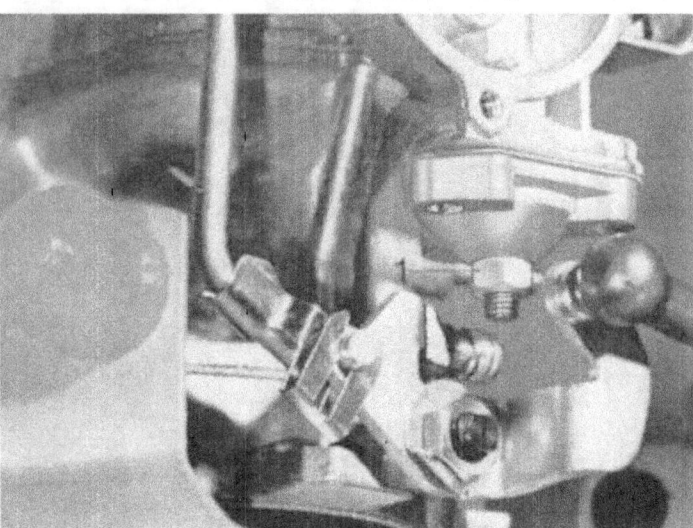

FIG 2:25 Choke control adjustment

FIG 2:26 Throttle control adjustment

Fuel pump:

This component cannot be repaired or adjusted and in the event of failure must be renewed. The pump is removed as follows:

Disconnect the battery and pull off the cable connector from the pump. There is a groove into which the plug must fit when reconnecting, this avoids incorrect polarity.

Remove the fuel hoses, noting that fuel loss can be prevented by plugging the hose from the tank which is the larger of the two.

Undo the attachment nuts and lift off the pump together with the expansion header container.

Fitting is carried out in the reverse order. Do not omit to check the filter element in the suction hose union.

Injection pump:

In the event of a breakdown in this very delicate component it is suggested that professional assistance should be obtained.

Drive belt renewal:

The injection pump is driven by a cogged belt which requires no attention in normal service. When it becomes necessary to fit a new belt it is essential to ensure that the correct timing of the pump is maintained.

Remove the front air filter hood, remove the four retaining screws and detach the upper dust cap.

Turn the engine until No. 1 cylinder is at TDC. In this position the notch in the V-belt pulley on the crankshaft must be in line with the marker on the dustcap, see **FIG 2:30**, and the notch in the cogged belt pulley on the injection pump must point to the marking rib on the timing case cover.

Slacken off the alternator mounting bolts to enable the V-belt to be removed and then take out the four securing screws and withdraw the V-belt pulley from its hub. Do not now permit the engine to be turned, otherwise the timing will be lost.

Unscrew the bolts attaching the lower dust cap over the cogged belt, slip the belt off the pulleys and then while holding the dust cap forwards, pull the belt out between the hub and the dust cap.

Reverse the above to fit the new belt.

Accelerator pedal linkage:

This is not likely to require adjustment in normal service, but if it has been dismantled for any reason, it must be correctly connected as follows. Refer to **FIG 2:31**.

Detach the pin joint 1 from the cranked lever 2 and then check the length of the two connecting rods A and B and adjust them if necessary to the correct dimensions. These are: A = 289 mm (11.378 inch), B = 85 mm (3.346 inch).

Now use the hooked tool 6075 to secure the pump regulating lever 3 in the bottom slotted hole as shown and adjust the stop screw 4 so that it just contacts the regulating lever.

Press down on the accelerator pedal 5 onto the full load stop 6 and adjust the joint pin 1 so that it may be easily inserted in the hole in the cranked lever 2 without any straining.

Secure the pin joint and remove the hooked tool.

Fuel tank:

The fuel tank on the BMW 2002 tii is larger than that on carburetter models and holds a little over 12 gallons (55 litres).

Lubrication:

The necessary lubrication for the injector pump is provided by the engine's lubrication system and so no additional attention is required. The pump carries a small amount of oil and if, for any reason, this may have been drained or a new pump fitted, 100 cc of engine oil should be added to the pump before the engine is started.

Solex 32/32 DIDTA carburetter
2 : 15 Operation & adjustment

This double barrel carburetter is fitted to later models of the 2002 Automatic and the main specifications are given in **Technical Data**. The carburetter includes an acceleration pump and an automatic choke and, although they are quite separate, the two barrels are fed by a common float chamber and feed into a common inlet manifold.

The primary barrel is controlled directly by the accelerator and operates on its own for all normal low-speed running, but when the demand exceeds the quantity of fuel which the primary system can supply, the secondary throttle opens automatically under the control of a vacuum valve and linkage and continues in action until the engine demands have reduced and can again be supplied by the primary barrel alone. In order to avoid any surge or hesitation as the secondary throttle comes into action, there are progression holes in the walls of the barrel which are uncovered as the throttle plate begins to open and supply the initial fuel required for a smooth transition to double channel operation.

Interference with the carburetter is not advised and adjustments should preferably be made using an exhaust gas analyzer. In many cases the adjustment screws are sealed by the manufacturers before delivery. In the event of a service station being out of reach, a temporary setting for the slow-running can be made as follows:

Bring the engine up to normal operating temperature and fit a reliable tachometer.

First, make sure that the throttle stop screw (3 in **FIG 2 : 32**) is correctly set; gently turn in screw 1 onto its seat and then use screw 3 to obtain an engine speed of 650 to 700 rev/min. Using screw 1, set the speed to 900 ± 50 rev/min and then use the mixture screw 2 to obtain the highest engine speed possible consistent with smooth running. Finally, use screw 1 to return to 900 rev/min. If a CO meter is available, use screw 2 to obtain a CO content of 0.8 to 1.2%.

2 : 16 Fault diagnosis

The following table of faults attributable to the fuel system applies to carburetter installations. The diagnosis of defects in a fuel injection system should be entrusted to a qualified service station.

(a) Leakage or insufficient fuel delivered

1. Air vent in tank restricted
2. Petrol pipes blocked
3. Air leaks at pipe connections
4. Pump or carburetter filters blocked
5. Pump gaskets faulty
6. Pump diaphragm defective
7. Pump valves sticking or seating badly
8. Fuel vaporizing in pipelines due to heat

FIG 2:27 Petrol tank mountings

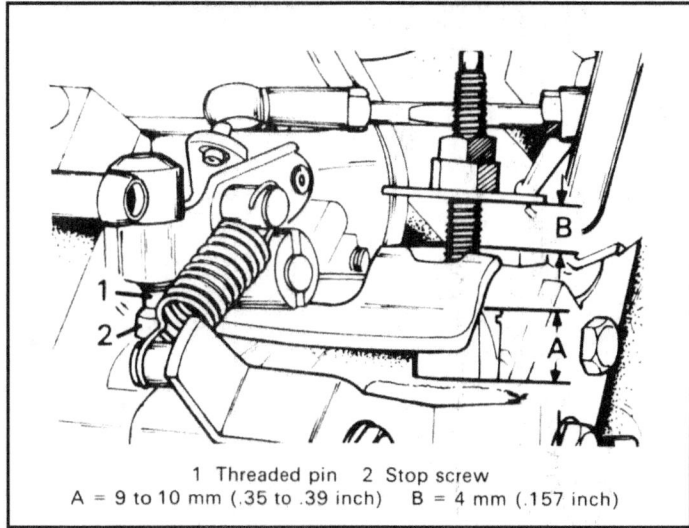

1 Threaded pin   2 Stop screw
A = 9 to 10 mm (.35 to .39 inch)   B = 4 mm (.157 inch)

FIG 2:28 Adjusting the slow-running, fuel injection

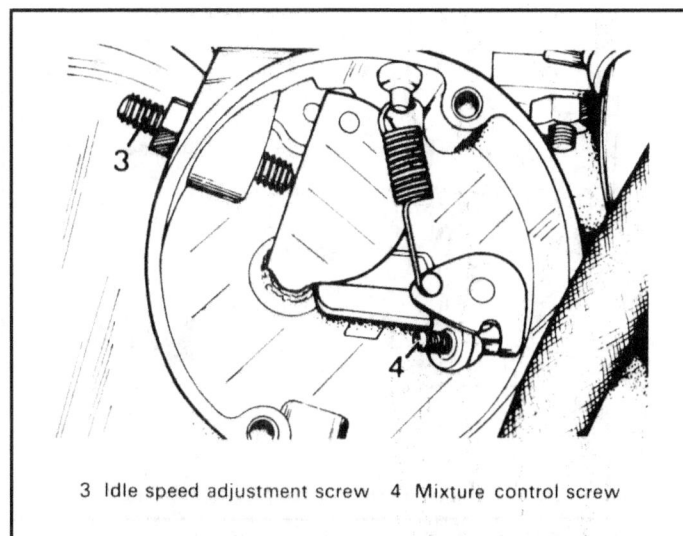

3 Idle speed adjustment screw   4 Mixture control screw

FIG 2:29 Adjusting the slow-running, fuel injection

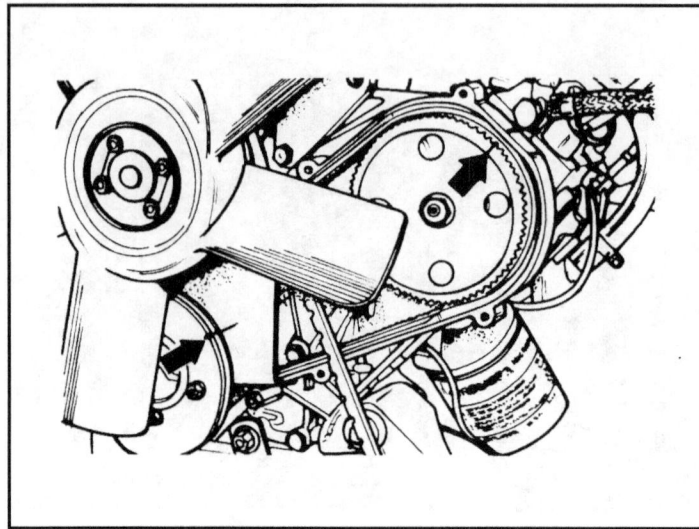

FIG 2:30 Showing the correct alignment of the belt pulleys when No. 1 is at TDC

(b) Excessive fuel consumption

1 Carburetter(s) need adjusting
2 Fuel leakage
3 Sticking controls or choke device
4 Dirty air cleaner(s)
5 Excessive engine temperature
6 Brakes binding
7 Tyres under-inflated
8 Idling speed too high
9 Car overloaded

(c) Idling speed too high

1 Rich fuel mixture
2 Carburetter controls sticking
3 Slow-running screws incorrectly adjusted
4 Worn carburetter butterfly valve

(d) Noisy fuel pump

1 Loose mountings
2 Air leaks on suction side and at diaphragm
3 Obstruction in fuel pipe
4 Clogged pump filter

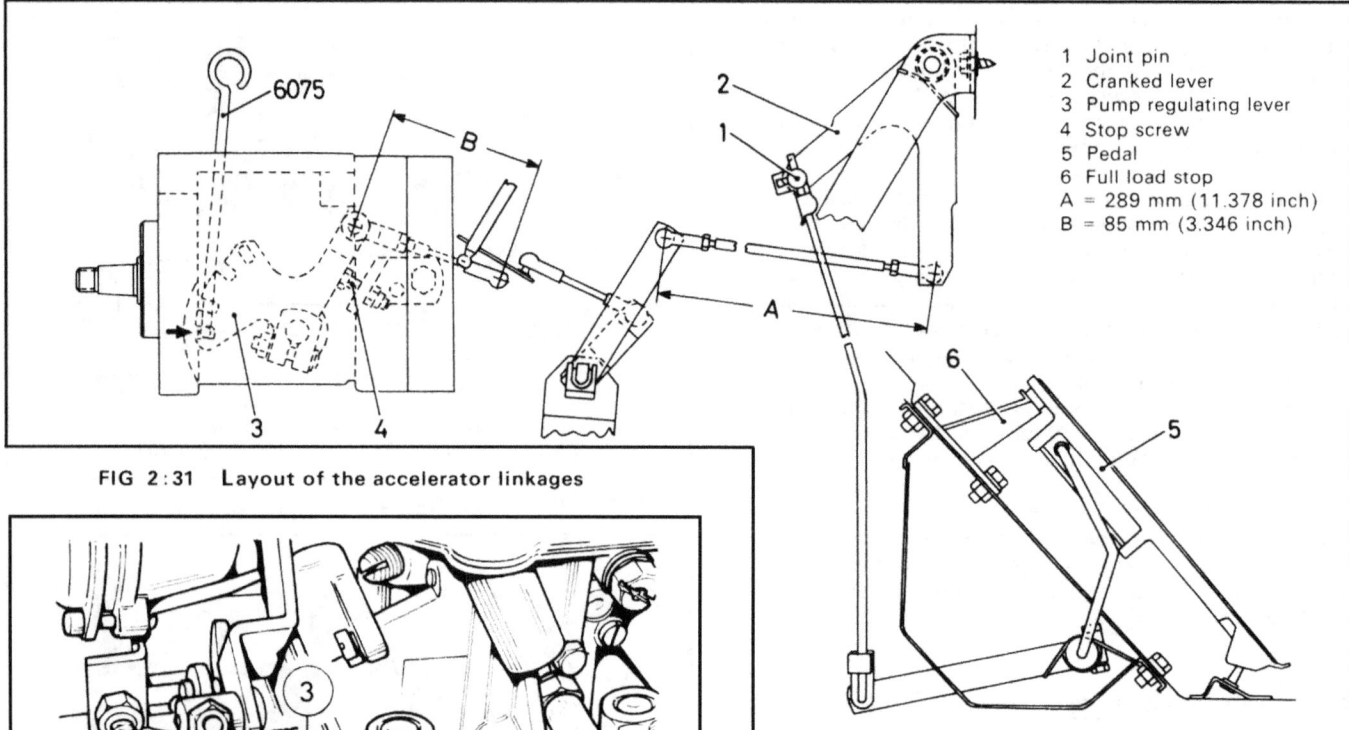

FIG 2:31 Layout of the accelerator linkages

1 Joint pin
2 Cranked lever
3 Pump regulating lever
4 Stop screw
5 Pedal
6 Full load stop
A = 289 mm (11.378 inch)
B = 85 mm (3.346 inch)

(e) No fuel delivery

1 Float needle stuck
2 Vent in tank blocked
3 Pipeline obstructed
4 Pump diaphragm stiff or damaged
5 Inlet valve in pump stuck open
6 Bad air leak on suction side of pump

1 Bypass screw 2 Mixture control screw 3 Throttle stop screw

FIG 2:32 Slow-running adjustment screws Solex 32/32 DIDTA carburetter

2 : 17 Technical data

Recommended fuel octane rating:
- 2002, 2000, 2000A, 2000CA 95
- 2000TI, 2000 TI Lux, 2000CS 99
- 2002, 2002TI, 2002Tii 97

Fuel tank capacity .. .. 12.1 gallons
Fuel system filter .. .. Fine mesh in fuel pump

Mechanical fuel pump:
- Type .. .. Pierburg PE
- Pressure at 1000 rev/min .. .. 2.99 to 3.56 lb/sq inch

Carburetters:

2002, 2000, 2000A, 2000CA, 2002A:
- Type .. .. Solex 40.PDSIT or 40.PDSI
- Main jet X155
- Air correction jet 130
- Venturi 30
- Pilot jet 45
- Idling air jet 100
- Rich mixture valve 100
- Port for air to mixing tube .. .. .50
- Float needle valve gasket .. .. .04
- Injection pump tube 100
- Quantity per stroke:
    - Automatic choke .. .. 1.9 ± .2 cc
    - Manual choke .. .. 2.0 ± .2 cc
- Float needle valve 2.0
- Butterfly valve angle .. .. 8 deg.
- Bypass drillways .. .. 1.1 to 1.2
- Depth of fuel below joint line .. .. .67 to .75

2000TI, 2000 TI Lux, 2000CS, 2002TI:
- Type .. .. Solex PE.40.PHH
- Main jet 130
- Air correction jet 155
- Venturi 34
- Pilot jet 52.5
- Idling jet air drillway .. .. 1.2 ± .05 calibrated
- Mixture tube ZK.6854
- Injection pump tube .. .. .5 calibrated
- Quantity per stroke .. .. .3 cc
- Float needle valve 2.0
- Butterfly valve angle .. .. 13 deg.
- Bypass drillways 1.3
- Depth of fuel below joint line .. .. Mark on float chamber housing
- Fuel injection pump .. .. Kugelfischer PLO4
- Injectors DLO-20D
- Fuel pump .. .. Bosch 0580364002

2002 Automatic (later):
- Type .. .. Solex 32/32.DIDTA

	Primary	Secondary
Choke tube	24 mm	28 mm
Main jet	117	140
Compensating jet	120	80
Idle jet	50	50
Accelerator pump	0.8/1.0	
Needle valve	2.0 mm	

NOTES

CHAPTER 3

IGNITION SYSTEM

3 : 1 Description
3 : 2 Maintaining the ignition system
3 : 3 Troubleshooting the ignition system
3 : 4 Distributor removing, overhaul & refitting
3 : 5 Timing the ignition
3 : 6 Spark plugs & H.T. leads
3 : 7 Fault diagnosis
3 : 8 Technical data

3 : 1 Description

All the cars covered by this manual use a Bosch distributor which incorporates automatic timing control by a centrifugal mechanism and a vacuum operated unit.

The weights of the centrifugal device fly out against the tension of small springs as engine speed rises. This movement advances the contact breaker cam relative to the distributor driving shaft to give advance ignition. The vacuum unit is connected by small bore pipe to the induction manifold. Depression in the manifold operates the vacuum unit, the suction varying with engine load. At small throttle openings, with no load on the engine, there is a high degree of vacuum in the induction manifold causing the vacuum unit to advance the ignition. When hill climbing on large throttle openings, the much reduced vacuum ensures that the unit will retard the ignition. The distributor unit is mounted to the rear of the cylinder head and can be seen in **FIG 3:1**.

3 : 2 Maintaining the ignition system

Refer to **FIG 3:2** and remove the distributor cap. Carefully pull up the rotor squarely off the end of the cam spindle. Squirt a few drops of oil between the cam spindle and the contact breaker base plate to lubricate the centrifugal advance mechanism, but take great care to avoid letting any oil onto the contact breaker base plate or the points themselves. Smear a little grease or engine oil on the cam and apply the tiniest drop of oil to the contact breaker pivot.

Contact breaker points:

1 Release the distributor cap retaining clips and lift away the cap. Carefully lift upwards the rotor arm.
2 Using the fan belt to turn the engine in the normal direction of rotation, turn the engine till the contact breaker arm has reached its fully open position on the apex of one of the cams. Using a set of feeler gauges check the contact breaker point gap. The correct gap should be .016 inch or if metric feeler gauges are available .4 mm.
3 Inspect the contact breaker points whilst they are open and if they show signs of excessive wear, pitting or corrosion on either or both of the contact breaker points they will have to be renewed.
4 Refer to **FIG 3:2** and loosen the nut 1 and carefully pull upwards the cable 2. Release the hairpin clip 3 and lift away the washer 4. Carefully push out the spring support 5 on the fixed contact plate 6 and remove the moving contact.
5 Refer to **FIG 3:3** and remove the fixed contact locking screw 7 using a screwdriver of suitable width blade. Lift away the fixed contact 6.
6 Reassembly is the reverse procedure to dismantling.

Cleaning the contact points:

If the contact breaker points are dirty or only very slightly pitted they must be cleaned by polishing them with a fine carborundum stone, taking care to keep the faces flat and square. Afterwards wipe away all dust with a clean cloth moistened in fuel. The contacts may be dismantled to assist cleaning as previously described in this section. If the moving contact is removed from its pivot, check that it is not sluggish. If it is tight, polish the pivot pin with a strip of fine emerycloth, clean off all dust and apply a tiny spot of oil to the top of the pin. If a spring testing gauge is available the contact breaker spring should have a tension of 15.9 to 19.5 oz measured at the points.

3 : 3 Troubleshooting the ignition system

If the engine runs unevenly set it to idle at a fast speed. Taking care not to touch any metal part of the sparking plug leads, pull up the insulator sleeves and short each plug in turn, using a screwdriver with an insulated handle, connect the screwdriver blade between the plug top and the cylinder head. Shorting a plug which is firing properly will make the uneven running more pronounced. Shorting a plug in a cylinder which is not firing will make no difference.

Having located the faulty cylinder, stop the engine and remove the plug lead. Start the engine and hold the lead carefully to avoid shocks so that the metal end is about $\frac{3}{16}$ inch away from the cylinder head. A strong regular spark shows that the fault might lie with the sparking plug. Remove and clean it according to the instructions in **Section 3:6**. Alternatively, substitute it with a new plug.

If the spark is weak and irregular, check that the lead is not perished or cracked. If it appears to be defective, renew it and try another test. If there is no improvement remove the distributor cap and wipe the inside clean and dry. Check that the main central carbon brush is free and that it protrudes from the moulding and moves correctly against the pressure of the internal spring. Examine the surface inside the cap for signs of 'tracking', which can be seen as a thin black line between the electrodes or some metal part in contact with the cap. This is caused by a breakdown in electrical insulation and the only cure is to fit a new distributor cap.

Testing the low-tension circuit:

Before carrying out electrical test, confirm that the contact breaker points are clean and correctly set. Then proceed as follows:
1 Disconnect the thin black cable from the contact breaker point terminal on the side of the coil marked 1 and also the other end of the cable from the side of the distributor body. Connect a test lamp between the two

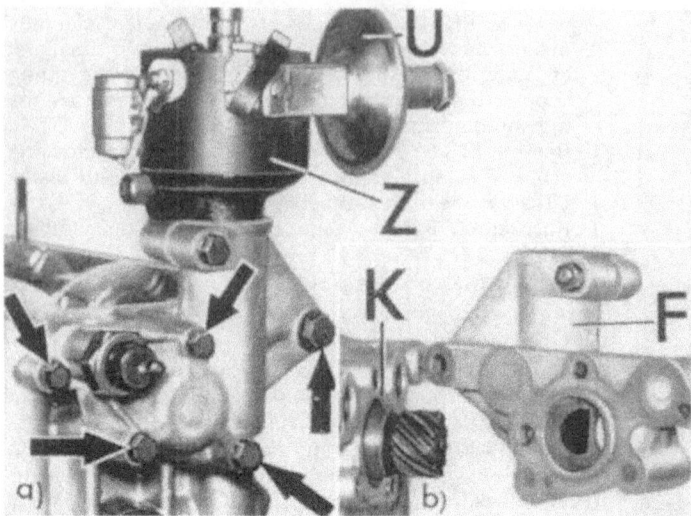

FIG 3:1 Distributor location

FIG 3:2 The contact breaker points

FIG 3:3 Contact breaker securing screw

terminals. Turn the engine over slowly. If the lamp lights when the contacts close and go out when they open, the low-tension circuit is in order. If the lamp fails to light, the contacts are dirty or there is a break or loose connection in the low-tension wiring.

2 If the fault lies in the low-tension circuit, switch on the ignition and turn the crankshaft until the contact breaker points are fully open. Refer to the wiring diagram in Technical Data and check the circuit with a 0-15 voltmeter. If the circuit is in order the meter should read approximately 6 or 12 volts depending on the electrical system used.

3 Battery to ignition switch terminal 30. Connect the voltmeter between terminal 30 on the back of the ignition switch and earth. No reading indicates a faulty cable or loose connection.

4 Ignition switch. Connect the meter between number 15 switch terminal and earth. Switch on the ignition when no reading indicates an internal fault within the switch.

5 Ignition switch to ignition coil. Connect the meter between terminal 15 on the ignition coil and earth. No reading indicates a damaged cable or loose connection.

6 Ignition coil. Disconnect the cable from the terminal 1 on the side of the ignition coil and connect the meter between this terminal and earth. No reading indicates a fault in the primary winding of the coil and a replacement coil must be fitted. If the reading is correct, remake the connections to the coil.

7 Contact breaker points and capacitor. Connect the meter across the contact breaker points. No reading indicates a fault in the capacitor.

Capacitor:

The best method of testing a capacitor (condenser) is by substitution. Disconnect the original capacitor and connect a new one between the low-tension terminal on the side of the distributor body and to earth.

If a new capacitor is needed, fit one complete with brackets, but if necessary, unsolder the original bracket and solder it onto the new capacitor using as little heat as possible.

3:4 Distributor removing, overhaul & refitting

Use **FIG 3:2** for reference. Before removing the distributor turn the crankshaft until the rotor arm is pointing to the brass segment in the cap which is connected to No. 1 cylinder plug lead at the fan end of the engine. This will supply a datum for replacement. Do not turn the crankshaft after this.

1 Remove the distributor cap and disconnect the cable from the low-tension terminal. Disconnect the vacuum pipe from the vacuum unit.

2 Release the distributor body clamp located at the top of the mounting bracket F (see **FIG 3:1**), and very carefully lift upwards the distributor body.

3 Carefully pull upwards the rotor arm.

4 Remove the nut 1 and dismantle the terminal assembly from the side of the distributor body. Remove the hairpin clip 3 together with the washer 4 (see **FIG 3:2**). Carefully push out the spring support 5 on the fixed contact plate 6 and lift away the moving contact.

5 Remove the fixed contact locking screw (see **FIG 3:3**) with a screwdriver and lift away the fixed contact.
6 Remove the contact breaker base plate screws and carefully withdraw the base assembly from the distributor housing. Care must be taken in releasing the vacuum central unit.
7 The location of the rotor arm driving slot and centrifugal weights must be noted to assist with retiming once the distributor is assembled. Remove other parts as necessary.

Inspection:

1 Thoroughly clean all the metal parts in fuel.
2 Thoroughly inspect the weight springs and if found to be weak in operation or signs of cracking, these must be renewed.
3 Examine the contact breaker points for wear and replace as necessary.
4 By the addition of shims eliminate any excessive end play in the distributor shaft or cam.

Reassembly:

Reassembly is the reverse procedure to dismantling but the following points should be noted:
1 Lubricate the parts of the centrifugal advance mechanism, the distributor shaft and that part of the shaft which accepts the cam, with thin engine oil.
2 When reassembling the distributor insert it so that the vacuum chamber is on the lefthand side when viewed from the front of the engine as shown in **FIG 3:1**.

Installation:

If for any reason the distributor has been removed from its mounting in the cylinder head it must be correctly meshed with the camshaft gear with the rotor arm pointing in the right direction once the timing marks have been realigned. This operation is fully described in **Section 3:5**.

FIG 3:4 Contact breaker point adjustments

FIG 3:5 Ignition timing marks locations

3:5 Timing the ignition

It is important that before the ignition timing is reset the distributor points are checked to ensure that they are in good condition and that the gap is correctly adjusted. To retime the ignition with the engine stationary proceed as follows:
1 Remove the distributor cap and rotor arm.
2 Carefully turn the engine in its normal direction of rotation until the contact breaker arm is fully open. Recheck the contact breaker point gap. This should be .0157 inch or .4mm.
3 Turn the engine until it is in the firing position for No. 1 cylinder. This is shown in **FIG 3:5** and also in **Chapter 1, FIGS 1:47** and **1:49**. On 2000 TI and 2002 TI models the firing point is TDC. The notch marked on the distributor rotor should coincide with the marking cut into the top face of the side of the distributor body.
4 Connect a test lamp between the terminal on the side of the distributor body and earth. Switch on the ignition. If the ignition timing is correctly adjusted the contact breaker points should have just separated at this point. The test lamp will be alight. To check the setting turn the crankshaft through approximately 45 deg. in an anticlockwise direction. The test light should be extinguished. Turn the crankshaft back again in a clockwise direction and the test lamp should light at the moment when the pointer on the gear case cover is opposite to the appropriate notch in the belt pulley.
5 To adjust the ignition timing or reset it as required, loosen the clamping screw on the distributor flange and rotate the distributor as necessary.

Stroboscopic timing:

With this method do not let the engine speed rise above approximately 600 rev/min or the centrifugal advance plate will start to operate. If the vacuum advance pipe is connected direct to the inlet manifold, disconnect this first or the timing will be retarded. See also **Section 1:16**.

3 : 6 Spark plugs & H.T. leads

Inspect, clean and adjust sparking plugs regularly. The inspection of the deposits on the electrodes is particularly useful because the type of colour of the deposit gives a clue to conditions inside the combustion chamber and is therefore most helpful when tuning.

Remove the sparking plugs by loosening them a couple of turns and then blowing away loose dirt from the plug recesses with compressed air or a tyre pump. Store them in the order of removal.

Examine the gaskets. If they are about half their original thickness they may be used again.

Examine the firing end of the plugs to note the type of deposit. Normally, it should be powdery and ranging from brown to greyish tan in colour. There will also be slight wear of the electrodes, and the general effect is one which comes from mixed periods or high-speed and low-speed driving. Cleaning and resetting the gap is all that will be required. If the deposits are white or yellowish they indicate long periods of constant-speed driving or much low-speed driving about town. Again, the treatment is straightforward.

Black, wet deposits are caused by oil entering the combustion chamber passed worn pistons, rings or down valve stems. Sparking plugs of a type which run hotter may be of assistance in alleviating the problem. The cure of course, is an overhaul.

Dry black fluffy deposits are usually the result of running with a rich mixture. Incomplete combustion may also be a cause and this might be traced to defective ignition or excessive idling.

Overheated sparking plugs have a white, blistered look about the centre electrode and the side electrode may be erroded. This may be caused by poor cooling, wrong ignition, or sustained high speeds with heavy loads.

Have the sparking plugs cleaned on an abrasive-blasting machine and tested under pressure after attention to the electrodes. File these till they are clean, bright and parallel. Set the electrode gap to .024 to .027 inch (.014 inch platinum tipped plugs). **Do not try to bend the centre electrode.**

Before replacing the plugs clean the threads with a hand wire brush. Do not use a wire brush on the electrodes. If it is found that the plugs cannot be screwed in by hand, run a tap down the threads in the cylinder head. Failing a tap, use an old sparking plug with cross cuts down the threads. Tighten the spark plugs using a normal box spanner through half a turn.

Sparking plug leads:

The high-tension cables must be examined carefully and any which have the insulation cracked, perished or damaged in any way must be renewed. Fitting new plug leads is a straightforward operation but it is recommended that the lead sockets in the distributor cap are smeared with a silicone grease before the cable is inserted to prevent water from entering. Ensure that the lead is pushed home as far as it will go and then secure firmly.

3 : 7 Fault diagnosis

(a) **Engine will not fire**

1 Battery discharged
2 Distributor contact points dirty, pitted or maladjusted
3 Distributor cap dirty, cracked or 'tracking'
4 Carbon brush inside distributor cap not touching rotor
5 Faulty cable or loose connection in low-tension circuit
6 Distributor rotor arm cracked
7 Faulty coil
8 Broken contact breaker spring
9 Contact points stuck open

(b) **Engine misfires**

1 Check 2, 3, 5 and 7 in (a)
2 Weak contact breaker spring
3 High-tension plug and coil leads cracked or perished
4 Sparking plug(s) loose
5 Sparking plug insulation cracked
6 Sparking plug gap incorrectly set
7 Ignition timing too far advanced

3 : 8 Technical data

See Technical data - **Chapter 11**

CHAPTER 4

COOLING SYSTEM

4 : 1 Description
4 : 2 Maintaining the cooling system
4 : 3 Troubleshooting the cooling system
4 : 4 Radiator removing & refitting
4 : 5 Fan belt adjusting & replacing
4 : 6 Water pump removing & refitting
4 : 7 Water pump overhaul
4 : 8 Thermostat removing & refitting
4 : 9 Cold weather precautions
4 : 10 Fault Diagnosis
4 : 11 Technical data

4 : 1 Description

All models which are covered by this manual have the same type of pressurised cooling system. The natural thermo-syphon action of the water is assisted by a centrifugal impeller mounted at the cylinder block end of the fan spindle, driven from the crankshaft by a V-belt.

A thermostat is fitted into the cooling system to enable the engine to quickly warm up to normal operating temperature by restricting the water circulation.

The induction manifold has waterways cast into it, so enabling good fuel vaporisation at ambient temperature thus enabling the engine to give good performance during all normal condition changes. A spring-loaded valve in the radiator filler cap pressurizes the system and so increases the temperature at which the coolant boils.

4 : 2 Maintaining the cooling system

There is only one lubrication point and this is a plug in the water pump casing. At approximately every 10,000 miles, remove the plug and introduce some recommended grade of grease into the pump. Do not force the lubricant in under pressure or it may pass through the bearings and get onto the pump seal, impairing the efficiency of the seal.

The cooling system should be drained, flushed through and refilled with clean water at regular intervals. Antifreeze may be used for two years providing that its concentration is checked during the cold weather. When draining the system filled with antifreeze, it should be collected for re-use during that period. Take care to separate any sediment in the bottom of the container, and not allow it to enter the radiator.

Draining:

Open both the radiator and cylinder block drain taps as shown in **FIG 4:1**. Remove the radiator pressure cap and set the heater control to 'hot'. Allow the system to completely drain into a clean container of a suitable size. Inspect the coolant for traces of oil or signs of excessive corrosion.

Flushing:

Introduce water from a hose into the top tank of the radiator and let it continue to run through the system and out through the draining plug holes until it runs clear.

If the radiator is blocked, remove it as detailed in **Section 4:4** and turn upside down. Reverse flush by inserting a hose into the bottom tank and allow water to flow through the radiator and out through the pressure cap neck.

Filling:

Before refilling the cooling system, the heater control lever must be set to the 'hot' position. Carefully fill with water through the radiator pressure cap neck and screw down the radiator cap until it is engaged on the second retaining notch. Start the engine and allow to warm up to normal operating temperature thus ensuring the thermostat has fully opened. Place a rag over the radiator pressure cap and release slowly to the first notch position. This will release the pressure. Finally remove the cap, check the water level and top up as necessary using hot water. Refit the radiator pressure cap firmly.

4 : 3 Troubleshooting the cooling system

The object of this test is to ensure that the pressure cap is seating correctly and that the spring rating has not changed with use over a period of time. Also it is designed to ensure that no coolant leaks from the system whilst it is operating under normal running pressure. The test requires special pressure testing equipment which is available at most service stations.

1 Fix the test equipment to the radiator pressure cap neck as shown in **FIG 4:2**, and pressurize the cooling system to 14.22 psi using the hand pump.
2 The gauge should be watched for a minimum period of two minutes during which time the gauge reading should not alter, thus indicating complete water tightness. Should the pressure fall, the cause must be investigated and rectified accordingly.
3 Remove the test gauge and fit the union S as shown in **FIG 4:3**. Screw the radiator pressure cap K to the union and using the hand pump P pressurize the tester. The opening pressure as indicated by the tester gauge should be compared with the opening pressure which is marked on the top of the radiator pressure cap under test. If the cap does not come to the required specification a new one must be fitted.

4 : 4 Radiator removing & refitting

To remove the radiator from the car proceed as follows:

1 Drain the coolant from the cooling system by opening the two drain taps as shown in **FIG 4:1**, and collect in a clean container of suitable size. Disconnect the automatic fluid cooler pipes, if fitted.
2 Remove the air filter and lift away together with the air preheater regulator housing.
3 Remove the radiator hose K from the thermostat housing T (see **FIG 4:4**), and also the radiator hose S from the water pump elbow W.
4 Release and unscrew the four radiator fixing bolts and very carefully lift the radiator upwards ensuring that the fan blades do not damage the radiator matrix.
5 Reassembly is the reverse procedure to dismantling. Refill the cooling system as described in **Section 4:2**. Check automatic fluid level.

FIG 4:1 Drain tap locations

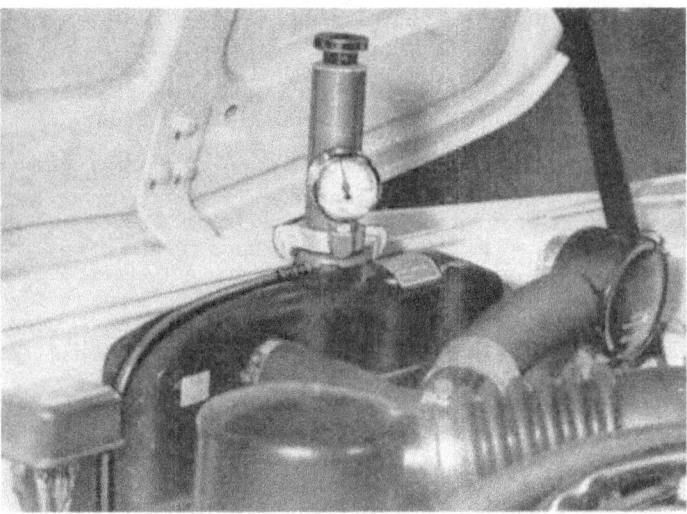

FIG 4:2 Pressure testing cooling system

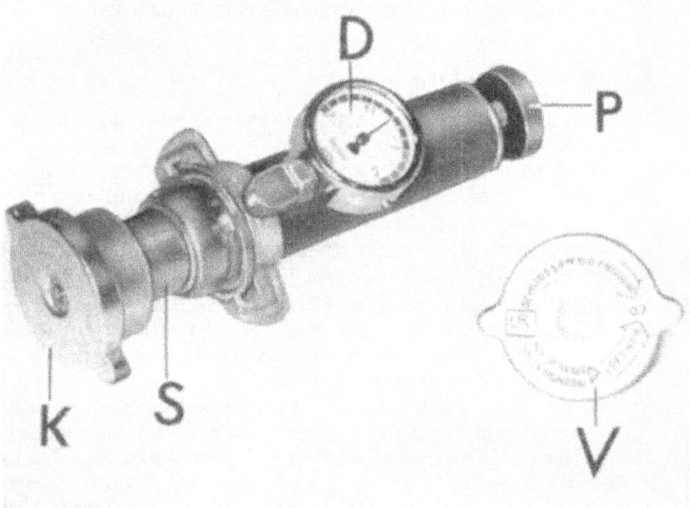

FIG 4:3 Pressure tester

4:5 Fan belt adjusting and replacing

1 Slacken the three tension bolts from the alternator end plates and push the alternator down towards the cylinder block.
2 Carefully lift the V-belt from the generator pulley, followed by the water pump pulley and the crankshaft pulley.
3 Upon reassembly the V-belt should be suitably adjusted by pulling upwards on the generator body. When correctly adjusted it should be possible to depress the V-belt between .179 and .394 inch on the longest run.

4:6 Water pump removing & refitting

This is shown in FIG 4:5, where the water impeller is on the lefthand end of the spindle and the flange mounting on the right. The bearing assembly can be seen and also the seal pressing against the inner face of the impeller boss. The face of the seal is spring-loaded thus ensuring a good quality seal between the shaft and pump body.

Removing the water pump:

1 Drain the coolant from the cooling system as described in **Section 4:2**.
2 Remove the air filter and front air filter cover.
3 Release the hose clip 3 (see **FIG 4:6**) and carefully ease the breather pipe from the cylinder head top cover. Carefully pull the air filter housing together with its hose 6 from the air preheater regulator housing.
4 Remove the radiator hose K (see **FIG 4:4**), from the thermostat housing T and the radiator hose S from the water pump elbow W.
5 Remove the radiator fixing bolts and carefully lift out the radiator ensuring that the fan blades do not damage the radiator matrix.
6 Using the hand, increase the V-belt tension so locking the water pump spindle and unscrew the fixing nut 1 (see **FIG 1:18**). Open the lockplates 2 and 3 and release the four fixing bolts 4–7.
7 Remove the fan blades and release the generator mounting bolts 8–10 as shown in **FIG 1:19**. Lift away the V-belt. Slacken the hose clip S on the return pipe as shown in **FIG 4:7**.
8 Using a universal puller with suitably tapped legs remove the pulley from the water pump as shown in **FIG 4:8**. Remove the seven fixing bolts as shown in **FIG 4:9** and carefully lift away the water pump.

Reassembly:

Reassembly is the reverse procedure to dismantling but the following points should be noted:
1 When refitting the water pump the copper gaskets must be renewed.
2 Refer to **Section 4:5** for the correct procedure for adjustment of the V-belt.
3 When tightening the fixing nut 1 as shown in **FIG 1:18** the V-belt tension must be increased by depressing it and the nut tightened to a torque wrench setting of 28.9 lb ft.

4 : 7 Water pump overhaul

Two types of water pump are fitted to the power unit. One has a flange pressed onto the main spindle and it is onto this that the fan blades and pulley are bolted. The second type of pump fitted as a detachable flange which is retained in place by a Woodruffe key and locked by a nut screwed onto the end of the shaft.

Water pump type 1—model without flange fitted

1 Using a suitably pointed tool remove the Woodruffe key 1 (see **FIG 4:10**) from the shaft. Release the circlip 2 using a pair of circlip pliers with pointed ends fitted. Carefully extract the spacing ring 3 and the seal ring 4.
2 Using a press and suitably sized drift carefully press the shaft with the grooved ballbearings from the impeller. Use a suitable sized drift and drive the seal ring 8 from its housing 9. Refer to **FIG 4:11** for seal location.
3 Carefully withdraw the grooved ballbearing races from the shaft 13 together with the securing ring 6.

Inspection:

Inspect the bearing races for discolouration or excessive wear and fit new as necessary. Ensure that the seals are in good condition although it is considered advisable to fit new if available. Inspect the impeller seal assembly if it shows signs of wear, excessive corrosion or damage. If there have been signs of water leakage from the water pump itself new impeller seals must be fitted.

Reassembly:

To reassemble the water pump proceed as follows:
1 Carefully insert the snap ring 7 into the groove and slide in the securing ring 6 over the top of it.
2 Carefully pack the grooved ballbearing race 10 with multi-purpose high melting point grease and press onto the spindle. Fit the spacer ring 11 and pack with grease. It should be noted that both the notches should be facing towards the grooved ballbearing race 10. Pack the grooved ballbearing race 12 with grease and also press onto shaft.
3 Carefully insert the sealing ring 5 into the housing and assemble the complete shaft into its housing. This operation must be carried out with care as the spacer ring must be in correct alignment. Insert the sealing ring 14 and spacer ring 15. Using circlip pliers insert the circlips 16 and ensure that it is correctly located.
4 Using a press carefully replace the impeller 17 ensuring that clearance A (.039 ± .008) is available between the housing 9 and impeller 17 as shown in **FIG 4:5**.

Water pump type 2—model with flange fitted:

1 Using a heavy duty universal puller or hydraulic press remove the boss from the shaft. Release the circlip (see **FIG 4:12**), using a pair of circlip pliers with pointed ends and carefully remove the spacer ring.
2 Using a press and suitably sized drift remove the impeller from the shaft and the water pump bearing from its housing.
3 Remove the axial friction seal from its housing using a hammer and suitably sized drift. The assembly is shown in **FIG 4:13**.

FIG 4:4 Cooling system parts identification

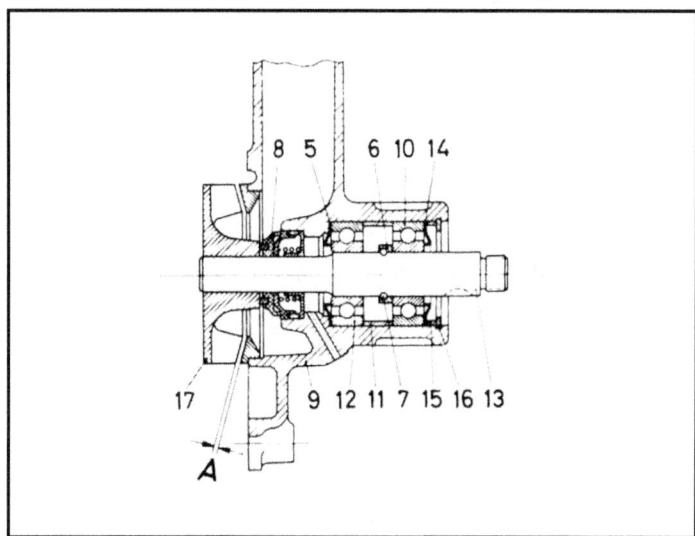

FIG 4:5 Water pump—sectional view

FIG 4:6 Air filter parts identification

FIG 4:7 Generator mounting bolts

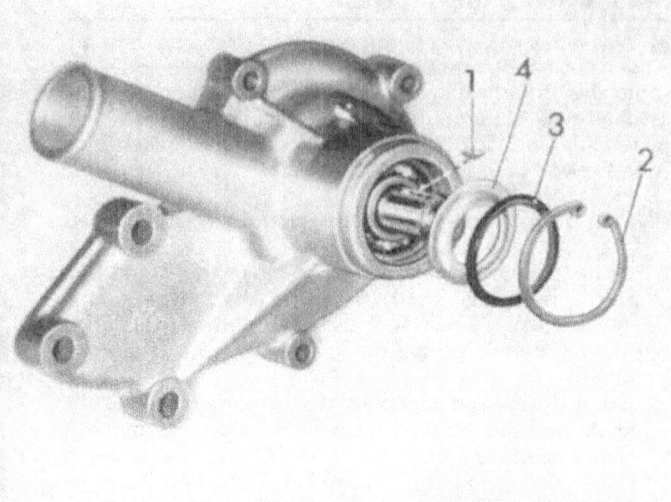

FIG 4:10 Water pump front end components

FIG 4:8 Water pump pulley removal

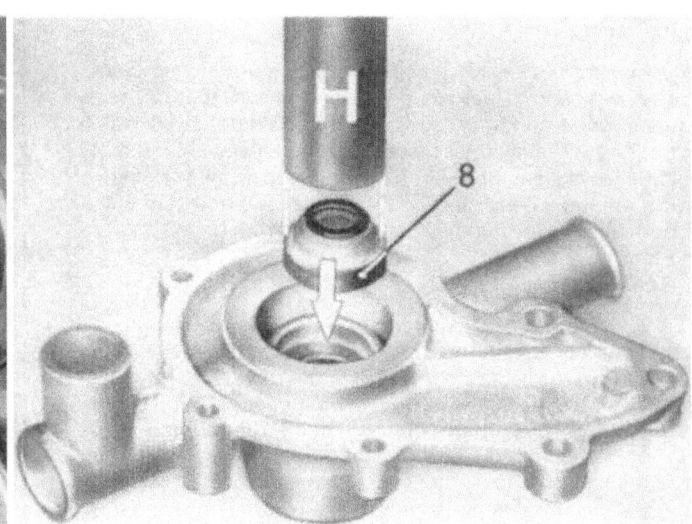

FIG 4:11 Water pump seal

FIG 4:9 Water pump retaining bolts

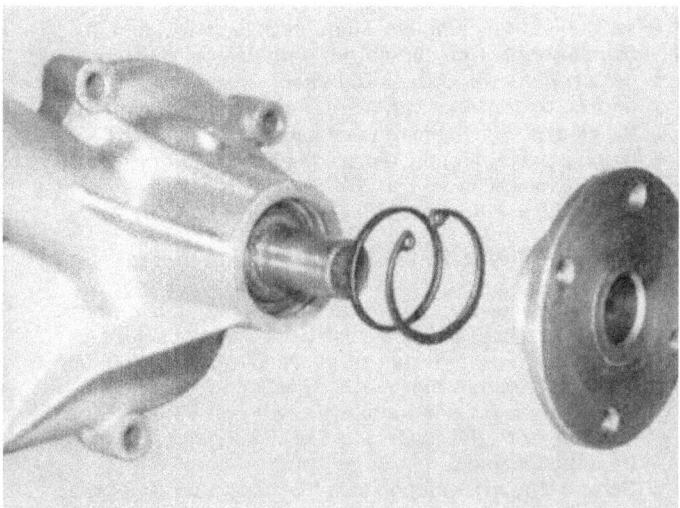

FIG 4:12 Water pump front end components

Inspection:

Inspect the bearing races for discolouration or excessive wear and fit new as necessary. Ensure that the seals are in good condition although it is considered advisable to fit new if available. Inspect the impeller seal assembly if it shows signs of wear, excessive corrosion or damage. If there have been signs of water leakage from the water pump itself a new impeller seal assembly must be fitted.

Reassembly:

Reassembly is the reverse procedure to dismantling but the following points should be noted:
1 Using a press and suitably sized drift, press in the water pump bearing 1 until it is up against its seating. Follow by inserting the axial friction seal 2 with a suitably sized tube.
2 Insert the spacer ring and refit the circlip ensuring that it is correctly seated in the pump body. Using a press carefully replace the flange ensuring that dimension A (see **FIG 4:14**) is $2.965 \pm .008$ inch.
3 Turn over the pump body and coat the face of the shaft with Loctite AVV and carefully press on the impeller until clearance B (see **FIG 4:15**), is $.039 \pm .008$ inch. It is recommended that this clearance be set using feeler gauges. As this assembly is an interference fit a press capable of exerting a pressure of at least 1100 lb is required.

4 : 8 Thermostat removing & refitting

The thermostat is located towards the forward end of the cylinder head (see 'T' in *FIG 4:4*). To remove the thermostat proceed as follows:
1 Unscrew the radiator cap 3 and also open the water drain tap on the radiator.
2 Referring to **FIG 4:16**, release the four bolts retaining the thermostat housing cover 1 and lift away the thermostat housing cover. Remove the thermostat 2 from its housing together with its joint gasket 3.
3 The thermostat can be tested by immersing it in water so that it does not touch the sides or bottom of the container. The temperature of the water is raised until the thermostat valve starts to open at the temperature given in Technical Data. If the valve does not open or sticks in the fully open position renew it. It is impossible to repair a defective thermostat.
4 Refitting is the reverse procedure to dismantling. It is recommended that a new joint gasket be fitted whenever the original one is disturbed.

4 : 9 Cold weather precautions

When a heater is fitted antifreeze must be used, as draining the cooling system does not automatically drain the heater.

To add antifreeze mixture the cooling system should first be drained and flushed through with water until it runs out clean. Pour in antifreeze first, followed by the water.

FIG 4:13 Water pump seal

FIG 4:14 Flange location

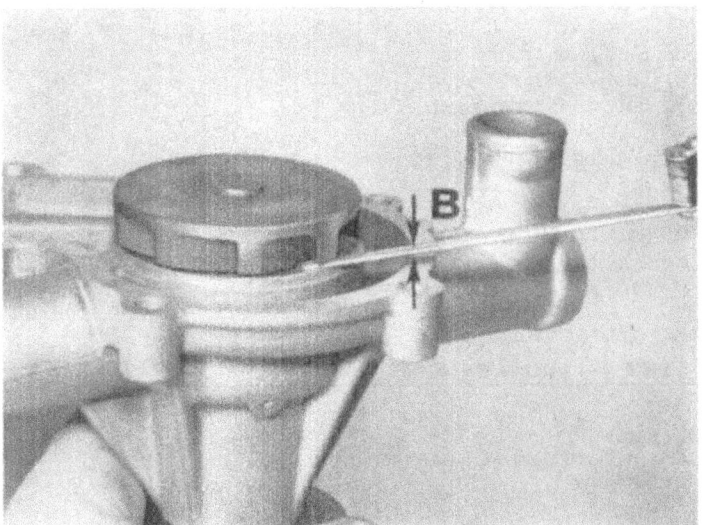

FIG 4:15 Impeller location

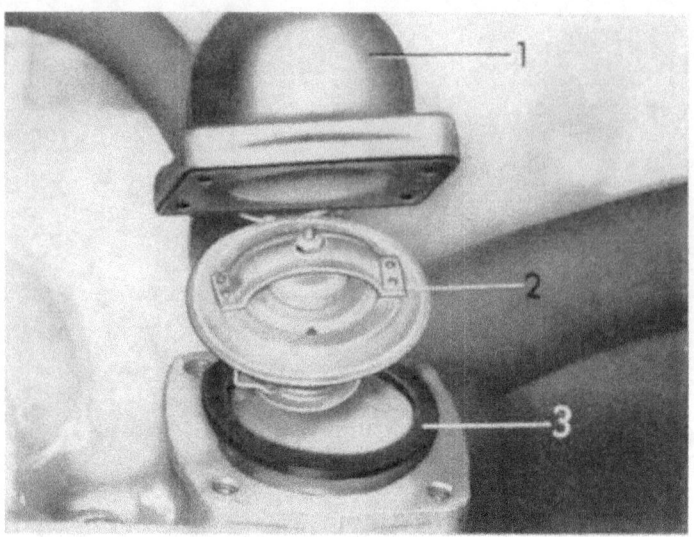

FIG 4:16 Thermostat

Use only antifreeze of the ethylene-glycol type which conforms to British Standards Specification BS.3151 or BS.3152. The mixture can remain in the system for two years providing that the SG is checked periodically and fresh antifreeze is added as required. After the second winter drain the system, flush out using water and refill with new antifreeze solution.

Do not use antifreeze in the windscreen washer container. Special additives are available for this purpose. The recommended quantities of antifreeze for different degrees of frost are:

Antifreeze	Starts freezing at	Absolute safe limit
1¾ pints	−9°C or 16°F	−19°C or −3°F
2 pints	−13°C or 9°F	−26°C or −15°F
2¼ pints	−16°C or 3°F	−33°C or −28°F

4 : 10 Fault diagnosis

(a) Internal water leakage

1 Cracked cylinder wall
2 Loose cylinder head nuts
3 Cracked cylinder head
4 Faulty head gasket

(b) Poor circulation

1 Radiator core blocked
2 Engine water passages restricted
3 Low water level
4 Loose fan belt
5 Defective thermostat
6 Perished or collapsed radiator hoses

(c) Corrosion

1 Impurities in the water
2 Infrequent draining and flushing

(d) Overheating

1 Check (b)
2 Sludge in crankcase
3 Faulty ignition timing
4 Low oil level in sump
5 Tight engine
6 Choked exhaust system
7 Binding brakes
8 Incorrect valve timing
9 Slipping clutch
10 Retarded ignition
11 Mixture too weak

4 : 11 Technical data

Thermostat opening temperature	75 ± 1°C
Radiator pressure cap	14.2 ± 2.1 lb/sq inch
Water pump clearance between housing and impeller	.039 ± .0008

CHAPTER 5

CLUTCH

5:1 Description
5:2 Removing & refitting the clutch
5:3 Servicing the clutch components
5:4 Servicing the hydraulic system
5:5 Bleeding the hydraulic system
5:6 Clutch pedal removing & refitting
5:7 Self-adjusting diaphragm clutch
5:8 Fault diagnosis
5:9 Technical data

5:1 Description

The two main driving members of the clutch assembly comprise the flywheel and pressure plate assembly as shown in **FIG 5:1**. The pressure plate is caused to rotate with the flywheel by a projection on the pressure plate engaging with slots in the cover which is bolted to the back of the flywheel. On earlier models a series of nine springs are located between the clutch cover and the pressure plate and these force the pressure plate towards the flywheel face, so trapping the friction-lined driven plate between the two machined surfaces. On later models (since 1969) a diaphragm spring replaces the nine coil springs (see **Section 5:7**).

The drive shaft sometimes called first motion shaft, is supported in the front of the gearbox by a journal bearing and in the flywheel by a ballbearing race. It is splined so enabling the hub of the clutch disc to have longitudinal movements and yet to be able to transmit the torque from the clutch disc to the gearbox. The clutch disc incorporates a spring-cushioned hub so minimizing transmission vibration being transmitted to the engine and car body.

The clutch is disengaged by withdrawing the pressure plate assembly from the clutch disc against the tension of the nine clutch springs or the diaphragm spring. On the earlier models this is accomplished by three specially shaped release levers which pivot at their centres on the clutch cover and engage with the pressure plate at one end and the clutch withdrawal bearing at the other end. On later models the withdrawal bearing acts directly upon the diaphragm spring. The clutch pedal operates the withdrawal bearing by using a pivoted fork lever which is operated by a simple hydraulic system. The withdrawal bearing comprises a special ball thrust race which bears onto a hardened steel plate that is carried by the outer track of the release bearing.

5:2 Removing & refitting the clutch

To remove the clutch from the car proceed as follows:
1 Remove the gearbox assembly as detailed in **Chapter 6**.
2 Carefully slacken the clutch cover retaining bolts in a diagonal pattern as shown in **FIG 5:2**. Carefully ease the cover assembly from the dowels located in the back of the flywheel and lift away the complete assembly.

Refitting:

Reassembly of the clutch unit is the reverse procedure to dismantling but the following points should be noted:
1 Refer to **FIG 5:3** and identify the correct lining location so that the driven plate may be assembled the correct way round to the flywheel. The T.450.W lining faces the engine, denoted by the letter 'M'. The T.50.S lining faces the gearbox denoted by the letter 'G'.
2 Before securing the clutch cover to the flywheel the driven plate should be centred to the flywheel by means of a dummy shaft BMW.603 which, if available, can easily be made out of wood or scrap metal rod. The clutch mounting screws should be tightened in the same diagonal pattern as previously described and tightened to a torque wrench setting of 12.3 ± 1.4 lb ft.
3 Lubricate the clutch shaft spigot bearing with a high melting point multi-purpose grease.
4 Adjust the clutch play on the withdrawal arm as indicated in **FIG 5:5**. The clearance 'S' should be between .12 and .14 inch.

5:3 Servicing the clutch components

1 Thoroughly clean all parts of the clutch assembly ensuring that no cleaning fluid comes into contact with the lining if the clutch disc is to be re-used.
2 Measure the thickness of the friction lining and if it is thinner than the minimum requirement of .315 inch (8.0mm), it must be renewed. Examine the lining for uneven wear or loose rivets and also ensure that the driven plate splines have not worn, distorted or show signs of fatigue cracks. It is considered essential to install a complete driven plate assembly when renewal of the friction surfaces is necessary.
3 Carefully examine the machined face of the pressure plate and if this shows signs of grooving or roughness the surface may be carefully reground until the grooves disappear.
4 Check the tips of the release levers which bear onto the release bearing. A small amount of worn flat surface is permissible but if this is excessive the levers must be renewed. Check for excessive wear in the groove in which the fulcrum action of the release levers operates. If the metal here has worn thin the lever must be renewed as it may break under load.
5 Examine the release bearing for cracks, pitting, signs of overheating or excessive wear and it should be renewed as necessary.
6 Examine the pressure springs for weakness, distortion or signs of cracks which, if evident, the springs must be renewed as a complete set. The correct spring rating is indicated by paint marks on the springs which are marked with blue/grey/blue paint mark for 2000 models or blue/white/blue with a yellow stripe on the outer edge for the 2002 model. The contact pressure should be approximately 925 lb for the 2000 models or 1075 ± 33 lb for the 2002 model.
7 Examine the clutch withdrawal fork for signs of wear at the contact point between the release bearing and the fork and also for signs of distortion or fatigue cracks. Renew as necessary.

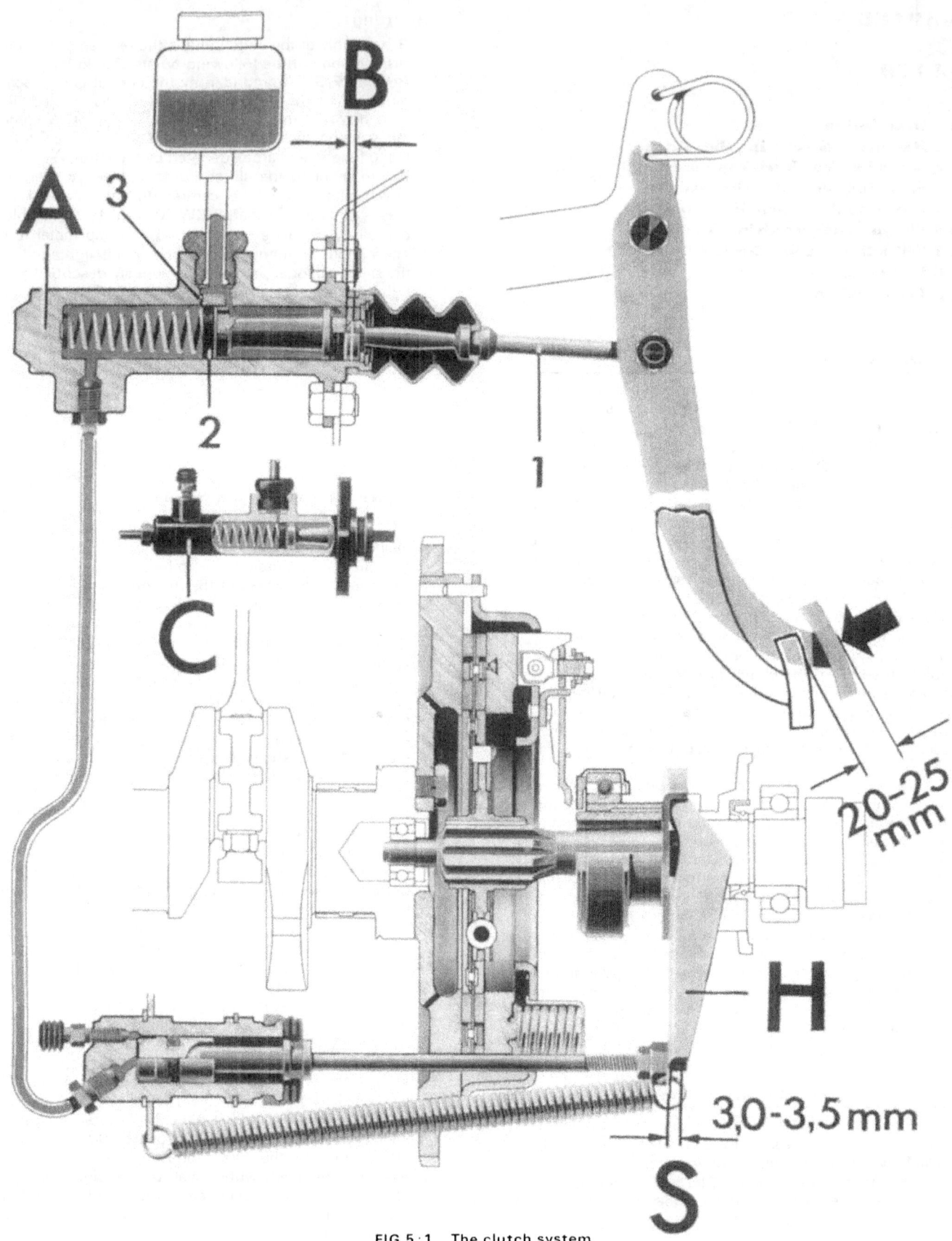

FIG 5:1 The clutch system

5 : 4 Servicing the hydraulic system

Description:

The clutch is operated hydraulically, the clutch pedal being connected to pushrod 1 as shown in **FIG 5:1**. The pushrod will press the piston and seal down the master cylinder bore when the pedal is depressed. Fluid in front of the piston will then be forced along the pipes until it reaches the slave cylinder. Here the piston will move down the bore in the body pushing the rod in front of it. This rod is connected to the clutch operating lever. Fluid leakage passed the pistons in both the master cylinder and slave cylinder is prevented by rubber seals or cups. When the master cylinder piston is fully retracted a small hole 3 in the master cylinder is uncovered. This communicates with the supply tank shown above the master cylinder in **FIG 5:1** and provides replenishing fluid to the system if there has been any loss. The hole is covered as soon as the piston starts to move.

Servicing operations must be carried out in conditions of great cleanliness as dirt will score the highly-finished bores and prevent the rubber cups from sealing properly.

Removing the master cylinder:

Remove the stud bolt 3 (see **FIG 5:6**), out of the clutch pedal 4 and the piston rod 5. Carefully lift away the bushes 6 and 7. Plug the reservoir outlet hole using a piece of tapered wood and release the connection pipe between the reservoir and master cylinder. Release the hydraulic pipe that connects the master cylinder to the slave cylinder at the master cylinder union. Remove the two retaining bolts holding the master cylinder to the body panel and carefully lift away.

Dismantling the master cylinder:

Refer to **FIG 5:1**. Carefully pull back the rubber boot and remove the circlip. Withdraw the pushrod 1 together with the dished washer. Extract all the internal parts. Gentle air pressure at the hydraulic line connection to slave cylinder may be used to blow out the parts taking extreme care in doing so. Remove the secondary cup washer from the piston using fingers only.

Reassembling the master cylinder:

Clean all the rubber parts in the correct grade of hydraulic fluid. Any solvents such as petrol, paraffin or trichlorethylene which may be used to clean the metal parts must be dried off completely before reassembling. Examine the rubber cups for damage or distortion, particularly to the knife-edges. The cups are available in kits of replacement parts and if they have seen considerable service it is wise to renew them even though they may seem to be satisfactory. Take care never to turn the cups inside out otherwise irreparable damage will be caused.

Start by dipping all internal parts in hydraulic brake fluid of the correct grade and assemble them wet. Stretch the secondary cup over the piston flange and work it about with the fingers until it is correctly seated. Insert the spring small-end first, making sure that the retainer is in place at the small-end. Also ensure that the retainer at the large end is in place. Insert the main cup lip first, taking great care not to damage or turn back the lip. Press it down the bore onto the spring retainer. Fit the washer followed by the piston. Refit the pushrod dished washer and circlip, followed by the rubber boot.

FIG 5:2 Clutch cover bolt location

FIG 5:3 Friction lining faces

FIG 5:4 Clutch disc centralization

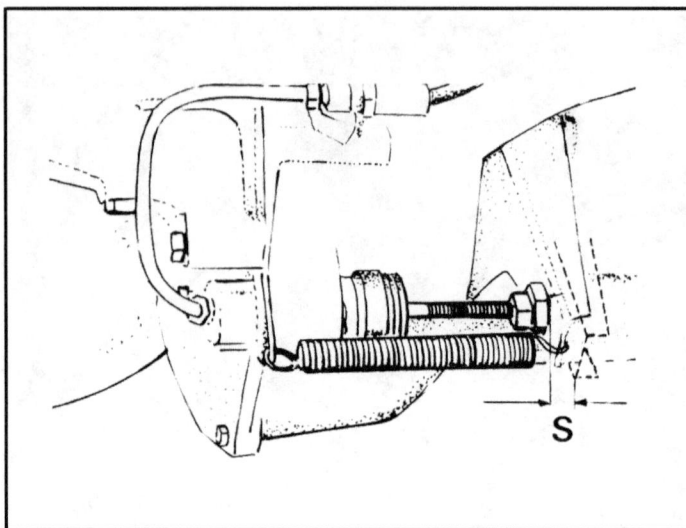

FIG 5:5 Clutch fork free play

FIG 5:6 Master cylinder pushrod to pedal mounting

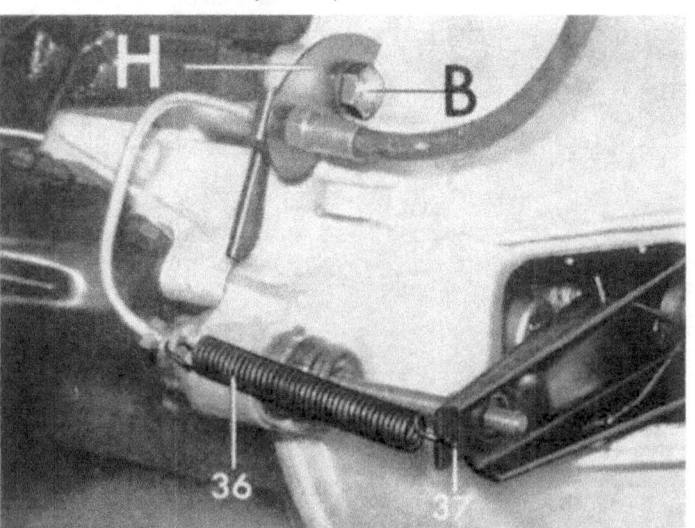

FIG 5:7 Slave cylinder retraction spring

Before refitting the assembly to the car, test it by refitting the supply tank to the master cylinder and pushing the piston up and down the bore several times letting it return on its own. After a few strokes, fluid should flow from the main outlet orifice.

Refitting the master cylinder:

Fit the master cylinder to the front panel and connect the pressure pipeline to the outlet from the cylinder. Line up the pushrod yoke with the end of the pedal lever and connect up with the shouldered bolt, bushes and nut. Refit the supply reservoir and bleed the hydraulic system as detailed in **Section 5:5**.

Removing the slave cylinder:

Fit a length of rubber tube to the nipple on the body of the slave cylinder and open the nipple screw three-quarters of a turn. Pump the clutch pedal until all the fluid has been transferred into a clean container.

Unscrew the pressure pipe from the cylinder taking care that the pipe does not turn otherwise it will either kink or fracture.

Release the adjustment nut and locknut from the control rod, disconnect the draw spring 36 (see **FIG 5:7**) from the withdrawal arm 37. Carefully ease back the rubber cap 38 (see **FIG 5:8**) and remove the circlip 39 from the slave cylinder 40 using a pair of pointed circlip pliers. Ease the slave cylinder forwards away from the withdrawal lever and take out the pushrod, followed by the slave cylinder itself.

Dismantling the slave cylinder:

Clean the exterior thoroughly and remove the rubber boot, using only the fingers to displace the boot retaining ring. Withdraw the parts from the interior of the slave cylinder or carefully blow them out with gentle air pressure.

Clean the internal parts with hydraulic fluid of the required specification and assembly the parts wet. It is always considered advisable to renew all the rubber parts particularly the piston sealing cup. Any solvents used for cleaning the metal parts must be completely dried off before reassembly.

Reassembly of the slave cylinder:

Carefully ease the rubber seal onto the piston and carefully insert the assembly into the bore. Take extra care to ensure that the seal is not damaged or turned back. Push the piston down the bore and refit the boot to the body ensuring that the lip of the boot is correctly located in its seating. Carefully replace the pushrod.

Refitting the slave cylinder to the hydraulic system is the reverse procedure to dismantling. Refill the hydraulic fluid reservoir and bleed the system as directed in **Section 5:5**. It will also be necessary to adjust the clutch slave cylinder pushrod details of this operation being described in **Section 5:6**.

5:5 Bleeding the hydraulic system

Fill the master cylinder reservoir with the correct grade hydraulic fluid and attach a rubber tube to the bleed screw nipple on the end of the slave cylinder. Immerse the open end of the tube in a small amount of the same brake fluid in a clean glass container. A second operator is needed to pump the clutch pedal after the bleed screw has been opened about threequarters of a turn. At the end of each down stroke of the clutch pedal close the bleed screw and let the pedal return to the 'off' position. At first, air bubbles will emerge from the immersed end of the tube. When clear fluid free from bubbles is delivered into the container, tighten the bleed screw on a down stroke of the pedal.

The operation of bleeding the system is necessary whenever the pipelines are disconnected or when the fluid in the supply tank has fallen so low that air has entered the system.

It is not advisable to use again hydraulic fluid which has been collected in the container unless it is clean beyond all doubt. Even then it must be allowed to stand for 24 hours to allow the air bubbles carried in the fluid to be released.

5:6 Clutch pedal removing & refitting

To remove the clutch pedal assembly from the car proceed as follows:

1 Refer to **FIG 5:9** and release the clamping screws 1 to 5 holding the lefthand cover 'L' in place. Also release the clamp screws 6 to 11 for the centre cover 'M'. Remove the heater booster motor switch plug connection and lift away the covering from below twisting it towards the left as shown in the arrow in **FIG 5:9**.
2 Remove the retaining nut 1 (see **FIG 5:6**) together with its spring washer and push the specially shaped stud bolt 3 from the clutch pedal and piston rod taking care not to misplace the bushes 6 and 7.
3 Using BMW clamping attachment 6021 comprising the clamp and sleeve, push the sleeve 8 (see **FIG 5:10**), into the torsion spring 9. Depress the clutch pedal to its maximum limit and insert the threaded part of the tool 10 through the torsion spring 9. Fit the thrust member 11 and washer onto the threaded member 10. Using the clamp handle 12 compress the torsion spring 9.
4 With the torsion spring compressed turn the torsion spring 9 (see **FIG 5:11**) with its plastic insert 14 upwards out of the clutch pedal assembly 4.
5 Remove the flexible locknut 15 (see **FIG 5:12**) and carefully pull the screw 16 out of the bearing support 17. Lift away the clutch pedal. Push the spacing sleeve 18 and bearing bush 19 from the clutch pedal arm 4. Release the BMW clamp attachment and remove the swivel spring.

Reassembly:

Reassembly is the reverse to dismantling. The following points should however be noted:

1 Always fit the swivel spring 20 and sleeve 21 onto the shaft as shown in **FIG 5:13**, before the spring compressor is fitted.
2 Always compress the swivel spring 20 until the plastic insert 23 slips into its special recess in the clutch pedal arm 4.

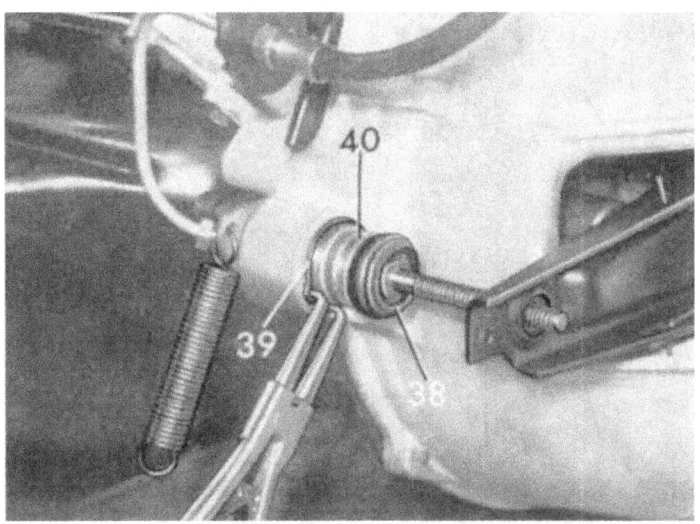

FIG 5:8 Slave cylinder retaining circlip removal

FIG 5:9 Under lining mounting screws

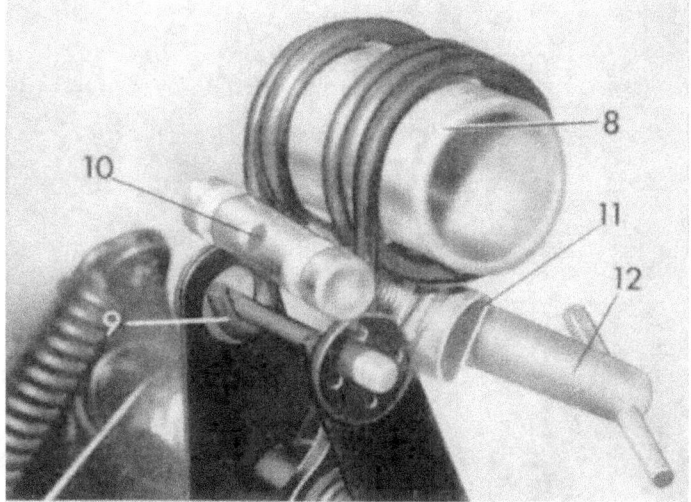

FIG 5:10 Torsion spring clamp location

FIG 5:11 Torsion spring removal

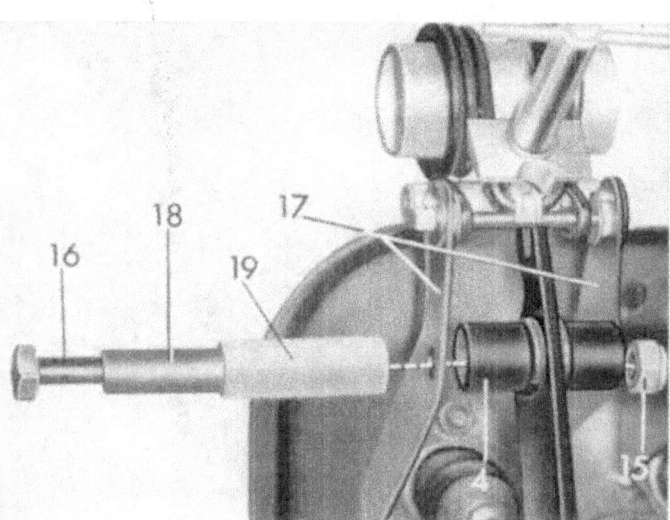

FIG 5:12 Pedal pivot assembly

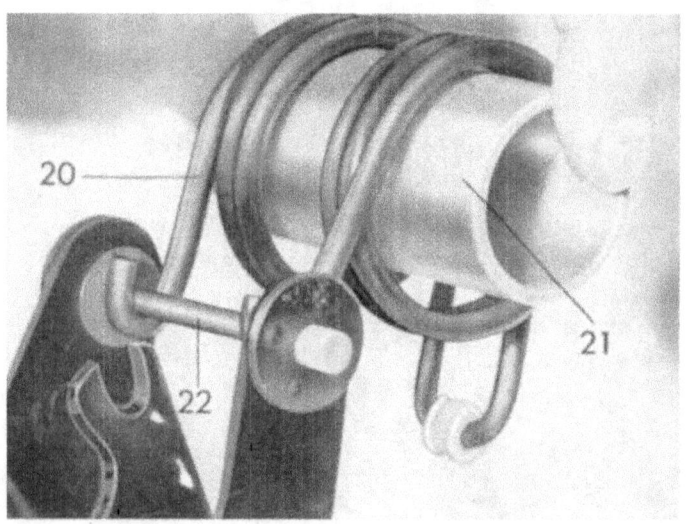

FIG 5:13 Torsion spring reassembly

Clutch adjustment:

1 Refer to **FIG 5:1**. When the clutch unit is in its disengaged position the clutch pedal must abut the special limit stop on the pivot assembly.
2 The clearance should be between 5.7 to 5.9 inch between the clutch pedal face and the lower horn ring assembly. Care must be taken to ensure that any obstruction in the form of carpets or sound deadening media placed underneath the clutch pedal do not affect its movement. Should the clearance be less than 5.3 inches a piston rod 1 (see **FIG 5:1**) having a length of 4.37 inches is to be fitted in place of the original. Should the clearance be between 5.3 and 5.5 inches a piston rod of 4.29 inches should be fitted. It is highly undesirable for the maximum clearance of 5.9 inches to be exceeded. Later cars have an adjustable pushrod.
3 Free travel of the piston rod to piston of the hydraulic master cylinder, dimension B (see **FIG 5:1**) should be .0394 inch.
  Should a piston rod of the wrong length be fitted the oil seal 2 will press into the compensation bore 3 whilst in its rest position, causing irreparable damage to the seal.
4 Inset 'C' shows the older type of master cylinder fitted with bleed valve. Later models do not have a bleed valve fitted. Whenever the clutch hydraulic system is being bled it should be done so from the slave cylinder position.
5 From Chassis No. 976909 and 985061 on the 2000 models the diameter of the master and slave cylinders was altered to .75 inch. Should repair or new units be fitted it is important that only master and slave cylinders of the same specification are fitted so making a matched pair.

5:7 Self-adjusting diaphragm clutch

2000 from chassis No. 1962745.
2000 TIL from chassis No. 1472294.
2000 CS from chassis No. 1109269.
2000 TII from introduction.

On later cars a diaphragm spring clutch is fitted of which the operating mechanism is self-adjusting. No attention is required other than an inspection every 8000 miles to measure the amount of wear on the clutch friction surfaces.

Push the clutch withdrawal lever forwards with the hand as shown in **FIG 5:14** until it contacts the slave cylinder, then measure the travel of the operating arm at **A**. On a new clutch this distance will be between 17 and 19mm, but will steadily decrease as the surfaces wear down.

When the dimension **A** is reduced to 5mm the clutch plate must be renewed.

5:8 Fault diagnosis

(a) Judder
1. Check 1 and 4 in (d)
2. Pressure plate incorrectly fitted to spring housing
3. Contact area of driven plate linings not evenly distributed
4. Faulty rubber mountings

(b) Fierceness or snatch
1. Check 1, 2, 4 and 5 in (d)
2. Worn clutch linings

(c) Slip
1. Check 1 in (d) and 2 in (b)
2. Weak pressure spring(s)
3. Seized piston in clutch slave cylinder
4. Operating lever stop has no clearance

(d) Drag or spin
1. Oil or grease on driven plate linings
2. Leaking master cylinder, slave cylinder or piping
3. Driven plate hub binding on splines
4. Distorted driven plate
5. Warped or damaged pressure plate
6. Broken driven plate linings
7. Air in the clutch hydraulic system

(e) Tick or knock
1. Badly worn driven plate hub splines
2. Worn release bearing
3. Faulty drive pinion on starter
4. Elongated holes in spring housing
5. Defective driven plate springs

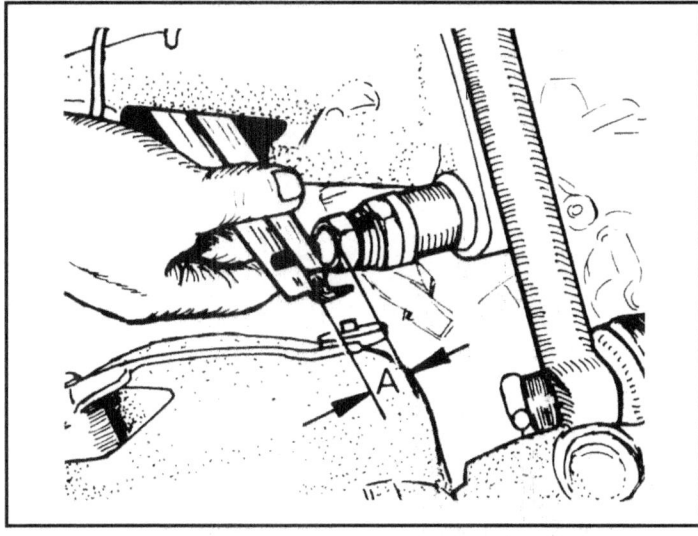

FIG 5:14 Measuring wear on self-adjusting clutch

5:9 Technical data

Type	Dry single plate with torsional damper
Model	HB 225 Sph, MF215K, MF228K Sph
Spring, colour coding:	
2002Tii	Yellow
All other models	Blue/grey/blue or none
Driving plate, external diameter, 2002:	
Up to 1973	8.98
From 1973	8.5
All other models	8.98
Driving plate, minimum thickness:	
2002	.32
All other models	.36
Maximum runout at circumference	.024
Withdrawal arm clearance:	
2002	.118 to .138
All other models	.158 to .177
Free travel at pedals:	
2002	.8 to 1.0
All other models	1.4 to 1.6
Clearance between thrust ring and arm ends:	
2002	.059
All other models	.079
Master cylinder:	
Bore	.75
Stroke	1.18
Slave cylinder:	
Bore	.75
Stroke	.945

NOTES

CHAPTER 6

MANUAL GEARBOX

6 : 1 Description
6 : 2 Gearbox removing & refitting
6 : 3 Gearbox disassembly
6 : 4 Synchromesh components
6 : 5 Output shaft & speedometer drive
6 : 6 Layshaft
6 : 7 Third & fourth speed pinion sets
6 : 8 Output shaft grooved bearing
6 : 9 Selector shafts & forks
6 : 10 Refitting input shaft
6 : 11 Fault diagnosis
6 : 12 Technical data

6 :1 Description

The cars covered in this manual may be fitted with any one of three different gearboxes. There are two four-speed boxes, one with Porsche type synchromesh units and one with Borg-Warner synchromesh. The third type of transmission is a five-speed and reverse box, also with Porsche baulk ring synchromesh.

The dismantling and reassembly of a gearbox is not an operation to be undertaken without a considerable degree of experience. This chapter will give details of the servicing procedures for a typical four-speed unit for those with the necessary skills and equipment, other gearboxes are similarly serviced.

The gearbox is in a single unit connected to the engine backplate. It consists of two detachable parts, (a) a front bell-mouthed housing and central body, (b) a rear end cover. The clutch shaft is supported by a ballbearing race located at the front of the gearbox housing whilst the constant mesh shaft is supported by a spigot bearing located on the inside of the clutch shaft and a ballrace located at the rear of the central section of the gearbox casing. A front and rear ballbearing race supports the layshaft located at the bottom of the gearbox.

6 : 2 Gearbox removing & refitting

To remove the gearbox from the vehicle proceed as follows:

1 Jack up the front of the vehicle so that the front wheels are well clear of the ground and place on firmly based stands. Refer to **FIG 6 : 1** and remove the attachment bolts on the triangular flange (1 to 3). Also remove the attachment bolts 4 and 5 from the exhaust bracket to gearbox support bracket. Remove the centre exhaust bracket mounting bolt and tie back the bracket. Remove the exhaust pipe to manifold mounting nuts.
2 Remove the four propeller shaft front flange to gearbox flange bolts, remove the centre bearing block, push the propeller shaft downwards and pull away from the centering pin.
3 Disconnect the battery positive terminal. Detach the reversing light switch plug connection 13 (see **FIG 6 : 2**), and slacken the bolt clamping the speedometer drive cable to the gearbox casing. Withdraw the cable.
4 Refer to **FIG 6 : 3** and slacken the fixing bolt 11 using an Allen key. Gently push out the kingpin 12.
5 Gently ease up the gaiter 1 (see **FIG 6 : 4**), the foam rubber ring 2 and using a pair of circlip pliers release circlip 13. Lift upwards the gearchange lever making a note of any shims present.
6 Disconnect the starter motor cables and remove the two retaining bolts. Lift away the motor.
7 Remove the clutch hydraulic pipe bracket from the gearbox cover and release the clutch withdrawal lever tension spring as shown in **FIG 6 : 5**. Carefully pull back the protective cap 20 and lift away the circlip 21. Remove the slave cylinder forwards and also push out the pushrod at the same time. When a self-adjusting mechanism is fitted, the retaining wire ring must first be removed, then the front collar and finally the circlip at the base of the slave cylinder.
8 Remove the steering control lever bracket retaining bolts, the location being shown in **FIG 9 : 17**. Turn the steering wheel to full righthand lock and rotate the bearing support towards the bulkhead. Gently turn the steering wheel back on the lefthand lock and at the same time lay the drop arm down and to the right onto the track arm.
9 Remove the three gearbox cover fixing bolts and lift away the coverplate.
10 Using an overhead hoist or garage crane support the engine from above, moving forward as far as is permitted by the silentbloc engine mountings.
11 Release the engine and gearbox mounting bolts and carefully withdraw the gearbox away from the engine downwards and towards the rear taking very great care that no load is put on the clutch shaft otherwise it will distort.

Refitting:

To refit the gearbox is the reverse procedure to dismantling but the following points should be noted:

1 When assembling the gearbox bellhousing to the engine back face, tighten the size M8 clamp bolts to a torque wrench setting of 18 lb ft, and the size M10 clamp bolts to a torque wrench setting of 34 lb ft.
2 The steering control lever bracket retaining bolts should be tightened to a torque wrench setting of 18 lb ft.
3 Tighten the starter motor retaining bolts to a torque of 34 lb ft.
4 Upon reassembling the gearchange lever always replace any shims fitted or fit further shims to ensure all play from the ball sockets is removed.
5 When assembling the gearchange lever the pivot pin must be inserted from the righthand side only. It is advisable to check the plastic bushes for wear and renew if necessary.
6 The propeller shaft to gearbox drive flange retaining bolts must be tightened to a torque wrench setting of 34 lb ft.

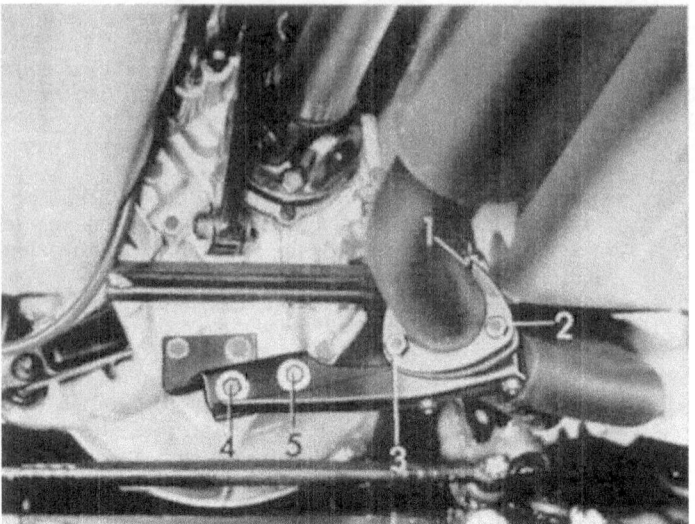

FIG 6:1 Exhaust system front mounting

FIG 6:2 Rear view of gearbox in position

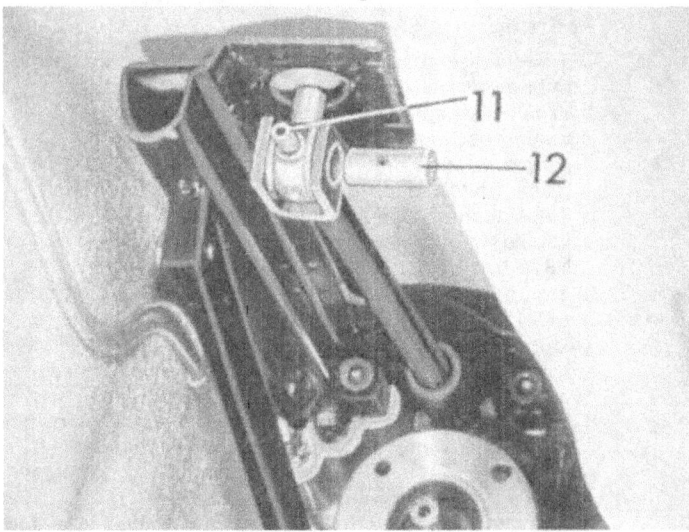

FIG 6:3 Gearchange lever lower linkage

6:3 Gearbox disassembly

1 Remove the oil drain pipe and allow all oil to drain out into a suitably sized container. Refer to **FIG 6:6** and remove the fixing bolts 1 to 3 on the bracket and stay. Lift away the bracket together with the stay. Engage second gear and push back the spacer sleeve 4 with a screwdriver.

2 Using a pin punch drive out the cylindrical pin from the selector shaft joint. Remove the selector shaft and joint from the rear of the gearbox.

3 Remove the two exhaust support bracket retaining bolts and lift away the bracket. Using a screwdriver remove the locking strip on the flanged nut of the output flange and remove the flanged nut on the output flange using a socket wrench whilst the flange is held tight.

4 Compress and lift away the spring for the clutch withdrawal lever and carefully lift away the withdrawal lever. Unscrew the three securing nuts for the guide sleeve and gently tap the side of the guide sleeve to loosen it from its seating. Lift away together with the gasket taking care to make a note of any shims that might be in place. Using a pair of circlip pliers remove the circlip together with any shims in place between the circlip and the ballrace.

5 Using a special ballrace extractor or Rillex 6206 tool as shown in **FIG 6:7** carefully withdraw the clutch shaft bearing. Note the location of any shims released.

6 Remove the gearbox housing cover retaining bolts and referring to **FIG 6:8** carefully heat up the gearbox housing around the sealing cover 'D' so that the grooved bearing on the layshaft slides out easily. Using a plastic faced hammer gently tap the gearbox housing and pull off. Remove the seal if it shows signs of wear.

7 Refer to **FIG 6:9** and slacken the screw plug 8 on the locking pin 9 and withdraw the locking pin and spring 10.

8 Using a pair of side cutters remove the locking wire for the selector fork retaining bolts and slacken these. Carefully withdraw the gearchange shaft 14 forwards as shown in **FIG 6:10**.

9 Set the selector shaft 15 (see **FIG 6:11**) to the fourth gear position and turn the guide sleeve until the locating pin 16 can be driven out using a suitably sized drift. Carefully pull the selector shaft 15 forwards until the selector fork 17 can be withdrawn from the selector sleeve. Take care not to lose any of the ballbearings.

10 Set the selector sleeve 19 (see **FIG 6:12**), to the neutral position and carefully push the selector shaft 18 to the second gear position and drive out the locating pin on the selector fork 20 using a suitably sized drift. Carefully withdraw the selector shaft 18 forwards until the selector fork 20 can be withdrawn from the selector sleeve. Take great care to note the location of any ballbearings that will be released during this operation.

11 Set the selector sleeve 21 (see **FIG 6:13**), to the neutral position and using a suitably sized drift drive out the locating pin 22 on the selector fork 23. To ensure that this is driven out correctly turn the guide sleeve until the locating pin is in a good working

FIG 6:4 Gearchange lever retaining circlip location

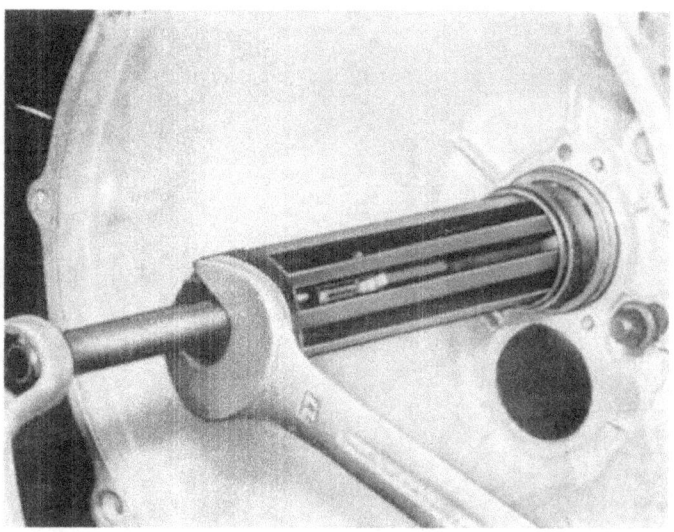

FIG 6:7 Clutch shaft bearing removal

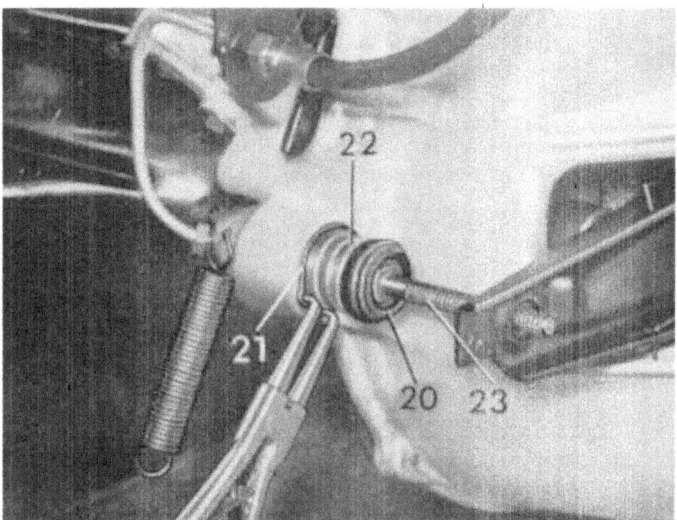

FIG 6:5 Clutch slave cylinder

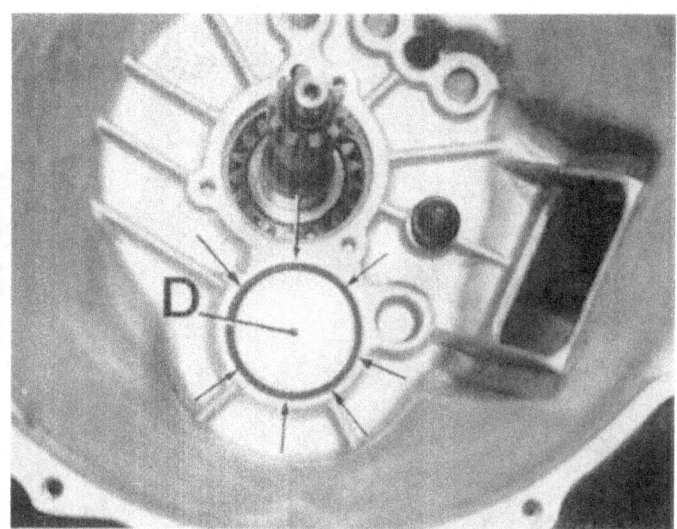

FIG 6:8 Front view of gearbox housing

FIG 6:6 Rear view of gearbox

FIG 6:9 Locking pin and spring removal

FIG 6:10 Gearchange shaft removal

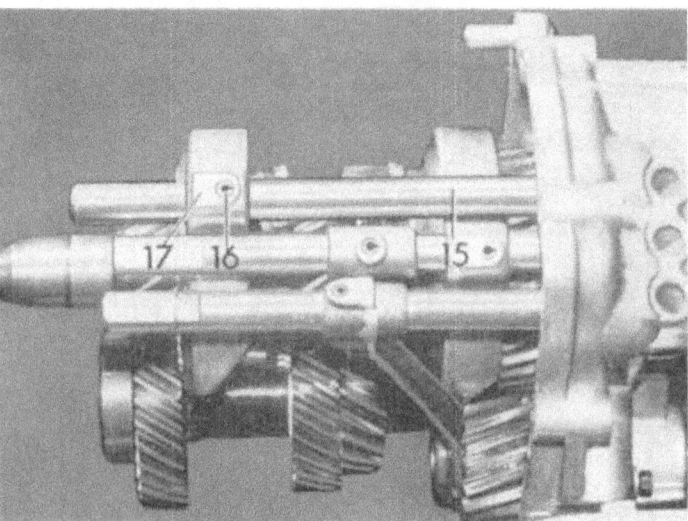

FIG 6:11 Selector shaft removal

FIG 6:12 Selector shaft removal

position. Carefully withdraw the selector shaft 24 forwards until the selector fork can be withdrawn from the reverse pinion. Again take great care to note the location of any ballbearings that will be released during this operation. Remove the five retaining bolts on the sealing cover and lift away the cover making a note of any shims. Using a special ballrace extractor or Rillex 6206 tool remove the grooved ballbearing from the rear of the output shaft. Carefully lift away the complete main shaft manipulating forwards and twisting slightly to the right.

12 Carefully heat the gearbox cover and pull off the layshaft and idler pinion from the gearbox housing cover taking care to note the location of any ballbearings that will be released during this operation.

13 Carefully pull off the drive shaft, the selector sleeve and needle roller bearing from the drive shaft. Using a pair of circlip pliers remove the circlip and carefully ease away the support disc from the guide sleeve. Pull off the guide sleeve and third gear pinion with the synchromesh unit. Extract the needle roller cage.

14 Using a press and suitably sized drift remove the speedometer drive 39 (see **FIG 6:14**), from the output shaft 38 together with the reverse gear pinion 40, first gear pinion 41 with the synchromesh unit, the selector sleeve 42 and the second gear pinion together with the synchromesh unit 43. Note the location of the shim between the speedometer drive and the reverse gear pinion.

6 : 4 Synchromesh components

The synchromesh assembly must be thoroughly inspected for signs of misuse which will show in the form of chipped teeth, hairline cracks and the tooth edges of the selector sleeve must have sharp edges and show no signs of chamfer.

Internal inspection and reassembly:

1 Using a pair of circlip pliers lift away the circlip 1 and lift off the synchromesh ring 2 as shown in **FIG 6:15**. Push the selector sleeve into the synchromesh ring 2. It should be noted that the front face of the selector sleeve be correctly aligned with the face of the synchromesh ring as shown in **FIG 6:16**. The synchromesh ring contact surface should be distributed as evenly as possible. It is important that at least 50 per cent of the circumference of the synchromesh ring must be in contact. The outer diameter of the unbiased synchromesh ring should measure $3.020 \pm .006$ inch.

2 Faulty synchromesh can be caused by a damaged locking band. The first gear is distinguishable by the block, in addition to which, it only contains one locking band whereas gears on second, third and fourth speeds are fitted with two locking bands.

3 Once the synchronizing ring has been reassembled to the synchromesh unit it must be easily turned by hand otherwise difficult gear changing will result.

FIG 6:13 Selector shaft removal

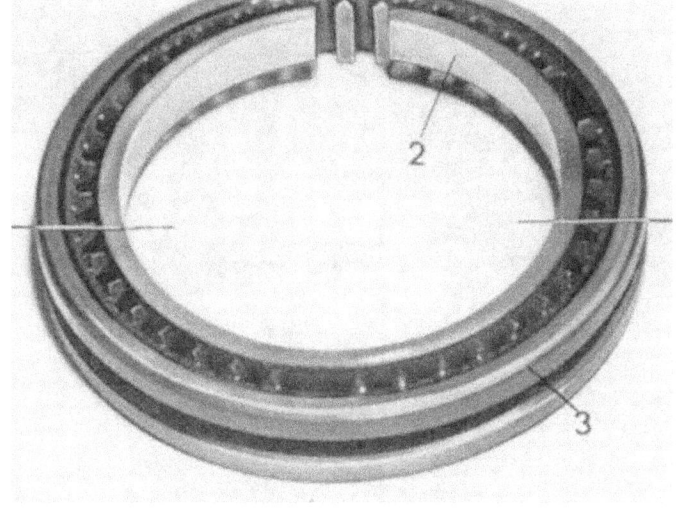

FIG 6:16 Synchromesh ring alignment

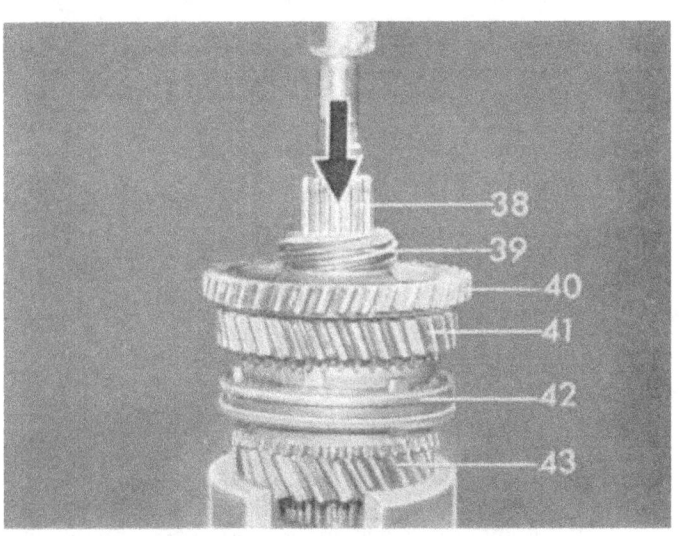

FIG 6:14 Speedometer drive gear removal

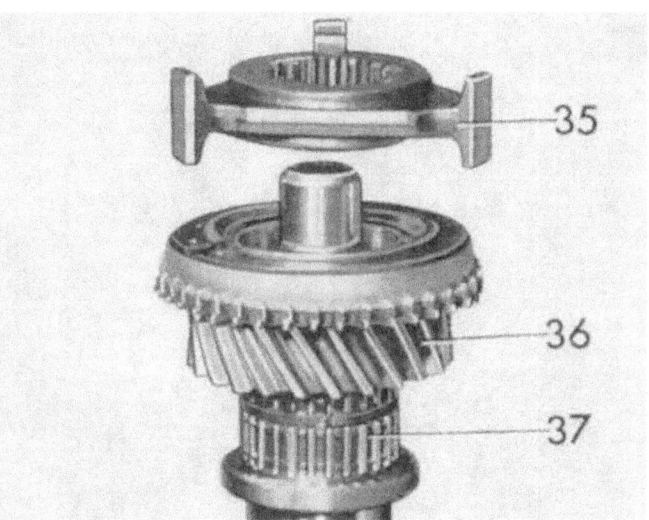

FIG 6:17 Third gear pinion reassembly

FIG 6:15 Synchromesh ring removal

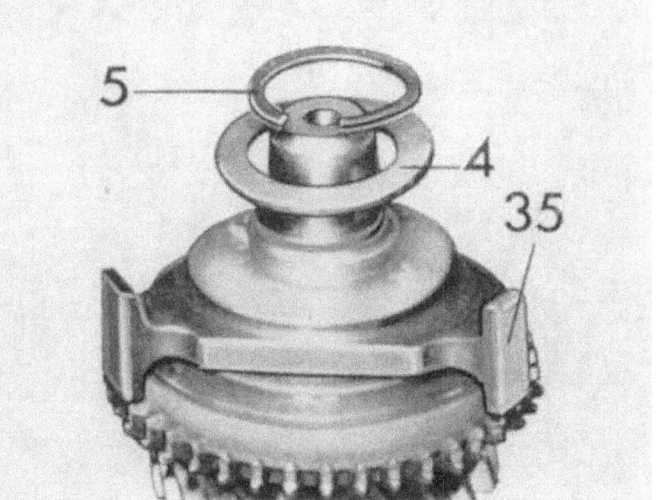

FIG 6:18 Refitting thrust washer & circlip to output shaft

6 : 5 Output shaft & speedometer drive

1. Carefully hold the output shaft between soft faces in a firm bench vice and place the needle roller cage 37 (see **FIG 6:17**), the third gear pinion 36 and the guide sleeve 35 onto the output shaft.
2. Place a .079 inch thick thrust washer 4 (see **FIG 6:18**), onto the guide sleeve 35 and spring the circlip into its groove using a pair of suitably sized circlip pliers.
3. Reverse the position of the output shaft in the vice and push the needle roller cage 6 (see **FIG 6:19**), the second gear pinion 7 and the guide sleeve 8 onto the output shaft.
4. Carefully push the spacer sleeve 9 (see **FIG 6:20**), onto the output shaft whilst it is cold with the aid of a suitably sized sleeve in conjunction with a spindle press. Place the needle roller cage 10, the selector sleeve 11 and the first gear pinion 12 into position. Place the reverse gear pinion 13 (see **FIG 6:21**), in position on the output shaft with the polished surface side towards the first gear pinion. Refer to **FIG 6:21** and check the overall dimension of the gear train. It should be noted that the overall dimension 'A' is measured from the surface ground face of the guide sleeve 35 up to the front face of the boss of the reverse gear pinion 13. This should be 5.433±.004 inch. Shims may be fitted to the front face of the boss of the reverse gear pinion 13 using shims of suitable thickness 'Y'.

FIG 6:19 Second gear pinion reassembly

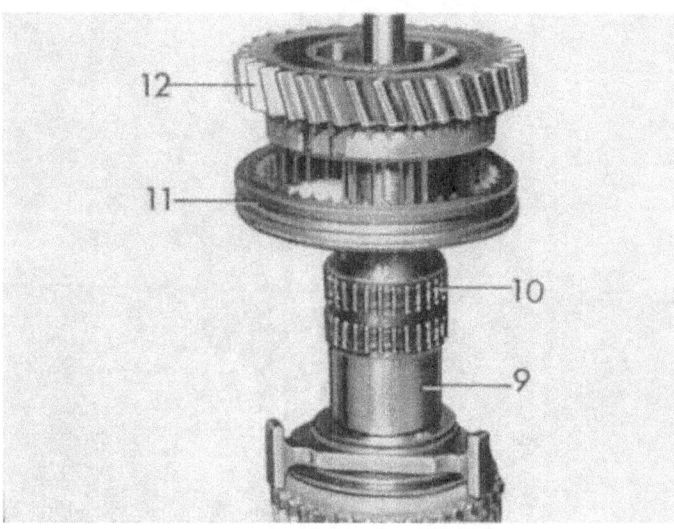

FIG 6:20 First gear pinion reassembly

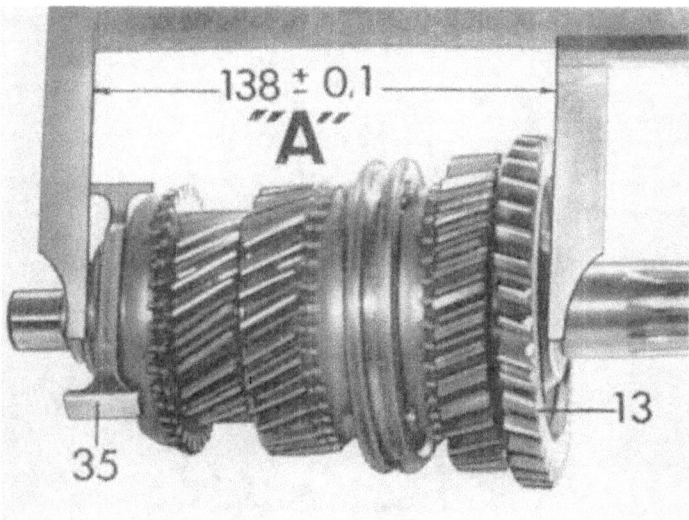

FIG 6:21 Gear train overall measurement

Example:

'A' Theoretical	=	5.433 inch
'A' Actual	=	5.394 inch
'Y'	=	.039 inch

5. Using an accurate vernier check the thickness 'B' of the speedometer pinion and make a note of its thickness. Press the speedometer pinion onto the output shaft using a suitably sized sleeve and a spindle press. Carefully drive the grooved bearing (see **FIG 6:22**) of the output shaft into the gearbox housing cover as far as it will go using a suitably sized sleeve on the outer track. Using a vernier depth gauge measure the distance 'C' from the gearbox housing cover with a gasket in place up to the grooved bearing outer race. This is shown in **FIG 6:21**. To determine the thickness of the shim calculate as in the following example:

'A' Theoretical	= 5.433 inch
+'B'	= .583 inch
	6.016 inch
−(C)	= 1.457 inch
'D' Actual selector sleeve	= 4.559 inch
'D' Theoretical gearbox housing cover	= 4.567 inch
'X' Shim thickness	= .008 inch

6. Remove the grooved bearing fit the shims of required thickness and refit the bearing.

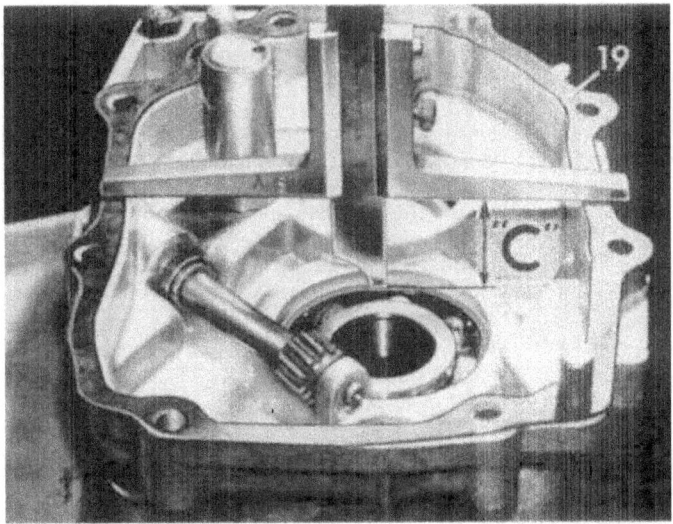

FIG 6:22 Gearbox grooved bearing measurement

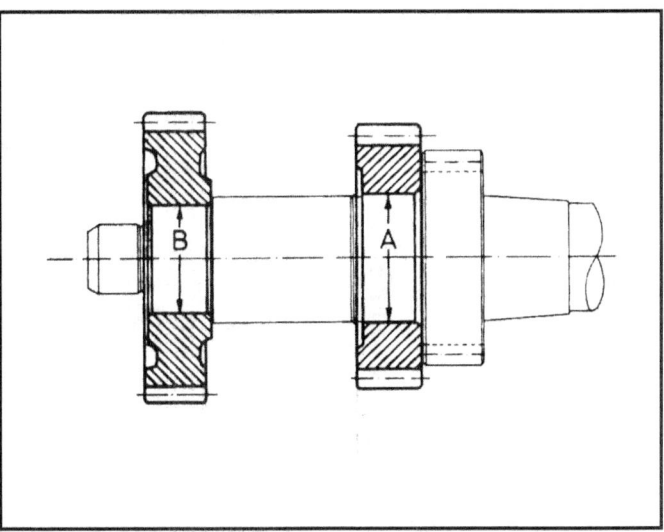

FIG 6:25 Third & fourth speed pinion internal dimensions

FIG 6:23 Grooved bearing shim location

FIG 6:26 Output shaft grooved bearing measurement

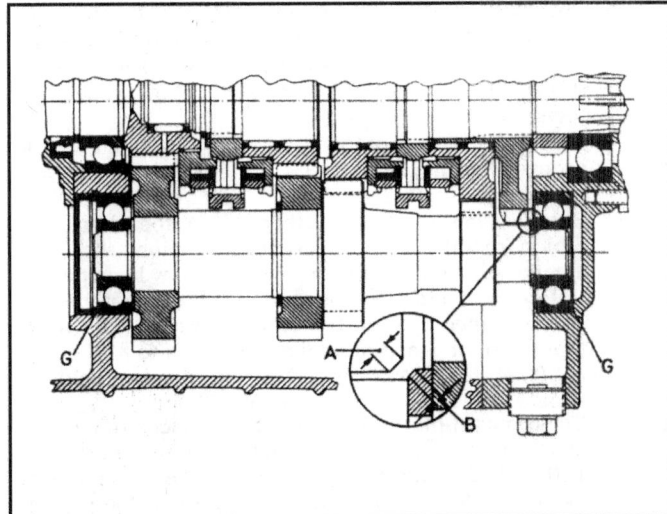

FIG 6:24 Reverse gear pinion & shim angle adjustment

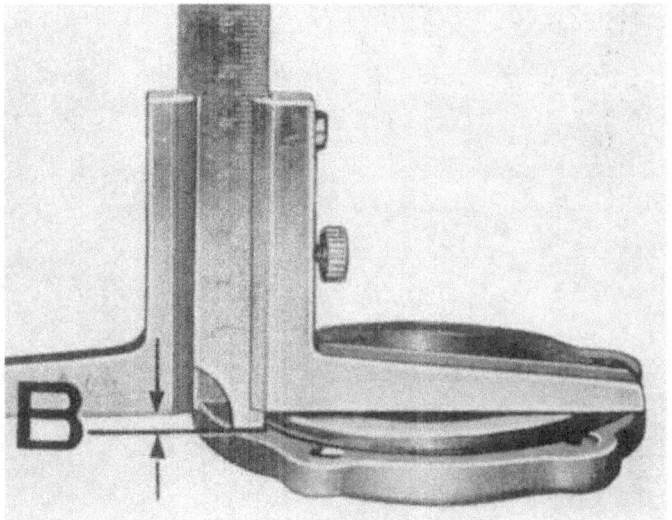

FIG 6:27 Gearbox housing cover measurement

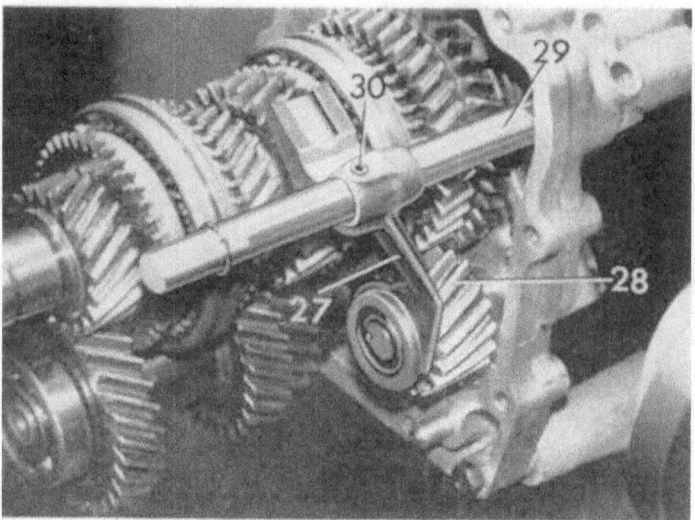

FIG 6:28 Idler pinion reassembly

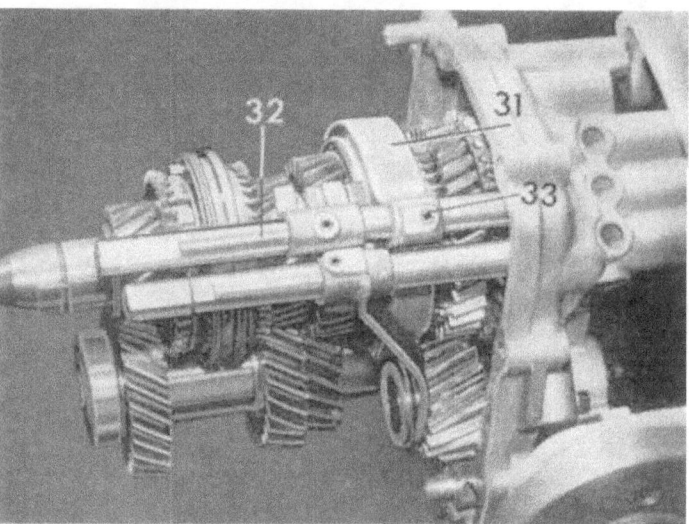

FIG 6:29 Selector fork and shaft reassembly

FIG 6:30 Selector fork and shaft reassembly

6 : 6 Layshaft

To ensure that the layshaft is correctly located within the gearbox housing proceed as follows:

1 Refer to **FIG 6:22** and using a depth gauge measure the dimension from the housing sealing face to the circlip. Make a note of this dimension 'F' for future reference.
2 Correctly refit the layshaft into the gearbox housing cover and establish dimension 'E' which is equal to the height of the layshaft with the gasket in place on the gearbox housing cover. Determine the thickness of the shim required 'G'.

Example:

F	housing depth	= 6.496 inch
—E	height of layshaft	= 6.480 inch
		.016 inch
	Subtract permissible axial play	= .008 inch
G	shim thickness	= .008 inch

3 Remove the layshaft and seal from the gearbox housing cover and insert the shim 'G' as previously calculated into the gearbox housing cover. Refit the idler pinion with the layshaft into the gearbox housing cover.
4 Carefully position the selector sleeve, the needle roller bearing and the drive shaft onto the output shaft. Carefully insert the drive and output shaft into the gearbox housing cover. Position the shim 'X' as previously calculated in the position shown in **FIG 6:23**. Carefully drive the grooved bearing 18 onto the output shaft using a suitably sized sleeve.
5 Using engineers 'Blue' check the tooth engagement which, of course, may be altered by the shim 'G' which, if necessary, may be inserted on the side in front of the grooved bearing of the layshaft.
6 Should the gearbox be dismantled to trace the cause of noisy operation check the reverse gear pinion and shim on layshaft for traces of wear and if necessary grind the reverse gear pinion down on the teeth on the driven side by .0551 ± .0118 inch and taper by 30 deg. (A) and shim on the layshaft by .051 to .0118 inch and taper by 30 deg. (B) (see **FIG 6:24**).

6 : 7 Third & fourth speed pinion sets

Should the fourth gear pinion (drive shaft) and third gear pinion (driven shaft) be renewed this must be carried out together with operations described in **Sections 6:3, 6:4, 6:5 and 6:6**. Then proceed as follows:

1 Using a universal grooved bearing puller remove the grooved bearing and press off the fourth gear pinion from the layshaft.
2 Remove the circlip and then press the third gear pinion from the layshaft. Inspect the pinions and using emerypaper smooth any grooves that may be apparent.
3 Before the pinions are pressed into place measure the overlap when cold and referring to **FIG 6:25** ensure that the third gear pinion dimension A is to a tolerance of .0031 to .00457 inch. The fourth gear pinion B should be within .00343 to .00508 inch.
4 Using a light machine oil coat the surfaces to be contacted on the layshaft and heat the pinions to between 120 to 150°C and using a hydraulic press capable of exerting a force of at least 8820 lb press the pinions into position. Finally check the toothed engagement and adjust as necessary.

6 : 8 Output shaft grooved bearing

1. Refer to *FIG 6:26* and using a depth gauge measure dimension A from the gearbox housing cover to the grooved bearing outer race.
2. Refer to **FIG 6:27** and using the vernier depth gauge determine dimension 'B' being the height of the sealing cover with the seal in position.
3. There should be no play between the outer race of the grooved bearing and the sealing cover, any play must be taken up with shims. To calculate the thickness of shims required:

Example:

A	= .120inch
—B	= .110inch
D shim thickness	= .010inch

4. Once the shim thickness D has been calculated place this in front of the grooved bearing and secure the sealing cover together with the seal to the gearbox housing cover.

6 : 9 Selector shafts & forks

To service the selector shaft and selector forks proceed as follows:

1. Disconnect the cables from the reversing light switch, the location being shown in **FIG 6:2** and unscrew the switch from the gearbox housing.
2. Using a suitably shaped punch drive out the sealing cap located next to the reversing light switch. The ballbearings should be pushed down with a screwdriver through the drillings exposed and also drilling next to reversing light switch drilling. Insert the arrester ballbearings and also the selector fork 27 (see **FIG 6:28**), into the guide slot in the idler pinion 28. Carefully push the selector shaft 29 through the selector fork 27 and into the gearbox housing cover. Correctly align the slot in the locating pin so that it is along the longitudinal axis of the selector shaft and knock in the locating pin 20.
3. Refer to **FIG 6:29** and insert the locking and arrester ballbearing. Correctly position the selector fork 31 in the selector sleeve and push the selector shaft 32 through the selector fork 31 and into the gearbox housing cover. Ensure that the slot in the locating pin points along the longitudinal axis of the selector shaft and carefully knock in the locating pin 33.
4. Refer to **FIG 6:30** and insert the locking and arrester ballbearing and also the selector shaft 34 into the selector sleeve. Carefully push the selector shaft 35 through the selector fork 34 and into the gearbox housing cover. Ensure that the slot in the locating pin points along the longitudinal axis of the selector shaft and carefully knock in the locating pin 33.
5. Refit the gearchange shaft 37 (see **FIG 6:31**), and tighten the square head tapered bolt and secure with soft iron wire. Refer to the inset in **FIG 6:31** and note the fitting position of the gearchange shaft 37, the taper bush K, the locking pin S and the selector finger 38. Refit the locking pin, the spring and screw plug.
6. Screw in the reversing light switch and finally drive the sealing cap into the gearbox housing cover.

FIG 6:31   Gearchange shaft refitting

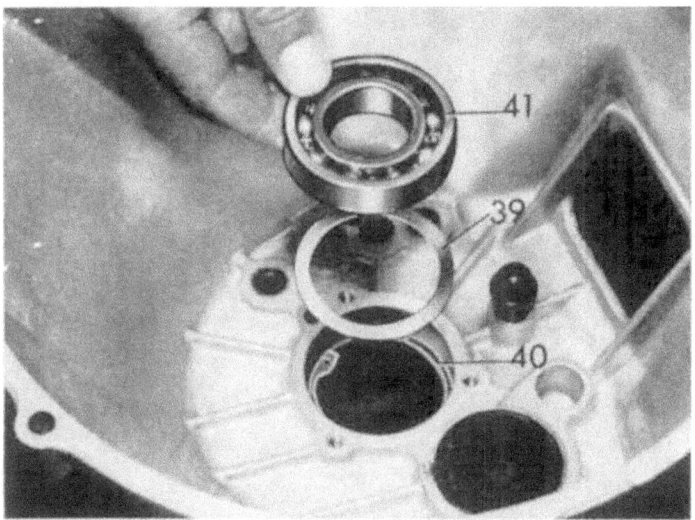

FIG 6:32   Input shaft bearing shim location

FIG 6:33   Inner ballbearing race measurement

FIG 6:34 Input shaft shim location

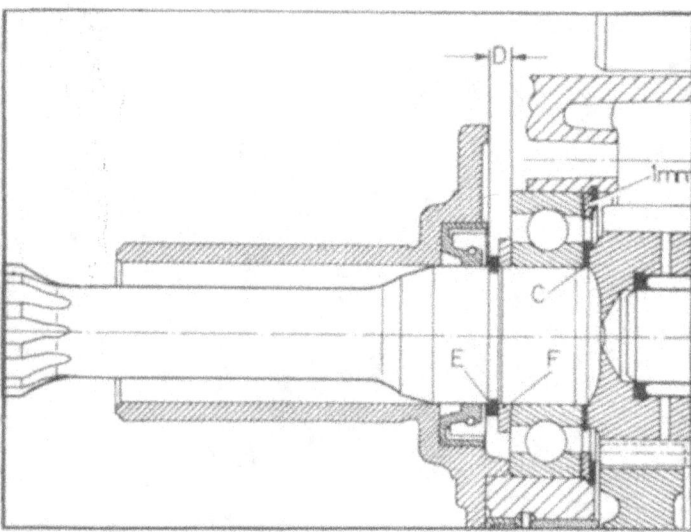

FIG 6:35 Input shaft circlip location

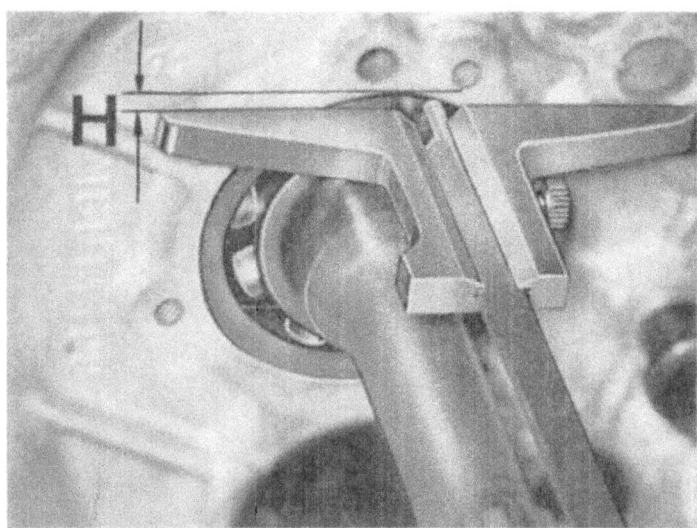

FIG 6:36 Outer bearing track to housing measurement

6:10 Refitting input shaft

1. Refer to **FIG 6:32** and with a packing washer .039 inch thick lay the packing washer 39 on the circlip 40 in the input shaft bearing seat.
2. Carefully drive the ballbearing 41 using a suitably sized sleeve into the gearbox housing until a tight fit is obtained.
3. Using a vernier depth gauge and referring to **FIG 6:33** determine dimension 'A' from the housing seal surface to the inner ballbearing race. Dimension 'B' is engraved on the input shaft and is to be read off on the shaft. The figures stated refer at all times to the dimension below the line.
4. Once dimensions 'A' and 'B' have been determined read off from column 'C' of the table below the required thickness of the shim to be positioned as shown in **FIG 6:34**. Place the shim on the input shaft, stick the shim C, as calculated earlier, on the grooved bearing with grease and lay the gasket 42 onto the gearbox housing cover. Carefully lower the gearbox housing over the gear assembly which if it is a tight fit, preheat the gearbox housings slightly.

A	ins.	B	mm	ins.	C	mm
153,9	(.9252)		23,5	(.0196)		0,5
(6.059)	(.9212)		23,4	(.0236)		0,6
	(.9173)		23,3	(.0276)		0,7
153,8	(.9252)		23,5	(.0157)		0,4
(6.055)	(.9212)		23,4	(.0196)		0,5
	(.9173)		23,3	(.0236)		0,6
153,7	(.9252)		23,5	(.0118)		0,3
(6.051)	(.9212)		23,4	(.0157)		0,4
	(.9173)		23,3	(.0196)		0,5
153,6	(.9252)		23,5	(.0078)		0,2
(6.047)	(.9212)		23,4	(.0118)		0,3
	(.9173)		23,3	(.0157)		0,4

5. Carefully press the input shaft into the ballbearing and the gearbox housing onto the gearbox housing cover and tighten the retaining bolts to a torque wrench setting of 18 lb ft.
6. Refer to **FIG 6:35** and using a pair of engineer's calipers determine dimension E, which is the thickness of the circlip. Secure the circlip in the input shaft groove and determine dimension D which is the distance from the circlip to the ballbearing inner race. This may be done by using a vernier depth gauge. Calculate the thickness of the shim F as shown by the following example.

Example:

D	= .157 inch
−E	= .078 inch
F shim thickness	= .079 inch

7. Take out the circlip and fit the appropriate shim F.
8. Carefully measure the distance 'H' between the gearbox housing and the outer ballbearing track using a vernier depth gauge as shown in **FIG 6:36** and determine the height K of the gearbox extension with the gasket seal in place again using a depth gauge. There should be no play between the outer ballbearing track and the gearbox extension.

Example:

```
  H  Housing/bearing outer track   = .204 inch
− K  Rim height                    = .196 inch
                                    ─────────
     Shim thickness                = .008 inch
```

9 Once the shim thickness has been ascertained fit the gearbox extension to the gearbox housing and reassemble all other parts in the reverse procedure to dismantling.

6 : 11 Fault diagnosis

(a) Jumping out of gear
1 Broken spring behind locating ball for selector rod
2 Excessively worn locating groove in selector rod
3 Worn coupling dogs

(b) Noisy gearbox
1 Insufficient oil
2 Excessive end play in laygear
3 Worn or damaged bearings
4 Worn or damaged gear teeth

(c) Difficulty in engaging gear
1 Incorrect clutch pedal adjustment
2 Worn synchromesh unit
3 Gearchange linkage wrongly adjusted

(d) Oil leaks
1 Damaged joint washers
2 Worn or damaged oil seals
3 Front guide bush loose or marked

6 : 12 Technical data

Type	Porsche synchromesh on all four forward speeds, one reverse speed
Ratios:	
First	3.835:1
Second	2.053:1
Third	1.345:1
Fourth	1.0:1
Reverse	4.18:1
Mainshaft end float	.024 maximum
Layshaft end float	.0079 maximum
Pinion tooth backlash	.0008 to .00591
Shaft runout	.0008 maximum
Type	Getrag 235/5, 5-speed and reverse
Ratios:	
First	3.368:1
Second	2.16:1
Third	1.579:1
Fourth	1.241:1
Fifth	1.0:1
Reverse	4.0:1

NOTES

CHAPTER 6A

AUTOMATIC GEARBOX

6A : 1 Description
6A : 2 Mechanical power flow
6A : 3 Troubleshooting & testing procedure
6A : 4 Throttle linkage adjustment
6A : 5 Gearchange point adjustment
6A : 6 Selector lever adjustment
6A : 7 Removing & refitting gearbox
6A : 8 Fault diagnosis
6A : 9 Technical data

6A : 1 Description

The automatic transmission incorporates a fluid torque converter coupling in place of the conventional clutch, and an hydraulically operated epicyclic gearbox in which all changes of ratio during normal driving are performed automatically in accordance with the speed of the car and the position of the accelerator pedal.

There are nominally three forward speeds and reverse but owing to the torque multiplication available in the converter there is perfectly smooth progression through the ratios from rest to maximum speed. Torque multiplication is infinitely variable from a minimum equivalent gear ratio of 1:1 to a maximum of approximately 2.2:1.

The gearbox is controlled by a selector lever mounted in a quadrant in the central console. This quadrant has six positions marked on it for the following functions:

P or Park	In this position the engine can be started and run without any drive being transmitted to the rear wheels. There is also a mechanical lock applied to the output shaft which prevents the car from moving in either direction.
R or Reverse	As the name implies.
O or Neutral	As for P, but the transmission lock is not applied.
A or Drive	In this position the car moves off in first gear and changes up to second and third automatically at speeds dependent upon throttle position and road speed. Downchanges are similarly made as circumstances require. This selection is used for all normal driving.
2	As for A but there is no change into third or top gear.
1	First gear only is available.

Ranges 2 and 1 are particularly useful when engine braking is required as when descending steep hills and may be selected at any time, but obviously must not be engaged at speeds greater than that possible in the lower gear or the engine will be overspeeded. A fluid cooler is fitted in the lower radiator chamber on some models.

6A : 2 Mechanical power flow

FIG 6A:1 shows how the various ratios are obtained. The crankshaft drives the outer casing of the torque converter and this is filled with a special hydraulic oil. An inner member called the stator can be induced to revolve within the outer casing of the torque converter by the action of vanes on the oil, so that eventually both parts of the converter may turn almost as one unit in the manner of a normal clutch. The drive down to the gear train is by way of an input gearshaft which runs along part of the longitudinal axis of the gearbox.

6A : 3 Troubleshooting & testing procedure

Various tests and adjustments which can be made by a reasonably competent owner are given, always assuming that a tachometer (revolution indicator) and an accurately calibrated oil pressure gauge, calibrated up to at least 125 lb/sq in are available. Serious trouble, which can only be cured by extensive dismantling, must be left to a properly equipped service station as specialist technical knowledge and equipment are necessary.

Before a suspect faulty automatic transmission unit is removed from the vehicle the cause of the trouble must be ascertained and for this a specific fault diagnosis routine has to be strictly adhered to. A summary of the road test procedure is given in this section for preliminary diagnosis purposes.

Road test procedure:

All suspected faults must be checked by road testing. In cases of slip or poor acceleration a special torque converter stall speed test must be completed.

Gearchange/road speed comparison:

With the selector lever in the normal drive position and the vehicle road tested the gears should automatically change as detailed below:

Gearchange	Road speed
1st to 2nd	27 to 34 mile/hr
2nd to 3rd	53 to 59 mile/hr

Hydraulic pressure check:

To assist with a mechanical or hydraulic system failure certain pressure checks should be carried out as are detailed below. Refer to **FIG 6A:2** and **FIG 6A:3** which give the location points for the pressure gauge to be connected into the system.

1. Converter oil pressure test. Pressure test point 1. Move the selector position to 0, with the accelerator linkage detached and the engine speed set at exactly 1000 rev/min. The oil pressure gauge should read 22.76 lb/sq in. With the accelerator linkage placed in the kickdown position using hand pressure, the oil pressure gauge should indicate 49.78 lb/sq in.
2. Clutch 'A' test. Pressure test point 2. Move the selector lever to position A with the accelerator linkage disconnected and the handbrake firmly on, together with the footbrake firmly depressed. Set the engine speed to 1000 rev/min and the oil pressure should be between 71.12 and 75.38 lb/sq in. With the accelerator linkage held in the kick-down position using hand pressure the pressure gauge reading should be between 99.56 and 103.83 lb/sq in.
3. Main pressure setting test. Pressure test point 3. Set the selector lever to position O with the accelerator linkage disconnected and the engine speed to 1000 rev/min. A pressure of 71.12 lb/sq in should be obtained. With the accelerator linkage moved to the kick-down position and held by hand, the pressure gauge should read 99.56 lb/sq in.

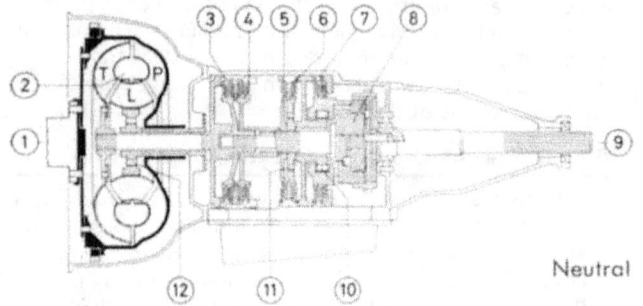
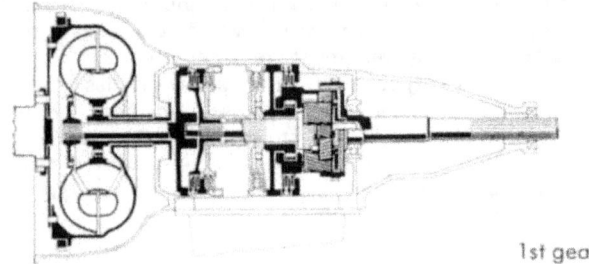
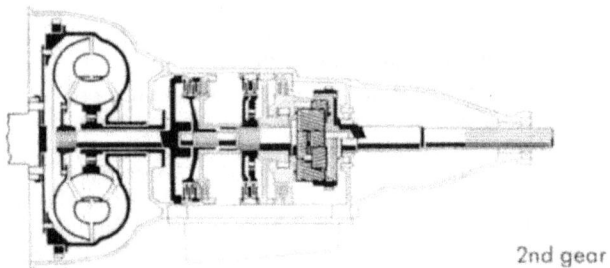
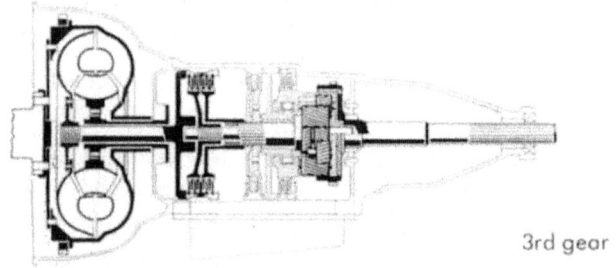
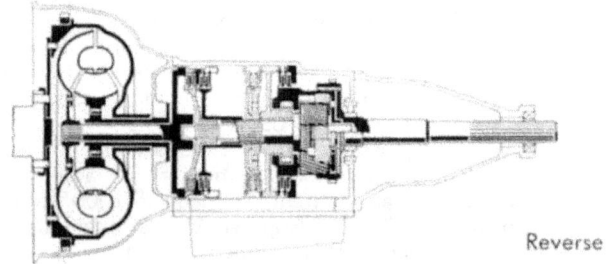
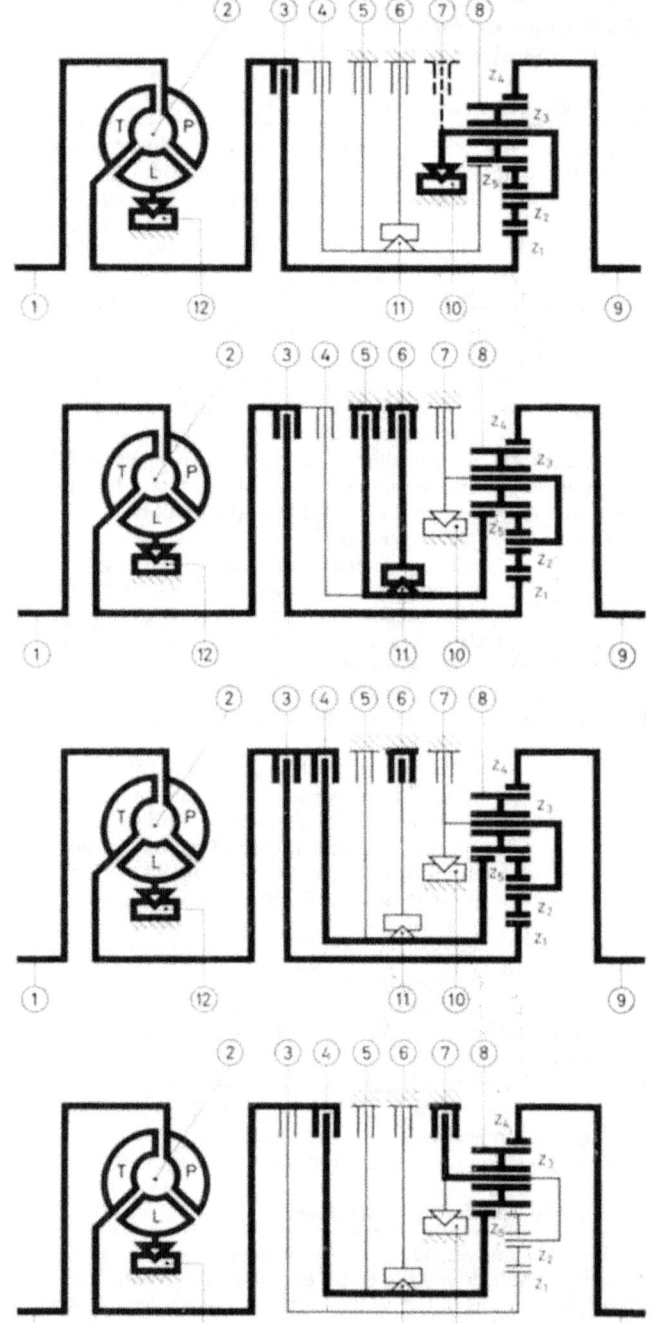

Power Flow (Mechanical)

1 Engine crankshaft
2 Torque converter
P Impeller
L Stator
T Turbine
3 Clutch A
4 Clutch B
5 Disc brake C'
6 Disc brake C
7 Disc brake D
8 Planetary gear train Z^1–Z^5
9 Input shaft
10 Free wheel
11 Free wheel
12 Free wheel

FIG 6A:1 Mechanical power train

4 Gearchange throttle valve pressure test. Pressure test point 4. Position the selector lever to position O with the accelerator disconnected. Set the engine speed to 1000 rev/min and the pressure gauge should indicate a reading between 12.80 and 17.07 lb/sq in. With the accelerator linkage in the kick-down position and held by hand the pressure gauge should indicate a reading of 12.08 and 17.07 lb/sq in. With the accelerator linkage in the kick-down position and held by hand the oil pressure should be between 49.78 and 52.63 lb/sq in.

5 Governor pressure test. Pressure test point 5. Move the selector lever to position A and with the vehicle being driven at a constant speed of 31.1 mile/hr the pressure should be between 4.27 and 7.11 lb/sq in.

6A : 4 Throttle linkage adjustment

1 Refer to **FIG 6A:4** and remove the kick-down switch stop 1 and adjust. It is recommended that for adjustment purposes the stop guide 1 should be set to a length of 2.618 in from the top edge of the bolt to the bottom edge of the stop guide.

2 When the throttle pedal is fully depressed the point F (see **FIG 6A:8**), may just touch the carpeting on the floor but the latter must not act as a stop.

3 Remove the locking clip 2 (see **FIG 6A:5**) at the ball joint and disengage the tie rod from the operating spindle. Detach the linking rod and open the throttle butterfly fully. The throttle butterfly must not open beyond the vertical position. Should this occur the stop A (see **FIG 6A:6**) must be bent to correct over adjustment.

4 Depress the throttle pedal plate right down from the idling position 9 (see **FIG 6A:7**), to the kick-down contact position 10. Open the throttle butterfly fully by rotating the shaft 6 and loosen the locknuts 11. Adjust the linking rod 4 to the correct length 'X' by turning the ball joint heads 12.

5 To check the adjustment connect the thrust rod 3 (see **FIG 6A:5**), to the operating shaft 6 (see **FIG 6A:7**), and depress the throttle pedal to the kick-down position 10. The throttle valve flap should now be fully open. Should further adjustment be required, adjust the linking rod length 4 until correct adjustment has been obtained. Tighten the locknuts to secure the ball joint heads 12 and refit the linking rod 4.

6A : 5 Gearchange point adjustment

To check that the time for gearchange compared with road speed is correct proceed as follows:

1 Check the adjustment of the linkage to the carburetter as detailed in **Section 6A:5**.

2 Refer to **FIG 6A:8** and with the pedal plate 13 fully depressed the joint F should not rest on the floor carpeting.

3 Move the hand selector lever to positon O. Depress the throttle pedal plate to the kick-down position 10 and in this position the length 'C' of the thrust rod E must be adjusted until the edge of the operating lever D is aligned with the mark B.

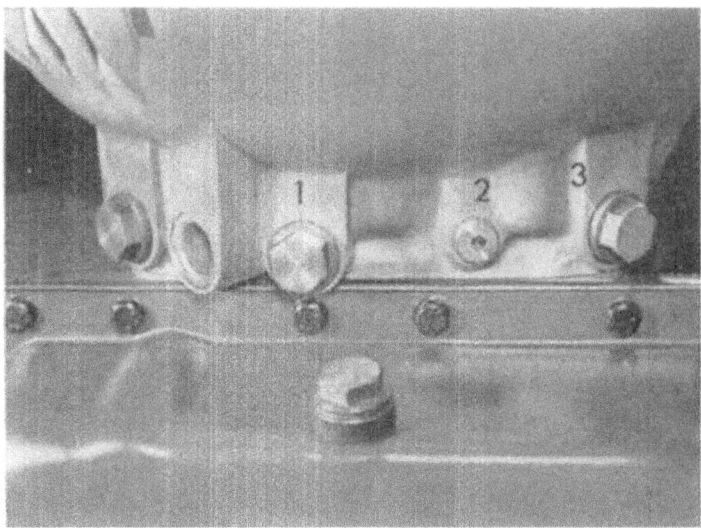

FIG 6A:2 Hydraulic pressure test points

FIG 6A:3 Hydraulic pressure test points

FIG 6A:4 Kick-down switch assembly

4 Release the ball joint securing clip and detach the thrust rod E. Slacken the locking nuts 14 and adjust the rod to length 'C' by means of the ball joints 15. Tighten and resecure the ball joints. Refit the thrust rod E and secure with spring clip. It is important to note that if any attempt is made to drive the vehicle with the thrust rod E disconnected damage to the gearbox will result.

5 Road test the vehicle and with the selector in position A and the throttle pedal fully depressed but not to the kick-down position, the gearbox should automatically change from 1st to 2nd speed at 27 to 34 mile/hr and into 3rd speed at 53 to 59 mile/hr. Should the gearchange occur too early the thrust rod E should be lengthened. Conversely if the gearchange occurs too late the thrust rod E must be shortened. By using the kick-down with the throttle pedal in position 13 the vehicle may be driven in each gear up to its maximum limited engine speed.

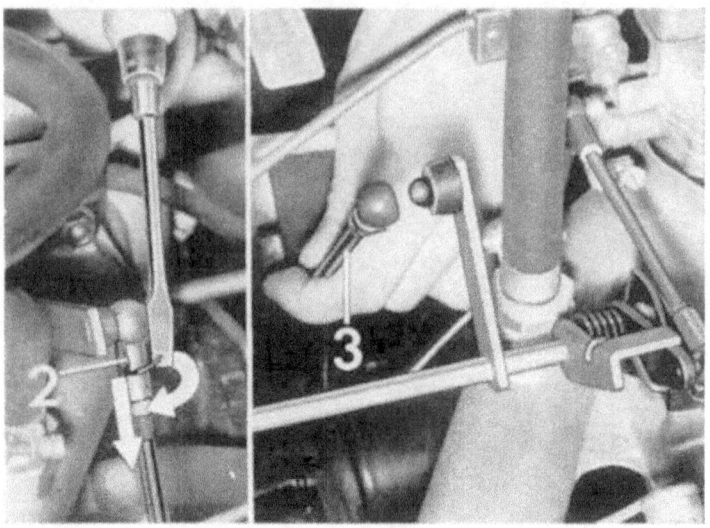

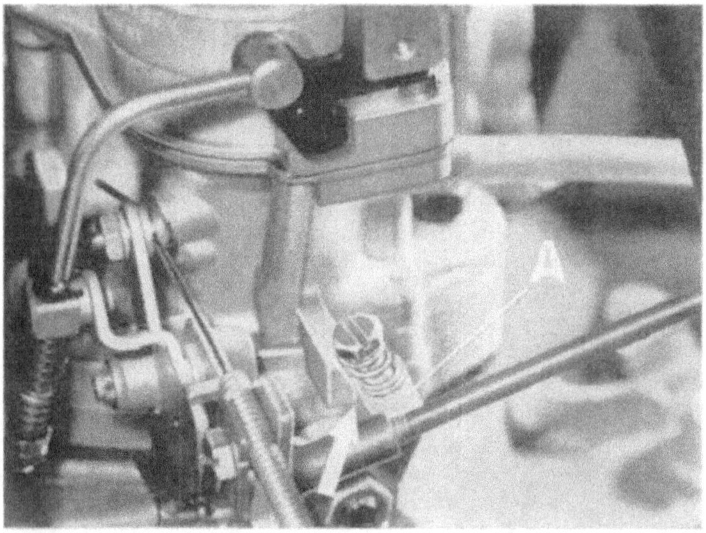

FIG 6A:5 Throttle linkage

FIG 6A:6 Throttle stop adjustment

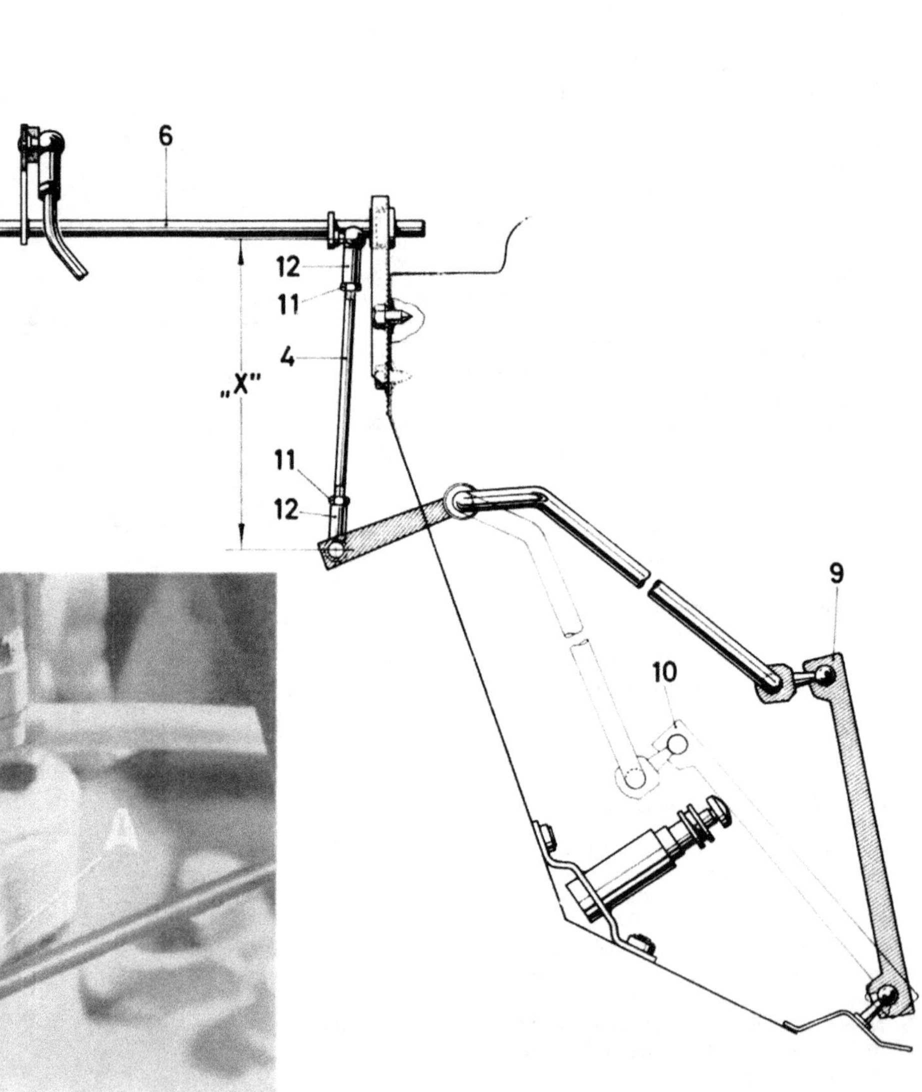

FIG 6A:7 Throttle linkage adjustment points

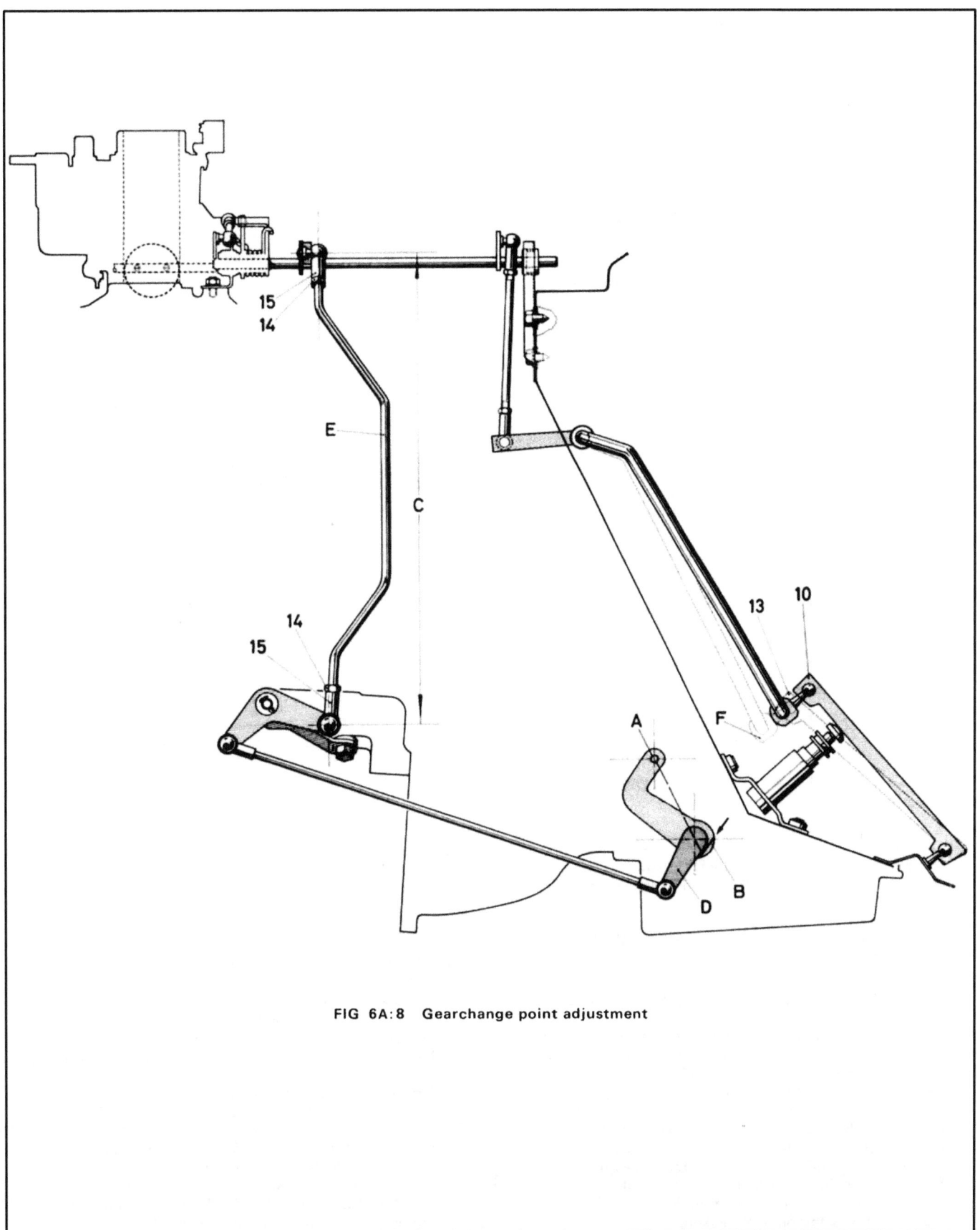

FIG 6A:8 Gearchange point adjustment

6A : 6 Selector lever adjustment

Type A version with single selector rod:

1. During this adjustment the vehicle must not be raised and the front and rear axles must carry the normal weight of the vehicle.
2. Check that the complete power unit mountings have not deteriorated causing excessive side movement.
3. Refer to **FIG 6A:9** and detach the selector rod S from the hand lever H. Move the selector quadrant to position O. It should be noted that the actual gear position is indicated not by stops 3 and 4 on the hand lever H but by engagement slots P–O–A–2–1–R in the gearbox as shown in **FIG 6A:9** inset.
4. Move the hand lever H to position O. It is important that a clearance of approximately .0394 inch should be maintained between the locking pin 7 and position stops 3 and 4. In this position 'Y' it should be possible to refit the selector S without difficulty.

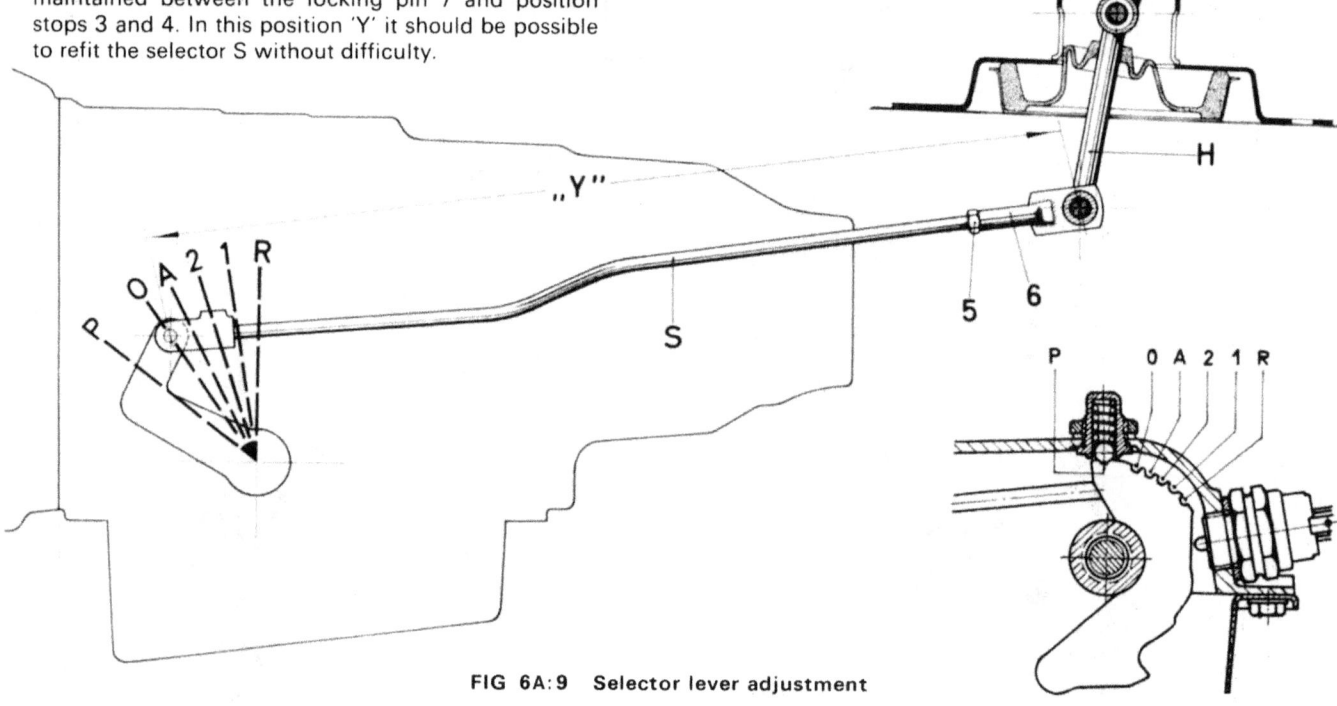

FIG 6A:9 Selector lever adjustment

5. Loosen the locknut 5 and turn the shackle 6 to adjust the length of rod S. Once correct adjustment has been made tighten the locknut 5 and refit selector rod S to the hand lever H.

Type B version with selector linkage with reverse motion lever:

1. During this adjustment the vehicle must not be raised and the front and rear axles must carry the normal weight of the vehicle.
2. Detach the selector rod 1 from the hand lever and move the selector quadrant to position O being the third notch from the bottom (see **FIG 6A:10**).
3. Check that a clearance A of .039 inch is present between the stop and the stop contacts in position O. Loosen the locknut 2 and turn the shackle 3 on the selector rod 1 until the distance Y measured between the reverse motion and the hand levers is as required. The stop positions are determined by notches on a modified ratchet A as shown in **FIG 6A:10** inset, whilst B shows the original version.

Gear selector lever adjustment:

In order for the driver to have complete control to obtain quiet and effective operation from the automatic transmission the gearlever must be correctly adjusted and to complete this operation proceed as follows:

1. Locate the spring catch at the bottom of the gear selector lever gate, push forward so releasing the gate. Lift out carefully.
2. Using a C-spanner loosen the selector lever sleeve nut 6 (see **FIG 6A:11**) and unscrew the selector lever handle 3 together with its rod 4 from the lever assembly 5.
3. Unscrew the selector lever sleeve nut 6 so that the locating stop 7 (see **FIG 6A:13**), can be lifted away from the lever 5. Refer to **FIG 6A:12** and remove the shaft retaining screw 8. Withdraw the pushbutton 9 and gearlever rod 4 from the lever handle 3. The locating stop 7 must correspond dimensionally with the inset shown in **FIG 6A:13** which, if signs of wear are evident, a new part must be fitted.

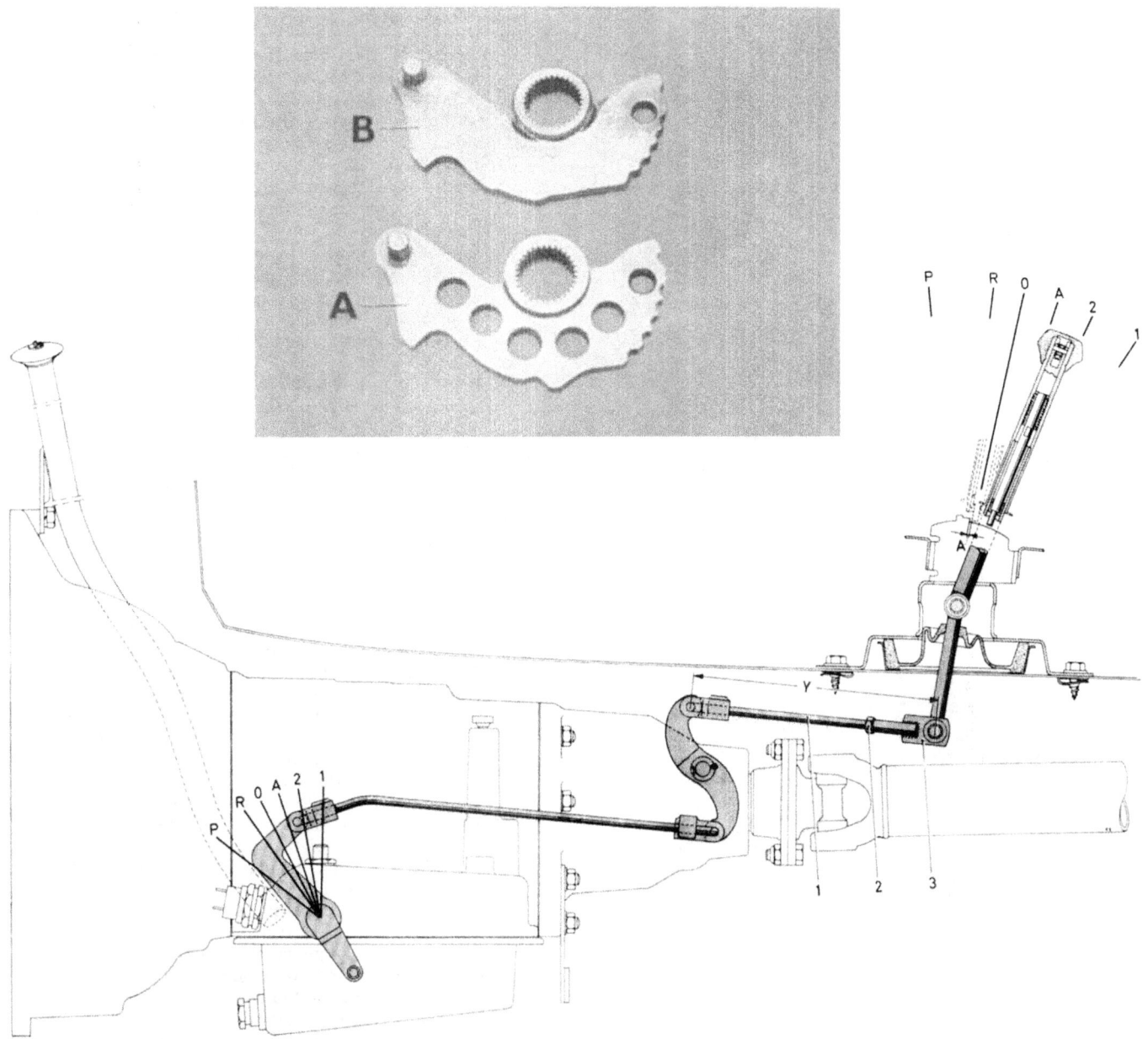

FIG 6A:10 Selector lever adjustment

4 Carefully slide the locating stop 7 into the selector lever 5 and place the bearing bush onto the selector lever rod 4. Apply a little molybdenum disulphide grease and screw down tight into the locating stop 7. Excessive care must be taken not to overtighten the gearlever rod 4 otherwise the bearing bush may be damaged or the thread on the stud stripped.

5 The slot of the fork head on the gearlever rod 4 must be located at exactly 90 degrees to the direction of travel. The selector lever shaft sleeve nut 6 should be screwed downwards until the distance between the flange and the gearchange gate is .393 inch. Screw on the selector lever handle 3.

6 Carefully screw down the selector lever handle until the press button 9 can be easily pushed into the fork head of the lever rod 4. The head of the pushbutton 9 must lift the locating stop 7 at least .011 to .019 inch by means of the roller at the top of the fork head slot.

7 Road test to ensure correct operation.

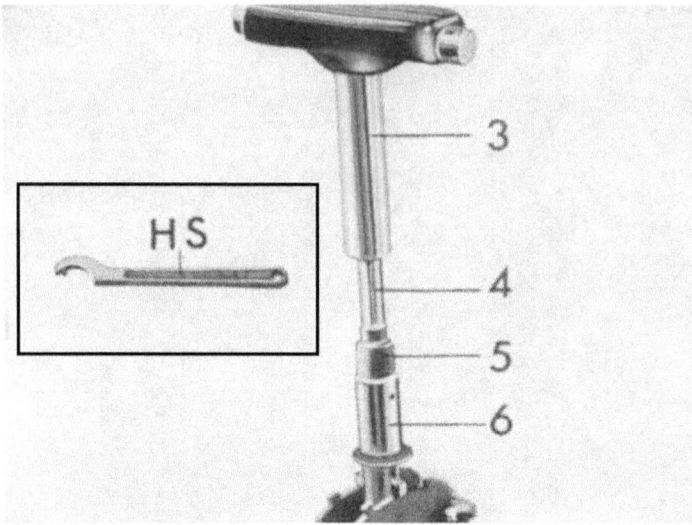

FIG 6A:11 Selector lever assembly

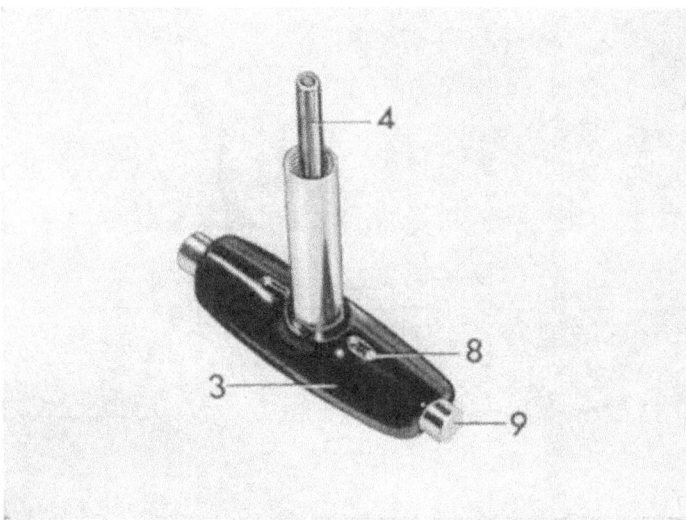

FIG 6A:12 Selector lever head

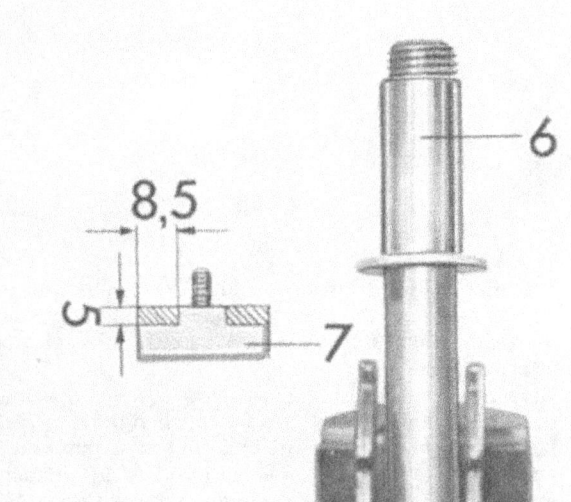

FIG 6A:13 Selector lever locating stop

6A : 7 Removing & refitting gearbox

1 Disconnect the negative cable from the battery and release the accelerator cable. Remove the exhaust downpipe from the triangular mounting flange and unscrew the exhaust support anchoring bolts. Detach the exhaust downpipe from the manifold flange and also remove the centre exhaust bracket. Tie the exhaust system securely to the rear drive shaft.
2 Remove the speedometer drive securing screw located at the rear end of the transmission casing and carefully lift away the speedometer drive. Detach the propeller shaft at the gearbox flange and place the propeller shaft as far as possible from the rear of the gear casing. Remove the retaining screw for the Bowden control cable located at the rear of the gear casing.
3 Disconnect the selector rod from the manual gearlever located at the side of the propeller shaft tunnel by the rear gearbox drive flange.
4 Remove the retaining spring clip from the ball joint at the link rod D (see **FIG 6A:8**). Disconnect the ball joint.
5 Release the cable terminals from the starter lock and reversing lamp switch which is shown in **FIG 6A:14**.
6 Release the steering guide lever bearing bracket retaining bolts as shown in **FIG 9:17**. Turn the steering wheel on full righthand lock and carefully rotate the bearing bracket until it is round against the bulkhead. Rotate the steering wheel slightly back towards the straight-ahead position and rest the steering arm on the top of the suspension wishbone.
7 Using a garage hydraulic crane or overhead hoist take the weight of the power unit and loosen the lefthand control lever mounting bracket located at the rear side of the engine. Also remove the retaining bolt holding this bracket to the torque converter housing.
8 Slacken the engine/torque converter securing bolts and withdraw the oil filler pipe from the gearbox. Plug immediately with a plastic stopper to prevent excessive loss of oil.
9 Remove the lower torque converter housing coverplate bolts shown by arrows in **FIG 6A:15a**. Remove the four diaphragm securing bolts shown in **FIG 6A:15b** which may be reached through the hole in the flywheel. Rotate the engine as necessary.
10 Carefully ease the engine upwards and towards the front as far as movement of the rubber engine mountings will allow. Remove the previously slackened gearbox to engine mounting bolts and take the weight of the gearbox using a garage hydraulic jack with a suitable cradle fitted to the saddle. It is important that the torque converter does not slip out from the gearbox. The torque converter should be pushed back using a screwdriver through the holes in the flywheel as the gearbox is withdrawn from the engine.

Reassembly:

Reassembly is the reverse procedure to dismantling but the following points should be noted:
1 When the gearbox is being renewed the two dowel sleeves located in the front face of the torque converter housing must also be renewed. Failure to do so will invite serious damage to the torque converter and driving disc.

2 Secure the four diaphragm securing bolts that are located through the hole in the flywheel to a torque wrench setting of 14.47 + 2.89 lb ft.
3 Tighten the steering guide lever bearing bracket securing bolts to a torque wrench setting of 18.1 lb ft.
4 When reassembling the cables to the starter lock and reversing lamps switch as shown in **FIG 6A:14** the two opposed pins furthest apart (8 and 9) should be connected to cables coloured green/black and green/white. The two pins closer together should be connected to cables brown/black and brown.
5 When reassembling the exhaust manifold flange to downpipe connection coat the threaded studs with Molykote paste.

6A : 8 Fault diagnosis

(a) Gearchange points too high
1 Accelerator linkage incorrectly adjusted
2 Leakage in governor inlet line
3 Leakage past governor piston rings
4 Governor bush jammed

(b) Gearchange points too low
1 Accelerator linkage incorrectly adjusted
2 Governor bush jammed
3 Throttle pressure too low

(c) Accelerator kick-down not available
1 Accelerator linkage incorrectly adjusted
2 Throttle pressure valve sticking

(d) Selector lever cannot be moved to P position
1 Selector linkage incorrectly adjusted
2 Parking lock mechanism defective

(e) Selector lever cannot be moved to R position
1 Selector linkage incorrectly adjusted

(f) Vehicle will not move forward or backwards
1 Selector linkage incorrectly adjusted
2 Oil level too low
3 Oil pressure too low
4 No drive to oil pump
5 Reducing passage in input shaft blocked

(g) Vehicle remains in 1st gear
1 Selector valve 1/2 jammed
2 Selector piston 1/2 jammed
3 Governor bush jammed

(h) Vehicle remains in 1st and 2nd gears
1 Selector valve 2/3 jammed
2 Selector piston 2/3 jammed
3 Latched sealing ring for clutch B leaking

(i) Vehicle remains in 2nd gear
1 Selector valves 1/2 and 2/3 jammed
2 Selector piston 1/2 and 2/3 jammed

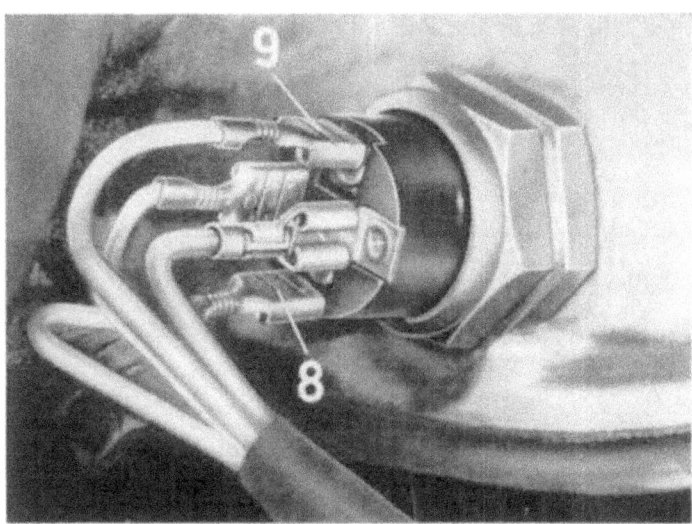

FIG 6A:14 Starter lock & reversing switch connections

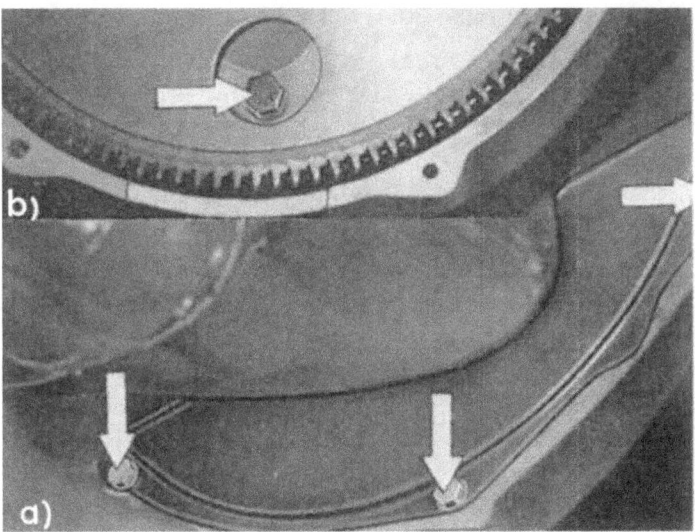

FIG 6A:15 Coverplate & diaphragm securing bolt location

(j) Vehicle remains in 3rd gear
1 Selector valves 1/2 and 2/3 jammed
2 Selector pistons 1/2 and 2/3 jammed
3 Governor bush jammed

(k) No reverse gear available
1 Forward/reverse locking valve jammed
2 Excessive end play on latched sealing ring for clutch B
3 Clutch B defective
4 Selector linkage incorrectly adjusted

(l) Slipping at gearchange points
1 Accelerator linkage disconnected
2 Oil pressure too low

(m) Slipping at 1st and 2nd gearchange points
1 Clutches C and C' slipping
2 Oil pressure too low
3 Oil inlet lines blocked
4 Freewheel C defective

(n) Slipping at 2nd and 3rd gearchange points
1 Excessive end float at latched sealing ring for clutch B
2 Oil pressure too low
3 Oil inlet lines blocked
4 Clutch B defective

(o) Slipping in 3rd gear
1 Excessive end float at latched sealing ring for clutch B
2 Oil pressure too low
3 Clutch B defective

(p) With selector lever in position A, 1st gear not receiving power from engine
1 Auxiliary freewheel defective

(q) With lever in position 2, very violent change from 2nd to 1st gear
1 Excessive clutch overlap between C', C and D
2 Pressure reducing valve D jammed

(r) With lever in position 1 or 2, no braking effect in 1st gear
1 Clutch D defective
2 Pressure reducing valve D jammed

(s) No braking effect in 2nd gear
1 Clutch C defective

(t) High-pitched whistling noise in neutral, disappears on accelerating
1 Torque converter plate whistling—hydraulic flow noise

(u) Whining sound at gearbox output, varying with speed and load
1 Squeaking from propeller shaft centre bearing

(v) Whining varying with speed and load change
1 Centre bearing of propeller shaft defective

(w) Knocking noise in neutral
1 Follower plate broken
2 Fixing eyelet on converter broken off

(x) Rattling noise in neutral, disappears when a gear is engaged or when the engine is revved up in the neutral position
1 Oil level not correct

(y) Whistling noise dependent on gear engaged
1 Planet wheel assembly noisy

(z) Torque converter bellhousing oily
1 Shaft sealing ring defective
2 O-ring on pump housing missing or defective
3 Torque converter leaking at weld seams

(aa) Oil loss occurs at shift lever or accelerator pedal
1 Shaft sealing ring in shift lever or O-ring on shift lever defective

(bb) Tachometer drive leaking
1 O-ring or sealing ring damaged

(cc) Inspection or drain plugs leaking
1 Sealing ring damaged

(dd) Driven flange oily
1 Shaft sealing ring defective

(ee) Oil leaking at filler neck
1 O-ring defective or missing

(ff) Oil leaks at breather
1 Incorrect oil level

6A : 9 Technical data

Type	ZF 3HP 12-10, 3-speed with hydrodynamic torque converter
Ratios:	
Converter	1 to 2.2:1
First	2.56:1
Second	1.52:1
Third	1.0:1
Reverse	2.0:1
Torque converter:	
Gearchange points:	
First to second	23 to 27 mile/hour
Second to third	60 to 64 mile/hour

CHAPTER 7

PROPELLER SHAFT
REAR AXLE & REAR SUSPENSION

7 : 1 Propeller shaft overhaul
7 : 2 Rear axle removing & refitting
7 : 3 Rear axle carrier removing & refitting
7 : 4 Trailing arm overhaul
7 : 5 Halfshaft overhaul
7 : 6 Shock absorber removing & refitting
7 : 7 Universal joint overhaul
7 : 8 Final drive unit removing & refitting
7 : 9 Differential housing removing & refitting
7 : 10 Differential overhaul
7 : 11 Crownwheel & pinion removing & refitting
7 : 12 Crownwheel & pinion set-up
7 : 13 Fault diagnosis
7 : 14 Technical data

7 : 1 Propeller shaft overhaul

1 Using a garage hydraulic jack raise the vehicle and support on firmly based stands
2 Detach the exhaust system at the three point coupling flange and the central suspension point and tie up the lower drilling in the downpipe flange so that the exhaust system may be swung to one side when necessary. Release the propeller shaft from the gearbox drive flange.
3 Release the rubber coupling from the differential unit leaving the rubber coupling on the propeller shaft. Carefully lift away from the underside of the body.

Propeller shaft self-centring bearing:

1 Refer to **FIG 7:1** and remove the centring bearing sealing cap using a screwdriver. Release the circlip using a pair of suitably pointed circlip pliers and extract the centring ring and ball socket using a Kukko extractor 22/1 or a universal two leg puller. The complete unit is shown in **FIG 7:2**.
2 To reassemble the centring ring and ball socket a suitable arbor and press must be used. Pack the centring seating with approximately .28 to .35 ounce of multi-purpose high melting point grease. Replace the parts in the following order. Referring to **FIG 7:2**, 1 spring, 2 ball socket, 3 centring ring, 4 ball socket, 5 retaining ring, 6 sealing cap.

Refitting propeller shaft assembly:

This operation is the reverse procedure to dismantling. The flexible coupling locknuts must be tightened to a torque wrench setting of 32.5 lb ft.

Propeller shaft centre bearing:

Removal:

1 Refer to **FIG 7:3** and remove the four fixing bolts as arrowed from the propeller shaft.
2 Remove the retaining bolts 2 (see **FIG 7:4**) from the centre bearing block. Carefully withdraw the propeller shaft 3 and the centre bearing block from the front.
3 Using a pair of pointed circlip pliers remove the circlip from the shaft. Press out the centre bearing block and ballbearing taking care not to press against the dust cap 5 (see **FIG 7:5**).
4 Press out the bearing from the centre bearing block.

Reassembly:

1 Wet the ballbearing reception bore with water and using a suitably sized drift press the new bearing into the centre bearing block. If the dust cap is disturbed it must be set to dimension 'A' (see **FIG 7:5**), which should be .23 inch.
2 Press the ballbearing and centre bearing block 2 (see **FIG 7:6**) tightly onto the propeller shaft flange. Install the distance piece 7, and insert the circlip 4 into the groove ensuring the inner side of the convex circlip faces the distance piece.
3 It should be noted that the propeller shafts and splined joints are matched and balanced together. Should non-matching parts be fitted the propeller shaft assembly may be out of balance causing vibration at certain speeds.
4 Refitting the propeller shaft is the reverse procedure to removal. Ensure that the centre bearing block is brought forward .08 inch (2 mm) as shown in **FIG 7:4**.

7 : 2 Rear axle removing & refitting

Removal:

1 Carefully ease back the protective rubber cap from the handbrake lever and remove the handbrake cable adjustment nuts.
2 Remove the wheel trims and carefully slacken the rear wheel nuts. Using a garage hydraulic jack raise the vehicle and support on firmly based stands.
3 Detach the exhaust system at the three point coupling flange and the centre suspension point. Release the exhaust silencer by removing the mounting bracket to silencer retaining bolt.
4 It is important that only one trailing suspension arm be supported by a jack at one time. Open the boot lid and remove the upper shock absorber locknut and retaining nut from the floor panel. It should be noted that the shock absorber also acts as a retaining member and if the upper shock absorber mounting on the boot compartment housing is removed before the vehicle is jacked up, it is essential to ensure that the driven shafts from the differential unit are released from the retaining bolts and suspended from the underside of the car using wire. The maximum bending angle of the halfshaft constant velocity joint is 18 deg. and only 14 deg. on the type with the sliding joint.
5 From the underside of the car withdraw the shock absorber from its upper mounting by retracting the upper half of the shock absorber. Gently lower the trailing arm assembly using the garage hydraulic jack. Lift away the helical spring together with the upper plate and damper rings.
6 Release the rubber coupling from the differential unit but not from the propeller shaft.
7 Release the flexible brake hose from the main brake pipe line as detailed in **Chapter 10** and cover the ends of the brake hoses to ensure no dirt enters into the hydraulic system.

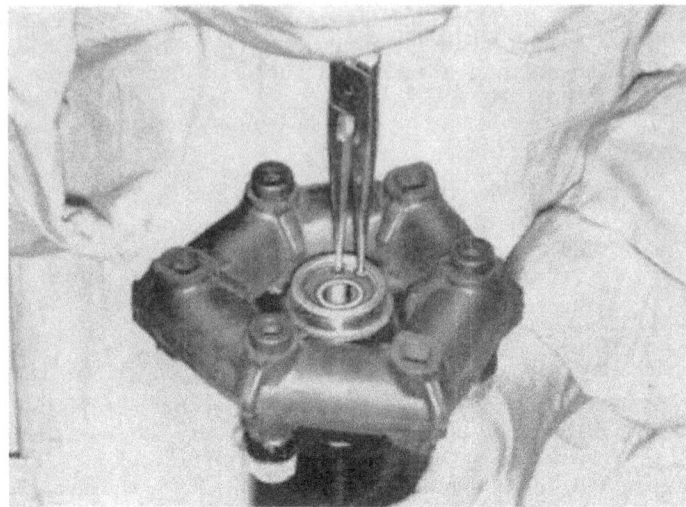

FIG 7:1 Circlip removal

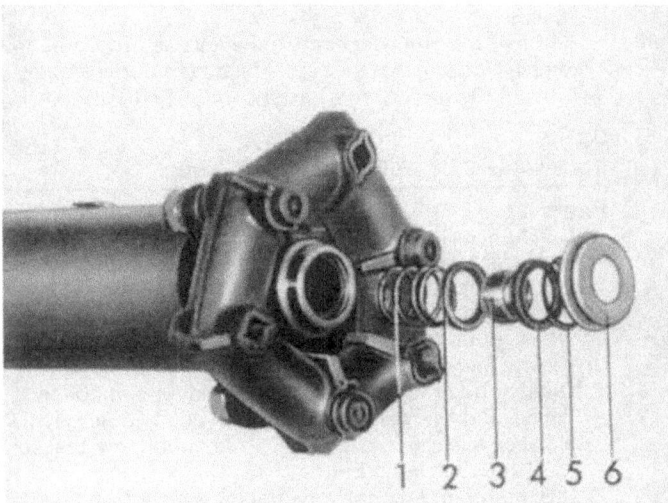

FIG 7:2 Centring ring removal

FIG 7:3 Propeller shaft flange bolts

8 Using a garage hydraulic jack together with a suitably shaped cradle, support the rear axle beam under the differential mounting. Detach the rear axle beam attachments from the body.
9 Remove the rear seat backrest and carefully knock out the bolts from the underside of the car using a soft faced hammer. Carefully detach the fastening bolt for the rear differential unit mounting and very carefully lower the rear axle assembly and at the same time withdrawing it backwards from the rear of the car (see **FIG 7:7**).

Refitting:

Refitting is the reverse procedure to dismantling but the following points should be noted:
1 Tighten the rear differential mounting retaining bolt to a torque wrench setting of 65.1 lb ft.
2 Tighten the rear axle beam retaining locknut to a torque wrench setting of 86.8 lb ft.
3 Once the rear brake hydraulic system has been refitted the complete system must be bled as described in **Chapter 10**.
4 Tighten the rubber coupling to differential drive flange from the propeller shaft retaining bolts to a torque wrench setting of 32.55 lb ft.
5 Tighten the halfshaft to differential unit universal joint locknuts to a torque wrench setting of 21.7 lb ft.

7 : 3 Rear axle carrier removing & refitting

Removal:

1 Remove the rear axle assembly as detailed in **Section 7 : 2**.
2 From the rear axle assembly remove the differential unit (see **FIG 7:8**), and also the trailing arm.
3 Detach both the rubber bearings from the rear axle beam by releasing the retaining bolts.

Reassembly:

Reassembly is the reverse procedure to dismantling but the following points should be noted:
1 The rubber bearing fastening holes are elongated so that when fitting always ensure that the rubber bearings are centred, otherwise the rear axle will not be correctly aligned to the body and therefore front axle, so causing the vehicle to move along the road in crab wise fashion.
2 Upon reassembly of the trailing arm the retaining bolts must be kept loose so that final tightening to a torque wrench setting of 54.25 lb ft may be performed once the vehicle is in its normal loaded position with all four wheels firmly on the ground.
3 When reassembling the differential unit, fit the distance bushes below the upper retainer plate with the collar towards the top. Tighten the retaining bolts to a torque wrench setting of 65.1 lb ft.
4 The rear axle carrier should always be fitted with both rubber bearings before mounting to the body otherwise the rear axle may become distorted in the three rubber mounting bearings.

7 : 4 Trailing arm overhaul

Removal:

1 Carefully push back the protective rubber cap on the handbrake lever and release the handbrake cable retaining nuts.
2 Remove the wheel trims and slacken the wheel nuts.

Jack up the rear of the vehicle and place on firmly based stands. Remove the road wheels.
3 Using a garage hydraulic jack carefully support the trailing arm. Open the boot compartment lid and remove the two nuts holding the shock absorber in position. It should be noted that the shock absorber functions as a support for the rear suspension. The inclination of the sliding universal joint must not exceed 14 degrees otherwise it may be strained.
4 Separate the driven shaft from the halfshaft and tie to the underside of the car with wire. Carefully withdraw the shock absorber from its upper mounting by compressing.
5 Carefully lower the trailing arm using the hydraulic garage jack and lift away the coil spring together with the upper spring plate.
6 Separate the flexible hydraulic brake hose from the main pipeline as detailed in **Chapter 10**, and cover the ends of the hose to ensure that no dirt finds its way into the hydraulic system.

Reassembly:

Reassembly is the reverse procedure to dismantling but the following points should be noted:
1 The trailing arm mounting retaining bolts should be left loose and only tightened to a torque wrench setting of 54.25 lb ft, when all four road wheels are firmly on the ground and the vehicle normally loaded.
2 Upon reassembly of the brake hydraulic system the system must be bled as detailed in **Chapter 10**.
3 When reassembling the coil spring ensure that the smooth ground spring end faces upwards. Rotate the cylindrical coil end of the spring into the channel in the trailing arm.

Trailing arm silentbloc bushes:

1 Remove and refit the trailing arms as previously described.
2 Using BMW tool 6011 extract the silentbloc bushes as shown in **FIG 7:9**.
3 Prepare the silentbloc bushes in the tool and coat the outer surface with glycerine.
4 Carefully pull the silentbloc bushes into the trailing arm until they are flush with the chamfered side.

Suspension arm silentbloc bushes:

1 Carefully slacken one bolt of the tie bar fixing and using a garage hydraulic jack carefully lower the suspension arm until the fixing bolts of the silentbloc bush can be slackened.
2 Remove the silentbloc bush. It should be noted that only solid rubber bushes may be fitted and in no circumstances may bushes with cavities be fitted (see **FIG 7:10**). Should a trailing arm with recessed spring mountings be encountered only rubber bushes with cavities in the sides should be fitted (see **FIG 7:11**).
3 Reassembly is the reverse procedure to dismantling.

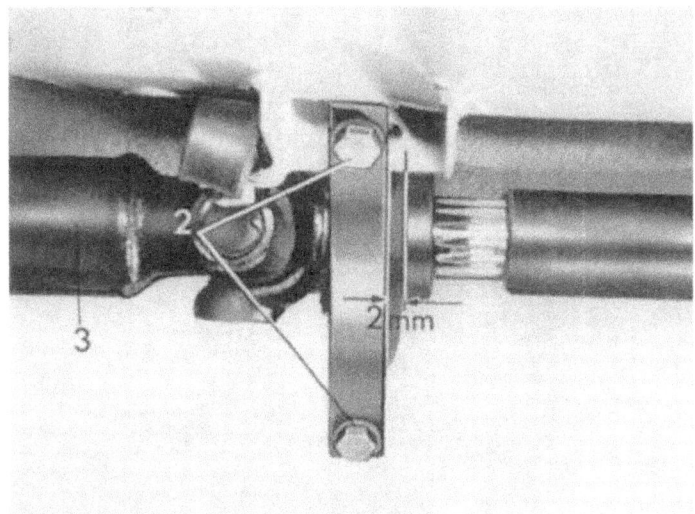

FIG 7:4 Centre bearing block

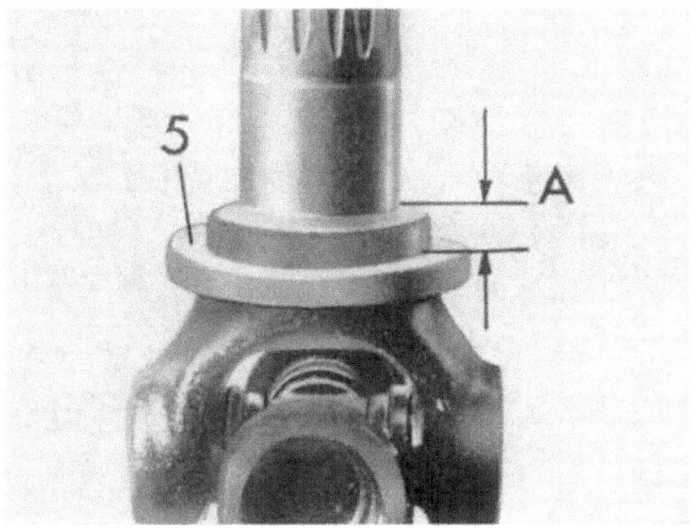

FIG 7:5 Dust cap position

FIG 7:6 Centre bearing spacer

FIG 7:7 Rear axle assembly removal

FIG 7:8 Differential unit removal

FIG 7:9 Silentbloc bush removal

7:5 Halfshaft overhaul

Removal:

1 It is important that if the halfshaft is to be removed the halfshaft nut should only be released with the handbrake fully applied and before the road wheel is removed. Remove the wheel trim and hub cap. Carefully extract the cotterpin from the shaft end and loosen the castellated nut on the halfshaft.
2 Loosen the wheel nuts and using a garage hydraulic jack raise the vehicle and place on firmly based stands. Remove the wheel and brake drum.
3 Release the retaining bolts from the driven shaft at the wheel hub end and also at the differential end having first marked the respective flange mating positions for correct reassembly.
4 Carefully lift away the drive shaft.
5 Using a soft faced hammer remove the driving flange and drive halfshaft from the trailing arm as shown in **FIG 7:12**. It is recommended that the castellated nut be screwed onto the threaded end of the halfshaft to ensure protection of the thread.
6 Remove the radial sealing ring and finally drive out the ball bearing races using a suitably sized drift.

Inspection and reassembly:

1 To inspect a ballbearing race first the bearing must be cleaned in petrol or white spirit, revolving it constantly until all impurities have been removed. Generally the bearing may be regarded as still serviceable if a visual inspection shows no traces or damage to the balls, race grooves, running faces or if there is no pronounced general wear. If bearing is defective or if there is any variation in axial play both bearings will have to be renewed. After a service life of 60,000 miles it is advisable to renew the bearings even if visual inspection indicates that they are apparently still serviceable. When installing new components the prescribed bearing play of .002 — .004 inch is to be obtained.
2 Replace the rear ballbearing and measure the depth of the front ballbearing contact surface in the hub to the rear outer ballbearing race (see **FIG 7:13**).
3 Carefully measure the length of the spacer bush using a vernier. Determine whether the unit can be assembled as it is or whether it is necessary to compensate to achieve the prescribed amount of bearing play. Any adjustment necessary should be performed by the use of shims.
4 Before finally inserting the bearings into the hub check the seating areas of the ballbearings on sliding tracks in the hub for any trace of slipping by the outer ballbearing race.
5 When refitting the hub it should be packed with approximately 2.47 ounce per wheel bearing of a multi-purpose high melting point grease.
6 Before refitting the halfshaft to the trailing arm, pack the sealing groove for the sealing ring with a graphite grease.
7 When tightening the halfshaft castellated nut it should be tightened to a correct torque wrench setting, as given in chapter **14**, with the road wheel assembled and the handbrake fully on.

7 : 6 Shock absorber removing & refitting

Removal:
1. Using a garage hydraulic jack raise the vehicle and place on firmly based stands. Support the trailing arm with a garage hydraulic jack.
2. Open the boot compartment lid and detach the upper shock absorber fastening nuts.
3. Release the lower shock absorber retaining nut. Compress the shock absorber and lift away from the underside of the vehicle.

Reassembly:
Reassembly is the reverse procedure to dismantling but the following points should be noted:
1. From Chassis No. 969552 shock absorbers are installed with a special comfort adjustment. This is indicated by a green spot on the sleeve in the vicinity of the shock absorber number. Shock absorbers should only be installed in matched pairs otherwise the road holding qualities of the car will be altered.
2. When refitting the lower shock absorber retaining nut the locknut should be tightened to a torque wrench setting of 54.25 lb ft when the vehicles road wheels are firmly on the ground and the vehicle normally loaded.
3. Modifications have been made to the top shock absorber mounting rubbers and it should be noted that if an old type rubber bearing is replaced by one of the new type it is necessary to fit the appropriate larger washers (see **FIG 7:14**).

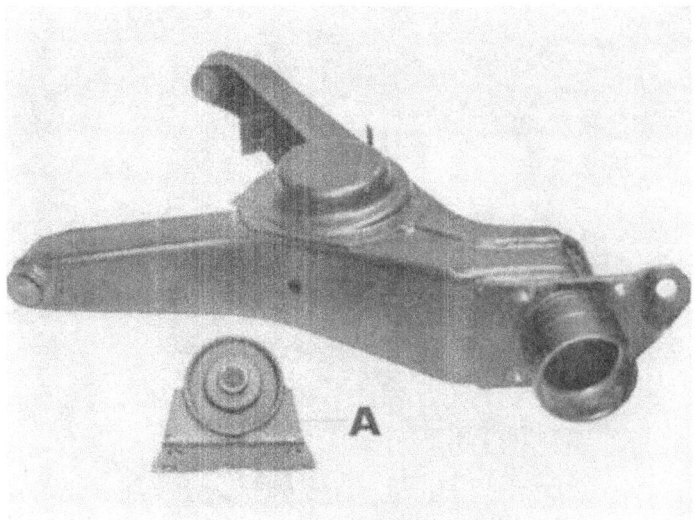

FIG 7:10 Silentbloc bush identification

7 : 7 Universal joint overhaul

Removal:
1. Mark the position of the two pairs of flanges relative to each other so that they may be correctly assembled.
2. Release the retaining bolt at both the differential drive flange and also the halfshaft flange and carefully lift away the halfshaft

Refitting:
Refitting is the reverse procedure to dismantling, but care should be taken to ensure that both pairs of flanges correctly line up and that the locknuts are tightened to a torque wrench setting of 22 lb ft.

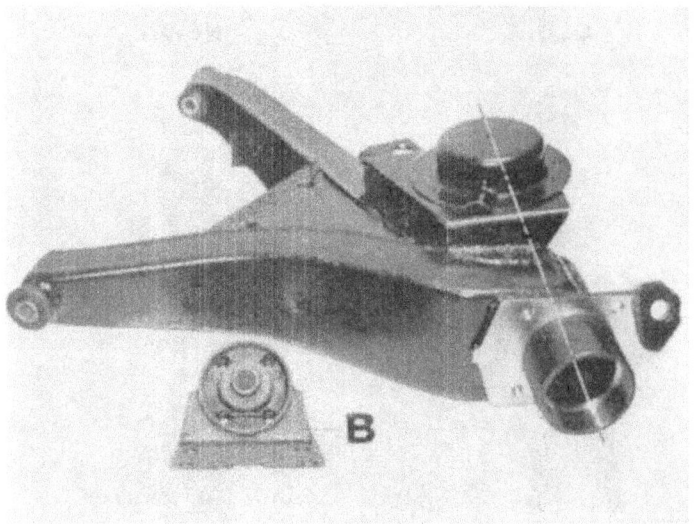

FIG 7:11 Silentbloc bush identification

Universal joint:
To overhaul the universal joint proceed as follows:
1. Lift out the circlip and lay the yoke of the universal flange on a sleeve suitably dimensioned so that the needle bearing bush may be pressed out.
2. With a suitably sized drift 'D' push down the needle bearing bush so pressing the needle bearing bush 1 out as far as it will move (see **FIG 7:15**).
3. Refer to **FIG 7:16**, turn the yoke around and lay the halfshaft on a suitably firm base and press the needle bearing bush 2 with sleeve 'H' out to limit stop.
4. Lift away the halfshaft flange. Lay the yoke of the driven shaft on sleeve 'B' and push the lower needle bearing bush 3 out as far as possible using the drift 'D' (see **FIG 7:17**).
5. Lay both bearing trunnions of the universal joint yoke on a suitable firm base and with the aid of the sleeve 'H' carefully push out the needle bearing 4 to its limit (see **FIG 7:18**).
6. Insert universal joint yoke ensuring that the grease nipple points towards the universal shaft flange. The needle bearing bush seals must be carefully checked

FIG 7:12 Removal of half shaft from trailing arm

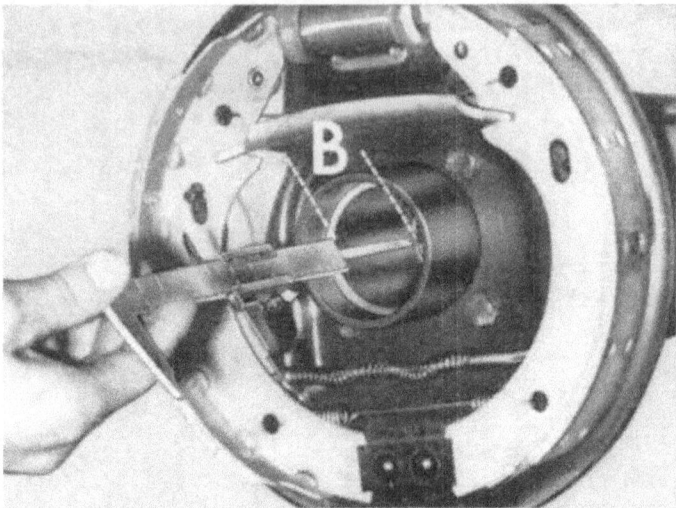

FIG 7:13 Measurement for bearing shim thickness

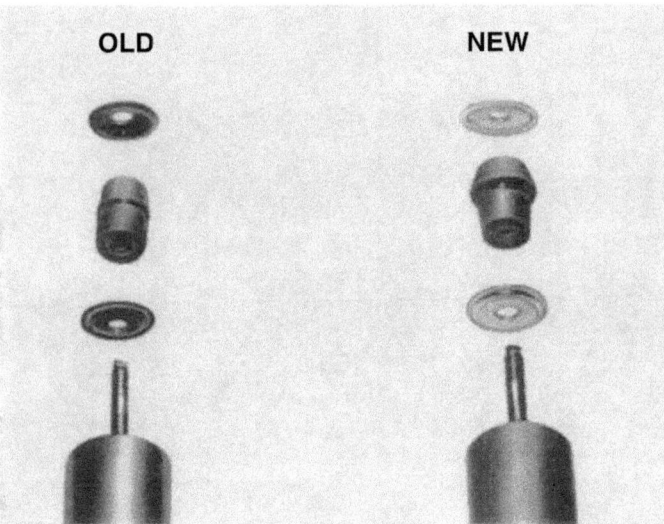

FIG 7:14 Shock absorber upper mounting bushes

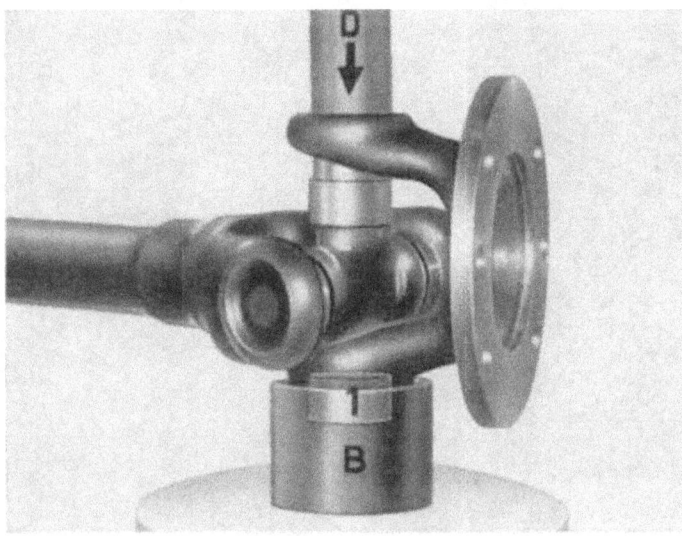

FIG 7:15 Needle bearing bush removal

for damage and renewed as necessary, otherwise rapid wear will occur due to lubrication failure.

7 Carefully press the needle bearing bush further in and insert the circlip with the aid of circlip pliers. Press inwards the opposing needle bearing bush and insert circlip with circlip pliers. Fit the remaining two needle bearing bushes in the same manner and lower the universal yoke on a suitably based stand and release any offset by one firm blow from a soft faced hammer. When the coupling is correctly aligned it should drop slowly under its own weight.
8 Finally fit driven shaft.

7 : 8 Final drive unit removing & refitting

There are several versions of the final drive used on the cars covered in this manual, including a limited-slip differential. The dismantling of these components should not be undertaken unless the operator is reasonably experienced and has access to the necessary equipment. Procedures are given here for servicing a typical installation, there will be detail differences for other versions.

Removal:

1 Using a garage hydraulic jack raise the vehicle and place on firmly based stands.
2 Detach the exhaust system at the three point coupling flange and also at its centre suspension. Release the exhaust silencer box from its two outside mounting brackets.
3 Disconnect the universal shaft from the final drive unit ensuring that the rubber coupling remains on the universal shaft. It should be noted that the universal shaft is not secured on the gearbox by the gearbox flange which means therefore that the shaft could slip out from the gearbox neck. It is therefore necessary to tie up the universal shaft.
4 Detach the halfshaft couplings at the final drive unit having first marked the two pairs of flanges for correct reassembly. Tie the halfshaft to the underside of the car ensuring that they are not angled in excess of 14 degrees.
5 Release the retaining bolts from the rear axle carrier and also the fastening bolt for the final drive mounting.
6 Carefully lift the final drive unit rearwards and down. Care must be taken to ensure that the three arm flange is so turned so that one arm of the flange is pointing vertically upwards as shown in **FIG 7:19**.

Reassembly:

Reassembly is the reverse procedure to dismantling but the following points should be noted:
1 Ensure that the three arm flange is turned so that one arm of the flange is pointing vertically upwards as shown in **FIG 7:19**.
2 Tighten the final drive mounting retaining bolt to a torque wrench setting of 65 lb ft.
3 When refitting the rear axle carrier retaining bolts always fit the spacer sleeve below the upper mounting plate with the collar facing upwards. Tighten the retaining bolts to a torque wrench setting of 65 lb ft.
4 Tighten the universal shaft locknuts to a torque wrench setting of 32.55 lb ft.

7 : 9 Differential housing removing & refitting

Removal:
1. Remove the final drive unit as detailed in **Section 7 : 8** and thoroughly clean the exterior of the unit. Drain the oil into a suitably sized container.
2. Remove the six rear cover retaining bolts and also the two driving flanges retaining bolts on either side of the final drive unit.
3. Mark the bearing caps and final drive unit casing to ensure correct reassembly and remove the four retaining bolts for each cap. Lift away the bearing cap.
4. Turn the differential housing until it is in the vertical position and remove the righthand bearing out through the aperture in the bearing cap as far as is possible and turn the pinion set clockwise to remove. This operation is shown in **FIG 7 : 20**.

Reassembly:
Reassembly is the reverse procedure to dismantling but the following points should be noted:
1. Should the differential unit taper roller bearings need renewing the cap must be heated to approximately 75°C before removing or replacing the new outer track. Once this operation has been completed the crownwheel and pinion mesh will have to be readjusted as detailed in **Section 7 : 11**. Ensure that the oil groove in the cap is facing downwards on reassembly.
2. Refit the driving flange bearing caps in their correct location as previously marked and tighten the retaining bolts to a torque wrench setting of 18 lb ft.
3. Tighten the driving flange bolts to a torque wrench setting of 72 lb ft.
4. Tighten the final drive unit rear cover bolts to a torque wrench setting of 36 lb ft.

7 : 10 Differential overhaul

1. Remove the final drive unit from the car as detailed in **Section 7:8**.
2. Remove the differential housing as detailed in **Section 7:9**.
3. Remove the securing bolts from the crownwheel to differential housing in a diagonal pattern and to separate the two strike the crownwheel with a soft faced hammer.
4. Using a hammer and suitably sized drift remove the differential shaft retaining pin (see **FIG 7 : 21**). Drive the differential shaft out of the differential housing using a suitably sized drift.
5. Lift away the halfshaft pinions and differential pinions through the opening in the differential housing.

Inspection and reassembly:
Reassembly is the reverse procedure to dismantling but the following points should be noted:
1. Check the bronze washers for wear and these should be renewed if necessary. There should be no play between the differential pinions. The lubricating groove machined in the bronze washers must face towards the contact surface of the pinions. Should new pinions be fitted they must be correctly paired and must always carry the same colour identification mark. Upon reassembly of the differential unit check the torque required to rotate the differential gears by fitting a driving flange and rotating using a torque wrench. After initial fitting the torque may reach 7.2 lb ft up to a maximum of 29 lb ft.

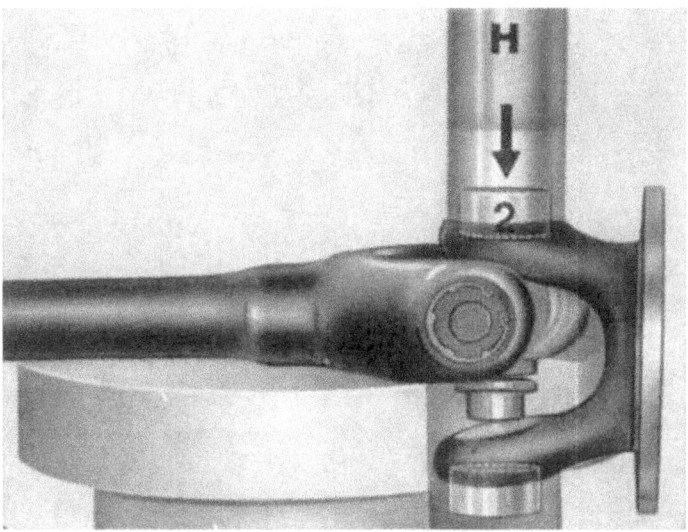

FIG 7 : 16 Needle bearing bush removal

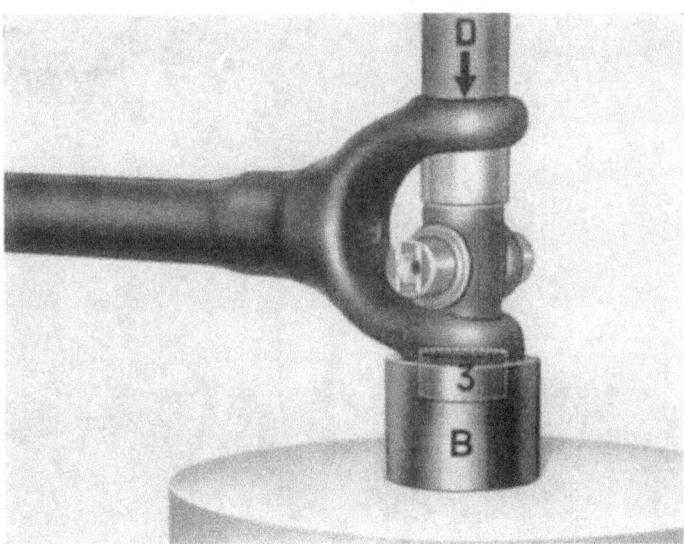

FIG 7 : 17 Needle bearing bush reassembly

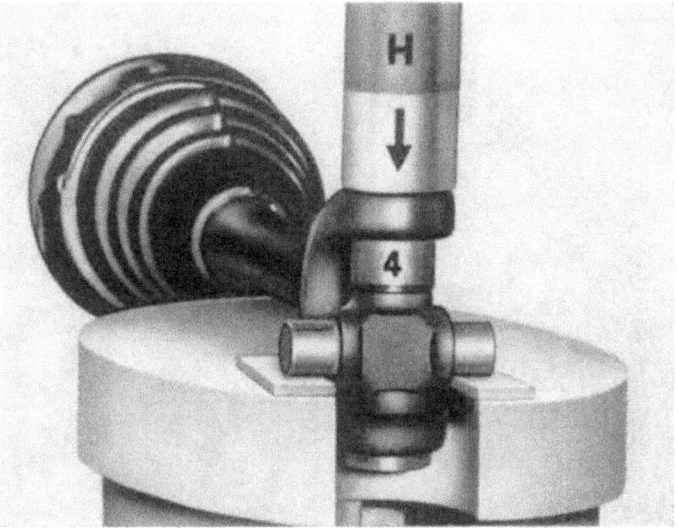

FIG 7 : 18 Needle bearing bush reassembly

FIG 7:19 Flange location for final drive unit removal

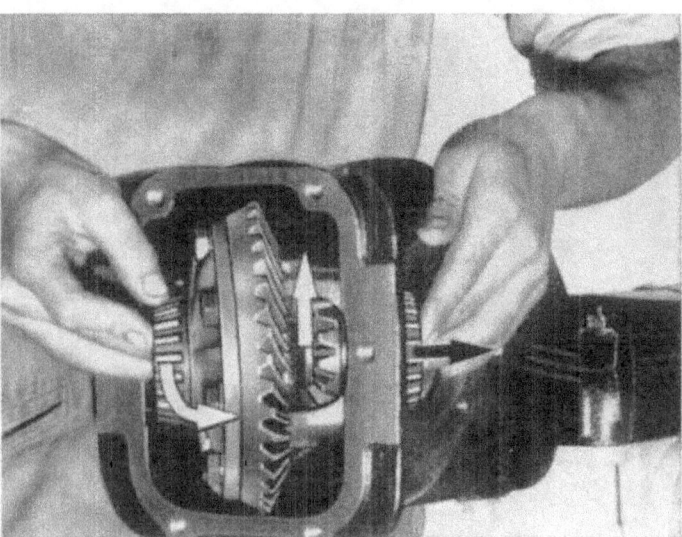

FIG 7:20 Differential removal

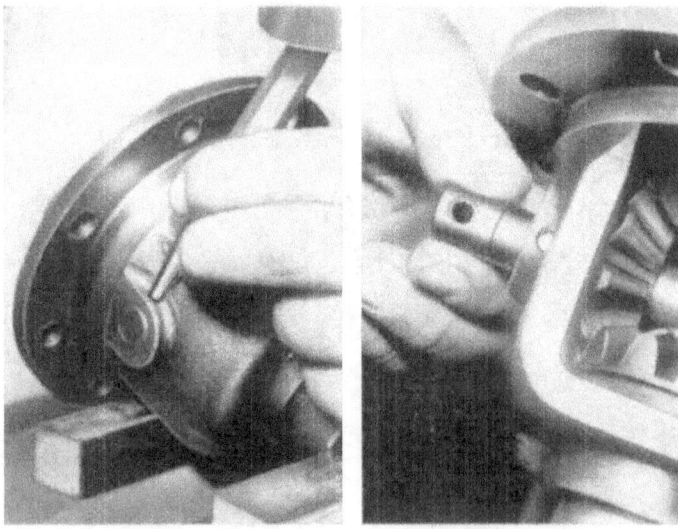

FIG 7:21 Differential shaft removal

2 When reassembling the crownwheel to the differential housing always heat the crownwheel in an electric oven to a temperature of 75°C. Allow the crownwheel with the two guide bolts to drop onto the differential housing. It is recommended that two or three threads of each of the securing bolts are coated with Loctite for additional security.

7:11 Crownwheel & pinion removing & refitting

Removal:
1 Remove the final drive unit as detailed in **Section 7:8**.
2 Remove the differential housing as detailed in **Section 7:9**.
3 Remove the nut from the three arm input flange and using a two leg universal puller remove the flange.
4 Remove the bearing cap retaining bolts on the front of the final drive casing and using a universal two leg puller pull off the bearing cap. Lift away the shim.
5 Place BMW tool 6046 socket wrench onto the elastic stop nut and push the three arm flange back onto the splines (see **FIG 7:19**). Hold the assembly with BMW tool 604 locking spanner to prevent from rotating and loosen the elastic stop nut.
6 Using a press remove the pinion from the final drive housing.
7 Carefully press the large taper roller bearing from the pinion. Using a long drift and hammer remove the bearing outer tracks from the final drive housing. Withdraw the taper roller bearing from the differential housing using a universal puller with wide feet.
8 Remove the crownwheel to differential housing retaining bolts in a diagonal pattern and using a soft faced hammer remove the crownwheel from the differential housing.

Reassembly:
Reassembly is the reverse procedure to dismantling but it should be pointed out that the pinion and crownwheel will have to be set so that the two gears are in correct mesh. For this information also see **Section 7:12**.

7:12 Crownwheel & pinion set-up

The pinion and crownwheel are carefully matched during manufacture and a serial number together with tolerances are inscribed on both components as shown in **FIG 7:22**. The number on the pinion is the deviation 'e' from the basic setting dimension 'D'. When fitting new crownwheel and pinion set the following procedure must be strictly adhered to:

1 Fit the crownwheel with the differential housing into the final drive casing and tighten down the bearing cap on the opposite side to a torque wrench setting of 18.1 lb ft.
2 Install the bearing cap on the crownwheel side and tighten the bolts evenly until the friction coefficient of the crownwheels seating amounts to approximately 17.4 to 24.3 lb in. Also screw in the driving flange fastening bolts into the differential shaft gears and tighten lightly against the differential pinion shaft.
3 Using a feeler gauge measure the distance which now exists between the bearing cap and the housing and fit shims the same thickness as the feeler gauges.
4 Turn the friction coefficient gauge several times against the operating direction and then read off the friction coefficient in the operating direction which should amount to between 17.4 and 24.3 lb in.

5 Remove the crownwheel and install the pinion without the distance bush with a shim 'X' between the pinion and the large taper roller bearing in the differential gearbox housing. Slide the three arm coupling onto the pinion splines and tighten the self-locking nut. Lightly tighten the three arm coupling retaining nut and using the friction gauge turn the drive pinion against the normal direction of rotation and then read off the friction coefficient in the direction of rotation. This should amount to approximately 10.42 to 14.76 lb in.
6 To determine the required thickness of the shim X:
Measure the distance A in **FIG 7:23**, between the face of the housing and the front face of the input bevel pinion.
Measure the bore diameter B in **FIG 7:24**, for the side cover plates. Divide this value by 2.
Measure the narrowest point C in **FIG 7:25**, between the side bore and the housing sealing face.
The basic setting dimension D is 52.52 mm (2.0677 inch). The deviation e, engraved on the face of the drive pinion is added, +, to D or subtracted, −.
D required is obtained from D basic + or − e.

Example 1:

(a)   B ÷ 2   41.50 mm   (1.6339 inch)
     + C   29.90 mm   (1.1771 inch)
       Y   71.40 mm   (2.8110 inch)

(b)   A   123.90 mm   (4.8779 inch)
     − Y   71.40 mm   (2.8110 inch)
     D actual   52.50 mm   (2.0669 inch)

(c)   D basic   52.52 mm   (2.0677 inch)
     − e   .18 mm   (.0071 inch)
     D required   52.34 mm   (2.0606 inch)

(d)   D actual   52.50 mm   (2.0669 inch)
     D required   52.34 mm   (2.0606 inch)
     X +   .16 mm   (.0063 inch)

The shim X to be fitted must be .16 mm (.0063 inch) thicker than the shim already in place.

Example 2:

If deviation e had a + value, the last two stages of the example above would be as follows:

(c)   D basic   52.52 mm   (2.0677 inch)
     + e   .25 mm   (.0098 inch)
     D required   52.77 mm   (2.0775 inch)

(d)   D required   52.77 mm   (2.0775 inch)
     D actual   52.50 mm   (2.0669 inch)
     X −   .27 mm   (.0106 inch)

The shim X to be fitted must be .27 mm (.0106 inch) thinner than the shim already in place.
From these examples it can be seen that if D required is larger than D actual, X must be subtracted from the shim X already in position and vice versa.
7 Refit the pinion and spacer bush together with the appropriate shim 'X'. Tighten the flexible locknut and using a soft faced hammer strike the end of the bearing trunnion sharply to seat the universal shaft centring. Apply the friction coefficient gauge and turn the pinion several times in the opposite direction to normal rotation and then read off the coefficient friction in the direction of rotation which should be in the order of 10 to 15 lb in.

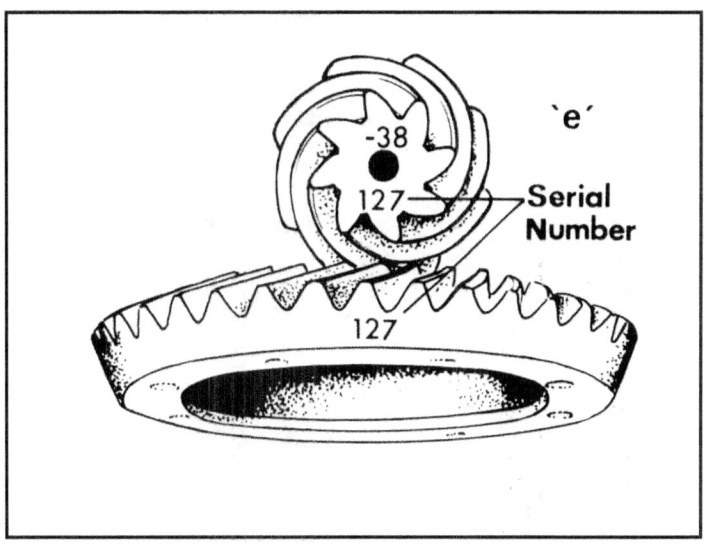

7:22 Crownwheel and pinion markings

FIG 7:23 Final drive casing measurement

FIG 7:24 Final drive casing measurement

87

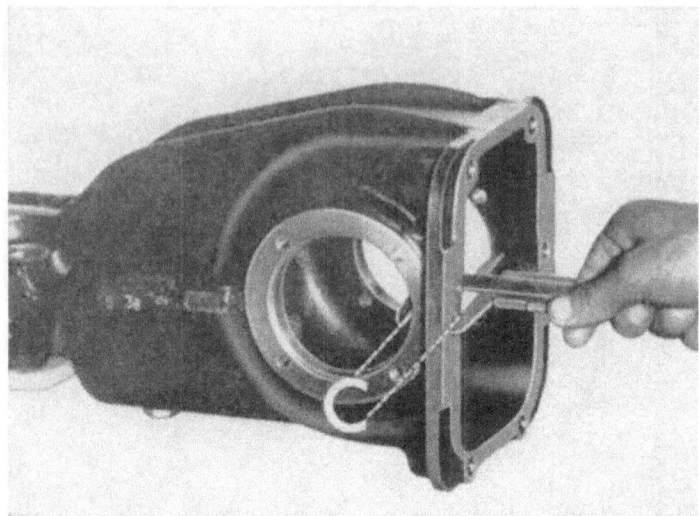

FIG 7:25 Final drive casing measurement

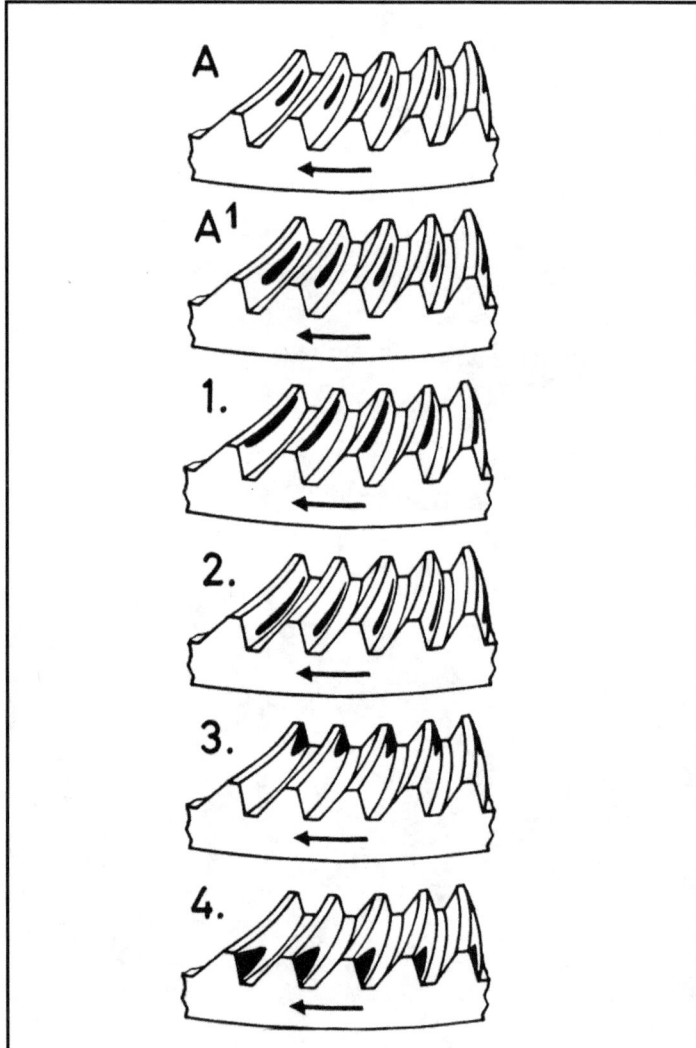

FIG 7:26 Crownwheel & pinion tooth mesh comparison

8 Fit the front bearing cap together with the slide spacer ring and three point coupling flange onto the pinion wheel teeth. Tighten the nut to a torque wrench setting of 108.5 lb ft.

9 Fit the crownwheel and measure the tooth backlash which should be between .07 and .12 mm (.0028 and .0047 inch). Referring to **FIG 7:26**, adjust the crownwheel position by altering around the shims from one bearing cap to another so that a correct tooth pattern as shown is obtained. To obtain this pattern use a small amount of engineers blue on the teeth and by adjustment obtain the pattern as shown in **FIG 7:26A**, for no load conditions, **A1** for the gears under load. Should difficulty be experienced in obtaining the correct tooth pattern the following notes should be of assistance.

(a) Refer to **FIG 7:26/1**. High narrow contact marking (tip contact) on crownwheel.

Correction:

Displace the pinion towards the crownwheel axis end, if necessary, correct backlash by moving the crownwheel away from the pinion.

(b) Refer to **FIG 7:26/2**. Deeper, narrow contact marking (root contact) on crownwheel.

Correction:

Move the pinion away from the crownwheel axis and, if necessary, correct backlash by pushing the crownwheel towards the pinion.

(c) Refer to **FIG 7:26/3**. Short contact marking on smallest tooth end (toe contact) of the crownwheel.

Correction:

Move the crownwheel away from the pinion and, if necessary move the pinion closer toward the crownwheel axis.

(d) Refer to **FIG 7:26/4**. Short contact marking on large tooth end (heel contact) of the crownwheel.

Correction:

Move the crownwheel towards the pinion and, if necessary, move the pinion away from the crownwheel axis.

7:13 Fault diagnosis

(a) **Noisy final drive**
1 Insufficient or incorrect lubricant
2 Worn bearings
3 Worn gears

(b) **Excessive backlash**
1 Worn gears, bearings or bearing housings
2 Worn halfshaft splines
3 Worn universal joints
4 Loose or broken wheel studs

(c) **Oil leakage**
1 Defective seals in hub
2 Defective pinion shaft seal
3 Defective seals on universal joint spiders

(d) **Vibration**
1 Propeller shaft or halfshafts out of balance
2 Worn universal joint bearings

(e) **Rattles**
1 Rubber bushes in damper links worn through
2 Dampers loose

(f) **'Settling'**
1 Weak or broken spring

7 : 14 Technical data

Number of teeth crownwheel/pinion:
- 2002, 2002A, 2002TI, 2002Tii .. 40:11
- 2000, 2000A, 2000CA .. 37:9
- 2000TI, 2000 Ti Lux .. 39:10

Ratios:
- 2002, 2002A, 2002TI, 2000Tii .. 3.64:1
- 2000, 2000A, 2000CA .. 4.11:1
- 2000TI, 2000 TI Lux .. 3.9:1

Backlash .. .0028 to .0047
Friction coefficient of input pinion bearing .. .87 to 1.23 lb ft
Total friction coefficient at 3-arm flange .. 1.23 to 1.74 lb ft
Crownwheel heating temperature for reassembly .. 75°C
Axial play between driving flange and axle case .. .0039 to .0059
Rear wheel bearing play .. .0020 to .0039
Toe-in .. .059 ± .059 (normally loaded)

Camber angle:
- 2002 .. 2° ± 30' negative
- All other models .. 2° negative

Coil spring free length:
- 2002 .. 12.93
- All other models .. 13.57

Coil spring rating:
- 2002:
  - Red .. 710 to 728
  - White .. 730 to 769
  - Green .. 772 to 789
- All other models:
  - Red .. 875 to 903
  - White .. 906 to 937
  - Green .. 939 to 968

Wire diameter:
- 2002 .. .484
- All other models .. .504

External coil diameter:
- 2002 .. 5.01
- All other models .. 5.03

Length of rubber auxiliary spring .. 3.15

Anti-roll bar diameter:
- 2002 .. .63
- All other models .. .67

Shock absorber:
- Makes .. Boge, Fichtel and Sachs, Koni or Bilstein
- 2002:
  - Type .. Boge 1
  - Colour code .. Finish, black
  - Maximum length .. 20.63 ± .098
  - Minimum length .. 13.15 ± .098
- 2000A, 2000TI, 2000 TI Lux:
  - Type .. Boge 1
  - Colour code .. Finish, grey
  - Maximum length .. 21.65 ± .098
  - Minimum length .. 13.82 ± .098
- 2000CS, 2000CA:
  - Type .. Boge 1
  - Colour code .. Finish, black or red/brown
  - Maximum length .. 21.65 ± .098
  - Minimum length .. 13.82 ± .098

NOTES

CHAPTER 8

FRONT SUSPENSION & HUBS

8 : 1 Description
8 : 2 Front axle carrier removing & refitting
8 : 3 Front axle carrier traction strut bearing
8 : 4 Wheel hub & bearing overhaul
8 : 5 Tie rod lever removing & refitting
8 : 6 Guide joint overhaul
8 : 7 Transverse swinging arm bearing
8 : 8 Anti roll bar removing & refitting
8 : 9 Shock absorber removing & refitting
8 : 10 Shock absorber support bearing overhaul
8 : 11 Shock absorber coil spring removing & refitting
8 : 12 Shock absorber removing & refitting
8 : 13 Fault diagnosis
8 : 14 Technical data

8 : 1 Description

The front suspension system is shown in **FIG 8:1** and comprises independent MacPherson type struts with integral dampers and co-axial coil springs fitted into a transverse lower wishbone. An anti-roll bar is attached to each suspension unit, which, together with the independent front suspension, gives the car its very good road handling qualities.

8 : 2 Front axle carrier removing & refitting

1 Remove the wheel trim and slacken the wheel nuts. Jack up the front of the car until the wheels are clear of the ground and support on firmly based stands. Remove the road wheels.
2 Refer to **FIG 8:1** for part identification and loosen the self-locking nuts from the guide joint 25. Release the steering gear 27 from the front axle carrier by removing the three retaining bolts 10, 11 and 12 as shown in **FIG 9:3**. Remove the bearing bracket for the steering guide lever by releasing three retaining bolts 1, 2 and 3 holding it to the front axle carrier as shown in **FIG 9:17**. It is recommended that the steering gear and also the steering guide lever bearing bracket be securely tied to a suitable component such as the gearbox.
3 Remove the front lefthand and righthand lower engine mounting retaining nuts and using a garage crane or overhead hoist, lift the engine upwards.
4 Using a garage hydraulic jack support the weight of the front axle carrier and release the fastening screws shown by arrows in **FIG 8:2** and carefully lower the front axle carrier and move the carrier forwards away from the underside of the vehicle.
5 Thoroughly clean down the axle carrier and then clamp firmly into a bench vice. Remove the cotterpins from the castellated nuts at the traction strut bearing of the front axle carrier and remove the castellated nuts. Also remove the cotterpins from the castellated nuts on the transverse swinging arm bearings at the front axle carrier and remove the transverse swinging arm bearing bolts at the front axle carrier. Gently ease out the traction struts from the rubber bearings. Take special note of the location of the spacer rings.
6 Remove the anti-roll bar by removing the locknut at the rubber bearings of the transverse swinging arms and release the fastening clips.

Reassembly:

Reassembly is the reverse procedure to dismantling but the following points should be noted:
1 When the anti-roll bar is being fitted the cranked centre section must face downwards.
2 When reassembling the transverse swinging arm bearings located at the front axle carrier the spacer rings that were previously removed must face the front axle carrier.
3 Tighten the castellated nuts located at the traction strut bearing of the front axle carrier to a torque wrench setting of 43.4 lb ft. This operation must be carried out with the vehicle under normal operating load, the specification of this being given in **Chapter 9, Section 9 : 7** Fit new cotterpins.
4 Tighten the front axle carrier retaining bolts to a torque wrench setting of 34 lb ft.
5 Tighten the steering gear mounting bolts to a torque wrench setting of 34 lb ft.
6 Tighten the self-locking stop nuts from the guide joint to a torque wrench setting of 18 lb ft.

8 : 3 Front axle carrier traction strut bearing

Removal:
1 Remove the self-locking stop nuts from the guide joints 25, (see **FIG 8:1**). Remove the cotterpins from the castellated nuts at the traction strut bearing of the front axle carrier and remove the castellated nuts. Carefully pull out traction struts from the rubber bearings and remove the anti-roll bar fitting as described in **Section 8:8**.
2 Refer to **FIG 8:3** and using BMW tool 6011 fit the threaded bolt 1 into the reception bore of the rubber bearings. Fit the sleeve 4 and washer 3 onto the threaded bolt and tighten the nut 2. Press the sleeve 5 over the rubber bearing against the front axle carrier and finally fit the discs 6 and 7 and nut 8. Tighten the nut and so pull out the rubber bearing.

Reassembly:
1 Coat the new rubber bearing with glycerine and press the rubber bearing 11 (see **FIG 8:4**) into the slip bush 7. Fit the threaded bolt 1 through the rubber bearing 11 into its location in the front axle carrier. Fit the thrust piece 8, the relief part of which should face the rubber bearing, and slide on the washer 9 and threaded bolt. Fit the nut 10 and place the bush 6 with the milled part at the rear top as shown in **FIG 8:4**, against the front axle carrier. Slide the bush 5 onto the threaded bolt and place the disc 4 with the milled part at the top against the bush 5. Finally place the washer 3 on the threaded bolt and fit the nut 2. Turn the nut 10 until the new bearing is correctly located.
2 Slacken the socket head screws of the slip bush 7 and remove the BMW tool 6011.
3 Refitting of the traction strut is the reverse procedure to dismantling as also is the fitting of the anti-roll bar. The car must be loaded to the specification as given in **Chapter 9, Section 9:7**.

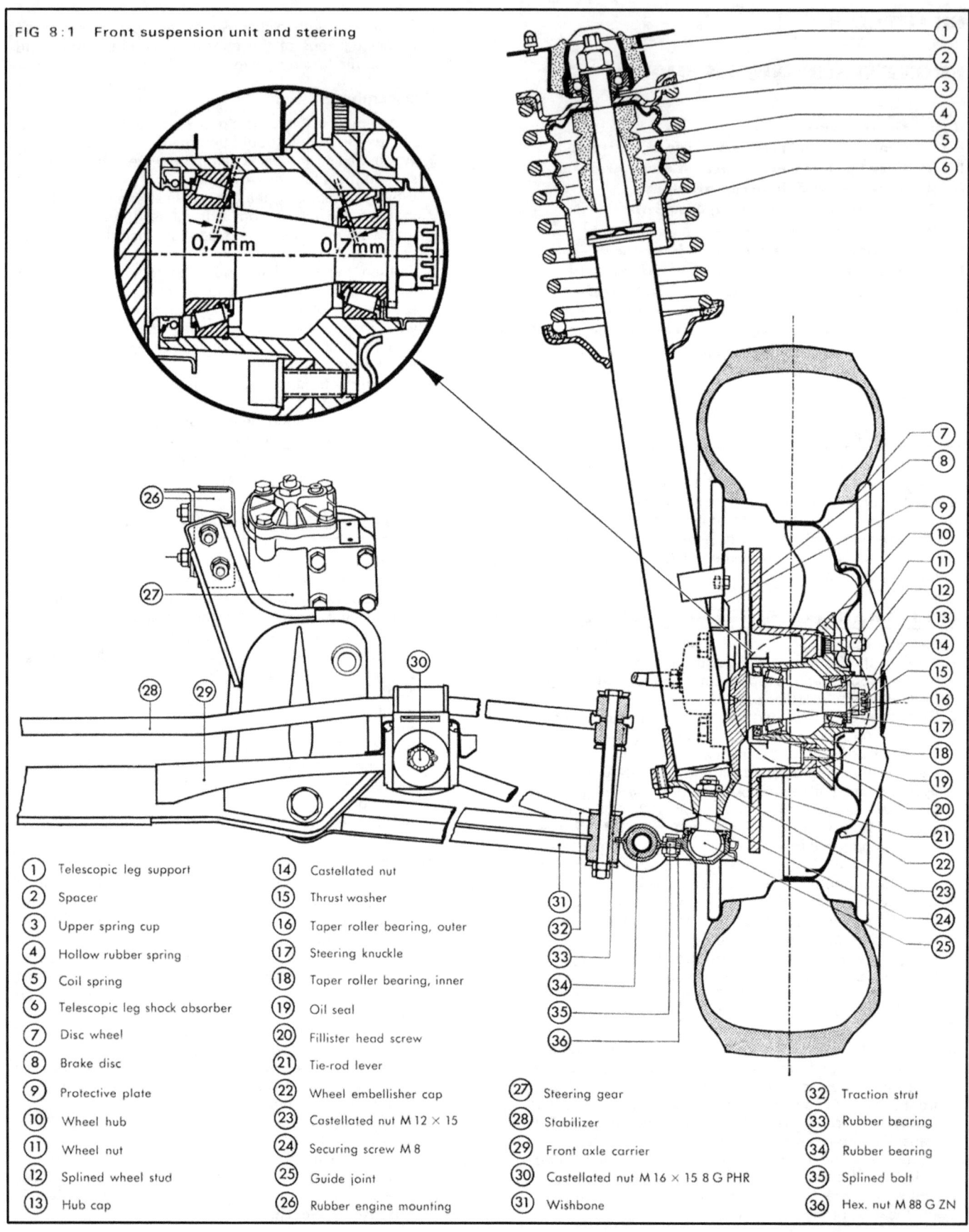

FIG 8:1 Front suspension unit and steering

1. Telescopic leg support
2. Spacer
3. Upper spring cup
4. Hollow rubber spring
5. Coil spring
6. Telescopic leg shock absorber
7. Disc wheel
8. Brake disc
9. Protective plate
10. Wheel hub
11. Wheel nut
12. Splined wheel stud
13. Hub cap
14. Castellated nut
15. Thrust washer
16. Taper roller bearing, outer
17. Steering knuckle
18. Taper roller bearing, inner
19. Oil seal
20. Fillister head screw
21. Tie-rod lever
22. Wheel embellisher cap
23. Castellated nut M 12 × 15
24. Securing screw M 8
25. Guide joint
26. Rubber engine mounting
27. Steering gear
28. Stabilizer
29. Front axle carrier
30. Castellated nut M 16 × 15 8 G PHR
31. Wishbone
32. Traction strut
33. Rubber bearing
34. Rubber bearing
35. Splined bolt
36. Hex. nut M 88 G ZN

8 : 4 Wheel hub & bearing overhaul

Wheel bearing removal:

1 Remove the wheel trim and slacken the wheel nuts. Jack up the car and place on firmly based stands and remove the road wheel.
2 Remove the front brake disc caliper retaining bolts from the telescopic leg shock absorber.
3 Remove the wheel hub cap and clean away the grease from around the castellated nut. Remove the cotterpin and castellated nut from the hub.
4 Carefully lift away the disc and hub assembly and clamp the disc between soft faces in a vice. Using a universal two leg puller carefully remove the wheel hub.
5 Using a suitably sized bearing extraction tool ease out the taper roller bearings. It is important that hub bearings be replaced in pairs even if only one is defective. Thoroughly clean the wheel hub and disc assembly in preparation for inspection and reassembly.

Reassembly:

1 Fill a new oil seal with Graphite grease and carefully locate the rear taper roller bearing in the hub, followed by the oil seal and press into position using a suitably sized drift.
2 Fit the wheel hub and disc assembly to the front axle. Tighten the castellated nut to a torque wrench setting of 7.2 lb ft and turn the wheel hub a few times in the forward and reverse direction of rotation to ensure correct grease distribution.
3 Slacken the castellated nut by one third of a turn and place a screwdriver into the recess of the thrust washer 15 (see **FIG 8:1**). This thrust washer must be easily movable both in the clockwise and anticlockwise direction.
4 Screw a universal dial indicator to the wheel hub using one of the threaded holes and align the dial gauge pointer to the front axle stub. Turn the wheel hub six turns in both directions and then firmly pull and push the hub assembly in the same axis as the steering knuckle assembly and read off the wheel bearing play from the dial gauge. Adjust the wheel bearing play to give a reading of .0008 to .002 inch.

Wheel hub removal:

1 Remove the wheel as previously described and clamp the wheel hub and brake disc between soft faces in a vice.
2 Remove the brake disc to hub retaining screws and carefully separate the brake disc from the wheel hub. Should difficulty be experienced in this operation because of excessive rust, it is recommended that the wheel hub is mounted to the road wheel and placed on the floor with the disc facing upwards. Rotate the brake disc forward and backwards and at the same time pulling upwards as firmly as possible.
3 Thoroughly clean down the brake disc and using a micrometer at approximately 8 points throughout the circumference the permissible deviation in thickness must not exceed .00079 inch. Should it be necessary to reface the rubbing area of the disc, the thickness of the disc must not fall below .354 inch otherwise overheating and distortion of the disc will occur.

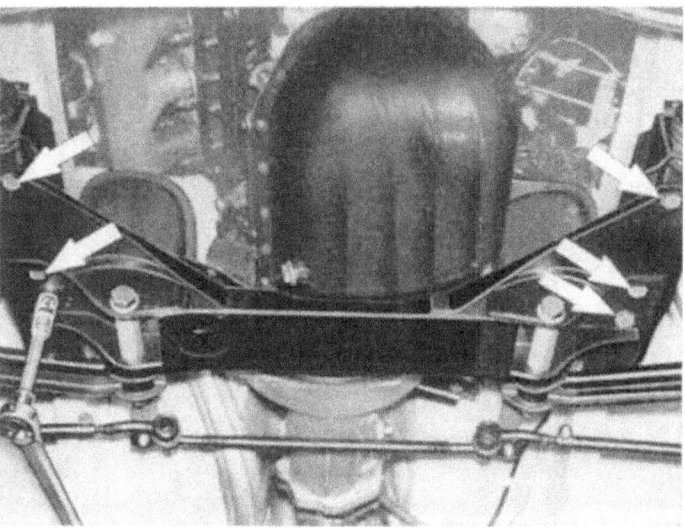

FIG 8:2 Front axle carrier

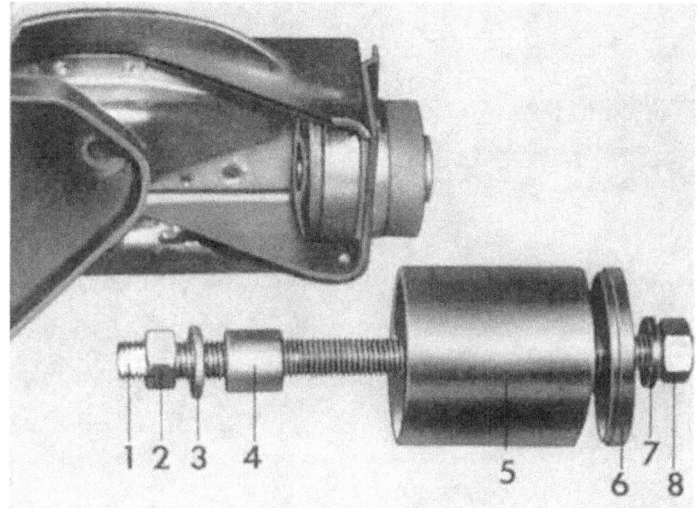

FIG 8:3 Traction strut bearing & withdrawal tool

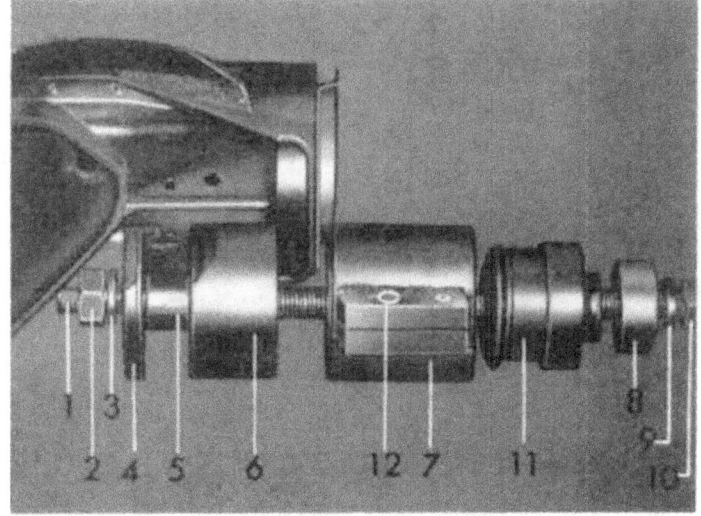

FIG 8:4 Rubber bearing & BMW tool 6011

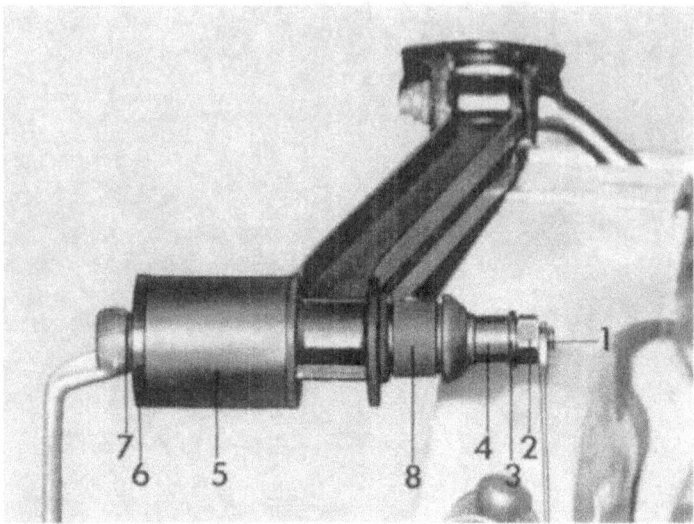

FIG 8:5 Swinging arm bearing removal & replacement

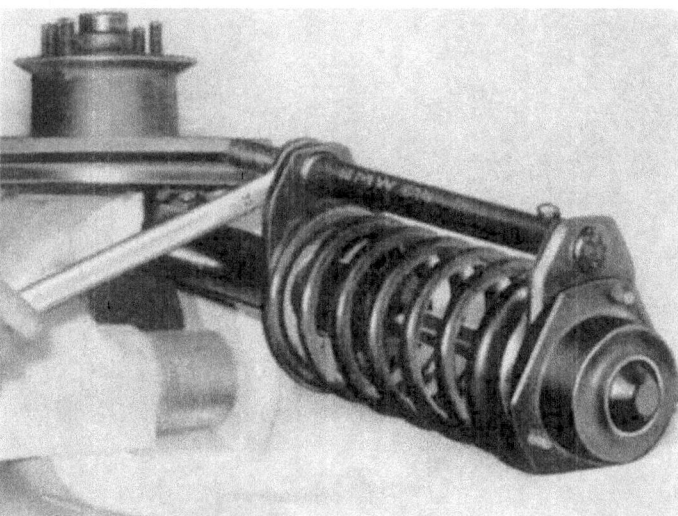

FIG 8:6 Compressing the coil spring using BMW tool 614

FIG 8:7 Shock absorber top assembly

4 If possible mount the disc in a lathe and check the lateral runout using a dial indicator gauge set. The runout must not exceed .002 inch and if this figure is exceeded a new disc must be fitted.

8 : 5 Tie rod lever removing & refitting

Removal:

Reassembly:

Reassembly is the reverse procedure to dismantling. The wheel hub to brake disc retaining screws must be tightened to a torque wrench setting of 43.4 lb ft.
1 Remove the wheel hub assembly as detailed in **Section 8:4**.
2 Remove the self-locking nuts from the guide joint.
3 Remove the securing wire locking the three retaining bolts of the tie rod lever to the steering knuckle assembly and remove the bolts. Carefully ease back the tie rod lever.
4 Remove the cotterpin from the castellated nut for the ball pivot and remove the castellated nut. Using BMW tool 6056 or a universal ball joint separator carefully press out the ball pivot.
5 Gently but firmly ease off the tie rod lever from the end of the telescopic leg shock absorber.

Reassembly:

Reassembly is the reverse procedure to dismantling but the following points should be noted:
1 The tie rod lever retaining bolts must be tightened to a torque wrench setting of 18 lb ft and finally locked using new soft iron wire.
2 The self-locking nuts for the guide joint must be tightened to a torque wrench setting of 18 lb ft.

8 : 6 Guide joint overhaul

Removal:
1 Remove the wheel hub as described in **Section 8:4**.
2 Remove the tie rod lever as described in **Section 8:5**.
3 Clamp the tie rod lever between soft faces in a vice. Remove the cotterpin from the castellated nut and remove the nut.
4 Using a suitably sized drift and a nut placed on the end of the screw thread press out the guide joint from the tie rod lever.

Reassembly:

Reassembly is the reverse procedure to dismantling but the following points should be noted:
1 The specially shaped knurled pins must be pressed into the new guide joint using a suitably sized drift.
2 The tie rod lever castellated nut must be tightened to a torque wrench setting of 50.6 lb ft and a new cotterpin fitted.
3 The wheel bearing play must be adjusted as described in **Section 8:4**.
4 If a new tie rod lever has been fitted the front wheel toe-in setting for the straight-ahead position and also the angle of toe-out on turns must be checked and adjusted as necessary. For this operation accurate steering geometry checking equipment is required and this work should be entrusted to the local service station.

8 : 7 Transverse swinging arm bearing

Removal:
1 Remove the wheel trim, slacken the wheel nuts and jack up the car and place on firmly based stands. Remove the road wheel.
2 Remove the cotterpin from the castellated nut of the strut bearing at the front axle carrier and remove the nut.
3 Remove the cotterpin from the castellated nut of the swinging arm at the front axle carrier and remove the nut.
4 Remove the self-locking nuts from the guide joints. Carefully withdraw the long bolt for centre of the swinging arm bearing from the front axle carrier. Take special note of the location of the spacer ring.
5 Withdraw the traction strut together with the transverse swinging arm towards the rear.
6 Clamp the transverse swinging arm between soft faces in a vice and using a sharp knife blade or hacksaw blade cut off as much rubber as possible from the rubber bearing at one side of the swinging arm. If the excess rubber is not removed the sleeve will be pulled together with the bearing and the swinging arm becomes unserviceable.
7 Refer to **FIG 8 : 5**, place the bush 4 of BMW tool 6011 at the side of the swinging arm at which the rubber bearing had been trimmed and fit the threaded bolt 1 together with the washer 3 and nut 2 through the rubber bearing 8. Place the bush 5 against the swinging arm and fit the disc 6 together with disc 7 onto the threaded bolt 1 and screw on the nut. Tighten the nut so pulling out the rubber bearings.

Reassembly:
Reassembly is the reverse procedure to dismantling but the following points should be noted:
1 Before refitting a new rubber bearing the outside must be coated with glycerine otherwise damage could result to the bearing.
2 Refit the special spacer ring so that it faces the front axle carrier.
3 Tighten the self-locking nuts at the drive joint to a torque wrench setting of 18 lb ft.
4 Tighten the castellated nut at the swinging arm and front axle carrier location with the vehicle loaded as specified in **Chapter 9, Section 9 : 7**. Tighten to a torque wrench setting of 108.5 lb ft.
5 Tighten the castellated nut of the strut bearing at the front axle carrier to a torque wrench setting of 43.4 lb ft, with the vehicle loaded as specified in **Chapter 9, Section 9 : 7**.

8 : 8 Anti roll bar removing & refitting

Removal:
1 Remove the locknut of the rubber bearings located at the transverse swinging arms position.
2 Carefully detach the fastening clip for the anti-roll bar located at either end of the anti-roll bar.

Reassembly:
Reassembly is the reverse procedure to dismantling. Ensure that the anti-roll bar is correctly refitted with the cranked centre section facing downwards.

8 : 9 Shock absorber removing & refitting

Removal:
1 Remove the wheel trim, slacken the wheel nuts and jack up the car and place on firmly based stands. Remove the road wheel.
2 Carefully remove the disc brake caliper and tie up the caliper away from the telescopic leg shock absorber.
3 Refer to **FIG 8 : 1** and remove the self-locking nuts from the guide joints. Remove the cotterpin from the castellated nut of the ball pivot and remove the castellated nut. Using BMW tool 6056 or a universal ball joint separator, carefully press out the ball pivot.
4 From the engine compartment slacken the three retaining nuts for the telescopic leg support.
5 Carefully withdraw the telescopic leg shock absorber from the underside of the car.

Reassembly:
Reassembly is the reverse procedure to dismantling but the following points should be noted:
1 When reassembling the telescopic leg support the three holes drilled in the body panel are specially offset so the support bearing must be rotated until correct location is obtained. Tighten the nuts to a torque wrench setting of 18 lb ft.
2 Tighten the self-locking nuts at the guide joint to a torque wrench setting of 18 lb ft.
3 Tighten the brake caliper mounting bolts to a torque wrench setting of 68.7 lb ft.

8 : 10 Shock absorber support bearing overhaul

Removal:
1 Remove the telescopic leg shock absorber as detailed in **Section 8 : 9**, items 1 to 5.
2 Clamp the telescopic leg shock absorber firmly in a vice and using the special BMW tool 614 compress the spring (see **FIG 8 : 6**). It is exceedingly dangerous to use any other means of compressing the spring otherwise should the spring slip from an improvization whilst compressed a considerable amount of damage or bodily harm can be unnecessarily caused.
3 Using a screwdriver carefully prise away the cap located at the top of the shock absorber. Remove the self-locking stop nut revealed by removal of the top cap and lift away the spring leg support bearing. This is shown in **FIG 8 : 7**.

Reassembly:
Reassembly is the reverse procedure to dismantling but the following points should be noted:
1 It is recommended that the complete spring leg support bearing be renewed if necessary and not just parts of it. Reassemble in the following order. Washer 1 (see **FIG 8 : 7**), sealing ring 2, support bearing 3, washer 4 and self-locking nut 5. Before finally tightening the self-locking nut ensure that the sealing ring 2 is correctly located in position.
2 Tighten the self-locking nut 5 to a torque wrench setting of 57.8 lb ft.

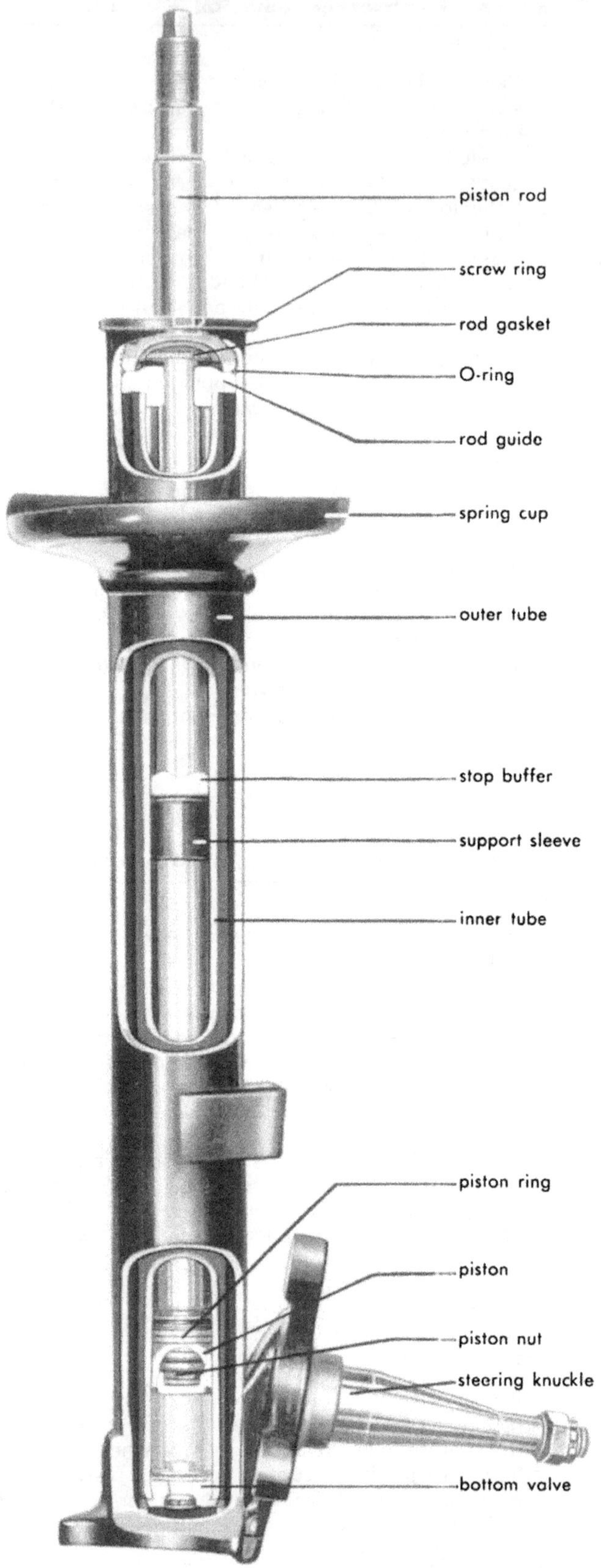

FIG 8:8 Sectional view – telescopic shock absorber

Labels (top to bottom): piston rod, screw ring, rod gasket, O-ring, rod guide, spring cup, outer tube, stop buffer, support sleeve, inner tube, piston ring, piston, piston nut, steering knuckle, bottom valve

8:11 Shock absorber coil spring

Removal:

1 Remove the telescopic leg shock absorber as detailed in **Section 8:9**, items 1 to 5.
2 Remove the support bearing as detailed in **Section 8:10**.
3 Carefully unscrew BMW tool 614 until the spring cup, rubber spring and the coil spring may be lifted out.
4 It should be noted that up to Chassis No. 917583 the spring length in the unloaded condition is 13.583 inch. The diameter of the wire being .4685 inch. From Chassis No. 917584 the spring length in the unloaded condition is 12.106 inch with a wire diameter of .4921 inch. In both specifications the spring rating is identical and as follows:

Red	640 to 660 lb	soft rating
White	662 to 682 lb	medium rating
Green	684 to 706 lb	hard rating

It is very important that identical springs be fitted to both front suspension assembly units.

Reassembly:

Reassembly is the reverse procedure to dismantling but it is important to ensure that both the spring ends are correctly located into the spring cups before compressing the spring.

8:12 Shock absorber removing & refitting

The telescopic leg shock assembly combined with the steering knuckle is shown in **FIG 8:8**.

Removal:

1 Remove the telescopic leg shock absorber assembly as detailed in **Section 8:9**, items 1 to 5.
2 Remove the support bearing as detailed in **Section 8:10**.
3 Carefully unscrew the BMW tool 614 until the coil spring and rubber spring may be lifted out.
4 Remove the hub grease cap and release the cotterpin from the castellated nut. Remove the nut. Carefully pull off the hub and thrust washer.
5 Release the tie rod lever retaining bolts securing wire and remove the bolts. Carefully separate the tie rod lever and guide joints from the telescopic leg, the assembly being shown in **FIG 8:9**. Loosen the brake backplate from the telescopic leg shock absorber by removing the retaining bolts.
6 It should be noted that it is important for the correct length telescopic leg shock absorber and matching coil spring to be fitted. Refer to Technical Data for the specification applicable to each model covered by this manual.

Reassembly:

Reassembly is the reverse procedure to dismantling but the following points should be noted:
1 Tighten the tie rod lever retaining bolts to a torque wrench setting of 18 lb ft and lock using a new soft iron wire.
2 When reassembling the hub assembly adjust the wheel bearing play as detailed in **Section 8:4**.
3 Ensure that the coil spring ends seat correctly into the spring cups before compressing the spring using BMW tool 614.

8 : 13 Fault diagnosis

(a) Wheel wobble
1 Worn hub bearings
2 Broken or weak front coil springs
3 Uneven tyre wear
4 Worn suspension strut
5 Loose wheel fixings

(b) 'Bottoming' of suspension
1 Check 2 in (a)
2 Telescopic leg shock absorber weak

(c) Heavy steering
1 Neglected swivel pin lubrication
2 Wrong suspension geometry

(d) Excessive tyre wear
1 Check 4 in (a); 2 in (b) and 2 in (c)

(e) Rattles
1 Check 2 in (a)
2 Pivot lubrication neglected, rubber bushes worn
3 Damper mountings loose or worn
4 Radius arm mountings loose, or worn
5 Anti-roll bar mountings loose, bearings worn

(f) Excessive 'rolling'
1 Check 2 in (a) and 2 in (b)
2 Anti-roll bar broken, mountings loose, bearings worn

FIG 8:9 Tie rod as fitted to telescopic shock absorber

8 : 14 Technical data

Toe-in, normal load :	
2000	Zero to .08
2002	.039 to .098
Toe-out, on 20 deg. turn	1° ± 30'
Camber angle :	
2000	0° 15' ± 30'
2002	0° 30' ± 30'
Kingpin inclination	8° 30'
Castor angle :	
2000	3° ± 30'
2002	4° ± 30'
Wheel bearing play	.00079 to .00236
Coil spring free length :	
2002	12.78
2000, 2000A	13.58
All other models	11.35
Wire diameter :	
2002	.465
2000, 2000A	.472
All other models	.516
External coil diameter :	
2002	4.99 ± .059
2000, 2000A	5.0
All other models	5.95 ± .051
Coil spring rating :	
2002 :	
Red	564 to 584
White	584 to 606
Green	606 to 626
All other models :	
Red	679 to 701
White	703 to 725
Green	727 to 750

Length of auxiliary spring	3.347
Diameter of anti-roll bar	.59 or .67
Shock absorber:	
Oil grade	Boge, Shell 4001, Fichtel and Sachs, Gasoline 1010
Capacity:	
2000	285 ± 3 cc
2002	395 ± 3 cc
Type	Boge 1 or Fichtel and Sachs
Colour code:	
2002	One white dot
2000, 2000A, 2000TI, 2000 TI Lux	One grey band
2000CS, 2000CA	Black finish
Stroke:	
2000	6.46
2002	6.85
Fitted length:	
2000	17.20
2002	18.27 ± .059 (later models, 21.89 ± .2)

CHAPTER 9

STEERING

9 : 1 Description
9 : 2 Steering box removing & refitting
9 : 3 Steering box overhaul
9 : 4 Steering mechanism adjustment
9 : 5 Steering spindle bearing replacement
9 : 6 Steering guide lever removing & refitting
9 : 7 Checking & adjusting tracking
9 : 8 Lubrication
9 : 9 Fault diagnosis
9 : 10 Technical data

9 : 1 Description

The ZF-Gemmer worm and roller steering gear with an overall gear ratio of 17.58:1 is fitted into a three-piece track rod system. A small splined universal joint is fitted between the spindle and the steering worm to accommodate for any adjustment necessary.

If, during maintenance, the front wheels are lifted clear of the ground do not move them forcefully from lock to lock otherwise serious damage to the steering system may result.

9 : 2 Steering box removing & refitting

1 Slacken the air filter attachment screw at the wheel arch inner panel and remove the air filter. Mark the position of the upper joint flange at the steering spindle using a scriber to ensure correct adjustment upon reassembly.
2 Refer to **FIG 9:1** and slacken the retaining screws 1 and 2 for the joint flanges. Loosen the self-locking nuts from the universal joint disc. Release the steering spindle earthing strap 3 and carefully slide the upper joint flange 4 upwards to the stop on the steering spindle 5. Finally remove the joint disc.
3 Jack up the front of the car until the road wheels are free to rotate and support on firmly based stands. Remove the cotterpin from the castellated nut located at the middle of the tie rod at the pitman arm. Refer to **FIG 9:2** and using a universal ball joint remover or BMW tool No. 6056 remove the middle tie rod from the pitman arm.
4 Slacken the fastening screws 10 and 12 (See **FIG 9:3**) for the steering gear front the front axle carrier. Carefully lift outwards the steering gear from the guide sleeves and take off from the underside of the car.

Reassembly:

Reassembly is the reverse procedure to dismantling but the following points should be noted:
1 When tightening the steering gear retaining screws as shown in **FIG 9:3**, tighten the screws to a torque wrench setting of 34 lb ft.
2 Tighten the castellated nut at the pitman arm and middle tie rod to a torque wrench setting of 25.3 lb ft and fit a new cotterpin.
3 When assembling the universal joint disc, ensure that the front wheels and steering wheel are in the straight-ahead position.
4 Tighten the universal joint disc self-locking nuts to a torque wrench setting of 10.8 lb ft.
5 Tighten the universal joint flange fastening screws 1 and 2 as shown in **FIG 9:1** to a torque wrench setting of 18 lb ft.
6 Upon reassembling the steering spindle bearing it should be fitted with an initial load of .079 to .098 inch. Ensure a firm pressure is placed onto the steering wheel in order to achieve this correct fitting position.

9 : 3 Steering box overhaul

1 Remove the steering gearbox as detailed in **Section 9:2**.
2 Carefully pull off the joint flange, lift out the oil drain plug and allow the oil to drain into a suitably sized container.
3 Clamp the steering gearbox into a vice and open the drop arm retaining nut locking plate. Remove the fastening nut from the pitman arm and using a universal puller remove the pitman arm.
4 Refer to **FIG 9:4** and remove the retaining screws 1 to 4 of the cover. Carefully lift away the case cover 5 and the steering shaft 6.
5 Slacken the adjustment locknut shown at the top of the cover in **FIG 9:4** and unscrew the adjusting screw from the housing cover.
6 Unscrew the fastening bolts 1 to 4 of the cover (see **FIG 9:5**), and it should be noted that the fastening screw 4 is of the socket head type for which an Allen key is required.
7 Refer to **FIG 9:6** and remove the cover 10, shim washers 11, ballrace 12, ballcage 13, worm 14 and the ballcage 15 from the steering gear case 16.

Adjustment and reassembly:

1 Refer to **FIG 9:7** and fit the worm assembly to the steering gear case with one shim 'X' to be located as shown. Whilst turning the worm continuously, slowly tighten the fastening screws using a torque wrench set to read between 13.0 to 14.5 lb ft.
2 Using a special friction coefficient gauge as shown in **FIG 9:8** determine the friction coefficient which should be between .072 and .181 lb ft. Should the friction coefficient be too low, reduce the thickness of the shim washers, or, conversely should the friction coefficient be too high the shim washer thickness should be increased.
3 Reassemble the cover to the steering gear case with the machined edge 'A' of the cover towards the bottom side as shown in **FIG 9:5**.
4 The head of the adjustment screw 5 (see **FIG 9:9**), is held into the steering roller shaft by a snapring. Maximum permissible play between the adjustment screw 5 and the steering roller shaft is .0021 inch and may be adjusted accordingly by guide washers. These are available in various thicknesses and may be ordered under spare part Nos. 2670144 and 2670149.
5 Reassemble the locknut and adjustment screw to the housing cover and assemble the steering shaft and case cover to the steering case ensuring that the mark 'A' (see **FIG 9:10**) scribed on the steering shaft 'W' is pointing towards the middle of the housing seam. Also ensure that the marking 'B' (see **FIG 9:11**) coincides with the mark 'C' on the steering gear face.

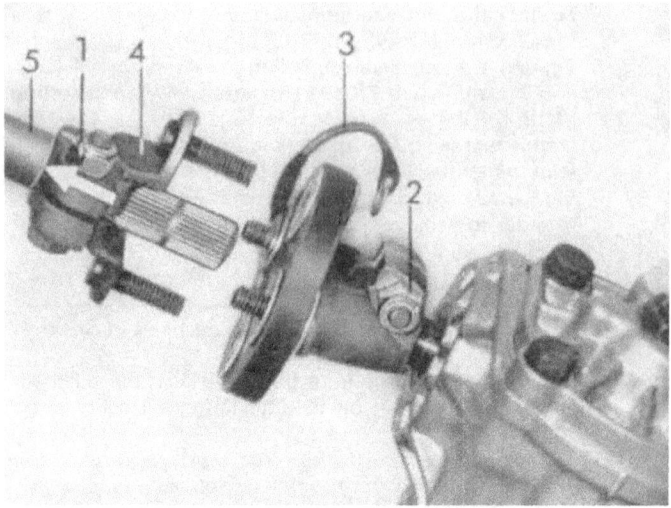

FIG 9:1 Steering shaft universal joint

FIG 9:4 Steering case cover removal

FIG 9:2 Separation of middle tie rod from pitman arm

FIG 9:5 Steering case side cover

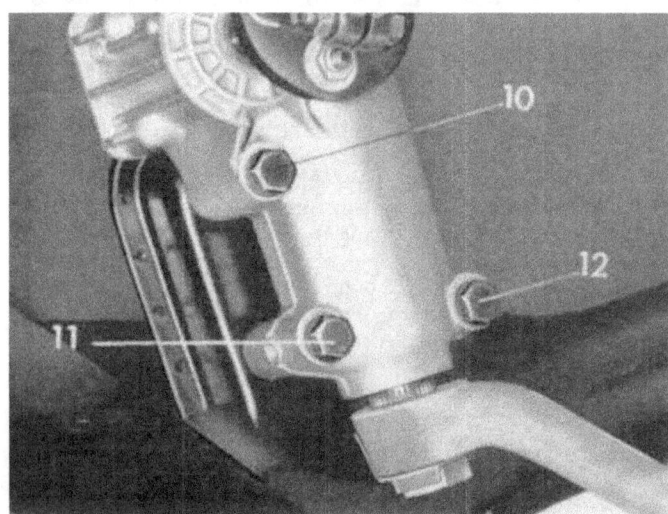

FIG 9:3 Steering gearbox mounting

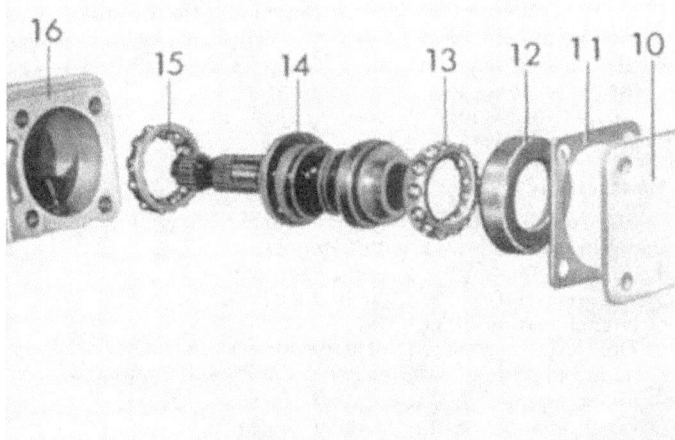

FIG 9:6 Steering worm assembly

6 Reassemble the pitman arm to the steering shaft ensuring that the mark on the steering shaft end is in line with the arrow on the pitman arm. Fit a new locking plate and tighten the nut and bend over the three locking plate tabs.
7 Fill the steering gearbox with .5 Imp pint of hypoid gear oil SAE.90. Refit the oil plug, the joint flange and reassemble to the car as detailed in **Section 9:2**.

9 : 4 Steering mechanism adjustment

1 Turn the steering wheel so that the front wheels are in the straight-ahead position taking care not to put excessive strain on the steering gear.
2 Refer to **FIG 9:11** and finally align the worm shaft marking with the marking on the steering gear case.
3 Jack up the front of the car until the road wheels are clear of the ground and support on firmly based stands. Remove the cotterpin from the castellated nut located at the middle of the tie rod at the pitman arm and remove the middle tie rod using a universal ball joint separator or BMW tool No. 6056.
4 Remove the steering wheel cover cap and turn the steering wheel approximately one turn to the left.
5 Using a friction coefficient gauge on the fastening nut of the wheel as shown in **FIG 9:12**, adjust the friction coefficient to between .72 and 1.16 lb ft.
Refer to **FIG 9:13** and slacken the locknut 1 and carefully turn the adjustment screw using a screwdriver until constant repetition of the friction coefficient test gives the required reading previously given.
6 When the test is complete, tighten the locknut 1 and reassemble in the reverse procedure to dismantling, tightening the castellated nut using a torque wrench setting of 25.3 lb ft.

9 : 5 Steering spindle bearing replacement

1 Disconnect the earth terminal from the battery and referring to **FIG 9:14** loosen the fastening screw 1 of the joint flange.
2 Lift off the steering wheel cover cap 2 (see **FIG 9:15**), remove the steering wheel retaining nut 3, washer 4 and carefully remove the steering wheel from the steering spindle.
3 Pull off the return cam and remove the under-covering fastening screws 1 to 5 as shown in **FIG 5:9** and carefully lift away the covering. Remove the fastening screws 6 to 11 for covering the centre panel M. Carefully pull the connectors from behind the heater fan switch and ease the covering downwards and turning towards the left as shown by the arrow.
4 Remove the fastening screws for the slip ring holder and carefully pull out the plug connection from the slip ring. Remove the underside switch covering. Carefully disconnect the plug connection from the starter control and loosen the fastening nuts for the top covering. Remove the top covering by lifting upwards.
5 Remove the fastening screws for the light and flasher switch and lift away. Carefully disconnect the plug connections from the steering/ignition lock. Make a careful note of their location
6 Remove the fastening screws for the steering column clamp bracket and remove the bracket together with its spacer. Remove the fastening screw for the clip at the base of the outer steering column and carefully ease upwards the steering tube together with the steering shaft away from the bearing bracket.

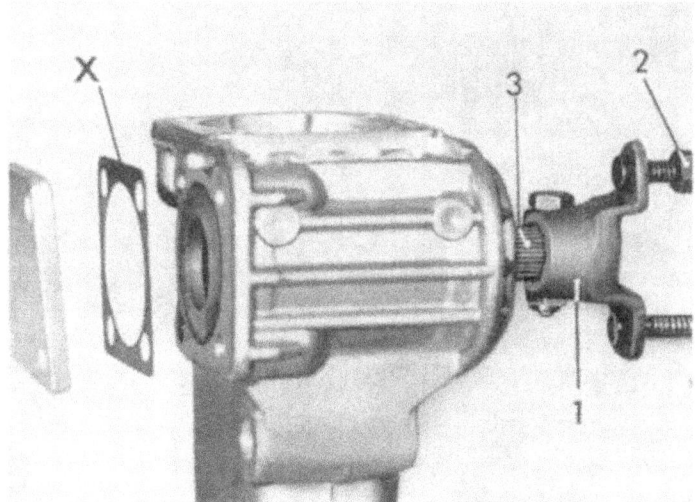

FIG 9:7 Steering case end cover shim

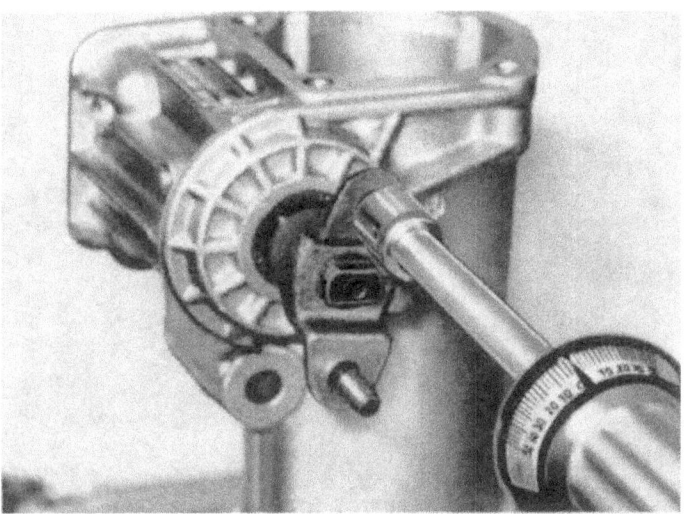

FIG 9:8 Checking friction coefficient of steering worm

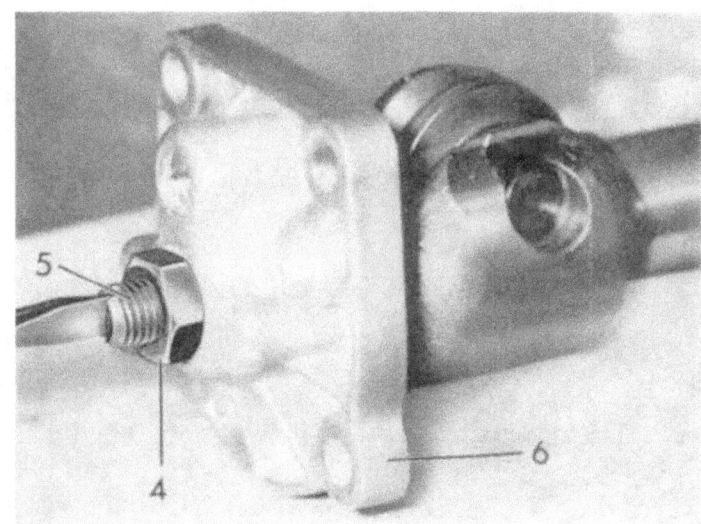

FIG 9:9 Steering case adjustment screw

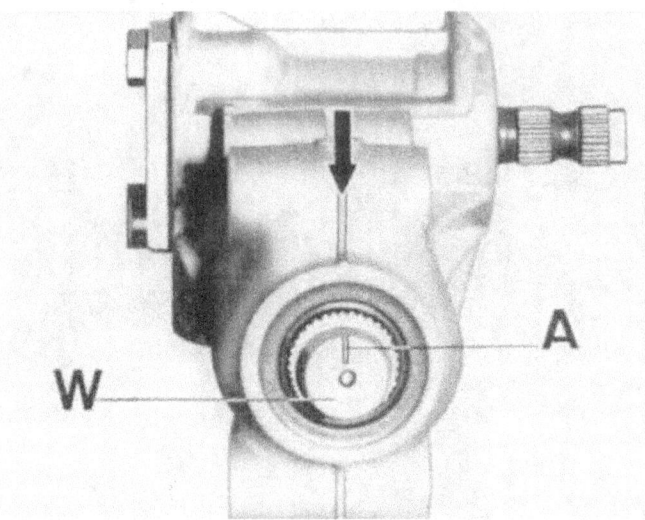

FIG 9:10 Steering shaft-to-steering case alignment

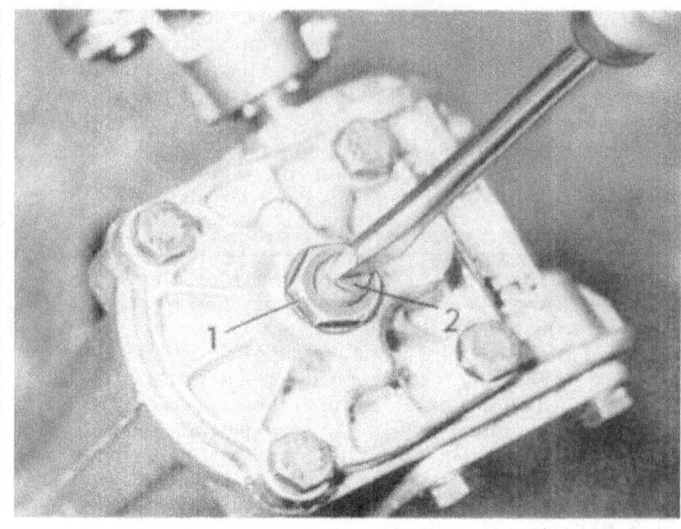

FIG 9:13 Steering shaft friction coefficient adjustment

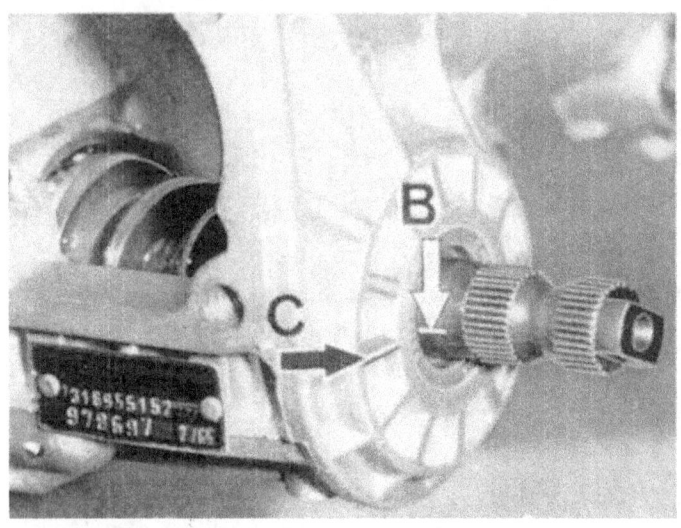

FIG 9:11 Steering gear-to-steering case alignment

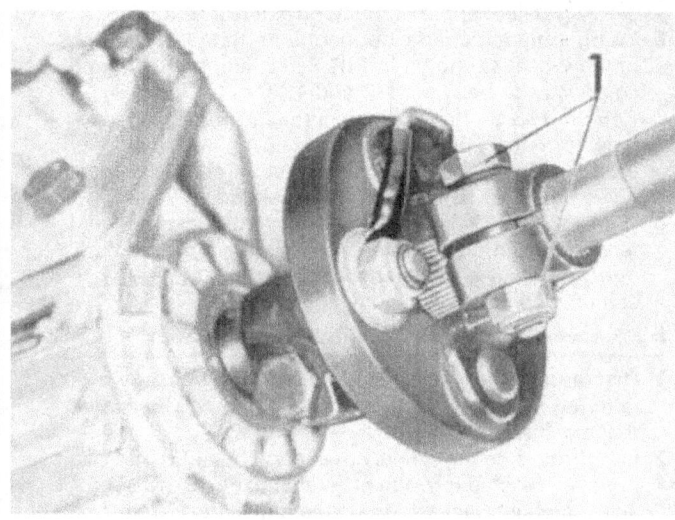

FIG 9:14 Steering shaft universal joint earth wire location

FIG 9:12 Friction gauge attached to steering shaft

FIG 9:15 Steering wheel cover cap

7 Refer to **FIG 9:16** and carefully pull off the collar 32. Using pointed nose pliers lift out the snap ring together with the washer, coil spring and seating ring. Using a screwdriver gently ease out the steering shaft bearing from the outer tube.

Reassembly:

Reassembly is the reverse procedure to dismantling but the following points should be noted:
1 Drive the steering shaft bearing into the tube using a suitably sized drift until it is a snug fit.
2 When reassembling the collar assembly the ring must have its shank inserted into the steering spindle bearing. Repack the recess in the collar with grease and reassemble to steering spindle.
3 Plug connections for steering/ignition lock.

Plug connection	Cable colour coding
30	red
50	black
15	green
R	yellow
P	grey

4 The steering wheel retaining nut should be tightened to a torque wrench setting of 28.9 lb ft.

9 : 6 Steering guide lever removing & refitting

1 Remove the cotterpin from the castellated nut at the middle tie rod and remove the castellated nut.
2 Remove the tie rod from the steering guide rod lever using a universal ball joint separator or BMW tool No. 6056.
3 Refer to **FIG 9:17** and remove the fastening screws 1 to 3 for the bearing bracket from the front axle carrier.

Reassembly:

Reassembly is the reverse procedure to dismantling but the following points should be noted:
1 The fastening screws 1 to 3 (see **FIG 9:17** must be tightened to a torque wrench setting of 18.1 lb ft.
2 Tighten the castellated nut of the middle tie rod to a torque wrench setting of 25.3 lb ft.

Bearing bracket dismantling and reassembly:

1 Carefully clamp the bearing bracket at both fastening plates into a vice and loosen the fastening screws for the cover 4 as shown in **FIG 9:18**. Remove the cover 4 and gasket 5.
2 Lift out the snap ring 6 using a pair of circlip pliers and also remove the washer 7. Carefully pull out the steering guide lever 8.
3 Reassembly is the reverse procedure to dismantling and the steering guide lever is adjusted by slackening the locknut located at the top of the cover and rotating the adjusting screw until it is free from vertical play. Lock the adjusting screw into the desired position.

9 : 7 Checking & adjusting tracking

The most accurate method of checking the front and rear wheel alignment is by special optical measuring equipment. This system is used by BMW service garages and, if these garages are locally situated, the owner should make every effort to have the wheel alignment checked and adjusted at one of these specialized establishments. If this is not possible, due to the locality or time, a temporary adjustment can be made.

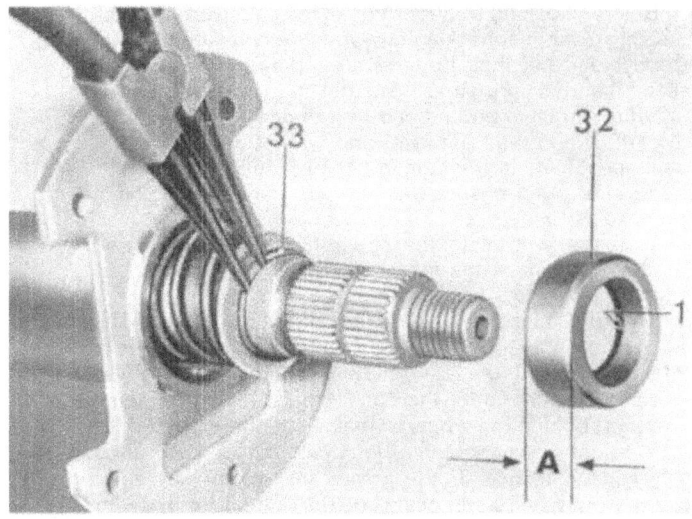

FIG 9:16 Steering spindle bearing assembly

FIG 9:17 Steering guide lever mounting

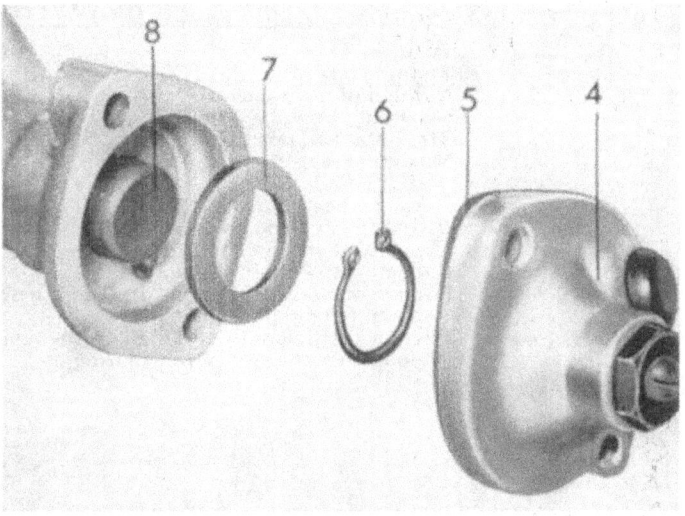

FIG 9:18 Bearing bracket end cover assembly

Before checking the front wheel toe-in ensure that the steering connections, kingpins and wheel bearings are in good order and that the tyres are inflated to the correct recommended pressures. Ensure that the vehicle is standing on level ground and that the car is loaded with 2 x 140 lbs on the front seats and 1 x 140 lbs on the rear seat and 65 lbs in the luggage compartment on the left-hand side. Also ensure that the fuel tank is full. Then proceed as follows:

1 Turn the wheels to the straight-ahead position and chalk a mark at the inner leading point of the wheel rims, i.e. wheel hub height.
2 Measure horizontally the exact distance between the two marks.
3 Carefully pull the car forward without moving the steering wheel until the chalk marks are at the same height behind the wheel as they were at the front.
4 Measure and compare the chalk marks with their original distance. If the marks are now wider apart the front wheels are toeing-in. The correct setting with the car loaded is a toe-in of 1 mm with a permitted tolerance of 1 mm either side (.04 inch ± .04).
5 If alignment is incorrect loosen the clamps of the rod sleeve adjusters and turn in or out both sleeves an equal amount so as to vary the rod length of the two outside track rods. Tighten the sleeve clamps ensuring a gap is left at the clamp ends and that the gaps in the sleeve adjuster and in the clamps are on the same side and flush.

9 : 8 Lubrication

No grease nipples are provided as the steering linkages are sealed for life. The steering gear has a capacity of .5 Imp pint and is filled with hypoid SAE.90 gear oil at a plug location in the gear casing. It is recommended that the oil be checked every 10,000 miles and topped up as necessary.

9 : 9 Fault diagnosis

(a) Wheel wobble

1 Unbalanced wheels and tyres
2 Slack steering connections
3 Incorrect steering geometry
4 Excessive play in steering gear
5 Broken or weak front springs
6 Worn hub bearings

(b) Wander

1 Check 2, 3 and 4 in (a)
2 Front suspension and rear axle mounting points out of line
3 Uneven tyre wear
4 Uneven tyre pressures
5 Weak dampers or springs

(c) Heavy steering

1 Check 3 in (a)
2 Very low tyre pressures
3 Neglected lubrication
4 Wheels out of track
5 Steering gear maladjusted
6 Steering column bent or misaligned
7 Steering column bushes tight

(d) Lost motion

1 End play in steering column
2 Loose steering wheel, worn splines
3 Worn steering box idler
4 Worn ball joints
5 Worn suspension system and swivel axle

9 : 10 Technical data

Type	ZF, Gemmer worm and roller
Steering box ratio	15.5:1
Number of turns lock to lock	3.5
Maximum free play at wheel rim	.79
Straightahead position	Mark on worm and steering box
Maximum lock:	
Inner wheel	42 deg.
Outer wheel	34 deg.
Oil grade (steering box and idler arm bearing)	SAE.90 hypoid gear oil
Capacity of steering box	300 cc approximately
Capacity of idler arm bearing	25 cc approximately
Friction coefficient (preload) of steering box in straightahead position	.72 to 1.15 lb ft
Friction coefficient (preload) of worm bearing	.07 to .18 lb ft
Preload on steering column bearing	.079 to .098 lb ft

CHAPTER 10

BRAKES (WHEELS & TYRES)

10 : 1   Description
10 : 2   General & preventative maintenance
10 : 3   Brake pads removing & refitting
10 : 4   Brake calipers removing & refitting
10 : 5   Disc brake overhaul
10 : 6   Drum brake overhaul
10 : 7   Bleeding the hydraulic system
10 : 8   Master cylinder overhaul
10 : 9   Wheel cylinder overhaul
10 : 10 Flexible hose removal
10 : 11 Handbrake cable removing & refitting
10 : 12 Servo unit overhaul
10 : 13 Fault diagnosis
10 : 14 Technical data (including wheels & tyres)

10 : 1 Description

Disc brakes are fitted to the front wheels and drum brakes to the rear. All four are hydraulically operated by the brake pedal and the handbrake lever operates the rear brakes only, through a mechanical linkage which normally requires no separate adjustment.

The front brakes on all the BMW models covered by this manual are of the rotating disc and rigidly mounted caliper type, each caliper comprising two friction assemblies between which the disc rotates. Early cars have a single circuit system, while later cars have a double twin-circuit brake system with servo assistance. Pressure exerted by the brake fluid is directed by way of duplicate brake lines to two pairs of wheel brake cylinders for each front brake disc, together with the wheel brake cylinders in each of the drum brakes at the rear. Should the circuit which supplies one pair of front wheel brake cylinders fail, braking effort is retained at all four wheels. If the other circuit, supplying all four wheels should fail the second pair of brake cylinders in the front wheels will continue to operate. Duplication of the front wheel brake cylinders by this means ensures that should failure of a brake circuit occur excessive braking effort should not be required to bring the vehicle safely to a halt.

Under normal operating conditions once the pressure is released from the footbrake pedal the pads are automatically retracted. Wear is taken up automatically and no adjustment is provided. The pistons in the caliper unit operate simultaneously to exert equal pressure onto the friction pads. This type of assembly is shown in **FIG 10 : 1**.

The rear brakes are of the internal expanding type with one leading and one trailing shoe to each brake. A double-ended cylinder expands both shoes into contact with the drum under hydraulic pressure from the master cylinder. When pedal pressure is released the shoes are retracted by springs. This type of assembly is shown diagrammatically in **FIG 10 : 22**. On some later cars the rear brakes include an automatic adjusting device that compensates for wear on the linings.

The brake pedal is directly coupled to the hydraulic master cylinder where pressure on the fluid is generated. This is transmitted to the braking units by a system of metal and flexible pipes.

10 : 2 General & preventative maintenance

Periodically check the level of fluid in the master cylinder supply tank and top up the tank to the required level. If frequent topping up is necessary there must be a leak in the system which should have immediate attention. Wipe dirt from around the cap before unscrewing it. Always use the recommended grade of hydraulic fluid.

Adjust the rear brake shoes when pedal travel becomes excessive. Full details of this operation are given in **Section 10:6**.

Preventative maintenance:

Regularly examine the friction pads, rear brake linings and all pipes, unions and hoses. If one front friction pad is more worn than the other do not change them over in an attempt to equalize the wear.

Change all the brake fluid every 10,000 miles or 12 months as brake fluid absorbs moisture through the supply tank vent hole. The boiling point of the fluid falls slowly from the original specification of 240°C to 160°-180°C. If the fluid is not renewed, bubbles of steam may form when the brakes are applied hard for long periods of time so causing brake failure.

Every 40,000 miles or four years check all flexible hoses and fluid seals in the complete system and renew if necessary. The bores of all cylinders should be highly polished and without signs of pitting or corrosion.

Never use anything but the recommended grade of hydraulic fluid (ATE Blue or Castrol/Girling Universal). Do not leave it in unsealed containers as it will absorb moisture which can be dangerous. Discard fluid drained from the system or after bleeding.

Observe absolute cleanliness when working on all parts of the hydraulic system.

10 : 3 Brake pads removing & refitting

Removal:

1 Before the caliper assembly is worked upon be sure that it has cooled down to normal room temperature.
2 Remove the wheel trim and slacken the wheel nuts. Lift up the front of the car and support on firmly based stands. Remove the wheel nuts and lift away the road wheel.
3 Using a compressed air jet carefully remove all signs of road dust from the caliper area. Carefully drive out the retaining pins from the caliper using a suitably sized drift and hammer. It is important that the original pins be discarded and new ones fitted. The pin locations are shown in **FIG 10 : 2**.
4 Carefully lift away the cross spring and using a suitably shaped hook carefully pull out the brake linings. Refer to **FIG 10 : 3**.
5 It is important that new brake pad linings are fitted if the original linings are worn down to a thickness of .08 inch or less. Only use brake pads coded by the same colour markings, if only one side is worn, renew the other side also.

Reassembly:

1 Ensure that the level in the brake master cylinder supply tank is below the recommended level and using a pair of piston press-back pliers return the pistons in the wheel cylinder.

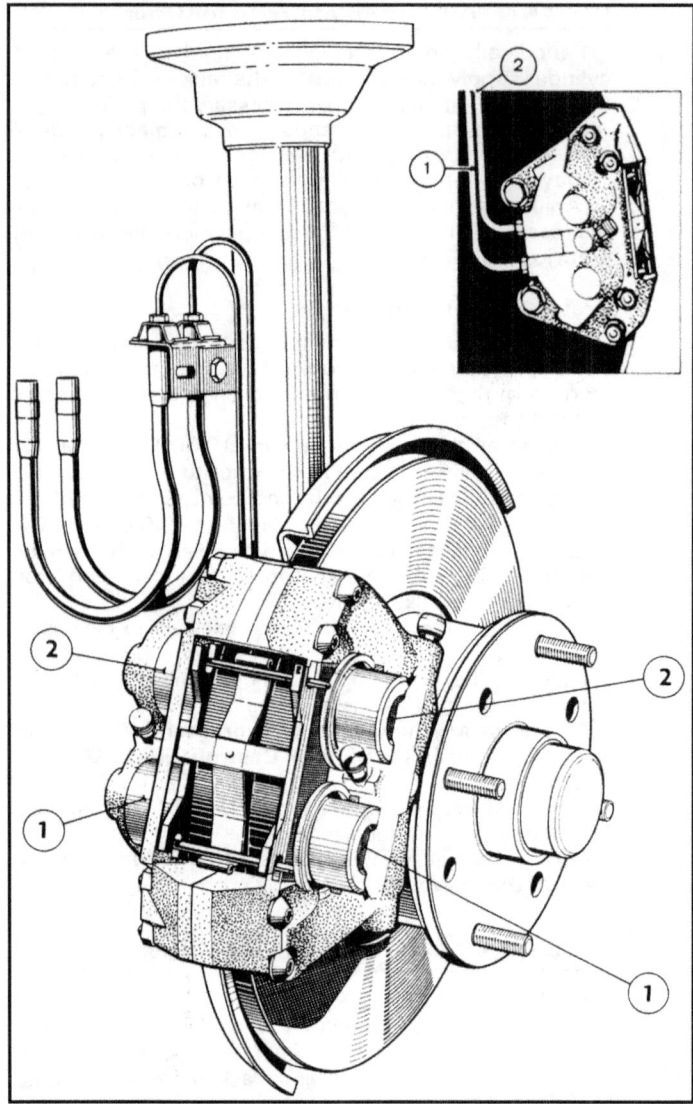

FIG 10:1 Front disc and caliper assembly

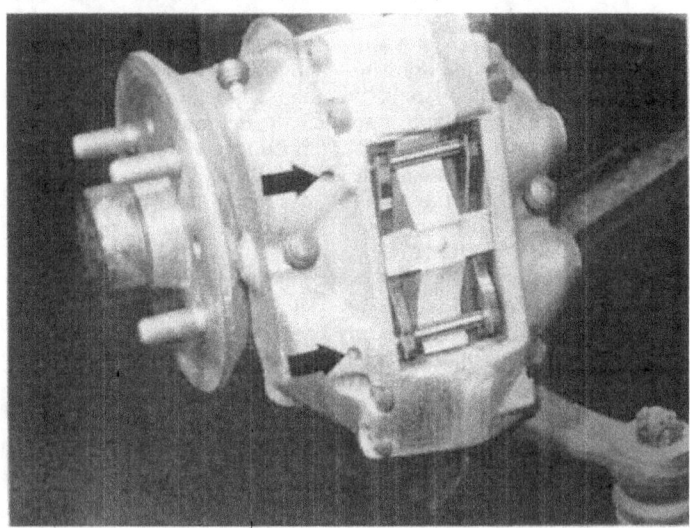

FIG 10:2 Disc pad retaining pins

2 As a matter of principle all four brake pads should be renewed as a set. Ensure that the pads are to correct specification as detailed by colour coding marked **B** (see **FIG 10:4**). Carefully insert the pads into the caliper and correctly locate the cross-shaped spring. Fit two new retaining pins and ensure that the open end is correctly splayed outwards so that there is no chance of the pin working out of the caliper.

3 Refit the road wheel, check the level of hydraulic fluid in the reservoir and finally road test the vehicle to ensure correct operation of the braking system.

10 : 4 Brake calipers removing & refitting

Removing and dismantling caliper:

1 Before the caliper assembly is removed ensure that it has cooled down to normal room temperature.
2 Remove the wheel trim and slacken the wheel nuts. Lift up the front of the car and support on firmly based stands. Remove the wheel nuts and lift away the road wheel.
3 Refer to **FIG 10:12** and seal off the reserve reservoir against escape of brake fluid by suitably plugging the two outlet pipes. Release the two brake lines at the back of the brake caliper unit at the two locations shown by the small arrows in **FIG 10:5**.
4 Release the caliper by removing the two retaining bolts, the location of which is indicated by the large arrows in **FIG 10:5** and finally carefully lift away the caliper unit.
5 Remove the friction linings as detailed in **Section 10:3**.
6 Thoroughly clean the exterior of the caliper, preferably using a compressed air jet and soft non-fluffy rag.
7 Carefully clamp the caliper between soft faces in a vice and using a screwdriver, very carefully lift away the clamp ring and rubber protective cap (see **FIG 10:6**).
8 Referring to **FIG 10:7**, secure one piston with the special piston retraction tool and insert a hard wood or felt pad in the stirrup recess. Push the piston out using a compressed air jet directed through the bleed hole as shown in **FIG 10:7**.
9 Very carefully remove the piston sealing ring using a pointed plastic rod or a discarded knitting needle.
10 If it is essential to split the caliper into two halves, remove the taper bolts 1 to 4 in the order shown in **FIG 10:8**. These must be discarded and new bolts fitted. Caliper separation is not advised.
11 Remove the two sealing rings as shown by the dark arrows in **FIG 10:9**.
12 Thoroughly clean all parts using methylated spirits or the correct grade hydraulic fluid. Never use any other fluid otherwise damage could result to the rubber seals. Ensure that all parts are spotlessly clean.

Reassembly:

Reassembly is the reverse procedure to dismantling but the following points should be noted:

1 Should the caliper body be parted new sealing rings must be fitted, also new bolts are to be used as they are made of a special ductile steel. Tighten the bolts in the sequence shown in **FIG 10:8** to the correct torque wrench setting of 21 to 24 lb ft. Set the torque wrench to 50 per cent of the final setting and tighten. Reset the torque wrench to final setting and retighten.

2 When reassembling the pistons ensure that they are correctly located in the bores and that they are well lubricated with the correct grade hydraulic fluid.
3 Lubricate well the two bore rubber sealing rings with the correct grade hydraulic fluid to stop tilting when the piston is replaced.
4 Always fit a new protection cap to ensure that no road dust will find its way into the piston assembly.

Refitting caliper:

To refit the caliper is the reverse procedure to dismantling but the following points should be noted:
1 The caliper must only be refitted when it is at normal room temperature.
2 Tighten the two caliper retaining screws to the correct torque wrench setting.
3 Special attention must be given to the bleeding of the brake system and the procedure described in **Section 10:7** carefully observed, otherwise it is possible for air bubbles to be retained with consequent unsatisfactory operation.

10 : 5 Disc brake overhaul

Removal:

1 Before the caliper assembly is removed ensure that it has cooled down to normal room temperature.
2 Remove the wheel trim and slacken the wheel nuts. Lift up the front of the car and support on firmly based stands. Remove the wheel nuts and lift away the road wheel.
3 Remove the caliper from the telescopic leg shock absorber assembly by removing the two retaining bolts. Remove the hub cap from the wheel hub and extract the cotter pin from the castellated nut. Remove the castellated nut and washer. Carefully pull the wheel hub and brake disc from the steering knuckle and clamp the wheel hub and brake disc assembly between the soft faces fitted between the jaws of a bench vice. Remove the Allen screws holding the brake disc to the hub assembly and part the two. If the brake disc is rusted to the wheel hub it is suggested that the wheel hub is screwed slightly in towards the rim and then turn the brake disc backwards and forwards whilst pulling.

Inspection:

1 Thoroughly inspect the brake disc for signs of overheating, hairline cracks or distortion. The maximum permissible runout measured at the circumference of the disc is .002 inch removed or .008 inch installed.
2 Should the contact faces be badly scored the disc may be refaced by turning on a centre lathe and skimming the areas affected provided that the thickness of the disc does not fall below the limits given in Technical Data.

Refitting:

Refitting is the reverse procedure to dismantling but the following points should be noted:
1 Tighten the Allen head screws holding the brake disc to hub assembly to a torque wrench setting of 43.4 lb ft.
2 Refit the brake disc and hub assembly to the stub axle as detailed in **Chapter 8, Section 8:4**.

FIG 10:3 Pad removal from caliper

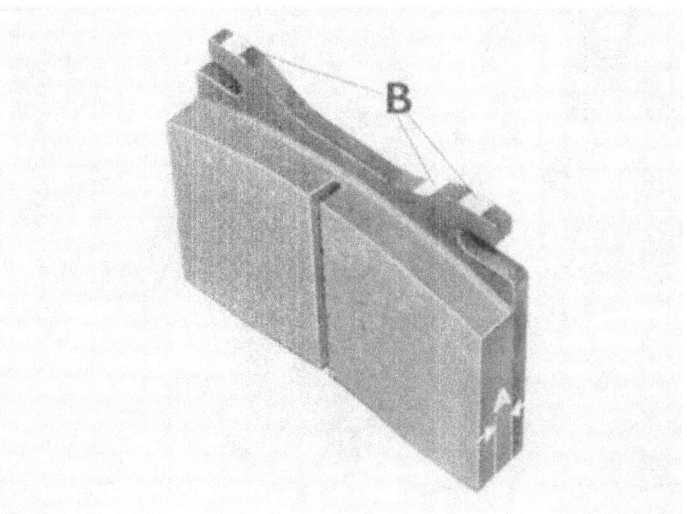

FIG 10:4 Pad identification

FIG 10:5 Caliper mounting bolts

FIG 10:6 Seal and dust cover removal

FIG 10:7 Piston clamp in location on caliper

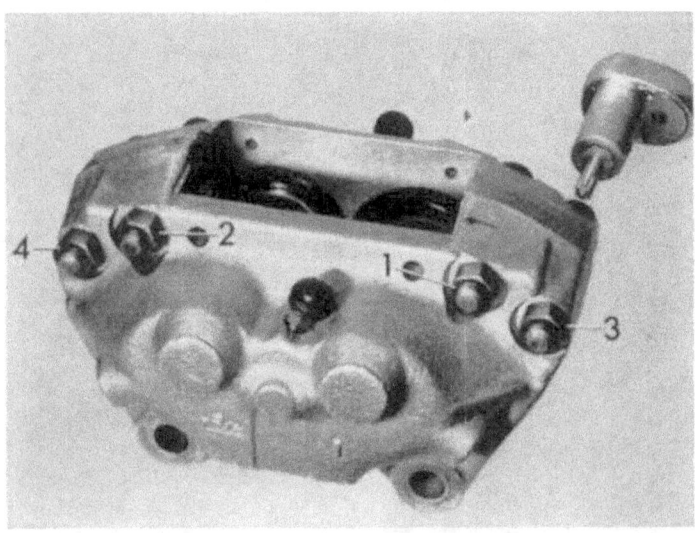

FIG 10:8 Caliper body clamping bolts

10:6 Drum brake overhaul

Dismantling:

1 Remove the wheel trim and slacken the wheel nuts. Lift up the rear end of the car and support on firmly based stands. Remove the wheel nuts and lift away the road wheel.
2 Remove the brake drum and carefully ease the two brake shoes from the anchor point at the bottom of the backplate assembly.
3 Carefully pull out the brake shoes from their locations in the wheel cylinder. Ease the handbrake Bowden cable from the brake lever and separate the brake shoes by detaching the return springs from the shoe webs having first made a note of the spring location. Do not press the brake pedal while the shoes are away from the backplate. It is considered a good idea to put wire or rubber bands around the wheel cylinder pistons to prevent accidental ejection and if the car is to be left without rear shoes for a long time a notice should be hung on the brake pedal to warn against the pressing of the pedal otherwise the wheel cylinder will have to be checked and the parts refitted.

Relining rear brake shoes:

If the linings are worn down to the rivets, renewal is necessary. It is not recommended that owners should reline brake shoes themselves. It is important that lining should be perfectly bedded down on the shoes and then ground to perfect concentricity with brake drums. For this reason it is best to obtain sets of replacement shoes already lined. The correct lining material is given in Technical Data. Do not fit odd shoes and do not mix material or unbalanced braking will occur.

Do not allow grease or paint to contact the friction lining. If the original linings are contaminated with oil or grease do not attempt to clean them with solvents as nothing useful can be done.

Refitting brake shoes:

This is the reverse procedure to dismantling. Ensure that the pull-off springs are correctly fitted to the holes in the webs and that the shoes register correctly in the slotted end of the pistons and adjusters. Before trying to fit the drum, slacken off the brake adjuster completely. Also fully release the handbrake. Readjust the shoes when assembly is completed. This will also set the handbrake correctly.

Brake shoe adjustment:

1 Jack up the rear end of the car and release the handbrake.
2 Refer to **FIG 10:10**. Acting on each adjusting nut in turn, turn it outwards until the wheel is locked and then back until the wheel just turns without any rubbing. Do not confuse axle drag with brake drag. Repeat on the other rear wheel.

10:7 Bleeding the hydraulic system

This is not routine maintenance and is only necessary if air has entered the hydraulic system because parts have been dismantled or because the fluid level in the master cylinder supply reservoir has dropped so low that air has been drawn in through the hole in the cylinder bore mentioned in **Section 10:8**.

1 Fill the master cylinder supply reservoir with correct grade hydraulic fluid. During bleeding operation fluid will be used and constant topping up of the supply reservoir will be needed. If this is not done it is possible for air to enter the master cylinder, which will nullify the operation and necessitate a fresh start.
2 Attach a length of rubber or plastic tube to the bleeder screw in a rear wheel cylinder, or to the screw on the caliper in the case of the front brakes. Immerse the free end of the tube in a small volume of correct grade hydraulic fluid in a clean glass jar.
3 Open the bleed screw one turn and with the assistance of a second operator press down slowly on the brake pedal. After a full stroke let the pedal return without assistance, pause a moment and repeat the down stroke. At first there will be air bubbles issuing from the bleed tube, but when fluid alone is ejected, hold the pedal firmly down on the floor boards and tighten the bleeder screw. Repeat this on both rear brakes and then do both the front. Note that there are three bleed screws on the four piston calipers, an upper and two lower. Bleeding must be carried out on all three otherwise air bubbles might remain in the caliper. Use the upper bleed screw first and then the two lower ones, always leaving the outboard screw to the last.
4 On completion, top up the fluid in the supply reservoir to the correct level. Discard all dirty fluid. If the fluid is perfectly clean, let it stand for twenty four hours to become clear of air bubbles before using again.

10 : 8 Master cylinder overhaul

This is shown in sectional form in **FIG 10:11**. When the brake pedal is applied the piston 1 is moved forwards so causing the primary sleeve 2 to travel past the compensation passage 3. This enables the pressure in chamber A to be built up and transferred to piston 4. As the piston 1 is being pushed further down the bore the primary sleeve 5 travels past the compensation passage 6. Under these conditions the pressure will be equal in Chambers A and B. Chamber A is connected to the front wheel caliper assembly whilst chamber B operates both the rear wheel hydraulic wheel cylinders and also the second pair of pistons within the front wheel caliper. This will ensure that should a failure occur on one of the brake circuits although considerably more travel may be experienced when depressing the brake pedal the braking system will still be partly in operation.

When the second brake circuit is inoperative due to a hydraulic line or seal failure the piston 4 in the chamber B not under pressure is pressed against the tandem master housing with the piston 1 as a result of the pressure building up in chamber A and the first brake circuit is set into operation.

When the front brake hydraulic circuit is not operative the piston 1 in chamber A will be at atmospheric pressure and is pressed against the spring cap 7 and the second brake circuit becomes fully operative through chamber B.

Removing master cylinder:

1 Refer to **FIG 10:12** and plug the hoses with two tapered pieces of wood approximately .24 inch diameter. Carefully withdraw the hoses from the tandem master cylinder and fold upwards as shown in **FIG 10:12**.

FIG 10:9 Caliper sealing rings location

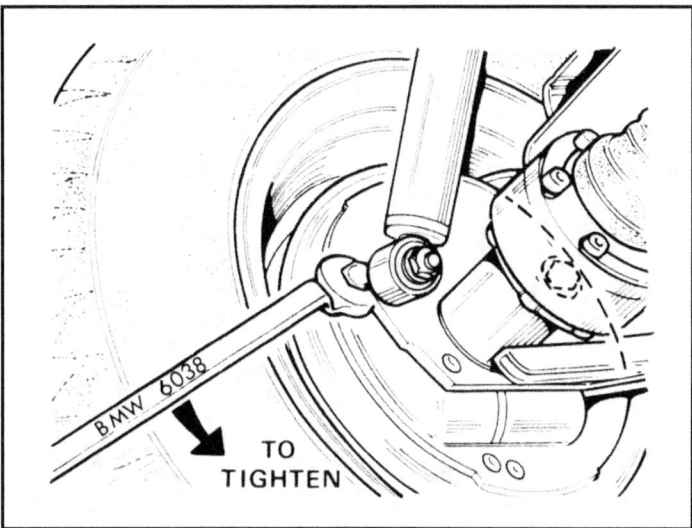

FIG 10:10 Rear brake adjustment

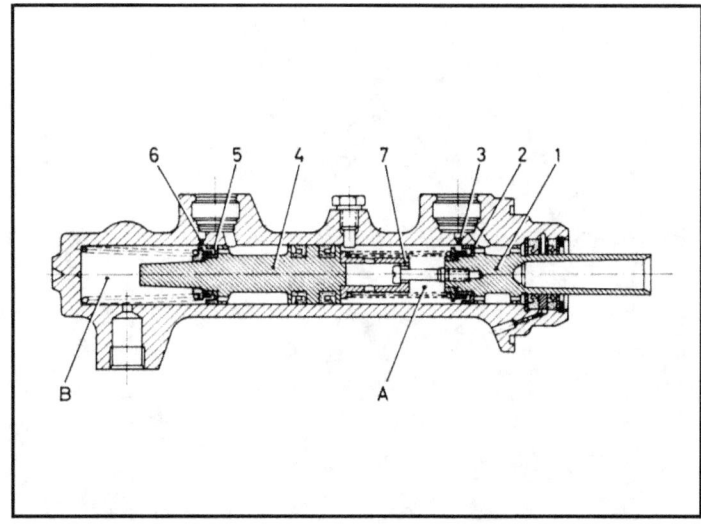

FIG 10:11 Sectional view of master cylinder

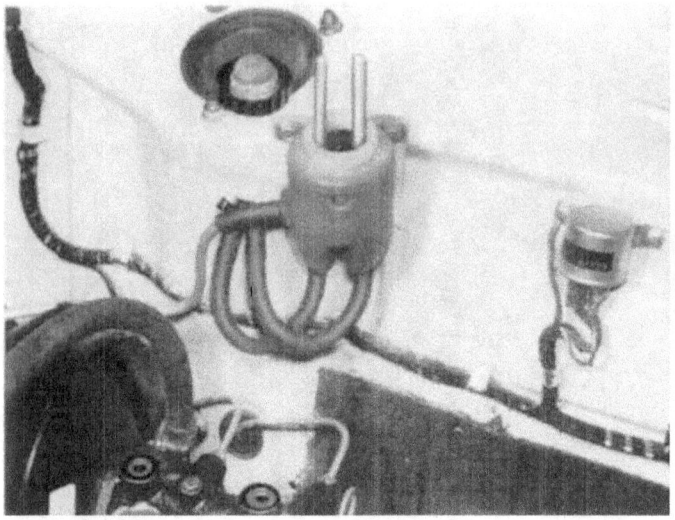

FIG 10:12 Master cylinder reservoir feed pipes plugged

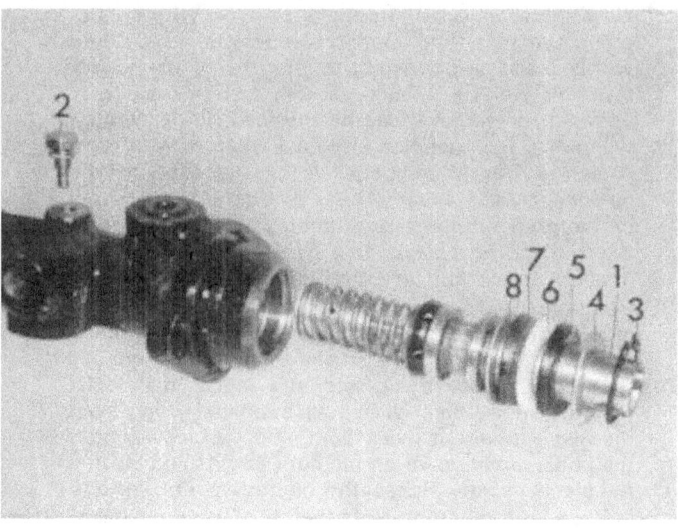

FIG 10:15 Master cylinder front piston assembly

FIG 10:13 Master cylinder sealing ring and pushrod shim

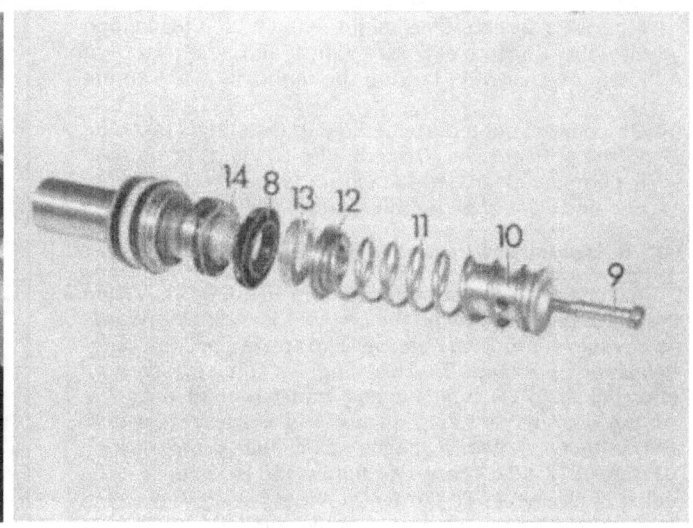

FIG 10:16 Master cylinder rear piston assembly

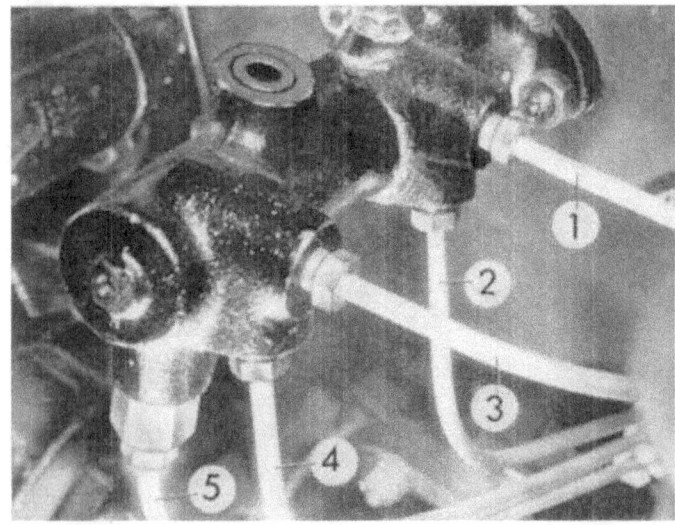

FIG 10:14 Master cylinder hydraulic pipe connections

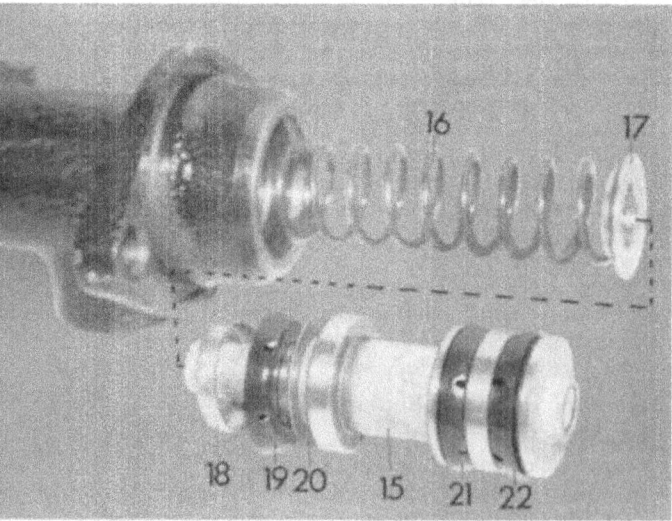

FIG 10:17 Rear piston sealing rubbers

110

2 Release the brake lines in the following order referring to **FIG 10:14** for the correct sequence.

Second brake circuit:
(1) Lefthand front.
(2) Righthand front.

First brake circuit.
(3) Lefthand front.
(4) Righthand front.
(5) Rear wheel brake.

3 Release the two master cylinder retaining bolt nuts and carefully withdraw the master cylinder.

Refitting:

1 Inspect the rubber sealing ring on the face of the master cylinder to ensure that it is not damaged and fit a new ring as necessary. This is shown in **FIG 10:13**.

2 If a new tandem master cylinder is fitted check the clearance between the master cylinder piston and the pushrod with plastigage and if necessary adjust to .002 inch by means of shims 2 (see **FIG 10:13**), placed behind the mushroomed shaped head.

3 Reassembly of the various brake lines is the reverse procedure to dismantling and upon completion, the braking system should be bled as detailed in **Section 10:7**.

Overhaul:

1 Refer to **FIG 10:15** and exert a slight pressure on the piston 1 which will enable the stop bolt 2 to be unscrewed.

2 Remove the circlip 3 and extract the piston 1.

3 Carefully pull off the stop washer 4, secondary sleeve 5, spacer ring 6, secondary sleeve 7 and stop ring 8.

4 To dismantle the primary sleeve 8 from the assembly unscrew the special bolt 9 as shown in **FIG 10:16**. Remove the spring cap 10, spring 11, spring cup 12, pressure cup 13 and packing washer 14.

5 Using a compressed air jet carefully push out the piston assembly 15 from the tandem master cylinder body. Refer to **FIG 10:17** and carefully withdraw spring 16, spring cup 17, pressure cup 18, primary sleeve 19 and packing washer 20. Also remove the secondary sleeve 21 and primary sleeve 22 from the piston.

6 Thoroughly clean all parts removed in correct hydraulic fluid and dry using compressed air. Inspect all parts for scoring, signs of seizure, rust spots or other kinds of superficial damage. If any part is suspect it must be renewed. Always renew the rubber parts when overhauling the master cylinder. Master cylinders with surface defects in the cylinder bore should not be refitted. It should be noted that all the drillings must be completely open, there must be no signs of sharp edges.

7 Reassembly of the parts is the reverse procedure to dismantling and it is recommended that **FIG 10:15**, **FIG 10:16** and **FIG 10:17** be carefully inspected to ensure that the correct sequence is obtained. It is recommended that the piston shank be smeared with silicone grease and also that the copper sealing ring under the stop bolt head 2 is renewed to ensure no hydraulic fluid leaks occur.

FIG 10:18 Wheel cylinder retaining screws

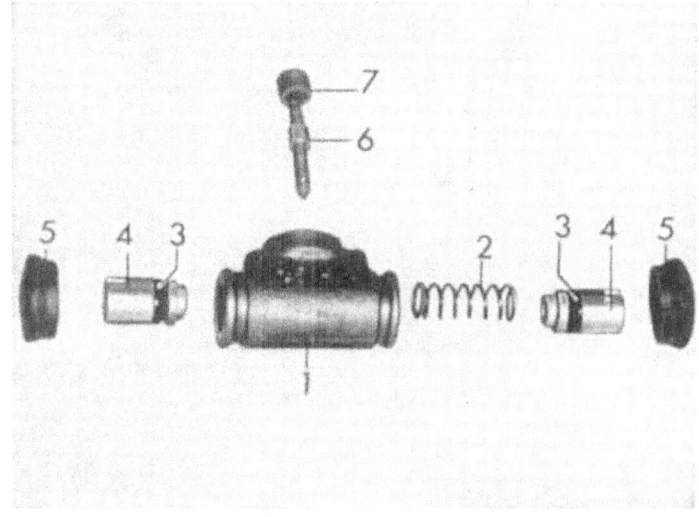

FIG 10:19 Wheel cylinder component parts

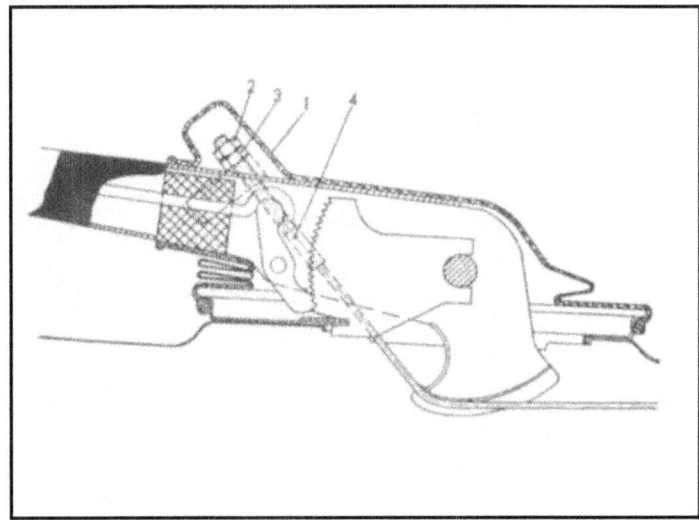

FIG 10:20 Handbrake lever assembly

111

10:9 Wheel cylinder overhaul

Removal:

1. Remove the wheel trim and slacken the wheel nuts. Lift the rear of the car and support on firmly based stands. Remove the wheel nuts and lift away the road wheel.
2. Remove the brake drum and detach the brake hoses at the bottom. These should be suitably plugged to ensure that total loss of the hydraulic brake fluid does not occur due to syphoning action.
3. Move the brake shoes fully outwards by means of the adjustment screw. Remove the wheel cylinder retaining screws indicated in **FIG 10:18** and press together both wheel cylinder pistons. Move the wheel cylinder to the right as far as it will travel, tilt forwards and carefully pull out.

Overhaul:

1. Refer to **FIG 10:19** and remove the protection caps 5, piston assemblies 4, spring 2 and bleeder valve 6 with dust cap 7.
2. Clean all the internal parts with correct grade hydraulic fluid. If any other solvents such as petrol have been used to clean the metal parts every trace must be dried off before reassembly.
3. Renew the rubber seals at every overhaul, or if there is any sign of leakage. Inspect the pistons and cylinder bore and renew parts which are worn or pitted with corrosion.
4. Fit the new seals using the fingers only. Assemble all internal parts after wetting with correct grade of hydraulic fluid. Refit the cylinder to the backplate in the reverse order to dismantling. Upon completion the brake shoes must be adjusted as detailed in **Section 10:6**, after the system has been bled according to the instructions in **Section 10:7**.

10:10 Flexible hose removal

Never try to release a flexible hose by turning the ends with a spanner. The correct procedure is as follows:

Unscrew the metal pipeline union nut from its connection with the hose. Hold the adjacent hexagon on the hose with a spanner and remove the locknut which secures the hose to the bracket. The hose can now be turned without twisting the flexible part, by using a spanner on the hexagon at the other end.

10:11 Handbrake cable removing & refitting

Removal:

1. Remove the wheel trims and slacken the wheel nuts of the two rear wheels. Lift the rear of the car and support on firmly based stands. Remove the wheel nuts and lift away the road wheel.
2. Remove the brake drum and referring to **FIG 10:20** slide off the rubber cap 1 from the handbrake lever. Remove the locknut 2 and adjustment nut 3 from the handbrake cable 4.
3. Remove the brake shoes 5 and 6 (see **FIG 10:21**), from the brake carrier 7. Release the handbrake cable 8 from the brake lever 9. Slacken the fastening clip at the longitudinal swinging suspension arm and carefully pull out the handbrake cable 10 from the pipe 11 together with the rubber grommet 12.

Refitting:

Refitting is the reverse procedure to dismantling but the following points should be noted.

1. The collar of the handbrake cable 13 (see **FIG 10:21**), must locate against the brake backplate 7 and collar 14 must align correctly with the pipe end 11. Ensure that the two rubber grommets 12 and 15 are correctly fitted.
2. To adjust the handbrake cable after refitting first adjust the brake shoes as detailed in **Section 10:6**. Adjust the handbrake cable at the handbrake lever making sure that the brakes are equally tight on the fourth tooth of the toothed ratchet.

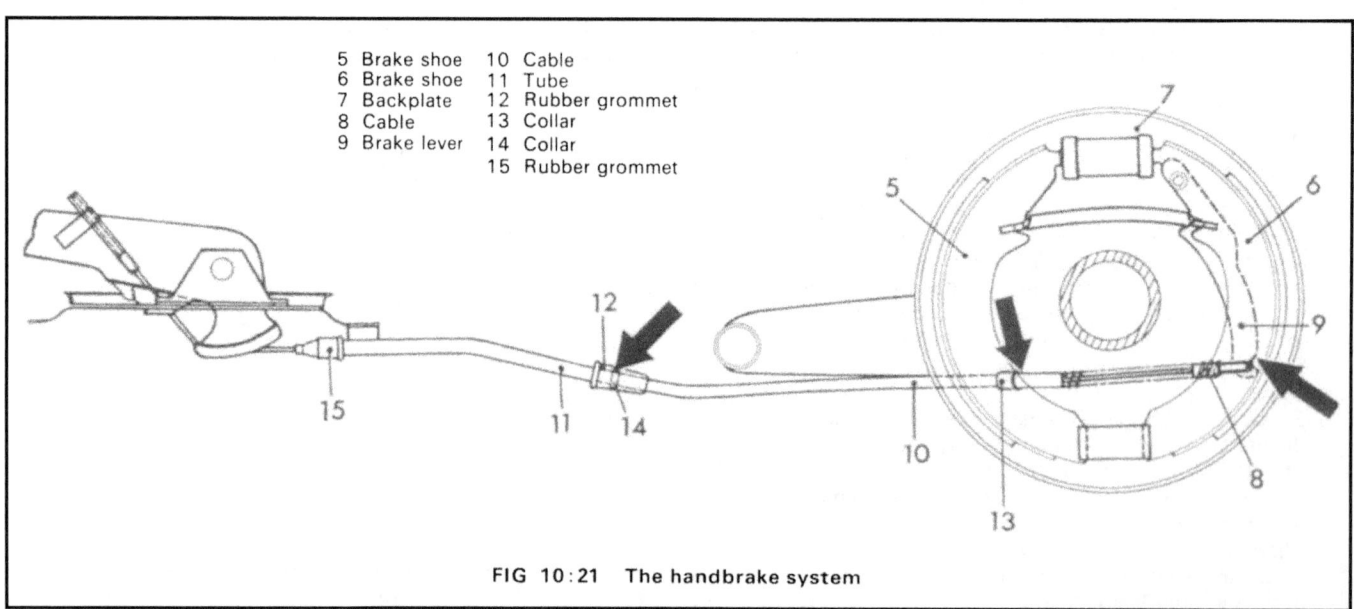

5 Brake shoe
6 Brake shoe
7 Backplate
8 Cable
9 Brake lever
10 Cable
11 Tube
12 Rubber grommet
13 Collar
14 Collar
15 Rubber grommet

FIG 10:21 The handbrake system

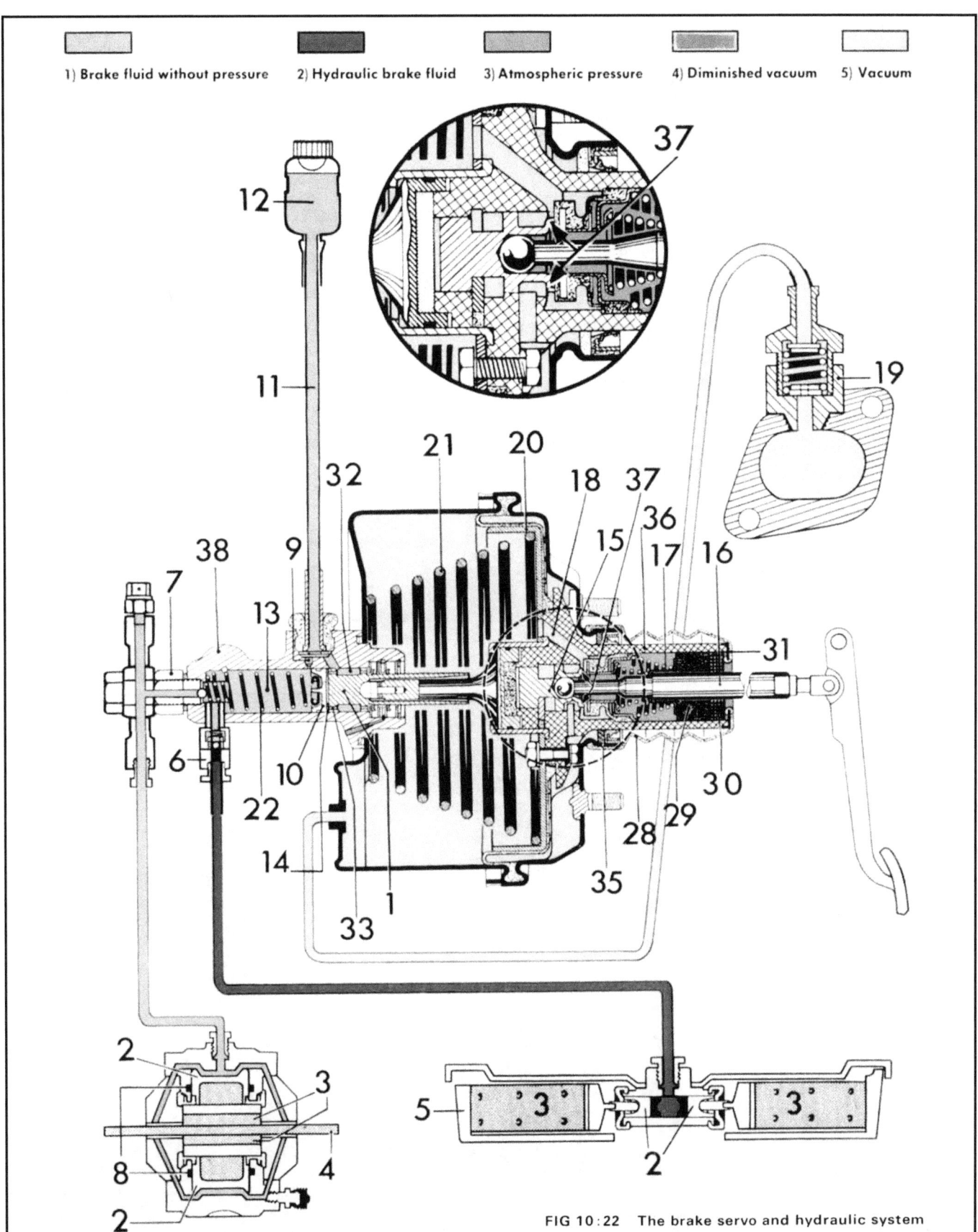

FIG 10:22 The brake servo and hydraulic system

10 : 12 Servo unit overhaul

Description:

When the brake pedal is depressed the piston 1 (see **FIG 10:22**), in the master cylinder is moved forward. Pressure that is applied to the hydraulic fluid is transmitted throughout all the pipelines so that the brake shoes are applied to the brake discs 4 and the brake drums 5 by the pistons 2. When the brake pedal is released, the return springs will move the brake shoes back to their rest position. The disc brakes are automatically returned by pressures released through the special bottom valve 7 in connection with the pre-loaded sealing rings 8. The pre-pressure valve 6 is designed to maintain a pressure reserve of approximately 11.6 lb/sq inch for the drum brakes.

Fluid compensation in the master cylinder is effected by the compensating bore 9 which is situated in front of the primary sleeve 10 and providing a connection between the compensating reservoir 12 and the pressure chamber of the cylinder 13. To avoid the possible ingress of air into the hydraulic system because of the pressure drop when the brake pedal is released, a fluid space 32 is arranged in the rear of the primary sleeve 10 at the circumference of the piston 1 so allowing the brake fluid to flow into the brake line system via the special filling bore 33 and filling valve 14.

Servicing:

The brake servo unit is a non-repairable component and cannot be supplied on a unit for unit exchange basis. Only the vacuum check valve, the protective cap 28, the filter 29 and silencer 30 may be exchanged. If the protective cap 28 is renewed it is essential that the filter 29 and silencer 30 are renewed at the same time. To perform this operation proceed as follows:

1. Carefully pull off the protective cap 28 from the neck of the vacuum cylinder 35 and disconnect from the silencer holder.
2. Lift the silencer holder 31 away from the control casing 36 using a screwdriver.
3. Remove the silencer 30 and filter 29 from the control casing 36.
4. Upon reassembly fit the plastic foam strip filter 29 over the piston rod 16 and then insert the silencer 30 into the control casing 36. After fitting the silencer holder 31 fit the protective cap 28 and connect to silencer holder and ensure that it is well over the neck of the vacuum cylinder.
5. For hydraulic brake servo units equipped with a vacuum check valve, press the vacuum valve against the bottom of the vacuum cylinder when removing. Then turn to the left using a spanner to disengage from the bayonet catch. Upon reassembly of a new vacuum check valve together with its sealing ring coat both parts with a multi-purpose grease.

Brake pedal adjustment:

When a new brake servo unit has been fitted it is important that the piston rod (see **FIG 10:23**), is correctly adjusted so that distance **A** is exactly 8.091 inch. Also ensure that the brake pedal dimension **B** is 8.661 inch and the play between the pushrod and piston dimension **C** is .02 inch. The stoplight switch adjustment **D** should be .197 + .04 inch to ensure correct brake light operation.

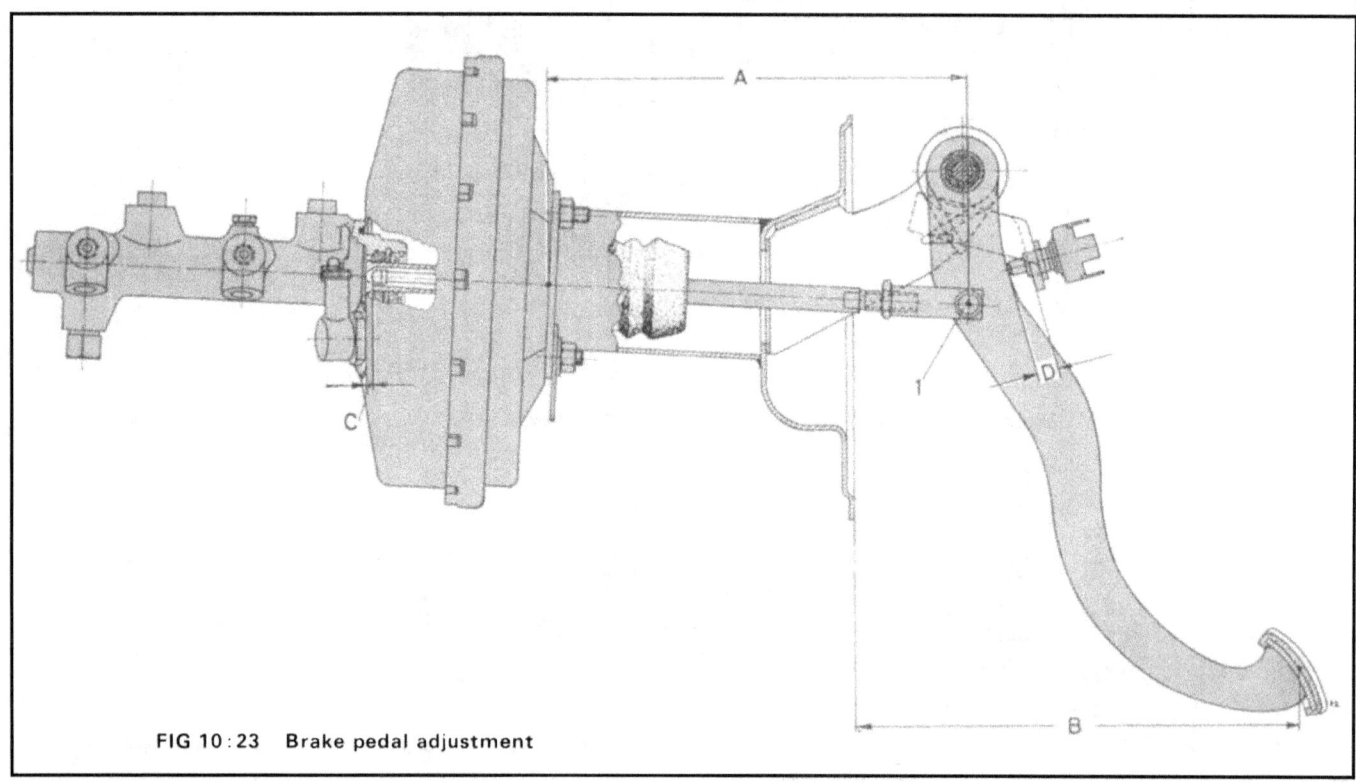

FIG 10:23 Brake pedal adjustment

10 : 13 Fault diagnosis

(a) Spongy pedal

1 Leak in the system
2 Worn master cylinder
3 Leaking wheel cylinders
4 Air gap in the fluid system
5 Gaps between rear shoes and underside of linings

(b) Excessive pedal movement

1 Check 1 and 4 in (a)
2 Excessive lining wear

(c) Brakes grab or pull to one side

1 Distorted discs or drums
2 Wet or oily pads or linings
3 Rear brakes backplate loose
4 Disc loose on hub
5 Worn suspension or steering connections
6 Mixed linings of different grades
7 Uneven tyre pressures
8 Broken shoe return springs
9 Seized handbrake cable
10 Seized piston in wheel cylinder
11 Loose caliper fixings

10 : 14 Technical data

Single circuit system:
- Front .. ATE fixed caliper disc with automatic adjustment
- Rear .. Drum with leading and trailing shoes

Maximum free travel at brake pedal .. $\frac{1}{4}$ to $\frac{1}{3}$ of total travel
Brake servo type .. T50 or T51

Master cylinder diameter:
- 2002 .. $\frac{7}{8}$
- All other models .. $\frac{15}{16}$

Front wheel cylinder piston diameter:
- 2002 .. 1.89
- All other models .. 2.13

Piston offset .. 20 deg.
Rear wheel cylinder piston diameter .. $\frac{11}{16}$

Brake disc diameter:
- 2002 .. 9.45
- All other models .. 10.71

Maximum brake disc runout .. .0039
Maximum disc thickness variation .. .00079

Minimum brake disc thickness:
- 2002 .. .374
- All other models .. .461

Front brake pad lining .. Necto 244 (green/white/green)
Minimum front brake pad lining thickness .. .079

Brake drum diameter:
- 2002:
  - Standard .. 9.06
  - First oversize .. 9.06 + .0197
  - Second oversize .. 9.06 + .0394
- All other models:
  - Standard .. 9.84
  - First oversize .. 9.84 + .0197
  - Second oversize .. 9.84 + .0394

Maximum ovality .. .0039
Brake shoe width .. 1.575
Minimum brake lining thickness .. .118

Twin circuit brake system:
- Front .. ATE 4 piston fixed caliper disc brake with automatic pad wear compensator
- Rear .. Internal expanding drums with leading and trailing brakes
- Pedal free travel .. ¼ to ½ total travel
- Tandem master cylinder piston diameter .. .937
- Wheel cylinder front piston diameter .. 1.34
- Wheel cylinder rear piston diameter .. .625 or .685
- Brake disc diameter .. 9.45
- Maximum disc runout at circumference .. .0020
- Maximum disc thickness variation in rubbed area .. .0008
- Minimum brake disc thickness .. .354 (2002) or .461 (2002TI)
- Front brake lining material .. Necto 248GG, white/green/white; or Textar V1431FF, green/yellow/green
- Minimum pad thickness .. .28
- Brake drum diameter:
  - Standard .. 9.06
  - First oversize .. +.0197
  - Second oversize .. +.0394
- Maximum ovality .. .002
- Brake shoe width .. .16
- Minimum shoe lining thickness .. .12
- Shoe lining material (do not mix makes) .. Bremsit 5620GG or Energit 335
- Hydraulic fluid .. ATE Blue or Lockheed HD

Wheels & Tyres

- **Type** .. Steel disc
- **Rim size:**
  - 2002 .. 4½J x 13
  - 2000, 2000A .. 5JK x 14
  - All other models .. 5½JK x 14
- **Maximum runout:**
  - Lateral .. .039
  - Radial .. .039
- **Tyres:**
  - 2002:
    - Radial ply tubed .. 165SR13
  - 2002TI, 2002Tii:
    - Radial ply tubed .. 165HR13
  - 2000, 2000A:
    - Standard tubeless .. 6.45S x 14
    - Radial ply tubed .. 165SR x 14
  - 2000TI, 2000 TI Lux:
    - Standard tubeless .. 6.95H x 14
    - Radial ply .. 175SR x 14
  - 2000CS:
    - Standard tubeless .. 6.95H x 14
    - Radial ply .. 175HR x 14
  - 2000CA:
    - Standard tubeless .. 6.95S x 14
    - Radial ply .. 175SR x 14
- **Tyre pressures:**
  - All models, except 2000CS, 2000CA:
    - Up to four persons:
      - Standard .. Front 24 .. Rear 27
      - Radial ply .. Front 26 .. Rear 26
    - Up to five persons and luggage:
      - Standard .. Front 24 .. Rear 27
      - Radial ply .. Front 26 .. Rear 28
  - 2000CS:
    - Up to two persons:
      - Standard .. Front 26 .. Rear 26
      - Radial ply .. Front 26 .. Rear 26
    - Up to four persons and luggage:
      - Standard .. Front 26 .. Rear 28
      - Radial ply .. Front 26 .. Rear 28
  - 2000CA:
    - Up to two persons:
      - Standard .. Front 24 .. Rear 24
      - Radial ply .. Front 26 .. Rear 26
    - Up to four persons and luggage:
      - Standard .. Front 26 .. Rear 27
      - Radial ply .. Front 26 .. Rear 28

CHAPTER 11

ELECTRICAL SYSTEM

11:1 Description
11:2 Battery maintenance
11:3 Alternator
11:4 Starter motor overhaul
11:5 Windscreen wiper motor removing & refitting
11:6 Fuel tank sender unit removing & refitting
11:7 Heated rear windshield
11:8 Headlamps maintenance
11:9 Lighting circuits troubleshooting
11:10 External electronic tuning system
11:11 Instrument panel
11:12 Fault diagnosis
11:13 Technical data
11:14 Wiring diagrams

11:1 Description

All models covered by this manual have 12 volt electrical systems in which the negative battery terminal is earthed. To enable many of the electrical diagnosis procedures to be completed accurate moving coil meters are necessary. Cheap and unreliable instruments will make accurate adjustments virtually impossible.

There are wiring diagrams in Technical Data at the end of this chapter to enable those with electrical experience to trace and rectify wiring faults.

For the UK market the headlamps are of the double filament separate bulb and reflector type with adjustments for beam settings.

The electrical system on early cars is protected by six fuses, housed in a box under the bonnet. On later models the number of fuses is increased to twelve. Further details can be seen in the wiring diagrams.

Detailed instructions are given for servicing the electrical equipment but it must be emphasized that in many cases it is not worthwhile to try to repair equipment which is seriously mechanically or electrically defective. Such items should be replaced by new units which can be easily obtained.

11:2 Battery maintenance

This is of the 12 volt lead/acid type and has to meet heavy demands for current particularly in the winter. To maintain the performance of the battery at its maximum it is essential to carry out the following operations.

The top of the battery and the surrounding parts must be kept dry and clean. Clean off corrosion from the metal parts of the battery mounting with diluted ammonia and paint them with anti-sulphuric paint. If the terminal posts are corroded, remove the cables and clean with diluted ammonia. Smear the posts with petroleum jelly before making the connections and fit the terminal clamps securely. High electrical resistance due to corrosion at the terminal posts is often responsible for lack of sufficient current to operate the starter motor.

During battery operation distilled water must be periodically added so that the separators do not emerge from the electrolyte. Never add neat acid. If it is necessary to make new electrolyte due to loss by spillage, add sulphuric acid to distilled water. It is highly dangerous to add water to acid. The final level of the electrolyte should be approximately .25 inch above the top of the plates.

To test the condition of the cells use an hydrometer to check the specific gravity of the electrolyte and this reading is proportional to the state of charge as shown below.

For climates below 27°C or 80°F

Cell fully charged	Specific gravity 1.270 to 1.290
Cell half charged	Specific gravity 1.190 to 1.210
Cell discharged	Specific gravity 1.110 to 1.130

For climates above 27°C or 80°F

Cell fully charged	Specific gravity 1.210 to 1.230
Cell half charged	Specific gravity 1.130 to 1.150
Cell discharged	Specific gravity 1.050 to 1.070

These figures are given assuming an electrolyte temperature of 16°C or 60°F. If the temperature of the electrolyte exceeds this add .002 to the readings for each 3°C or 5°F rise. Subtract .002 if it drops below 16°C or 60°F.

All six cells should read approximately the same. If one differs radically from the rest it may be due to an internal fault or to spillage or leakage of the electrolyte.

If the battery is in a low state of charge take the car for a long daylight run or put it on charge at 4 amps until it gases freely. When putting a battery on charge, take out the vent plugs and refrain from using a naked light when it is gasing.

If the battery is to stand unused for long periods give a freshening up charge every month. It will be ruined if left unused.

11:3 Alternator

Description:

Due to the development of the generator design over a period of time substantial reductions in size and weight for output ratings have been made. Unfortunately now their design has reached a stage whereby any further development to improve the normal low speed output and maximum rating would necessitate a large and far more complicated and heavier machine. Alternators can be designed to meet both requirements and yet at the same time be reduced in size and weight by comparison. Although the alternator is a somewhat different form of generator, it should be understood that from the point of view of the other items of the electrical equipment of the car nothing is changed.

An alternator as its name suggests produces alternating current and this is converted to direct current before being connected to the car electrical system. It is in this respect that the alternator and the d.c. generator are similar. The current generated in the armature winding of the normal generator is also alternating in nature and has to be changed to direct current before it can be connected

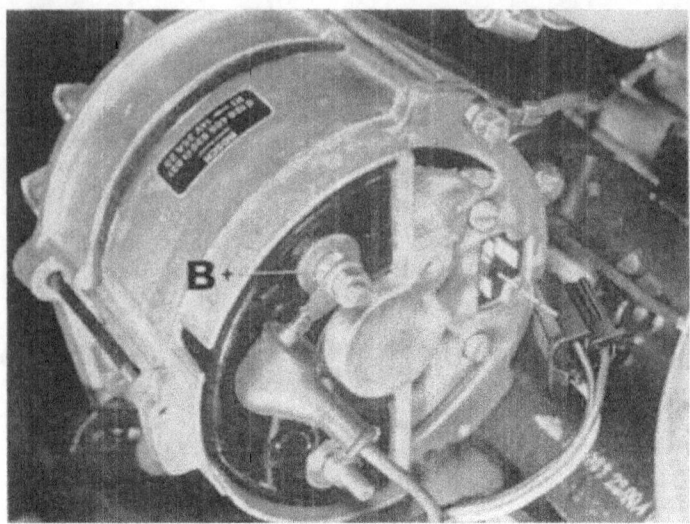

FIG 11:1 Alternator cable disconnection

FIG 11:2 Alternator mounting bushes

FIG 11:3 Fan belt tension with alternator fitted

to the other electrical circuits. It is the method by which conversion, sometimes known as rectification, is accomplished which differs.

To test or overhaul an alternator requires specialist knowledge and equipment so that it is recommended if the alternator performance is suspect the vehicle be taken along to the local automobile electricians who will have the necessary equipment to give a full diagnostic check.

Alternator removal:

1 Disconnect the negative lead from the battery terminal. Carefully ease off the flat pin plug from the back of the alternator (see **FIG 11:1**).
2 Unscrew the cable from the back of the alternator making a note that the brown cable is connected to earth and the red cable to B+ terminal.
3 Unscrew the retaining bolt at the tension plate and also at the mounting and carefully lift out the alternator.
4 Refer to **FIG 11:2** and check the mounting bushes for wear and fit new as necessary.
5 Upon refitting adjust the tension of the V-belt and by between .2 and .4 inch as shown in **FIG 11:3**.

11:4 Starter motor overhaul

Test for starter which does not operate:

Check the condition of the battery and particularly the connection to the terminals and earth. If the battery is fully charged, switch on the headlights and operate the starter motor control. If the lights go dim but the starter does not turn, it shows that current is reaching the starter motor. If the lamps do not dim, check the starter switch. At the same time check all the connections and cables from the battery to the switch and starter motor. If the starter still does not operate, remove it from the engine.

Removal:

1 Remove the negative terminal from the battery, also the plug connection and main supply cable to the starter motor switch.
2 Remove the starter motor from the engine by removing the two retaining bolts.

Starter solenoid:

The solenoid should be removed once the starter motor has been removed from the engine. Unscrew the cable to the field coil of the solenoid and unscrew the solenoid from its mounting. Lift upwards so disconnecting the engagement arm and draw the solenoid backwards. Refer to **FIG 11:4**. Reassembly is the reverse procedure to dismantling.

Renewing carbon brushes:

1 Refer to **FIG 11:5** and remove the support bracket and dust cap.
2 Detach the lockwasher 1, shim 2 and seal 3. Unscrew the pole housing bolts 5. Gently ease away the end cover.

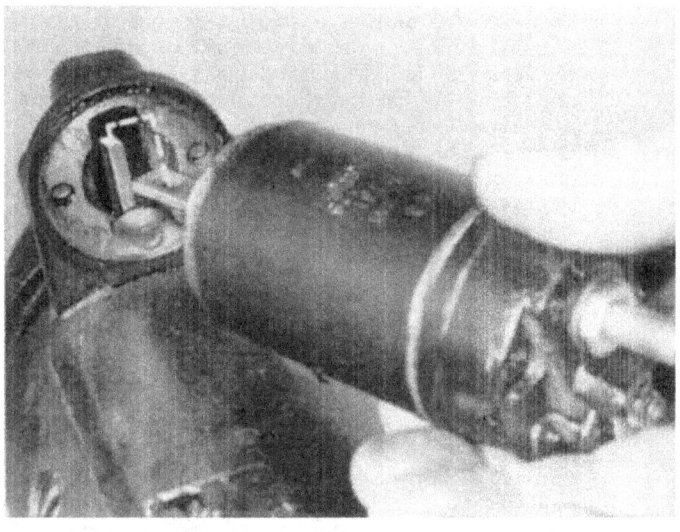

FIG 11:4 Solenoid removal

FIG 11:7 Armature and pinion assembly

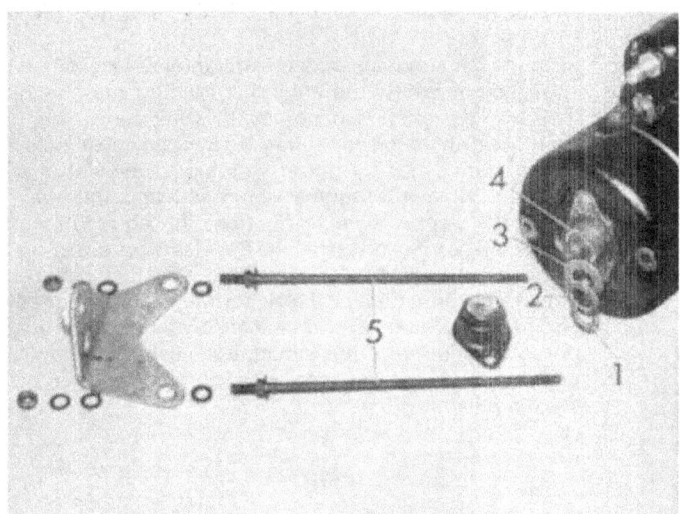

FIG 11:5 Starter motor rear end components

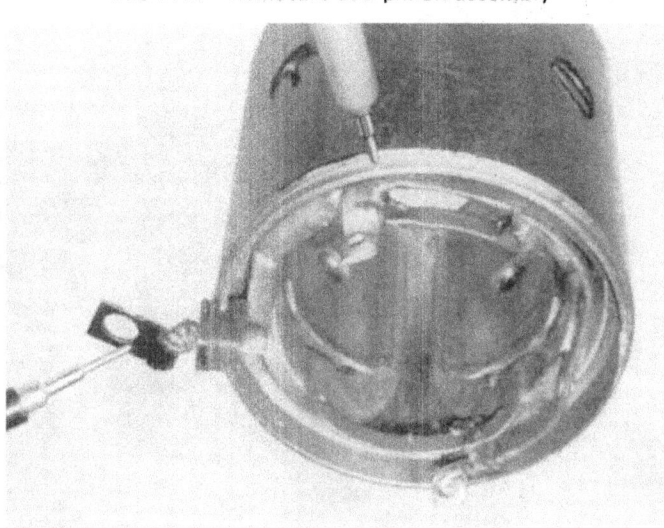

FIG 11:8 Field coil insulation test

FIG 11:6 The brush gear

FIG 11:9 The pinion assembly

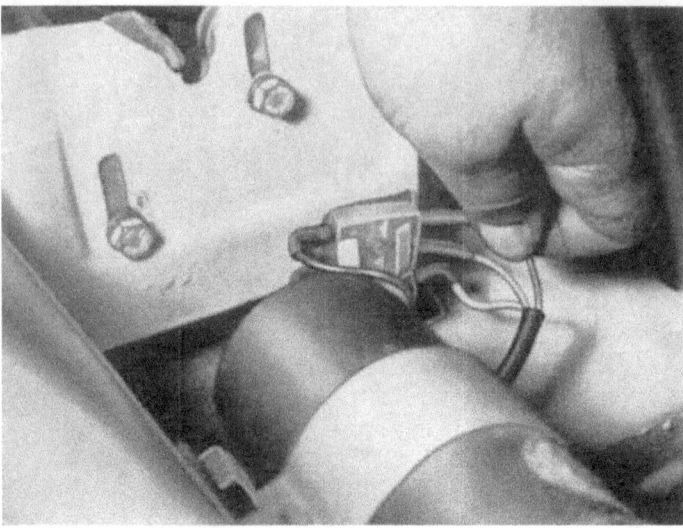

FIG 11:10 Screen wiper cable removal

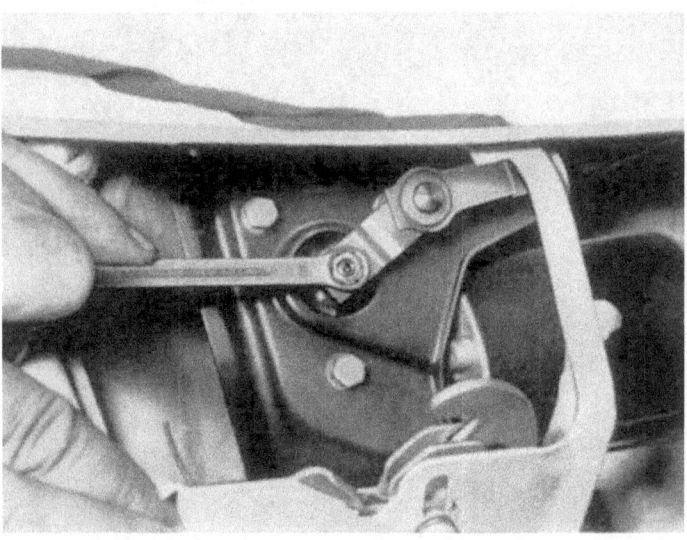

FIG 11:11 Screen wiper linkage disconnection

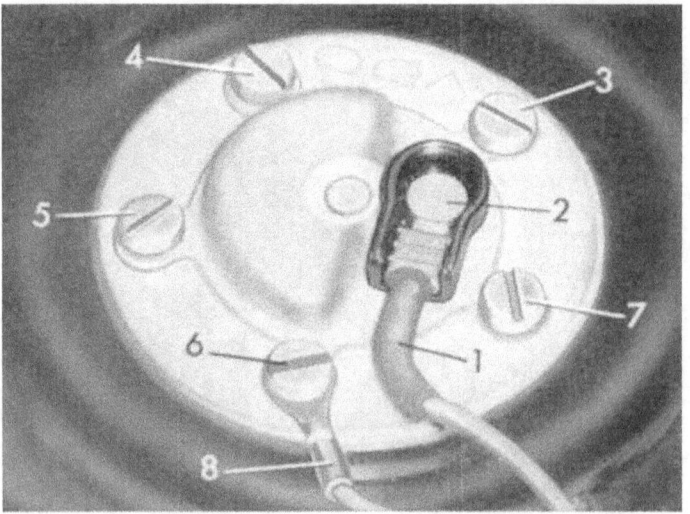

FIG 11:12 Tank sender unit Type 1

3 To renew the brushes unsolder them one at a time. Secure each new brush in place taking care not to let the solder run along the flexible lead. The brushes are pre-formed so that they do not need bedding into the curvature of the commutator.

4 On reassembly ensure that the axial play of the armature does not exceed .0039 to .0059 inch and it should be shimmed as necessary, **FIG 11:6** shows location of shims 1 and 2. At the same time ensure that the commutator bearing 4 (see **FIG 11:5**) is in a serviceable condition.

The armature:

1 To remove the armature, first remove the solenoid as previously described in this section.
2 Lift out the positive brushes and detach the brush holder plate.
3 Part the pole housing from the drive bearing and unscrew the pivot bolt on the engagement arm. Extract the armature with the engagement arm (see **FIG 11:7**).
4 Examine the armature shaft for straightness, accidental engagement whilst the engine is running may bend the armature shaft. Do not try to straighten a bent shaft or machine the armature core to obtain clearance.

The starter may be run at very high speeds if it is engaged while the engine is running and this may cause the copper wire to lift from the commutator. This could be a reason for failure. Besides reconditioning the commutator there is very little else that can be done to the armature itself. Any further testing requires equipment which a normal car owner would not possess, therefore if the armature is suspect the only check that he can do is to substitute an armature of known reliability.

Field coil test:

Using a test lamp connected to a battery and two wander leads connect one wander lead to the terminal and the other to earth (see **FIG 11:8**). The test light must not light up. If the lamp does light this means that there is a shortcircuit between the field coils and earth.

To test for continuity of the windings within the field coils use a test lamp and battery connecting the leads so that the coil windings are in series. If the bulb does not light there is a break in the field coil windings.

The pinion drive:

Remove the armature as previously described and referring to **FIG 11:9** push back the thrust ring and lift out the small circlip. Carefully ease forward the starter pinion assembly. Check for worn, cracked or broken springs. If the screwed sleeve is worn, or damaged it is necessary to renew both the sleeve and the pinion assembly. After cleaning, assemble the drive smearing a slight trace of silicone grease on the thread and engagement ring. This will ensure smooth operation.

11:5 Windscreen wiper motor

To remove the windscreen wiper motor proceed as follows:

1. Open the engine bonnet and protect the wing panels with covers.
2. Separate the cable connections at the windscreen wiper motor as shown in **FIG 11:10**, making a note that the sequence of the cables from top to bottom is, black (top), green (middle) and yellow (bottom).
3. Refer to **FIG 11:11** and remove the fastening nut from the crank guide.
4. Remove the windscreen wiper motor attaching bolts and carefully manipulate the wiper motor from the attachment bracket into the free space towards the heater, thereafter moving it downwards.
5. Refitting is the reverse procedure to dismantling. Ensure that the windscreen wiper is in the parked position before attempting to refit the drive crank.

11:6 Fuel tank sender unit removing & refitting

Type 1 – removal and refitting:

1. Refer to **FIG 11:12** and remove the rear floor panel.
2. Detach the positive lead 1 from the socket 2.
3. Release the clamp screws 3 to 7 together with the earth lead 8. Carefully lift out the immersed tube indicator and cover the hole with a clean metal plate to ensure that no dirt finds its way into the fuel tank.
4. Refitting is the reverse procedure to dismantling.

Type 2—removal and refitting:

1. Remove the rear floor panel.
2. Detach the fuel hose and cables making a note that the cable coloured blue/yellow is the positive lead, whilst the brown cable is the earthing lead.
3. Using two crossed screwdrivers as shown in **FIG 11:13** carefully unscrew the sender unit in an anti-clockwise direction.
4. Cover the hole with a metal plate to stop any dirt from finding its way into the fuel tank.
5. Refitting is the reverse procedure to dismantling. Always fit a new seal to ensure that there is no possibility of a fuel or vapour leak into the boot compartment.

Testing:

The most effective way of testing the fuel gauge sender unit is by substituting with one of known reliability.

11:7 Heated rear windshield

Full removal and fitting details are given in **Chapter 12, Section 12:7**.

11:8 Headlamps maintenance

Type 1 – circular:
Lens replacement:

1. Remove the radiator grill by releasing the retaining screws as shown in **FIG 11:14**.
2. Using a small wide blade screwdriver gently ease the lens forwards away from its circular mounting.
3. Upon refitting smear the lens to housing contact area with glycerine to ensure a weatherproof joint.

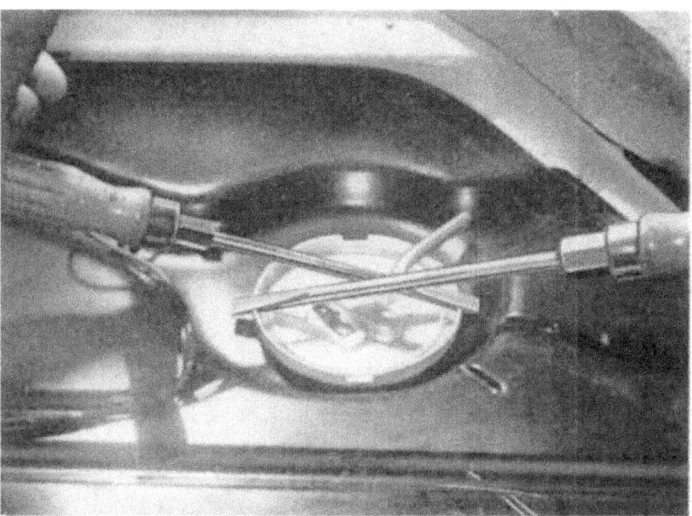

FIG 11:13   Tank sender unit removal Type 2

FIG 11:14   Front grille retaining screw locations

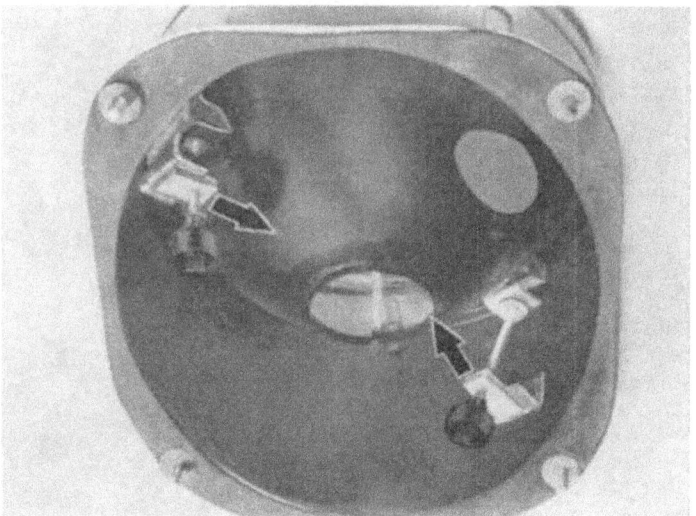

FIG 11:15   Headlamp relfector removal

FIG 11:16 Headlamp retaining bracket

FIG 11:17 Beam setting adjustment screws

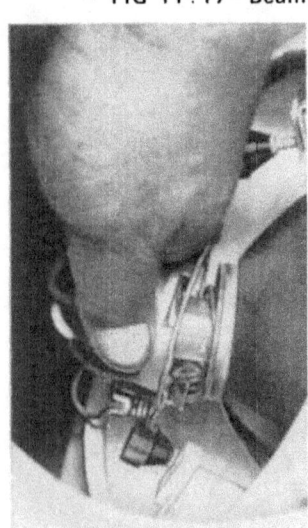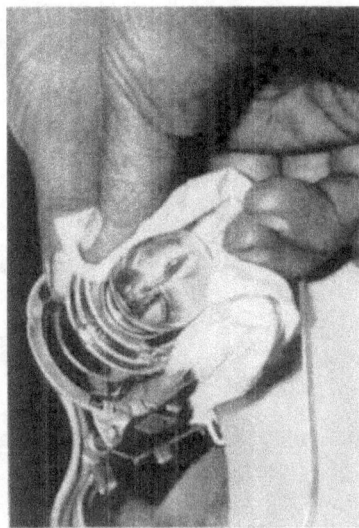

FIG 11:18 Headlamp bulb removal

Reflector:

To remove the reflector proceed as follows:
1. Remove the radiator grille, the mounting points being shown in **FIG 11:14**.
2. Remove the terminal cover cap and bulb.
3. Carefully unscrew the headlamp housing and remove.
4. If the Hella reflector is fitted, push out the two setting screws together with the guides. Gently push the reflector together with its rubber mounting out of the housing (see **FIG 11:15**).
5. If the Bosch reflector is fitted unscrew the bearing bracket from the housing. Push out the threaded plate from the rubber mounting and lift the reflector together with the rubber mounting out of the housing (see **FIG 11:16**).
6. In both cases the reflector setting should be carried out with the vehicle in its normal position suitably loaded with 2 x 143 lb weights on the back seat and 143 lb on the front seat and 67 lb in the boot compartment and the fuel tank full of petrol. Refer to **FIG 11:17** in which screw 1 is for the lateral adjustment and screw 2 is for the vertical adjustment.

Headlamp bulb renewal:

1. Remove the headlamp cover cap using a screwdriver.
2. Turn the bulb holders slightly to the left and lift away from the back of the headlight reflector.
3. Using a clean cloth or piece of paper so that the fingers do not touch the glass turn the bulb towards the left and remove as shown in **FIG 11:18**.
4. Reassembly is the reverse procedure to dismantling. Take care that the three cover cap retaining lugs fully engage.

Type 2—rectangular:

Lens replacement:

1. Remove the radiator grille by releasing the retaining screws as shown by the arrows in **FIG 11:21**.
2. Using a screwdriver carefully push off the spring clips so releasing the lens from its mounting.
3. Upon refitting place small pieces of insulation tape onto the lens itself where the retaining clips will locate so that when they are replaced the glass will not be damaged.

Reflector:

To remove the reflector proceed as follows:
1. Remove the cover cap and also the bulb and lens.
2. Referring to **FIG 11:22** completely unscrew the beam setting screws 1 and 2 from the threaded plates and carefully push the reflector forwards out of its rubber mounting. Note the position of the special locating dowels and slots for correct reassembly.
3. The setting screw 1 as shown in **FIG 11:23** is to adjust the lateral position of the headlamp beam whilst setting screw 2 adjusts the vertical setting. Reassembly is the reverse procedure to dismantling.

Type 3—rectangular headlamp fitted to 2000 C/CA/CS models:

Lens replacement:

1. Open the door and carefully unscrew the trim bar and remove the trim strip. Refer to **FIG 11:24** and remove the screw 1.

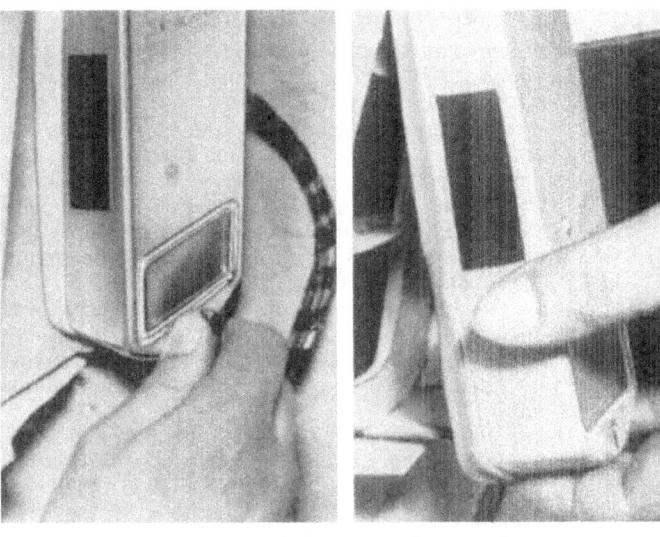

FIG 11:19 Rear light cluster removal

FIG 11:22 Beam setting screws

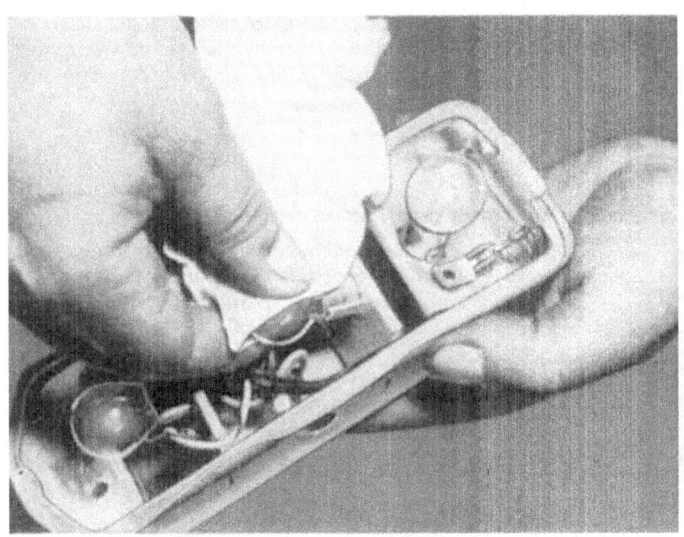

FIG 11:20 Cluster bulb removal

FIG 11:23 Location of lateral & vertical setting screws

FIG 11:21 Location of radiator grille retaining screws

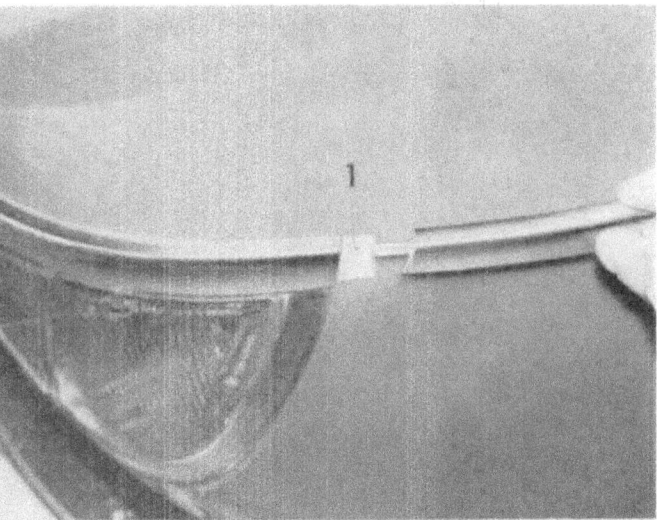

FIG 11:24 Removing of trim bar

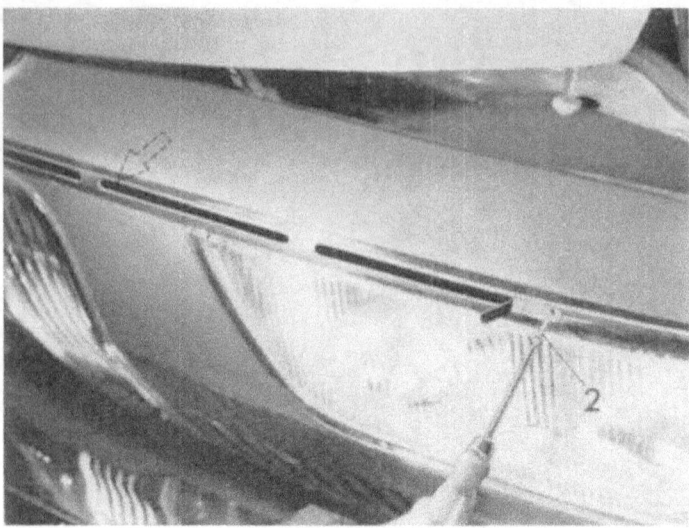

FIG 11:25 Fixing nut location

FIG 11:26 Headlamp mounting under the wheel arch

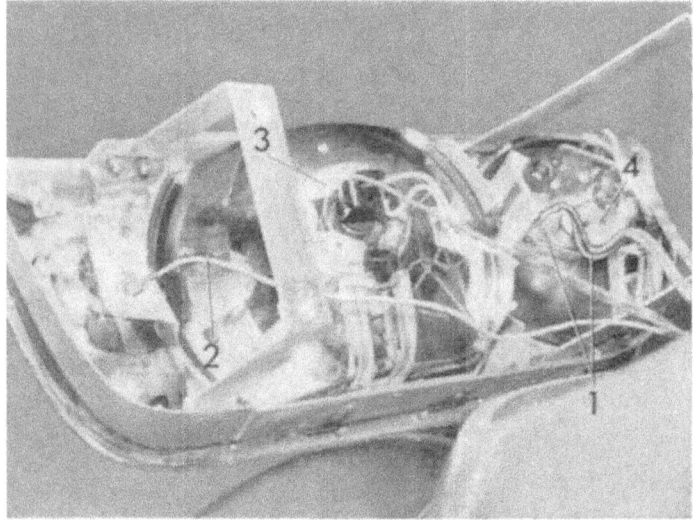

FIG 11:27 Cable location

2 Refer to **FIG 11:25** and carefully remove part of the adhesive strip. Remove the screw 2 and also the fixing nut onto the trim strip behind the facia, the location being shown by the dotted arrow.

3 With the engine compartment lid raised remove the cover of the headlamp dome and if working on the lefthand headlight unit remove the battery. Release the headlamp mounting from the engine compartment and also from under the wheel arch as shown by the arrows in **FIG 11:26**. Carefully remove the headlight unit forwards and pull off the cables. **FIG 11:27** shows the correct location of the main cables, cable 1 being coloured brown and cable 2 being coloured blue/red. Remove these two cables from their joints in the headlight cluster. Also remove the bulb holders 3 and 4.

4 Remove the sealing strip from the front of the headlight unit and also the surround from the holder housing. Slacken the top spring clips 7 (see **FIG 11:28**), and swing round to the side. Very carefully lift the lens from the bottom spring clips.

5 Reassembly is the reverse procedure to dismantling. Ensure that the sealing strip 8 (see **FIG 11:29**), is correctly positioned and finally before inserting the headlight unit insert the screw holding clip into the body panel.

Main headlamp reflector renewal:

1 Remove the wide lens headlamp unit as previously described in this section and carefully extract the specially shaped threaded plate from the rubber mountings.

2 Clip the reflector downwards and lift out of the housing together with the rubber mountings.

3 Refitting is the reverse procedure to dismantling. The headlight units will need to be reset which should be done so by rotating screws shown in **FIG 11:29**.

Additional headlamp reflector renewal:

1 Remove the wide lens headlamp unit as previously described in this section.

2 Carefully extract the threaded plate from the rubber mounting and lift the reflector together with the rubber mounting on the outside of the housing.

3 Refitting is the reverse procedure to dismantling. As the headlight unit will have been disturbed the beam setting will be incorrect and should be readjusted.

Rear light bulb renewal:

1 Release the milled nut on the bulb holder and pull the bulb holder off at the bottom and push upwards from the mounting as shown in **FIG 11:19**.

2 Use a piece of clean cloth or piece of paper between the fingers and the glass of the bulb and release the bulb from the holder by turning to the left and lifting away as shown in **FIG 11:20**.

3 Refitting is the reverse procedure to dismantling.

11:9 Lighting circuits troubleshooting

Lamp gives insufficient light

Test the state of charge of the battery and recharge it if necessary from an independent supply. Check the setting of the lamps. If the bulbs have darkened through age fit new ones.

Bulbs burn out frequently:

If this is accompanied by a need for frequent topping up of the battery and high hydrometer readings, check the charging rate with an ammeter when the car is running. Any reading in excess of the normal charging rate indicates that adjustment of the alternator is required.

Lamps light when switched on but gradually fade:

Check the battery as it is incapable of supplying current for any length of time.

Lamp brilliance varies with the speed of car:

Check the condition of the battery. Examine the battery connections. Make sure they are tight and fit new cables should faulty cables be found.

FIG 11:28 Spring clip location

11:10 External electronic tuning system

On late model cars, after 1970, provision is made for the connection of an external electronic tuning equipment for the engine. This consists of two multi-pin connecting sockets, one located above the water pump and the other at the rear of the engine compartment.

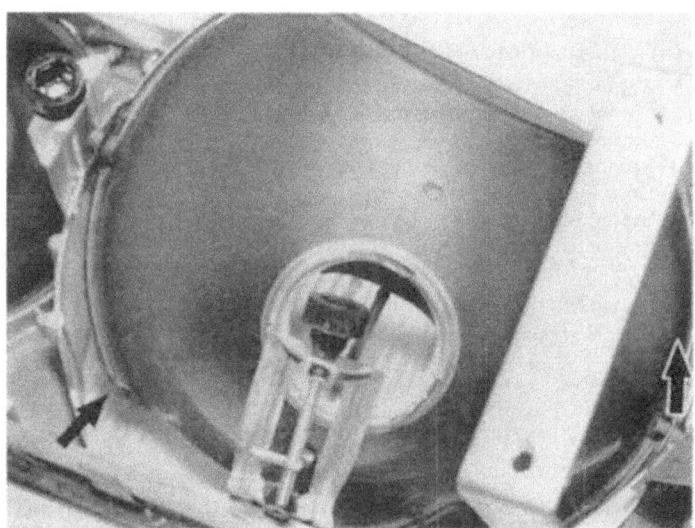

FIG 11:29 Resetting of headlights

11:11 Instrument panel

If it should be necessary to obtain access to the back of the instrument panel, it may be removed as follows:

Early cars:

First disconnect the battery, then undo the retaining screws in the panel above the instrument dials.

Remove seven cross-headed screws and withdraw the under casing panel.

Unscrew the knurled nut and remove the speedometer drive cable.

Push the instrument panel out towards the front to give access for pulling out the two multi-pin electrical connectors. Lift away the panel.

Later cars:

Disconnect the battery. Remove the lower section of the steering column surround, this is retained by four screws.

Remove the seven securing screws and withdraw the lower trim panel from below.

Unscrew the two knurled retaining nuts and the speedometer drive cable. On some models, it may be necessary to remove the hood retaining screws.

Push the instrument panel outwards and pull out the circular multi-pin connector.

11 : 12 Fault diagnosis

(a) Battery discharged
1 Terminals loose or dirty
2 Lighting circuit shorted
3 Battery internally defective

(b) Insufficient charging current
1 Loose or corroded battery terminal

(c) Battery will not hold a charge
1 Low electrolyte level
2 Battery plates sulphated
3 Electrolyte leakage from cracked casing of top sealing compound
4 Plate separators ineffective

(d) Battery overcharged
1 Voltage regulator needs adjusting

(e) Starter motor lacks power or will not operate
1 Battery discharged, loose cable connections
2 Starter pinion jammed in mesh with flywheel gear
3 Starter switch faulty
4 Brushes worn or sticking, leads detached or shorting
5 Commutator dirty or worn
6 Starter shaft bent
7 Engine abnormally stiff

(f) Starter motor runs but does not turn engine
1 Pinion sticking on screwed sleeve
2 Broken teeth on pinion or flywheel gears

(g) Noisy starter pinion when engine is running
1 Restraining spring weak or broken

(h) Starter motor inoperative
1 Check 1 and 4 in (e)
2 Armature or field coils faulty

(i) Starter motor rough or noisy
1 Mounting bolts loose
2 Damaged pinion or flywheel gear teeth
3 Main pinion spring broken

(j) Lamps inoperative or erratic
1 Battery low, bulbs burned out
2 Faulty earthing of lamps or battery
3 Lighting switch faulty, loose or broken wiring connections

(k) Wiper motor sluggish, taking high current
1 Faulty armature
2 Bearings out of alignment
3 Commutator dirty or shortcircuited
4 Wheelbox spindle binding, linkage joints stiff

(l) Wiper motor operates but does not drive arm
1 Wheelbox gear and spindle worn
2 Linkage faulty
3 Gearbox components worn

(m) Fuel gauge does not register
1 No battery supply to gauge
2 Gauge casing not earthed
3 Cable between gauge and tank unit earthed

(n) Fuel gauge registers 'Full'
1 Cable between gauge and tank unit broken or disconnected

11 : 13 Technical data

Battery:
Voltage	12-volt
Capacity	44 amp/hr
Earth lead	Negative
Lowest starting voltage	8.5

Starter:
Type	Bosch
Model	GF(R) 12-volt
Starting shortcircuit current	380 amps
Output	1 hp

Alternator:
Type	Bosch
Model	K1 14V 35A 20
Maximum output	490 watts
Maximum current	35 amps (Tii, 45 amps)
Charging begins	900 rev/min

Regulator:
Type	Bosch
Model	ADN 1/14V

Coil:
Type	Bosch
Model	K12V
Ignition voltage	15,000 volts

Spark plugs:

Thread	14 mm x 1.25
Type	Beru 230/14/3A, Bosch W200T31, Bosch W230T30
Electrode gap	.023 to .027 (.6 to .7 mm)

Distributor:

Type	Bosch
Model:	
2002, 2000, 2000A, 2000CA	FFUR4
2000CS, 2000TI, 2000 TI Lux, 2002TI, 2002Tii	JFR4
2002A	JFUD
2000Tii	JFDR4

Ignition point on belt pulley, engine cold:

2002, 2000, 2000A, 2000CA, 2002A	3 deg. BTDC
2000CS, 2000TI, 2000 TI Lux, 2000Tii, 2002TI, 2002Tii	TDC

Firing order .. 1-3-4-2

Contact breaker points gap:

2000	.016
2002	.014

Dwell angle:

2002TI	59 to 61
Others	59 to 65

Lighting: *Watts*

Long-range headlight (2000CS, 2000CA)	35
Dipped and main beam	45/40
Flashing indicators	21
Side and parking light	4
Stoplight	21
Reversing light	21 (previously 15)
Tail and parking light	10 (previously 5)
Licence plate light	5
Interior light	5
Instrument lights	3
Warning lights	3
Selector gate light	2
Hazard warning switch	1.2
Engine compartment light	5
Luggage compartment light	10

Fuse box:

2000, 2000A	6 pole, 4X8A, 2X25A
2000TI, 2000 TI Lux	6 pole, 3X8A, 3X25A
2000CS, 2000CA	8 pole, 5X8A, 1X16A, 2X25A
2000Tii, 2000, 2000A, 2000 TI Lux with hazard warning	10 pole, 3X5A, 3X8A, 4X16A
2002TI, 2002, 2002A up to 1971	6 pole, 5X8A, 1X16A
2002, 2002Tii:	
Early	12 pole, 4X5A, 4X8A, 4X16A
Late	12 pole, 7X8A, 5X16A

11 : 14 Wiring diagrams (see following pages)

BMW 2000/69 USA
BMW 2000/2000 A/2000 TILUX
BMW 2000 RE/2000 A-RE/2000 TILUX-RE
BMW 2000 Ti
BMW 2000 C/CA/CS
BMW 2002 from chassis No. 2.616.110 & Automatic from 2.504.463
BMW 2002 Ti from chassis No. 1.692.216
BMW 2002 Tii
BMW 2002 Tii USA
Rear fog warning lights diagram

BMW 2000/69 USA

1 Turn indicator and parking light front RH
2 High beam headlight (1) RH
3 Headlight (2)
4 Horn RH
5 Horn LH
6 Headlight (2)
7 High beam headlight (1) LH
8 Turn indicator and parking light front LH
9 High beam relay
10 Coil
11 Distributor
12 Alternator
13 Starter
14 Voltage regulator
15 Battery 12 V
16 Horn relay
17 Plug for foglamp relay
18 Windshield washer pump
19 Oil pressure contact
20 Remote thermometer contact
21 Automatic choke (Automatic only)
22 Screenwiper motor
23 Delay relay
24 Heater flower motor
25 Turn indicator/parking light/ windshield washer switch
26 Ignition/starter switch
27 Horn ring
28 Switch lighting
29 Dip switch and headlight flasher
30 Starter relay (Automatic only)
31 Light switch
32 Cigar lighter
33 Wiper switch
34 Blower switch (continuously variable)
35 Hazard warning flasher unit
36 Hazard warning flasher switch
37 Fuse box
38 Combined instrument:
  a Instrument lighting
  b Fuel gauge
  c Thermometer
  d High beam telltale (blue)
  e Fuel reserve and choke telltale (white)
  f Turn indicator telltale (green)
  g Oil pressure telltale (green)
  h Charge telltale (red)
39 Clock
40 Speedometer
41 Choke cable switch (not Automatic)
42 Door switch RH
43 Stop light switch
44 Door switch LH
45 Interior light
46 Fuel gauge tank mechanism
47 Selector lever illumination (Automatic only)
48 Switch for reversing light and starter lock (Automatic)
49 Heated rear window connection
50 Rear light RH
51 Rear light LH
  A Turn indicator
  B Rear light
  C Reversing light
  D Stop light
52 License plate light
53 Brake fluid level switch
54 Brake fluid level telltale
Firing order 1-3-4-2

Cable coding:
1.5 sq. mm cross-section
Basic colour:
  BL = blue
  BR = brown
  GE = yellow
  GN = green
  GR = grey
  RT = red
  SW = black
  WS = white

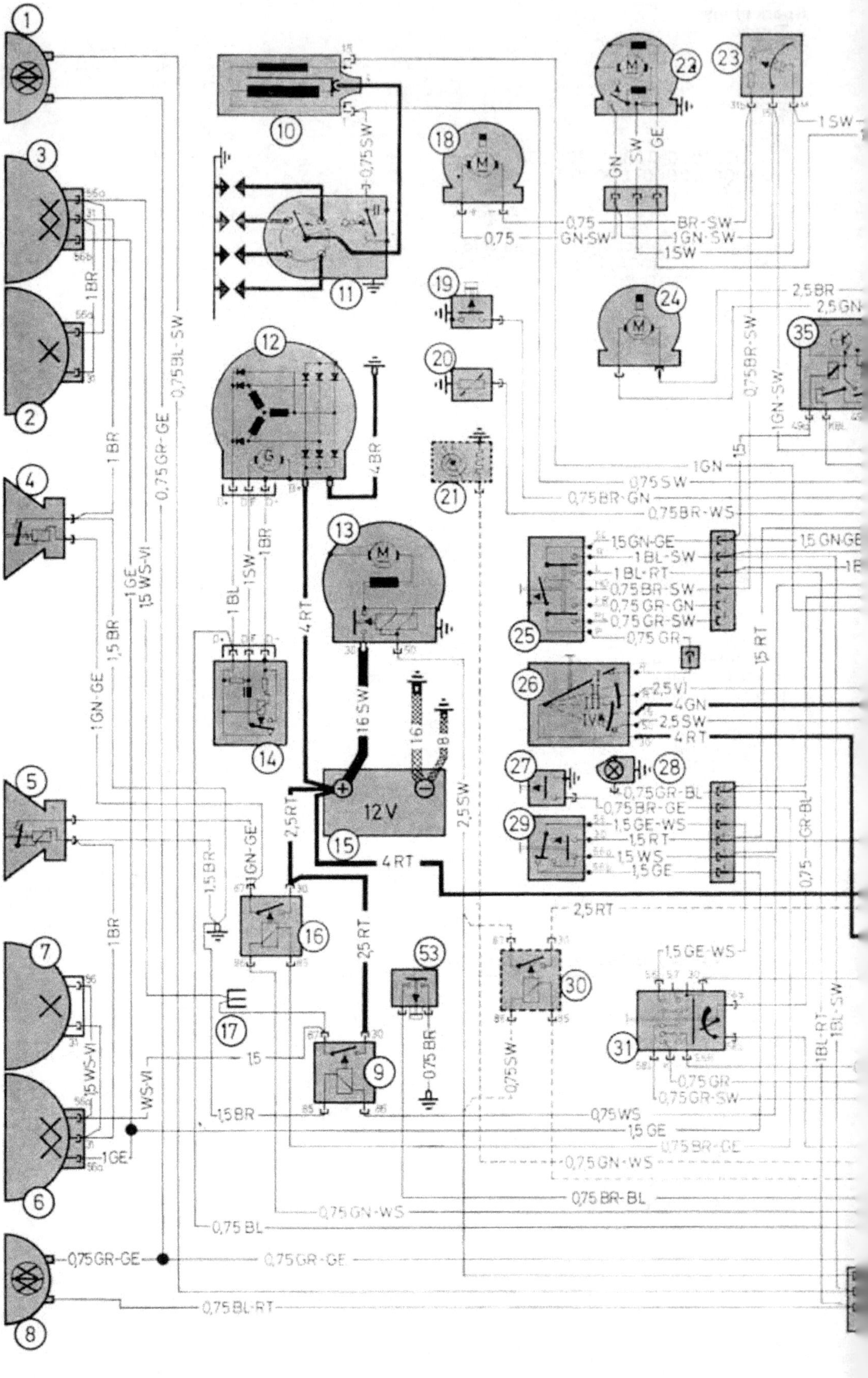

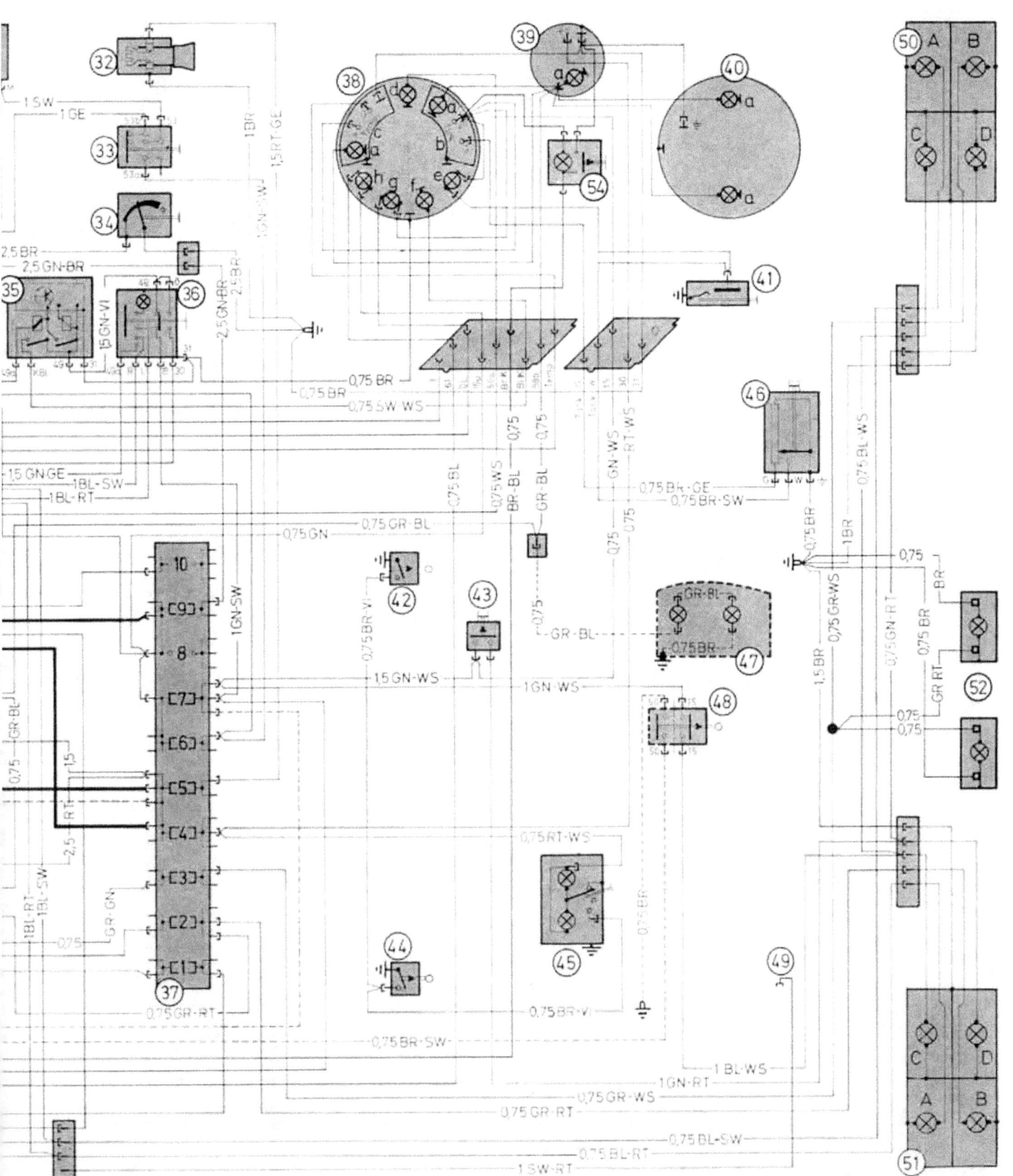

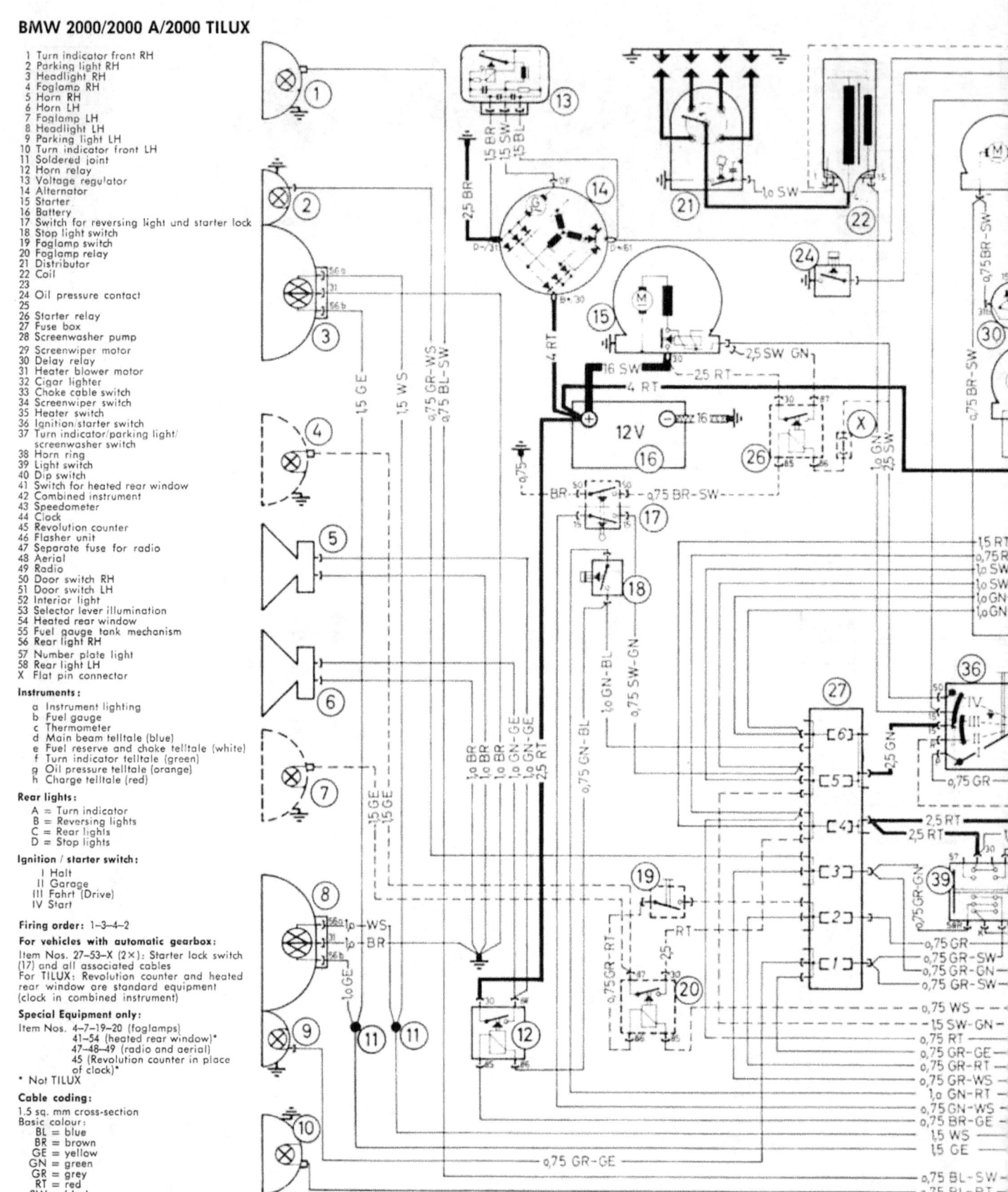

BMW 2000/2000 A/2000 TILUX

1 Turn indicator front RH
2 Parking light RH
3 Headlight RH
4 Foglamp RH
5 Horn RH
6 Horn LH
7 Foglamp LH
8 Headlight LH
9 Parking light LH
10 Turn indicator front LH
11 Soldered joint
12 Horn relay
13 Voltage regulator
14 Alternator
15 Starter
16 Battery
17 Switch for reversing light und starter lock
18 Stop light switch
19 Foglamp switch
20 Foglamp relay
21 Distributor
22 Coil
23
24 Oil pressure contact
25
26 Starter relay
27 Fuse box
28 Screenwasher pump
29 Screenwiper motor
30 Delay relay
31 Heater blower motor
32 Cigar lighter
33 Choke cable switch
34 Screenwiper switch
35 Heater switch
36 Ignition/starter switch
37 Turn indicator/parking light/ screenwasher switch
38 Horn ring
39 Light switch
40 Dip switch
41 Switch for heated rear window
42 Combined instrument
43 Speedometer
44 Clock
45 Revolution counter
46 Flasher unit
47 Separate fuse for radio
48 Aerial
49 Radio
50 Door switch RH
51 Door switch LH
52 Interior light
53 Selector lever illumination
54 Heated rear window
55 Fuel gauge tank mechanism
56 Rear light RH
57 Number plate light
58 Rear light LH
X Flat pin connector

Instruments:
a Instrument lighting
b Fuel gauge
c Thermometer
d Main beam telltale (blue)
e Fuel reserve and choke telltale (white)
f Turn indicator telltale (green)
g Oil pressure telltale (orange)
h Charge telltale (red)

Rear lights:
A = Turn indicator
B = Reversing lights
C = Rear lights
D = Stop lights

Ignition / starter switch:
I Halt
II Garage
III Fahrt (Drive)
IV Start

Firing order: 1–3–4–2

For vehicles with automatic gearbox:
Item Nos. 27–53–X (2×): Starter lock switch (17) and all associated cables
For TILUX: Revolution counter and heated rear window are standard equipment (clock in combined instrument)

Special Equipment only:
Item Nos. 4–7–19–20 (foglamps)
41–54 (heated rear window)*
47–48–49 (radio and aerial)
45 (Revolution counter in place of clock)*
* Not TILUX

Cable coding:
1.5 sq. mm cross-section
Basic colour:
BL = blue
BR = brown
GE = yellow
GN = green
GR = grey
RT = red
SW = black
WS = white

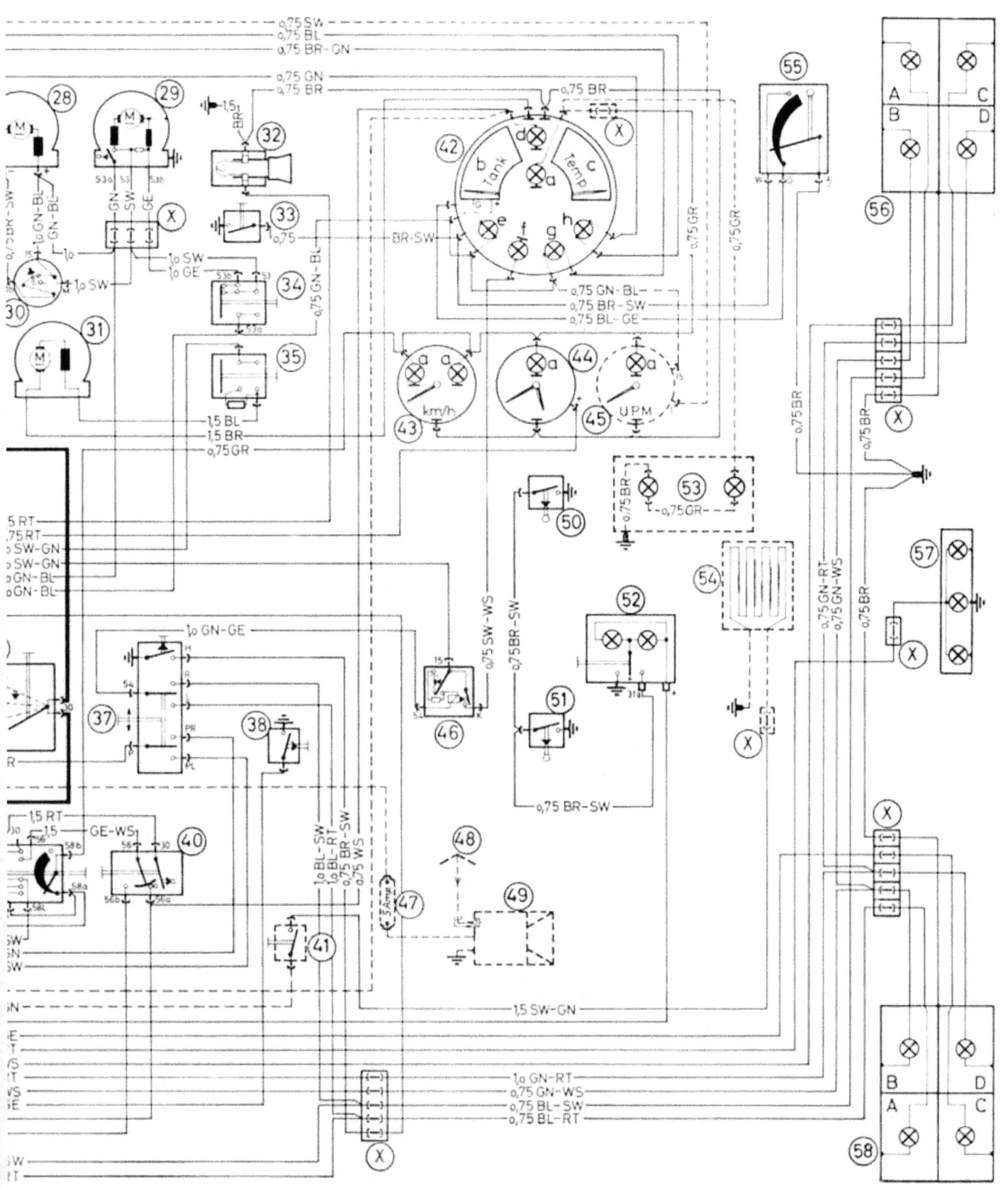

BMW 2000 RE/2000 A-RE/2000 TILUX-RE

1 Turn indicator front RH
2 Main headlight RH
3 Additional headlight (main beam) RH
4
5 Horn RH
6 Horn LH
7
8 Additional headlight (main beam) LH
9 Main headlight LH
10 Turn indicator front LH
11 Dip relay
12 Horn relay
13 Voltage regulator
14 Alternator
15 Starter
16 Battery
17 Reversing light and starter lock switch
18 Stop light switch
19
20
21 Distributor
22 Coil
23
24 Oil pressure contact
25
26 Starter relay
27 Fuse box
28 Screenwasher pump
29 Screenwiper motor
30 Delay relay
31 Heater blower motor
32 Cigar lighter
33 Choke cable switch
34 Screen wiper switch
35 Heater switch
36 Ignition/starter switch
37 Turn indicator/parking light/screenwasher switch
38 Horn ring
39 Light switch
40 Dip switch
41 Switch for heated rear window
42 Combined instrument
43 Speedometer
44 Clock
45 Revolution counter
46 Flasher unit
47 Separate fuse for radio
48 Aerial
49 Radio
50 Door switch RH
51 Door switch LH
52 Interior light
53 Selector lever illumination
54 Heated rear window
55 Fuel gauge tank mechanism
56 Rear light RH
57 Number plate light
58 Rear light LH
X Flat pin connector

Instruments:
a Instrument lighting
b Fuel gauge
c Thermometer
d Main beam telltale (blue)
e Fuel reserve and choke telltale (white)
f Turn indicator telltale (green)
g Oil pressure telltale (orange)
h Charge telltale (red)

Rear lights:
A = Turn indicator
B = Reversing lights
C = Rear lights
D = Stop lights

Ignition / starter switch:
I Halt
II Garage
III Fahrt (Drive)
IV Start

Firing order: 1-3-4-2

For vehicles with automatic gearbox:
Item. Nos. 26-53-X (2×): Starter lock switch
(17) with all associated cables

Special Equipment only:
* Standard on 2000 TILUX-RE
Item Nos. 41-54 (heated rear window)*
47-48-49 (radio and aerial)
45 (Revolution counter in place of clock)*

Cable coding:
1.5 sq. mm cross-section
Basic colour:
BL = blue
BR = brown
GE = yellow
GN = green
GR = grey
RT = red
SW = black
WS = white

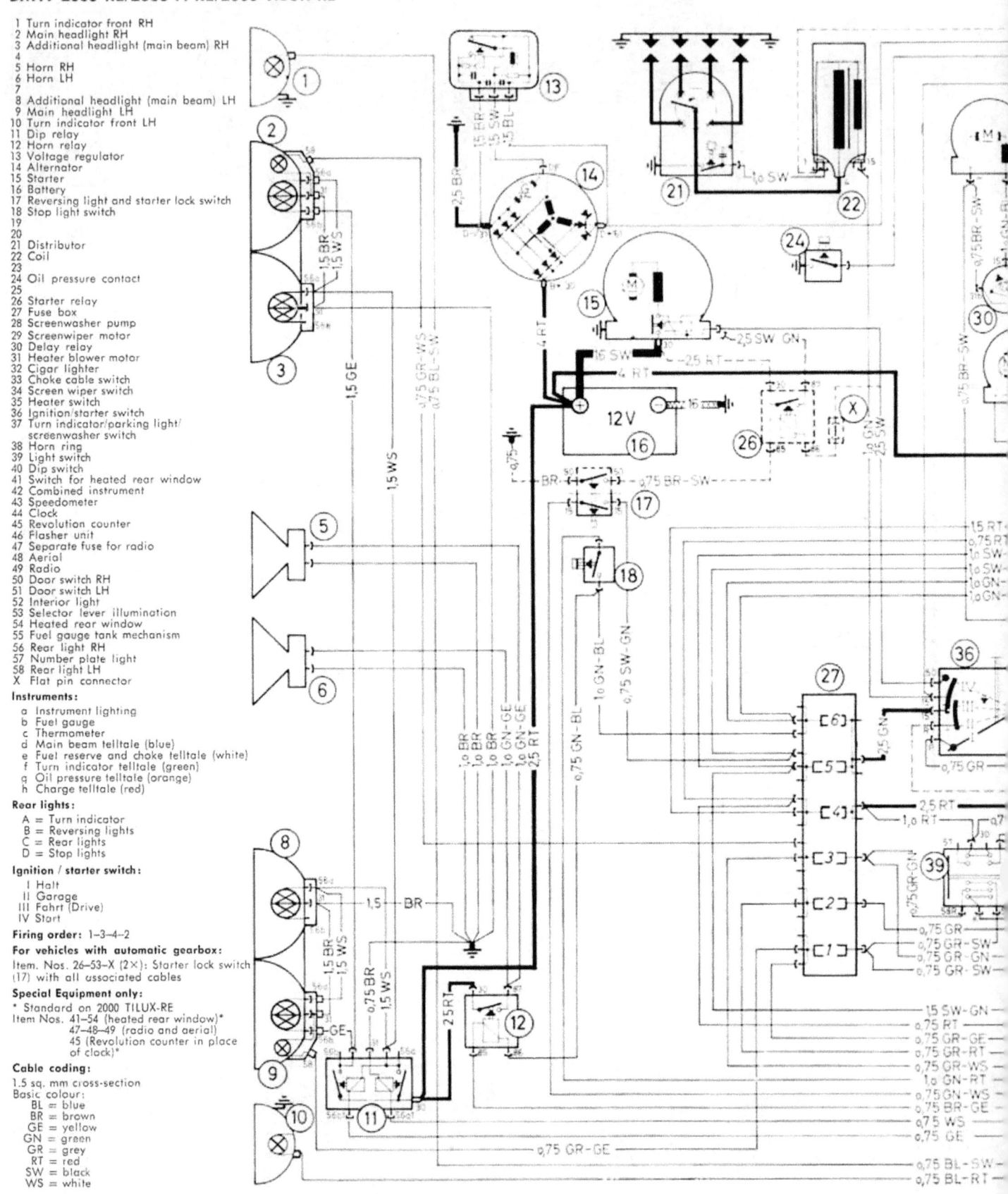

132

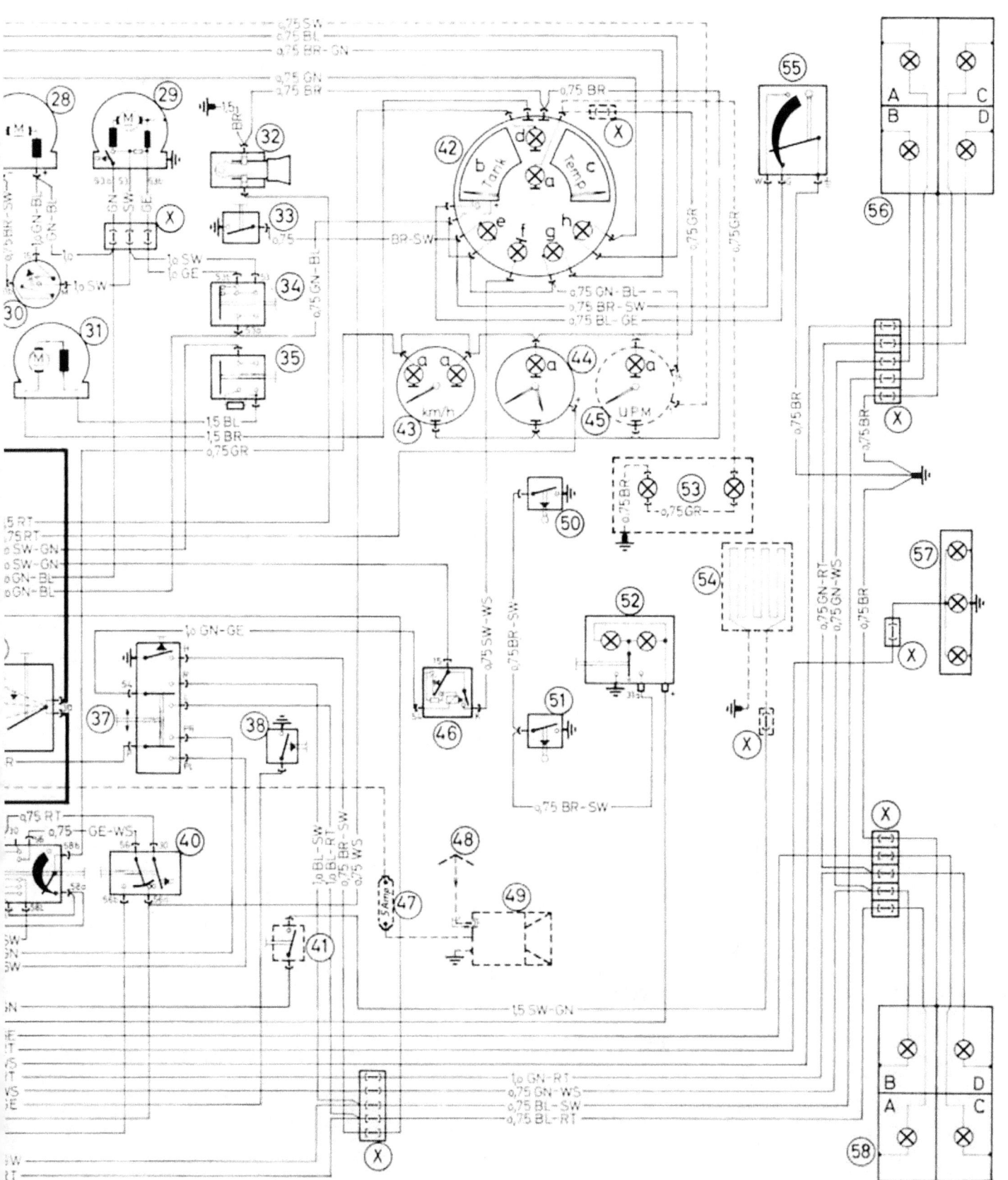

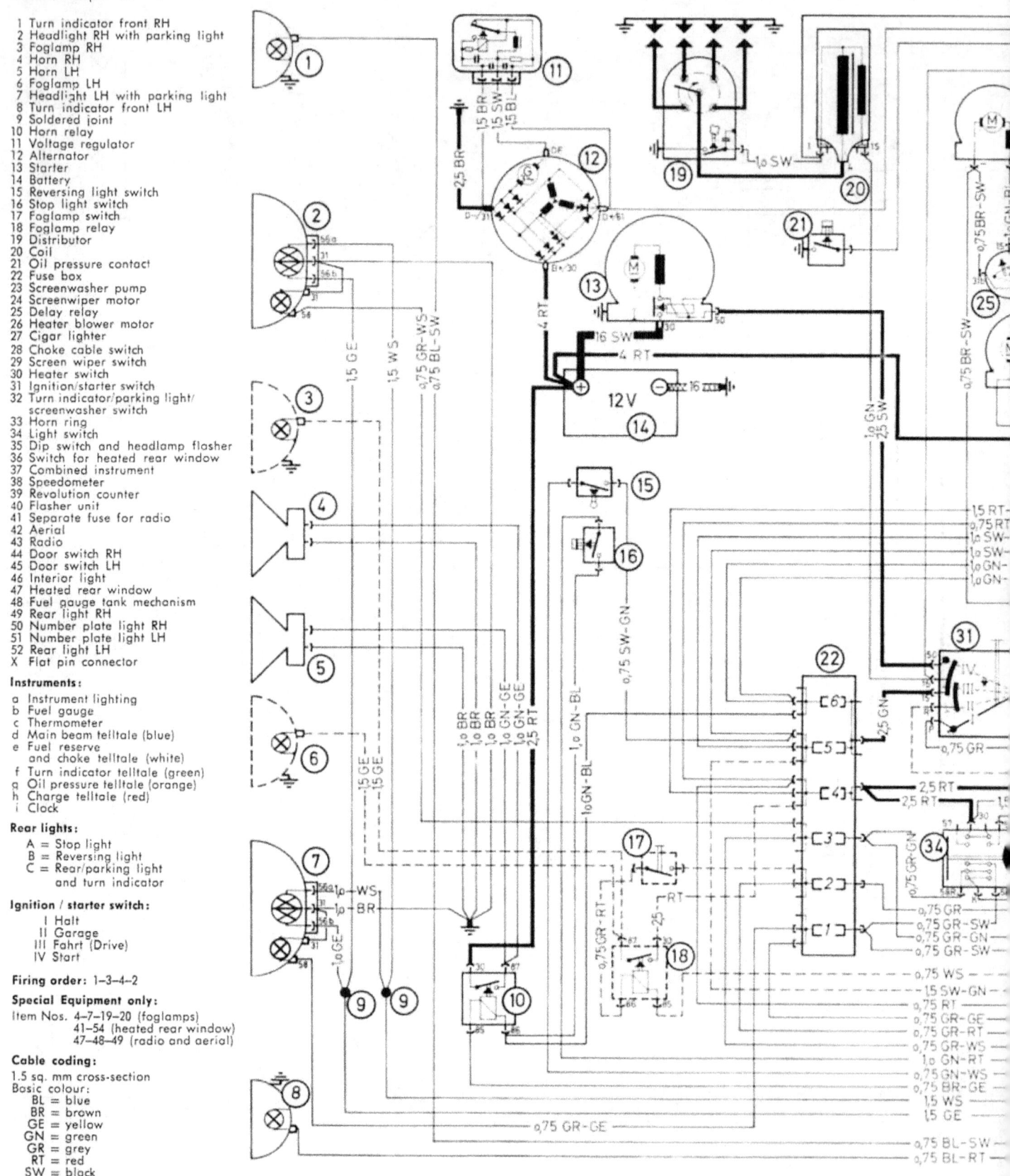

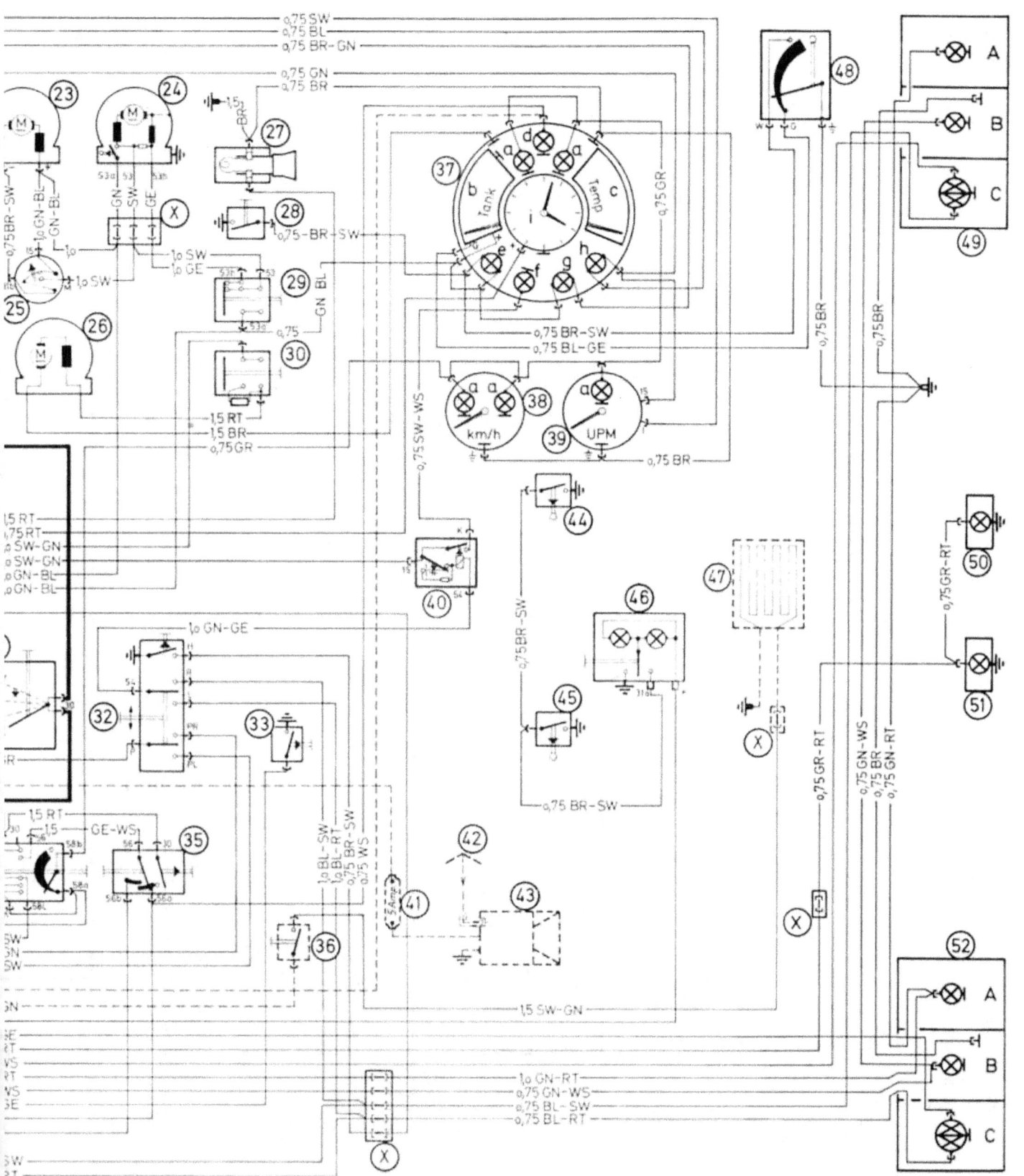

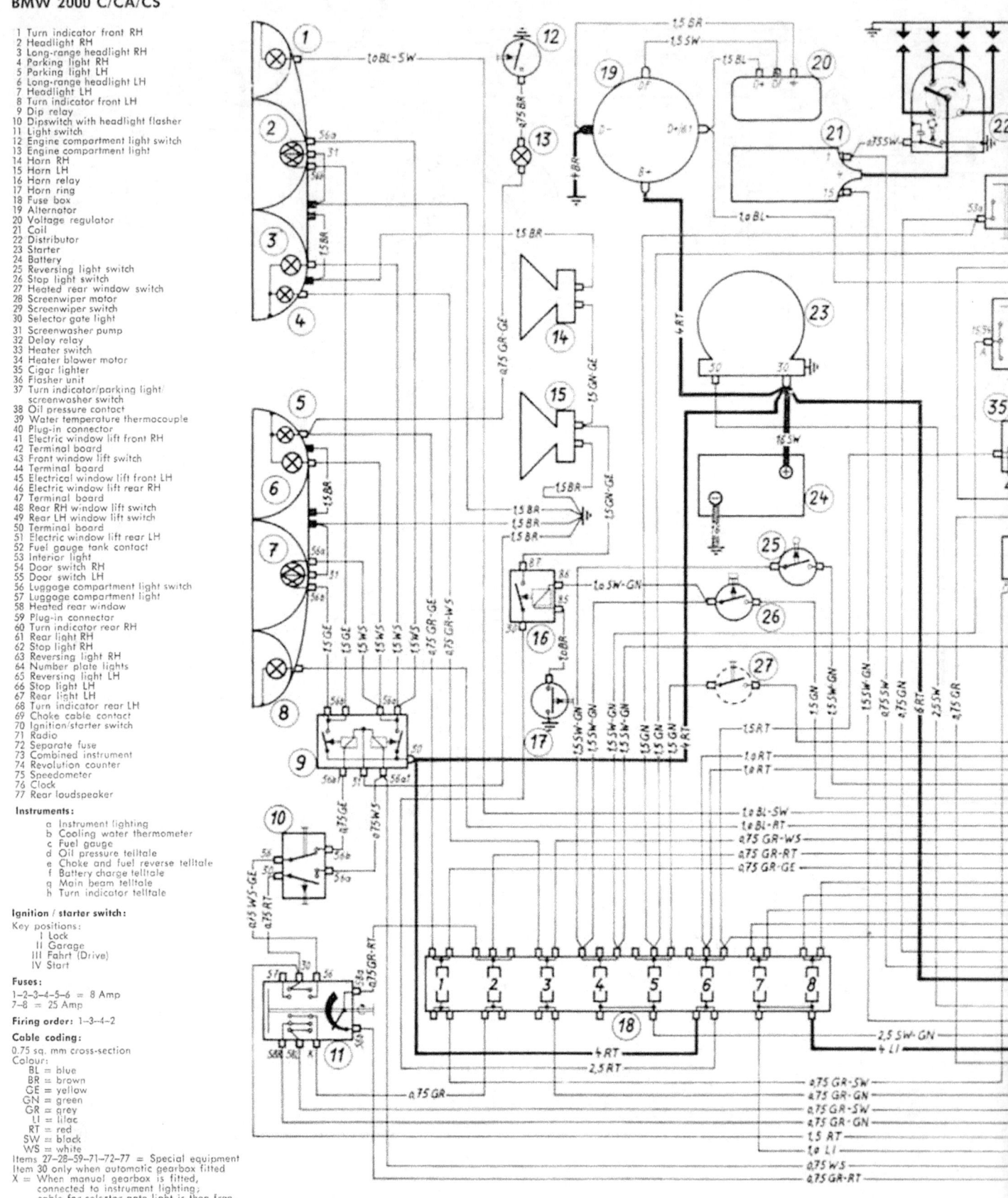

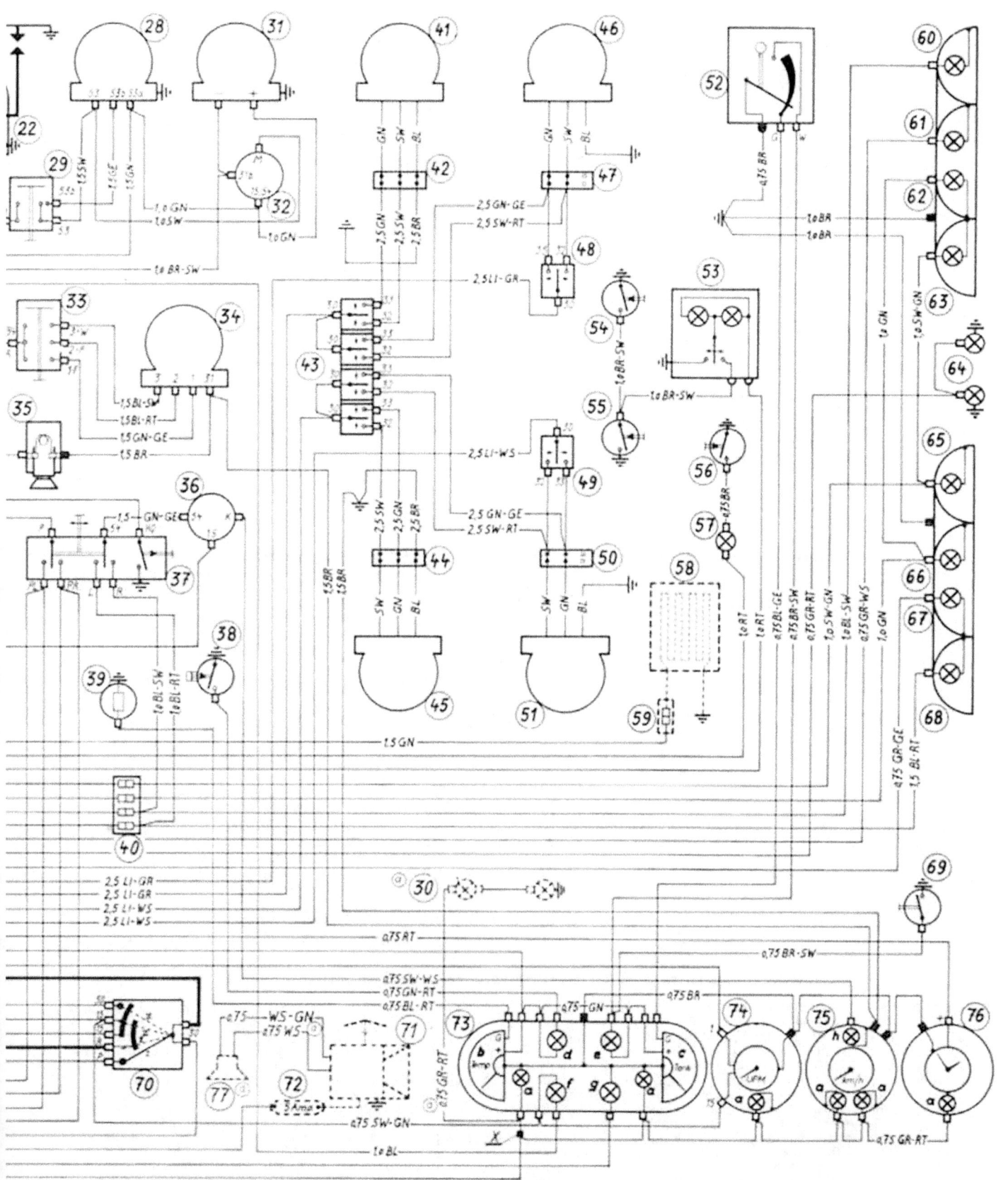

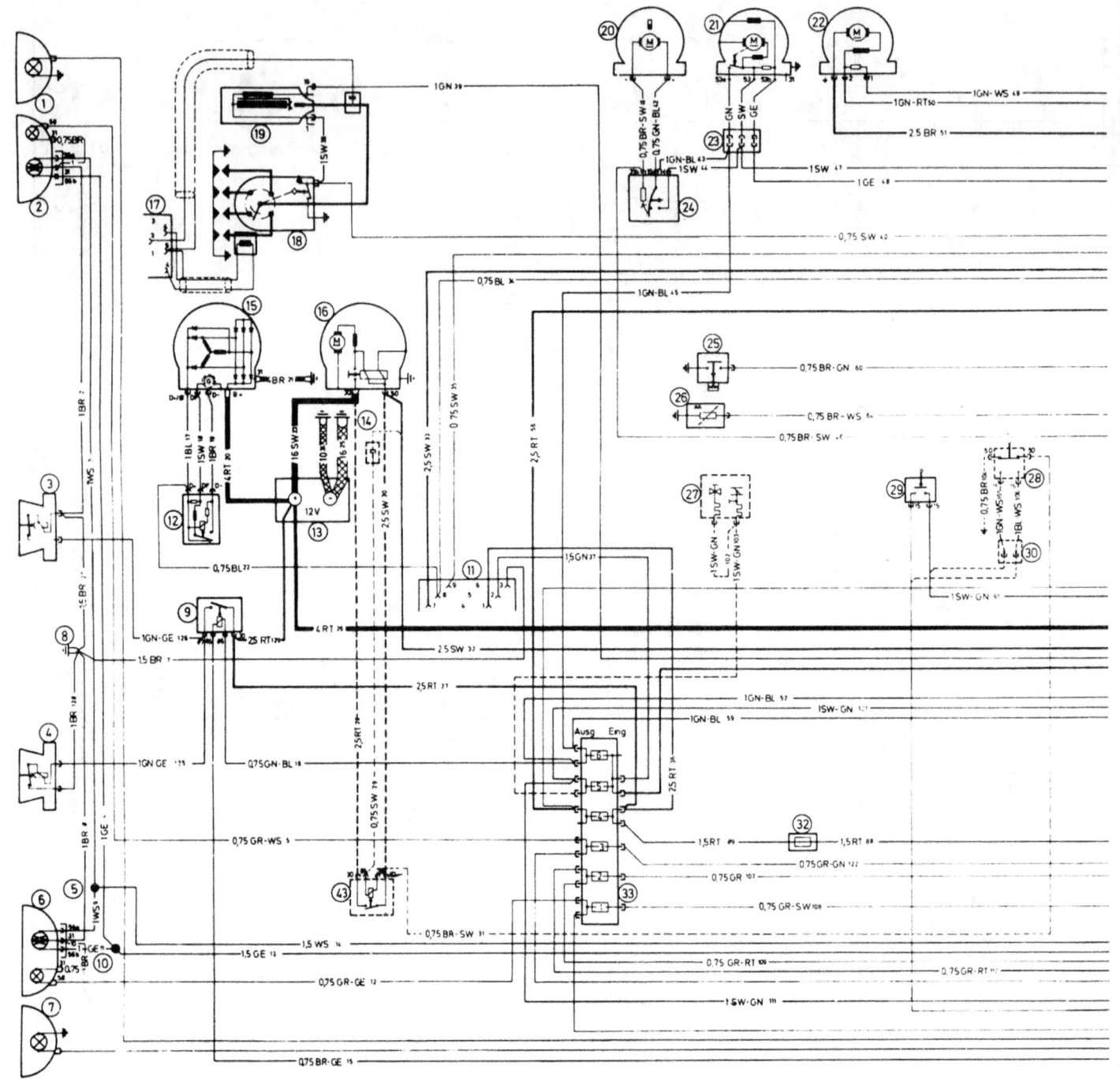

BMW 2002 from chassis No. 2.616.110, 2002 Automatic from chassis No. 2.504.463

Key to Diagram: 1 Front righthand flasher 2 Righthand headlight with parking light 3 Righthand fanfare 4 Lefthand fanfare 5 Solder point (56a) 6 Lefthand headlight with parking light 7 Front lefthand flasher 8 Earth (ground) 9 Fanfare relay 10 Solder point (56b) 11 Test equipment connection 12 Regulator 13 Battery 14 Starter relay plug connection 15 Generator 16 Starter 17 Connection for test equipment with lead and pick-up 18 Distributor 19 Ignition coil 20 Windshield washer pump 21 Windshield wiper motor 22 Blower motor 23 3-pin plug connection to wiper motor 24 Retard relay 25 Oil pressure switch 26 Remote thermometer transmitter 27 Automatic choke carburetter (only with automatic transmission) 28 Reversing light switch with starter lock 29 Reversing light switch 30 2-pin plug connection (only with automatic transmission) 32 Floating fuse 33 Fuse box 35 Earth (ground) 37 Cigar lighter 38 Wiper switch 40 Brake light switch 41 Instrument cluster 42 5-pin plug connection 43 Starter relay (only with automatic transmission) 44 Ignition switch 45 Light switch 46 Hazard flasher switch 47 4-pin plug connection 48 Turn indicator switch 50 Horn button 51 Dip switch 52 Earth (ground) 53 Lefthand door contact 54 Hazard flasher 55 Interior light 58 12-pin plug connection to instrument cluster 59 Revolution counter connection 60 Selector gate light (only with automatic transmission) 61 Fuel gauge level transmitter 62 Righthand door contact 63 Righthand rear light 64 Licence plate lights 65 Earth (ground) 66 Lefthand rear light

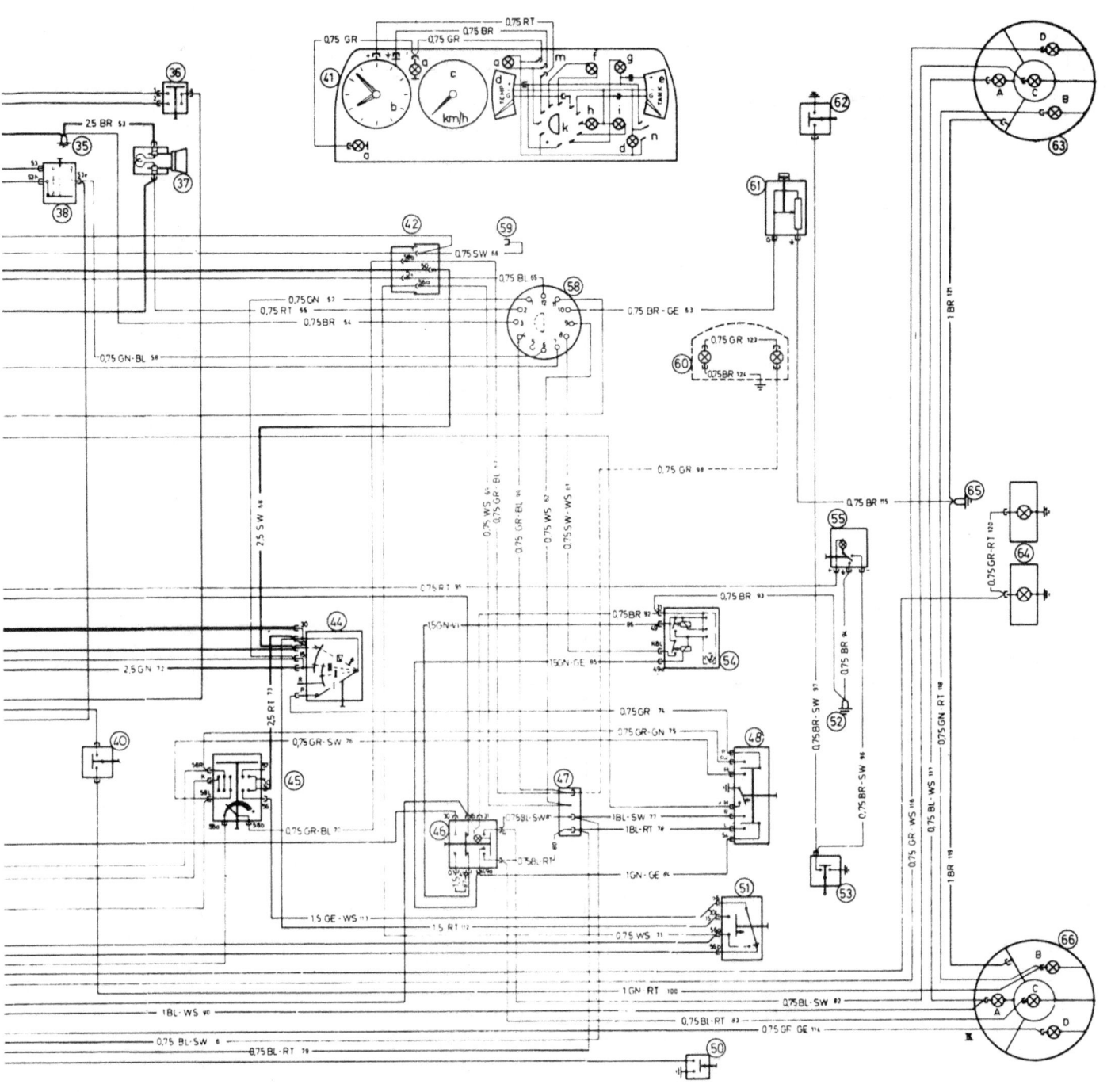

Instruments: **a** Dial illumination   **b** Clock   **c** Speedometer   **d** Coolant temperature gauge   **e** Fuel gauge   **f** Charging lamp (red)   **g** Oil pressure (orange)   **h** Headlight high beam telltale (blue)   **i** Flasher telltale (green)   **k** 12-pin plug connection   **m** 3-pin plug connection (clock)   **n** 3-pin plug connection (revolution counter)

Ignition switch: I Stop   II O   III Drive   IV Start

Righthand rear light: A Reversing light   B Brake light   C Flasher   D Tail light

Lefthand rear light: A Reversing light   B Brake light   C Flasher   D Tail light

Cable coding: BL Blue   BR Brown   GE Yellow   GN Green   GR Grey   RT Red   SW Black   VI Violet   WS White

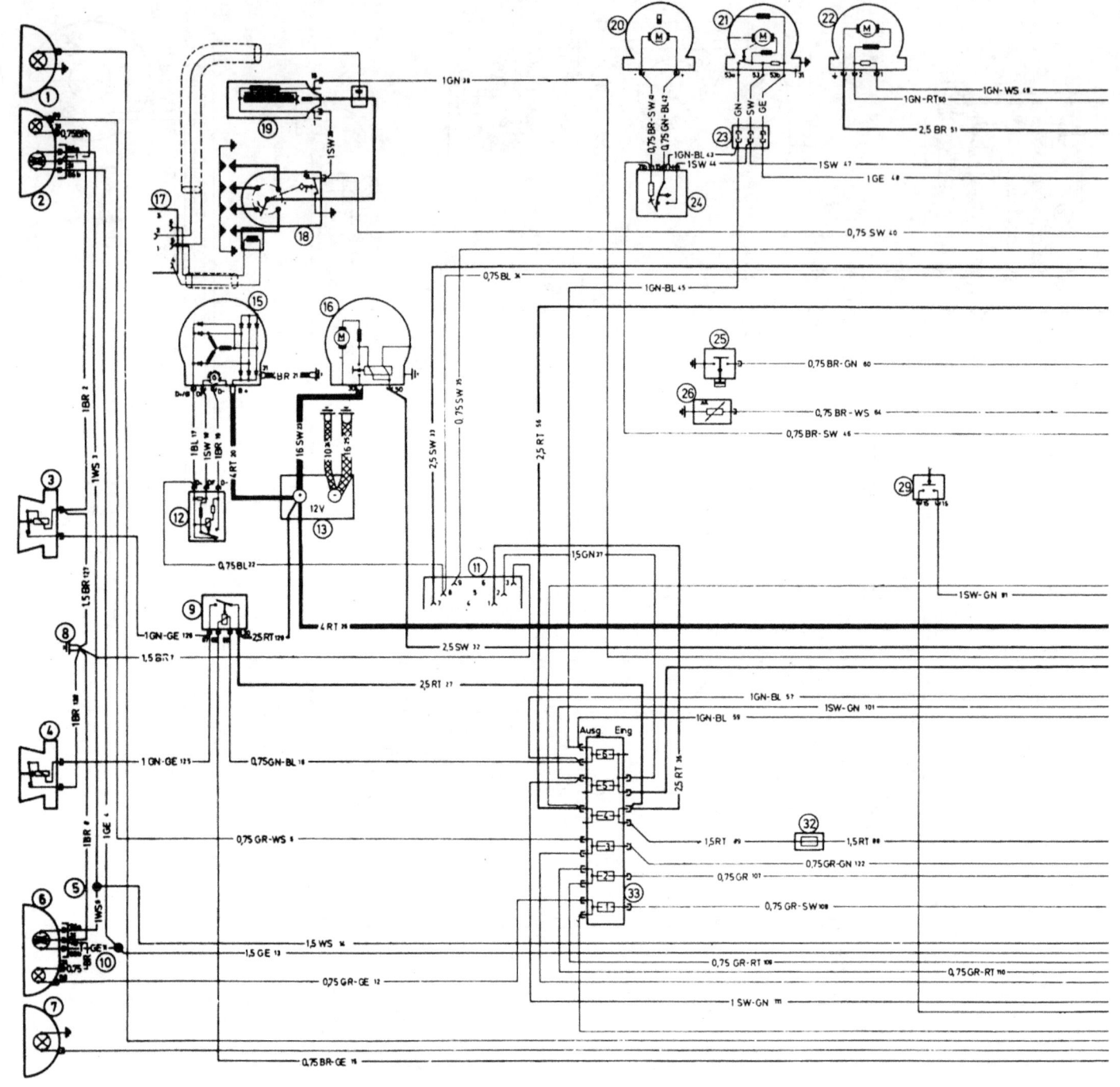

BMW 2002 TI from chassis No. 1.692.216

Key to Diagram: 1 Front righthand flasher 2 Righthand headlight with parking light 3 Righthand fanfare 4 Lefthand fanfare 5 Solder point (56a) 6 Lefthand headlight with parking light 7 Front lefthand flasher 8 Earth (ground) 9 Fanfare relay 10 Solder point (56b) 11 Test equipment connection 12 Regulator 13 Battery 15 Generator 16 Starter 17 Connection for test equipment with lead and pick-up 18 Distributor 19 Ignition coil 20 Windshield washer pump 21 Windshield wiper motor 22 Blower motor 23 3-pin plug connection to wiper motor 24 Retard relay 25 Oil pressure switch 26 Remote reading therm. transmitter 29 Reversing light switch 32 Floating fuse 33 Fuse box 35 Earth (ground) 36 Blower switch 37 Cigar lighter 38 Wiper switch 40 Brake light switch 41 Instrument set 42 5-pin plug connection 44 Ignition switch 45 Light switch 46 Hazard flasher switch 47 4-pin plug connection 48 Turn indicator switch 50 Horn button 51 Dip switch 52 Earth (ground) 53 Lefthand door contact 54 Hazard flasher 55 Interior light 58 12-pin plug connection to instrument cluster 59 Clock 61 Fuel gauge transmitter 62 Righthand door contact 63 Righthand rear light 64 Number plate lights 65 Earth (ground) 66 Lefthand rear light

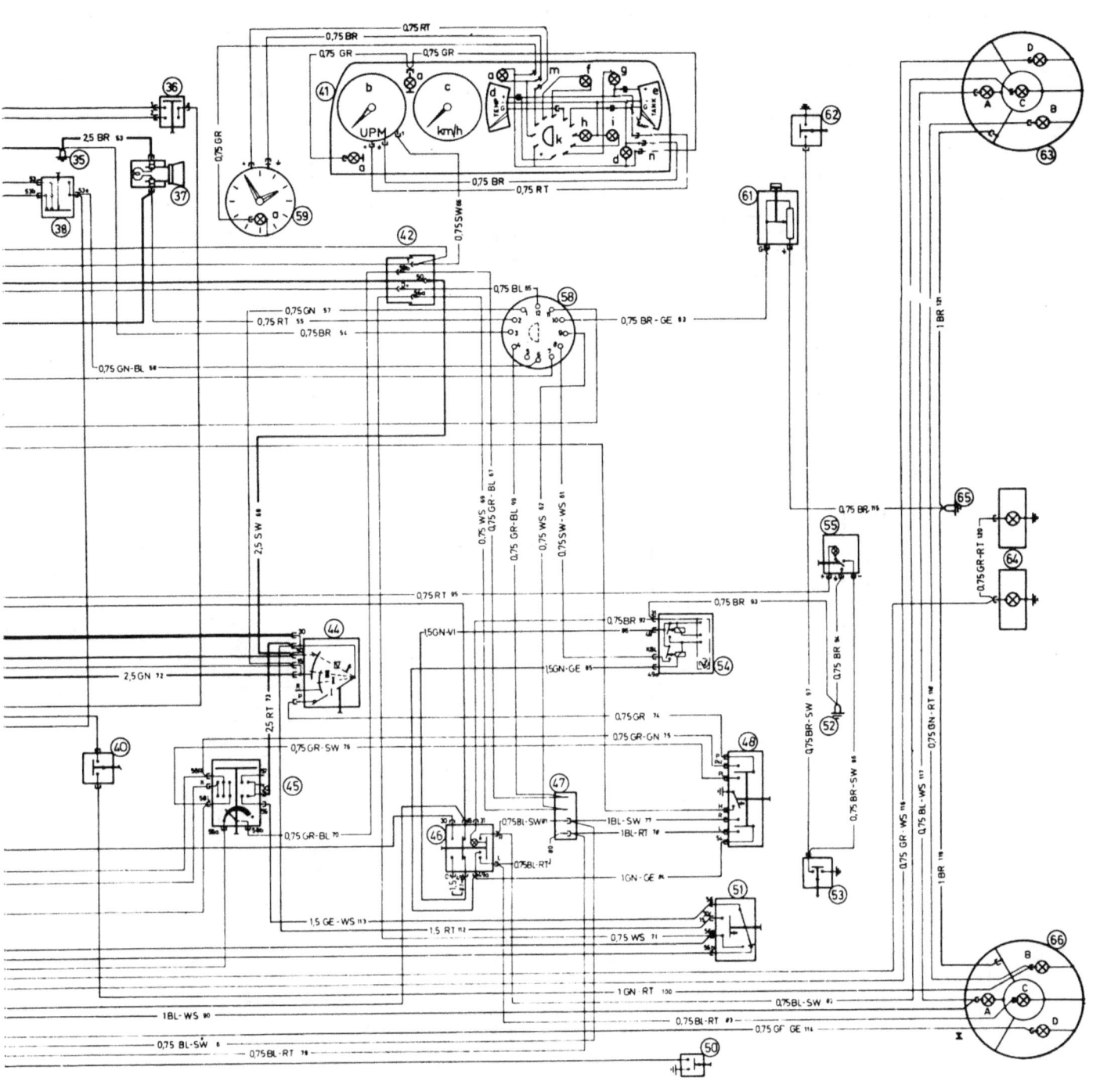

Instruments: **a** Illuminated scale   **b** Revolution counter   **c** Speedometer   **d** Coolant temperature gauge   **e** Fuel gauge   **f** Charging lamp (red)   **g** Oil pressure control (orange)   **h** Headlight beam control (blue)   **i** Flasher control (green)   **k** 12-pin plug connection   **m** 3-pin plug connection (clock)   **n** 3-pin plug (revolution counter)

Ignition switch: **I** Stop   **II** 0   **III** Drive   **IV** Start

Righthand rear light: **A** Reversing light   **B** Brake light   **C** Flasher   **D** Tail light

Lefthand rear light: **A** Reversing light   **B** Brake light   **C** Flasher   **D** Tail light

Cable coding: **BL** Blue   **BR** Brown   **GE** Yellow   **GN** Green   **GR** Grey   **RT** Red   **SW** Black   **VI** Violet   **WS** White

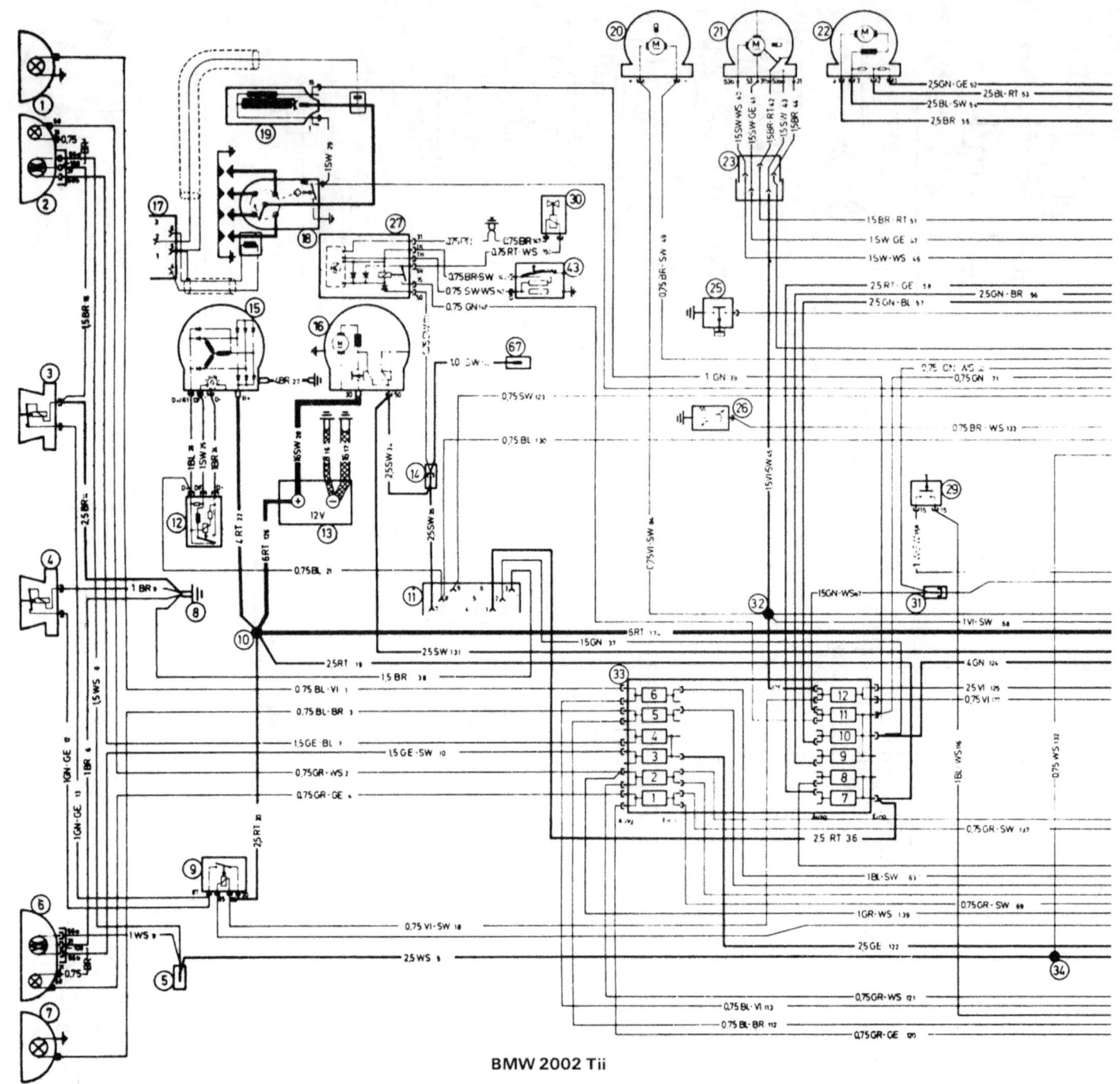

BMW 2002 Tii

Key to Diagram: 1 Front righthand flasher   2 Righthand headlight with parking light   3 Righthand fanfare   4 Lefthand fanfare   5 Fog lamp relay connection   6 Lefthand headlight with parking light   7 Front lefthand flasher   8 Earth (ground)   9 Fanfare relay   10 Solder point   11 Test equipment connection   12 Regulator   13 Battery   14 Connection for electrical system   15 Generator   16 Starter   17 Test equipment connection with lead and pick-up   18 Distributor   19 Ignition coil   20 Windshield washer pump   21 Windshield wiper motor   22 Blower motor   23 5-pin plug to wiper motor   24 Connection for radio   25 Oil pressure switch   26 Remote thermometer transitter   27 Time switch   29 Reversing light switch   30 Starting valve   31 Fuel pump connection   32 Solder point   33 Fuse box   34 Solder point   35 Earth (ground)   36 Blower switch   37 Cigar lighter   38 Wiper speed switch   39 Wiper/washer transmitter   40 Brake light switch   41 Instrument cluster   42 5-pin plug terminal   43 Temperature time switch   44 Ignition switch   45 Light switch   46 Hazard flasher switch   47 9-pin plug to turn indicator switch   48 Turn indicator switch   49 6-pin plug to dip switch   50 Signal button   51 Dip switch   52 Number plate light and fog lamp connection   53 Lefthand door contact   54 Hazard flasher   55 Interior light   56 Connection for heated rear window   57 Selector lever light connection   58 12-pin plug to instrument cluster   59 Heated rear window (SA)   60 Handbrake switch   61 Fuel gauge transmitter   62 Righthand door contact   63 Righthand rear light   64 Number plate light   65 Earth (ground)   66 Lefthand rear light   67 HT ignition system connection   68 Fuel pump   69 Plug connection to fuel pump   70 Clock   71 Choke connection   72 Solder point

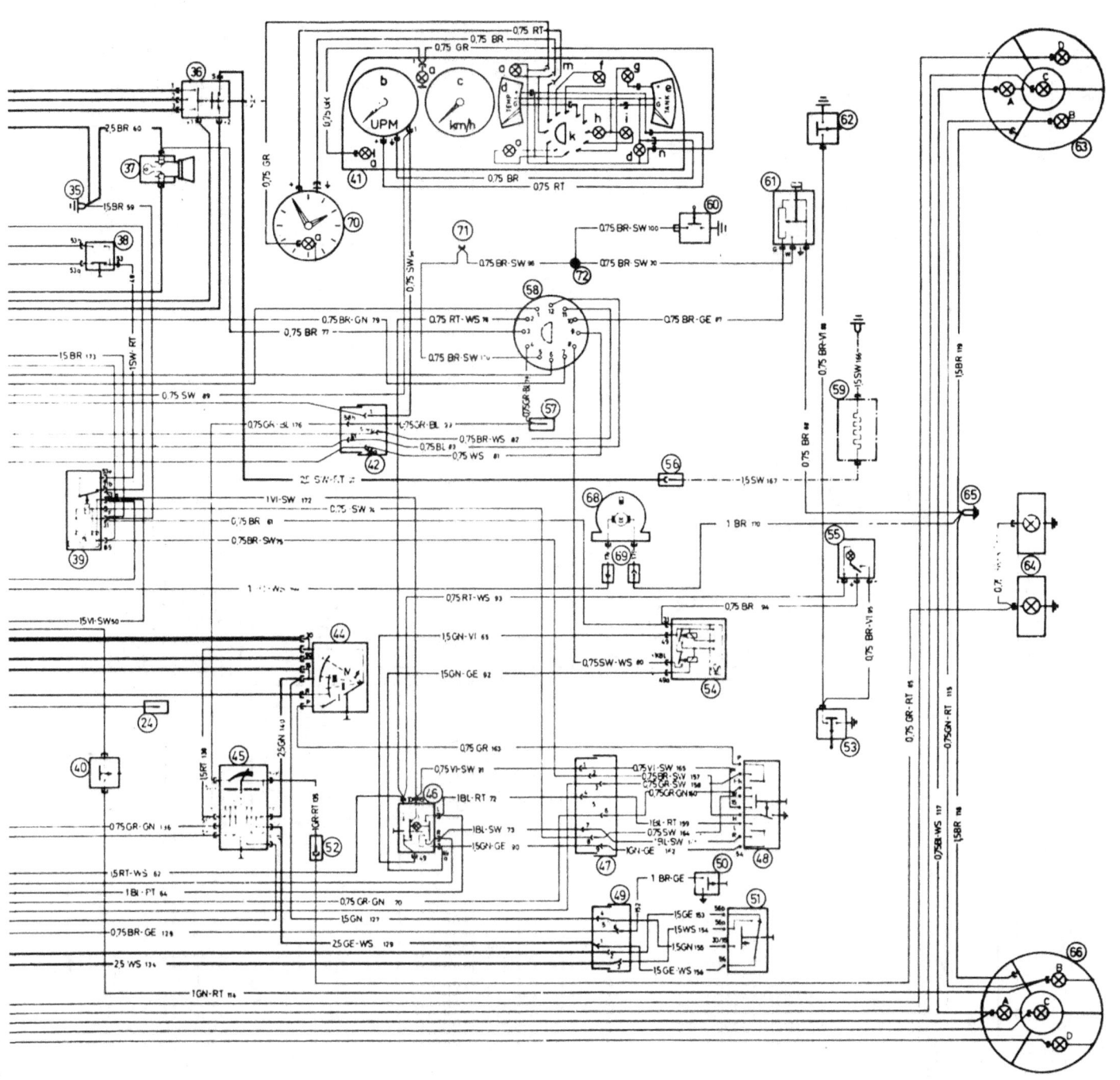

Instruments: **a** Illuminated scale   **b** Revolution counter   **c** Speedometer   **d** Coolant temperature gauge   **e** Fuel gauge   **f** Charging lamp (red)   **g** Oil pressure switch (orange)   **h** High beam telltale (blue)   **i** Flasher control (green)   **k** 12-pin plug   **m** 3-pin plug (clock)   **n** 3-pin plug (revolution counter)   **o** Central control lamp (choke, handbrake, petrol)

Ignition switch: I Off   II 0   III On   IV Start

Righthand rear light: A Reversing light   B Brake light   C Flasher   D Tail light

Lefthand rear light: A Reversing light   B Brake light   C Flasher   D Tail light

Cable coding: **BL** Blue   **BR** Brown   **GE** Yellow   **GN** Green   **GR** Grey   **RT** Red   **SW** Black   **VI** Violet   **WS** White

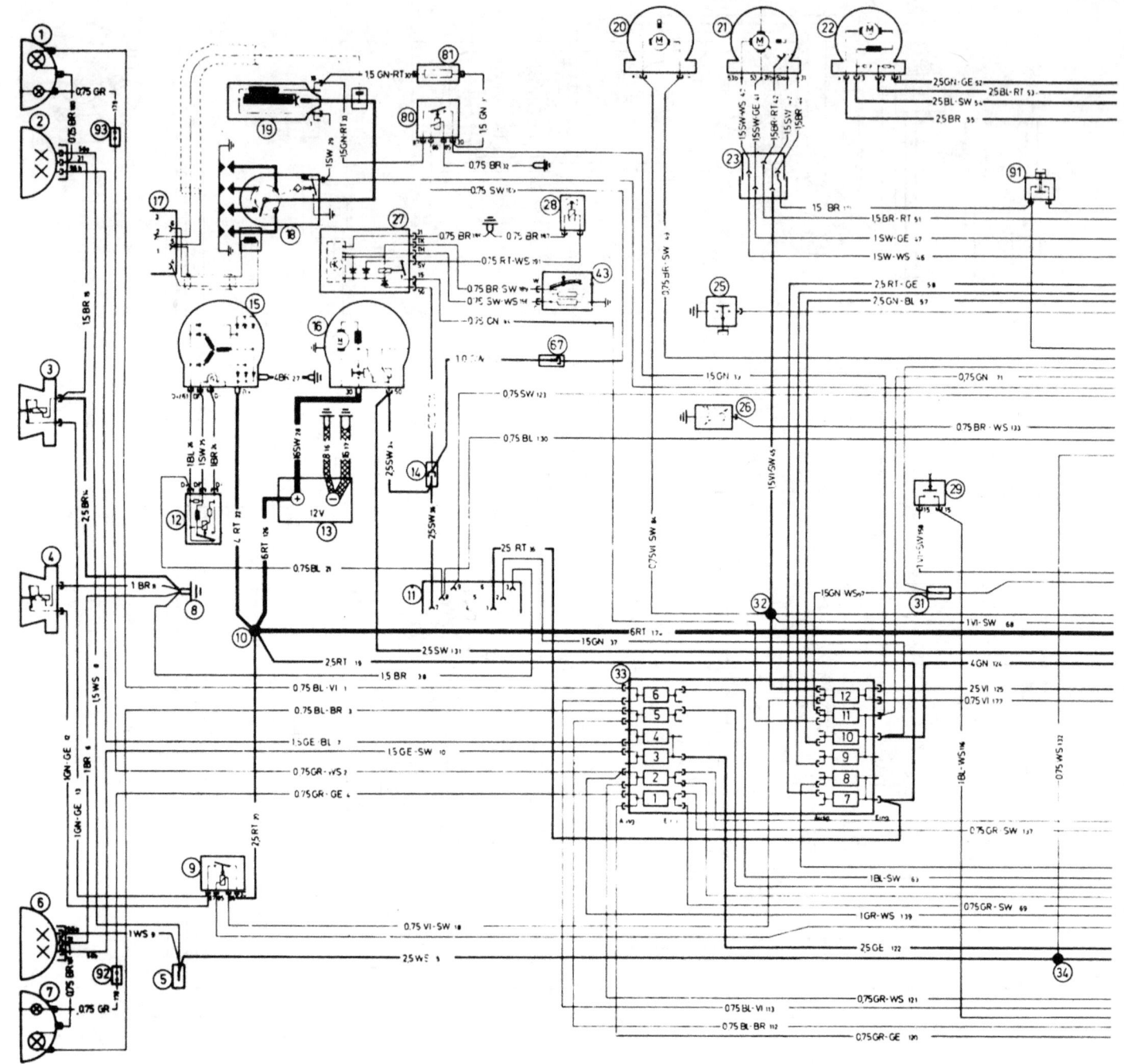

BMW 2002 Tii USA

Key to Diagram: 1 Front righthand flasher with parking light 2 Righthand headlight 3 Righthand fanfare 4 Lefthand fanfare 5 Fog lamp relay connection 6 Lefthand headlight 7 Front lefthand flasher with parking light 8 Earth (ground) 9 Fanfare relay 10 Solder point 11 Test equipment connection 12 Regulator 13 Battery 14 Connection for electrical equipment 15 Generator 16 Starter 17 Test equipment connection with lead and pick-up 18 Distributor 19 Ignition coil 20 Windshield washer pump 21 Windshield wiper motor 22 Blower motor 23 5-pin plug terminal to wiper motor 24 Radio connection 25 Oil pressure switch 26 Remote reading thermometer transmitter 27 Time switch 28 Starting valve 29 Reversing light switch 31 Fuel pump connection 32 Solder point 33 Fuse box 34 Solder point 35 Earth (ground) 36 Blower switch 37 Cigar lighter 38 Wiper speed switch 39 Wiper/washer transmitter 40 Brake light switch 41 Instrument cluster 42 5-pin plug terminal 43 Temperature time switch 44 Ignition switch 45 Light switch 46 Hazard flasher switch 47 9-pin plug terminal to turn indicator switch 48 Turn indicator switch 49 6-pin plug terminal to dip switch 50 Signal button 51 Dip switch 52 Number plate light and fog lamp connection 53 Door double contactor 54 Hazard flasher 55 Interior light 56 Heated rear window connection 57 Selector lever light connection 58 12-pin plug terminal to instrument cluster 59 Heated rear window 61 Fuel gauge transmitter 62 Door contact 63 Righthand rear light 64 Number plate lights 65 Earth (ground) 66 Lefthand rear light 67 HT ignition system connection 68 Fuel pump 69 Fuel pump plug connection

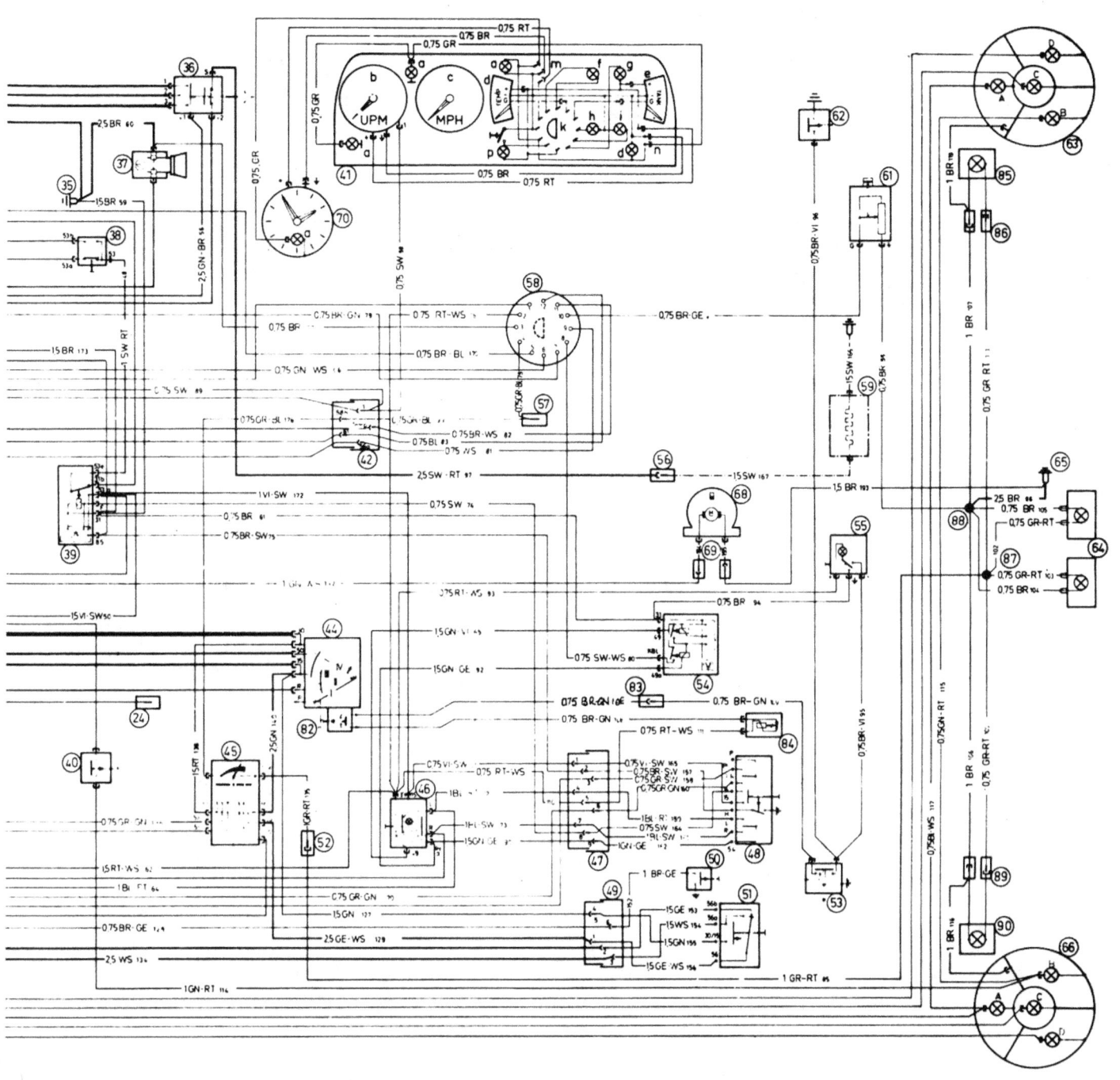

70 Clock	80 HT ignition system relay	81 Series resistance	82 Buzzer contact	83 Buzzer contact connection
84 Buzzer	85 Righthand side marker light	86 Righthand side marker light connection	87 Solder point (58K)	88 Solder point (31)
89 Lefthand side marker light connection	90 Lefthand side marker light	91 Brake fluid level switch	92 Cable connector	93 Cable connector

Instruments: **a** Illuminated scale **b** Revolution counter **c** Speedometer **d** Coolant temperature gauge **e** Fuel gauge **f** Charging lamp (red) **g** Oil pressure telltale (orange) **h** High beam telltale (blue) **i** Flasher telltale (green) **k** 12-pin plug **m** 3-pin plug (clock) **n** 3-pin plug (revolution counter) **p** Brake fluid control (red)

Ignition switch: I Off   II 0   III On   IV Start

Righthand rear light: A Reversing light   B Brake light   C Flasher   D Tail light

Lefthand rear light: A Reversing light   B Brake light   C Flasher   D Tail light

Cable coding: **BL** Blue   **BR** Brown   **GE** Yellow   **GN** Green   **GR** Grey   **RT** Red   **SW** Black   **VI** Violet

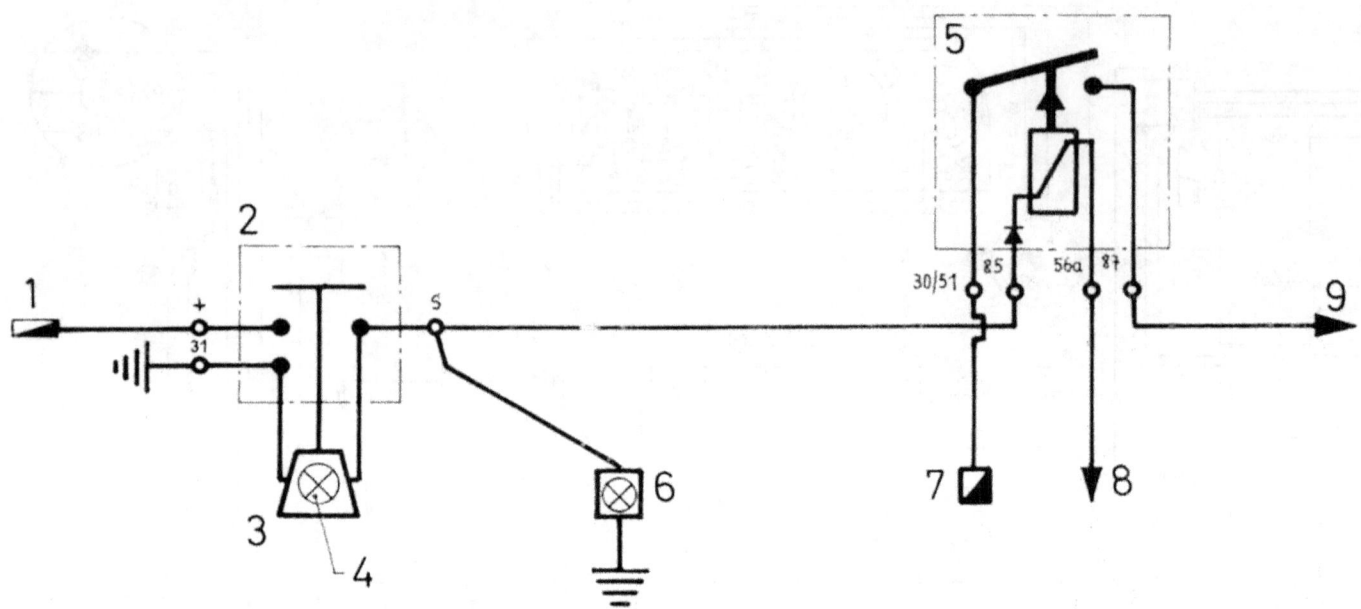

Wiring diagram for rear fog warning lights in conjunction with 12 Volt foglamps.

1. Fuse 2
2. Switch
3. Knob with telltale
4. Valve base bulb
5. Relay
6. Foglamp
7. Fuse 4
8. to main beam telltale
9. to foglamp

CHAPTER 12

BODYWORK

12 : 1 Bodywork & accident repairs
12 : 2 Front door removing & refitting
12 : 3 Rear door removing & refitting
12 : 4 Front & rear windshield removing & refitting
12 : 5 Bonnet removing & refitting
12 : 6 Boot lid removing & refitting
12 : 7 Heated rear windshield
12 : 8 Sun roof removing & refitting
12 : 9 Heater removing & refitting

12 : 1 Bodywork & accident repairs

Large scale repairs to body panels are best left to expert panel beaters. Even small dents can be tricky, as too much hammering will stretch the metal and make things worse instead of better. Filling minor dents and scratches is probably the best method of restoring the surface. The touching up of paintwork is well within the powers of most car owners particularly as self-spraying cans of paint in the correct colours are now readily available. It must be recommended, however, that paint changes colour with age and it is better to spray a whole wing rather than try to touch-up a small area.

Before spraying it is essential to remove all traces of wax polish with white spirit. More drastic treatment is required if silicone polishes have been applied. Use a primer surface or paste stopper according to the amount of filling required, and when it is dry, rub it down with 400 grade 'Wet or dry' paper until the surface is smooth, and flush with the surrounding area. Spend time on getting the best finish as this will control the final effect. Apply retouching paint, keeping it wet in the centre and light and dry round the edges.

After a few hours of drying, use a cutting compound to remove the dry spray and finish with a liquid polish.

12 : 2 Front door removing & refitting

Removal:
2000 models:
1 Mark the original position of the door hinges on the door pillar by marking the outline in pencil.
2 Using a chisel remove the lower flared end of the rivet of the door check strap and drive upwards the rivet body using a parallel pin punch.
3 With the assistance of a second operator take the weight of the door from the hinges and remove the upper and lower hinge retaining screws to the door pillar. Gently ease outwards the lower hinge and lift away the door assembly.

2002 models:
1 Remove door trim as explained later.
2 Remove Acella sheet as necessary.
3 Remove the door check strap pin.
4 Half open the door window.
5 Mark the position of the hinges.
6 Remove the six bolts and withdraw the door.

Refitting:
Refitting the door is the reverse procedure to removal. Ensure that the hinges are correctly aligned with the pencil marks previously made before final tightening. Always fit a new rivet with its head uppermost and pein over the lower end so that it does not work loose.

Adjustment:
2000 models:
Should difficulty be experienced in closing the door satisfactorily it should be correctly adjusted as follows:
1 Slacken the six retaining screws from the top and bottom hinges on the door pillar and adjust the position of the leading edge of the door inwards or outwards as required.
2 Slacken the three door catch screws and using a soft-faced hammer gently tap the door catch either inwards or outwards as required to give the required door closing action. It is important that the height of the door catch is not altered otherwise this will cause excessive strain on the catch mechanism.
3 Remove the inside door trim panel as detailed later in this section and carefully ease back the lining sheet from the apertures in the door panel.
4 Slacken the hinge clamp bolts 10 to 15 as shown in **FIG 12 : 1** and adjust the overall door clearance to ensure that it is correctly located in its position relative to the remainder of the body and also that the front and rear doors are in perfect alignment.

2002 models:
1 Remove the door trim as explained later.
2 Remove Acello sheet as necessary.
3 Half open the door window.
4 Loosen the hinge bolts and adjust the door backwards or forwards as necessary.
5 Loosen the four screws on the door lock striker and adjust as necessary.

When correctly fitted the door must be flush with the side panel. Adjust the door window glass if necessary as explained later.

Door interior trim panel:
To remove the door trim panel proceed as follows:
1 Unscrew the door safety lock button. Using a piece of bent wire insert this behind the hole 'B' (see **FIG 12 : 2**) and push out the coverplate 2. Remove the hand wheel clamp screw and washer if fitted and lift away the operating knob.
2 Push the coverplate of the window crank away from the handle using a screwdriver and lift away. Remove the window crank clamp screw and lift away the crank.
3 On 2002 models press off the cover of the door handle at rear and lift out forwards. On all models remove the clamp screw on the inside door handle and carefully pull off the door handle.
4 On 2000 models, remove the two armrest clamp screws and swing the armrest forwards pulling clear from the door lining panel. On 2002 models remove the coverplate screw and lift out the coverplate. Remove the two screws under the coverplate and the two bottom screws and lift off the armrest.

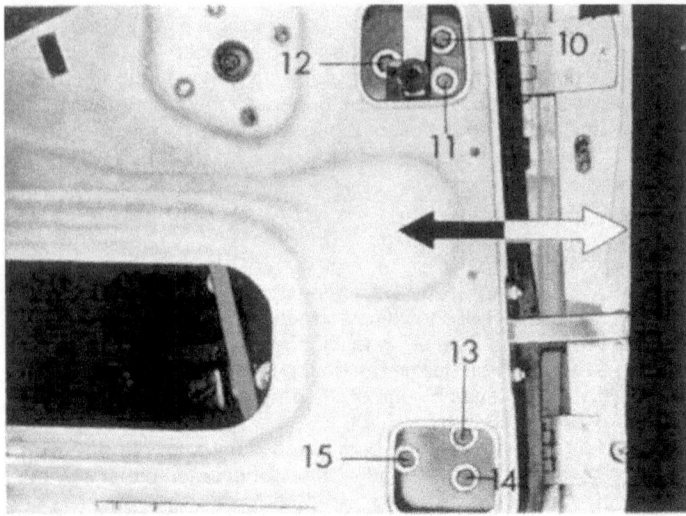

FIG 12:1 Front door hinge retaining bolts location

FIG 12:2 Pivoted quarter light hand wheel removal

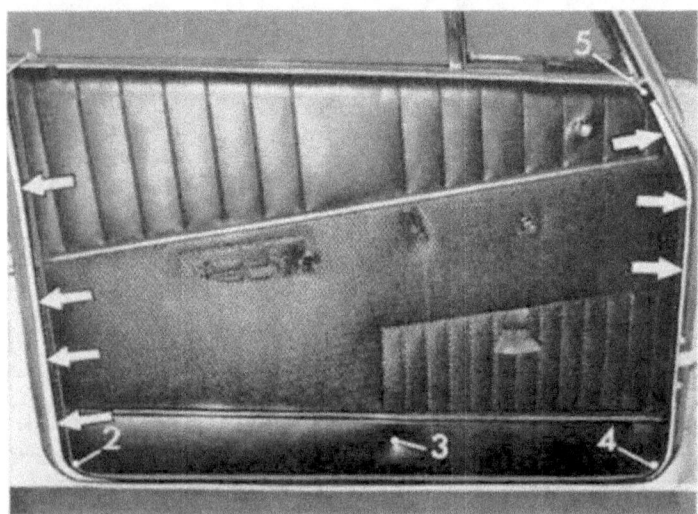

FIG 12:3 Front door trim clip & retaining screw location

5 On 2000 models, remove the five door lining fastening screws and ease the door lining away from the door using a wide blade screwdriver as a lever. The locations for the clips are shown by the arrows in **FIG 12:3**. On 2002 models lift the lining panel out of the bottom clips and remove upwards. Remove springs of window crank and hand wheel.

6 Reassembly is the reverse procedure to dismantling. The small end of the conical spring on the inside door handle on 2000 models should face towards the door, on 2002 models the larger coil diameter faces the door. When refitting the window crank on 2000 models ensure that the window is closed and the crank handle should point towards the armrest. On 2002 models do not forget the coverplate between the inner door handle and the lining panel, the knob on the window crank must point downwards.

Door glass:

2000 models:

To remove the door glass from the door proceed as follows:

1 Remove the door lining trim as previously described and also the lining sheet.
2 Carefully ease away the door weather strip from around the window frame and using a pencil mark the position of the window frame.
3 Loosen the window frame clamp bolts 1 to 6 (see **FIG 12:4**), and carefully wind the window down and release the breast rail 10 (see **FIG 12:5**). Mark the location of the spacer tabs between the door and the window frame with a pencil.
4 Using a wide blade screwdriver, carefully ease out the rubber seal and also the cover rail. Detach the window rail clamp bolts 13 and 14 (see **FIG 12:6**), from the holder 15. Carefully lift the window frame from the door by tilting to one side and disconnecting the window raising arm from the window rail.
5 Should it be necessary to fit a new glass remove all traces of old glass and coat the inside and outside surfaces of the sealing strip with Terokal 503 adhesive. Press in the new window glass and sealing strip into the thoroughly cleaned window rail ensuring that the clearance between the window rail and the front edge of the door glass is approximately $\frac{7}{8}$ inch.
6 Reassembly is the reverse procedure to dismantling. It should be noted that the window rail should be correctly located between the two plastic guide washers as shown in **FIG 12:7**. Terokal 2444 is recommended for re-attaching the door lining sheet and also the door weather strip.

Adjust the window and window frame as detailed in the following section.

2002 models:

1 Starting at the rear tap out the window well cover rail using a wedge of hardwood (see **FIG 12:8**).
2 Remove door trim panel as already described.
3 Disengage the retaining bracket from the lift rail (see **FIG 12:9**).
4 Loosen the screws indicated in **FIG 12:10**).
5 Open the window approximately 6 inch (150 mm) tilt forward and detach lift arm from lift rail, remove glass.

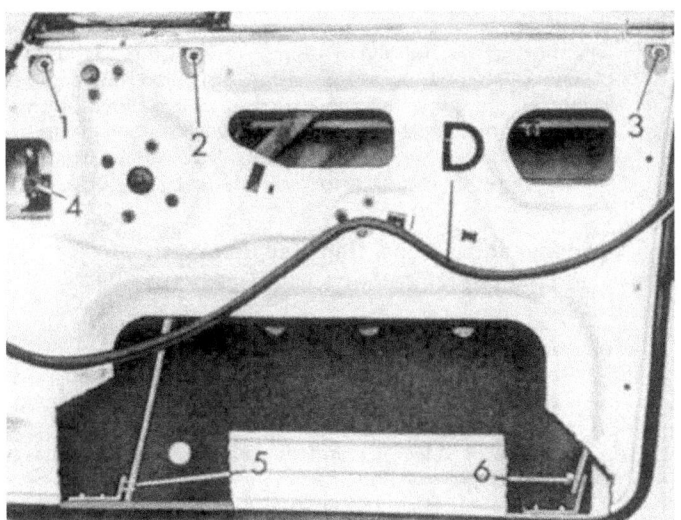

FIG 12:4 Window frame mounting locations

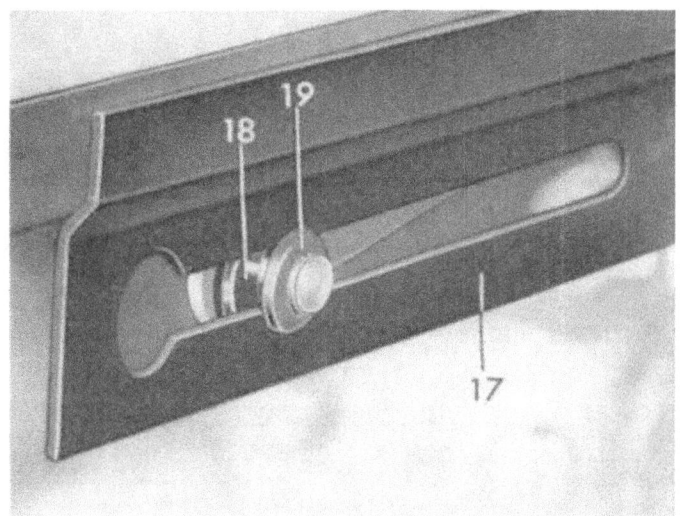

FIG 12:7 Window rail plastic guide washers

FIG 12:5 Window frame breast rail

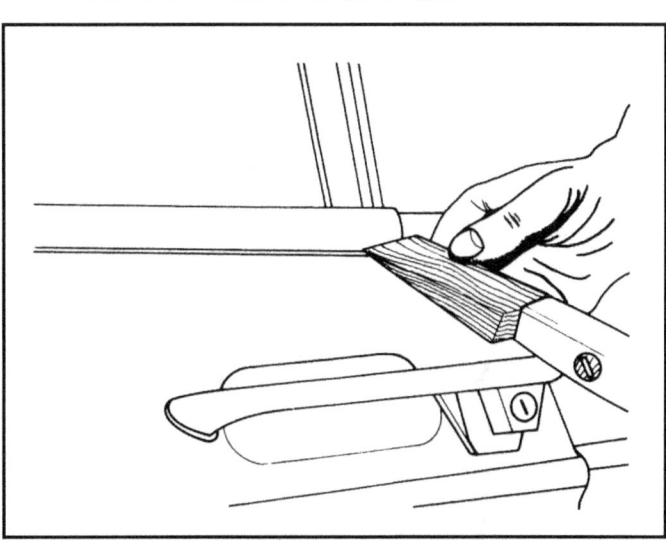

FIG 12:8 Cover rail removal

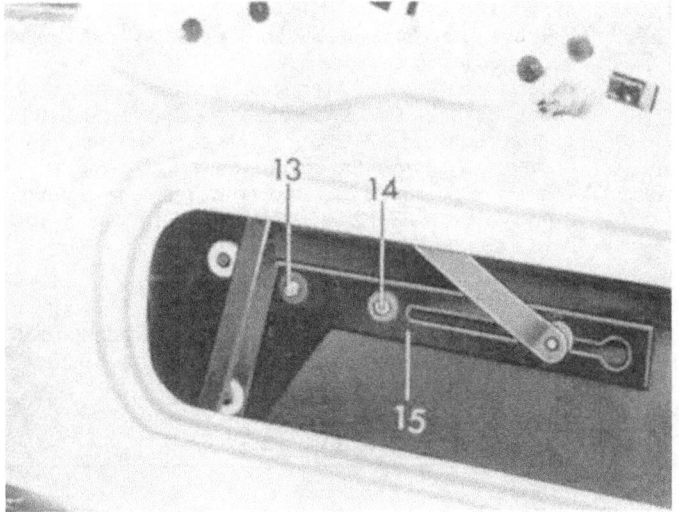

FIG 12:6 Window rail clamp

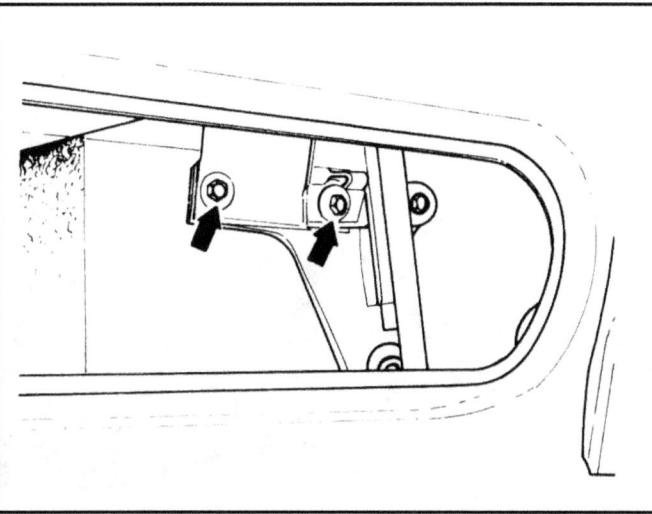

FIG 12:9 Lift rail retaining bracket

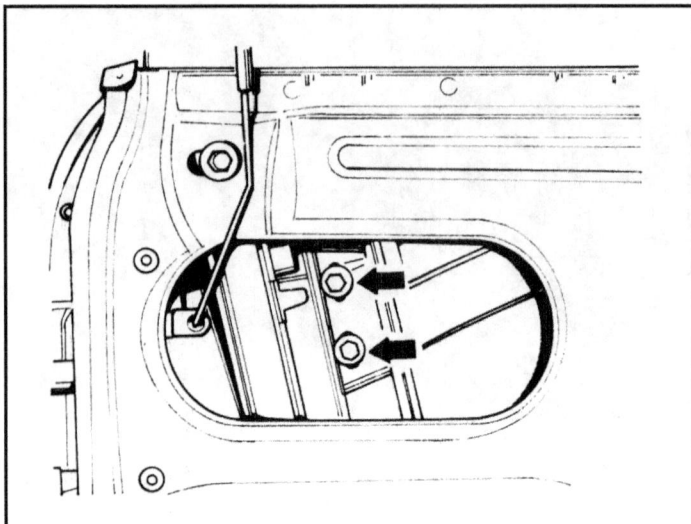

FIG 12:10 Front stop screws

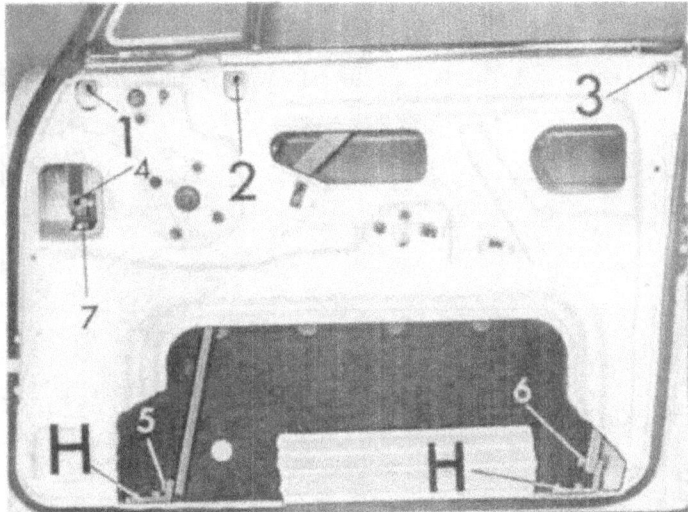

FIG 12:11 Window frame adjustment points

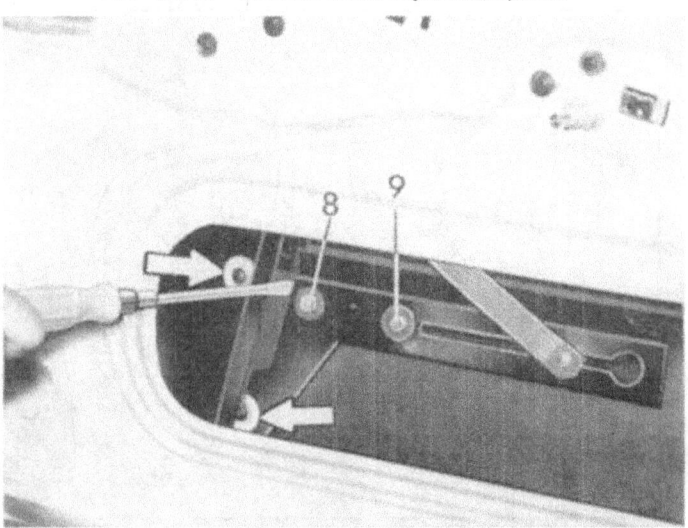

FIG 12:12 Door glass adjustment points

Reassemble in the reverse order to removal with attention to the following points, when fitting retaining bracket push the bracket upwards. Both guide rollers must locate on the guide rail, the lift rail must run between the two plastic washers, the large washer being fitted between lift arm and lift rail. There will be no requirement for adjustment if these instructions are followed correctly.

Window and window frame adjustment:

2000 models:

To adjust the window and window frame in the door panel proceed as follows:

1 Remove the door interior trim panel as detailed previously in this section. Detach the weatherproof lining sheet.
2 Refer to **FIG 12:11** and slacken the clamp screws 1 to 7 and the retaining brackets 'H'.
3 Close the door and ensure that its adjustment is correct. If not complete this operation next.
4 Adjust the clearance between the window frame and the body ensuring that there is equal clearance all the way round. Tighten the frame retaining bolts 1 to 3 (see **FIG 12:11**), and also the retaining brackets 'H'. The rubber weather strip and the window frames must press evenly against the body with sufficient force to eliminate any wind noise whilst the vehicle is in motion. Finally tighten down the fastening bolts 4 to 7 (see **FIG 12:11**).
5 Wind down the window and slacken the retaining bolts 8 and 9 (see **FIG 12:12**), and carefully push the window forward in its rubber frame. Using a wide blade screwdriver push the holder and rollers up against the lifting rail and tighten the clamp bolts.
6 Refit all parts disturbed in the reverse order of dismantling.

Pivoted quarter light:

2000 models:

To remove the pivoted quarter light proceed as follows:
1 Open the pivoted quarter light so that the trailing edge is away from the glass frame by approximately two inches.
2 Remove the door interior trim panel as previously described in this section.
3 Refer to **FIG 12:13** and slacken the worm gear clamp bolts 2 and 3. Carefully but firmly push the quarter light assembly downwards and then pull upwards away from the door frame.
4 The worm gear may be removed by removing screws 2 and 3 (see **FIG 12:13**), and the worm gear withdrawn downwards.

2002 models:

The quarter light is removed in a similar manner but refer to **FIG 12:14** and slacken screw 1, remove screws 2 and 3 to remove worm gear.

12:3 Rear door - 2000 models

Removal:

1 Mark the original position of the hinges on the door pillar by marking the outline in pencil.

2 Using a chisel remove the lower flared end of the rivet of the door check strap and drive upwards the rivet body using a parallel pin punch.
3 With the assistance of a second operator take the weight of the door from the hinges and remove the upper and lower hinge retaining screws to the door pillar. Carefully lift away the door assembly.

Refitting:

Refitting the door is the reverse procedure to removal. Ensure that the hinges are correctly aligned with the pencil marks previously made before final tightening. Always fit a new rivet with its head uppermost and peen over the lower end so that it does not work loose.

Adjustment:

Should difficulty be experienced in closing the door satisfactorily it should be correctly adjusted as follows:
1 Remove the inside door panel as detailed later in this section and carefully ease back the lining sheet from the apertures in the door panel.
2 Slacken the upper and lower hinge clamp screws on the door pillar and adjust the position of the leading edge of the door inwards or outwards as required.
3 Slacken the three door catch screws and using a soft-faced hammer gently tap the door catch either inwards or outwards as required to give the required door closing action. It is important that the height of the door catch is not altered otherwise this will cause excessive strain on the catch mechanism.
4 Slacken the hinge clamp bolts to the outer door panel and adjust the overall door clearance to ensure that it is correctly located in its position relative to the remainder of the body and also that the front and rear doors are in perfect alignment.

Door interior trim panel:

To remove the door trim panel proceed as follows:
1 Unscrew the door safety lock button.
2 Push the coverplate of the window crank away from the handle using a screwdriver and lift away. Remove the window crank clamp screw and lift away the crank.
3 Remove the clamp screw on the inside door handle and carefully pull off the door handle.
4 Remove the two armrest clamp screws and swing the armrest forwards pulling clear of the door lining panel.
5 Lift out the ashtray and remove the ashtray retainer clamp screws. Lift away the ashtray container.
6 Remove the three door interior trim panel clamp screws and ease the door lining away from the door using a wide blade screwdriver as a lever. The locations of the clips are shown by the arrows in **FIG 12:15**.

Window and window frame:

Adjustment:

To correctly adjust the window and window frame to the door panel proceed as follows:
1 Remove the door interior trim panel as previously described, and also the lining sheet.
2 Slacken the clamp bolts 1 to 6 (see **FIG 12:16**), and also the bracket.

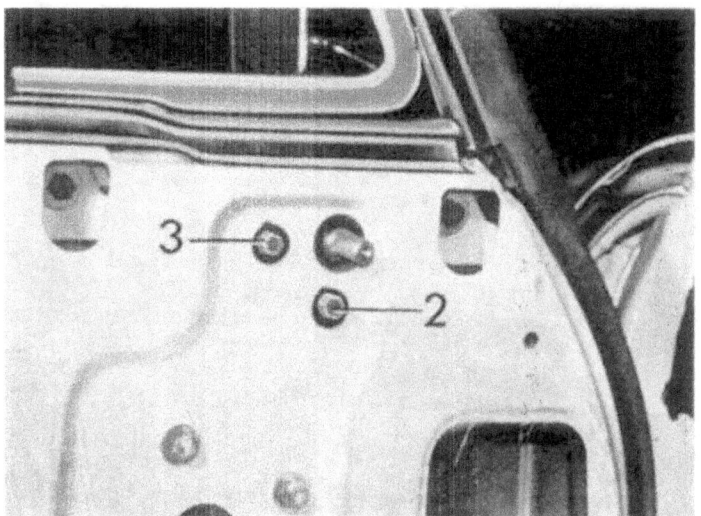

FIG 12:13 Worm gear retaining bolts

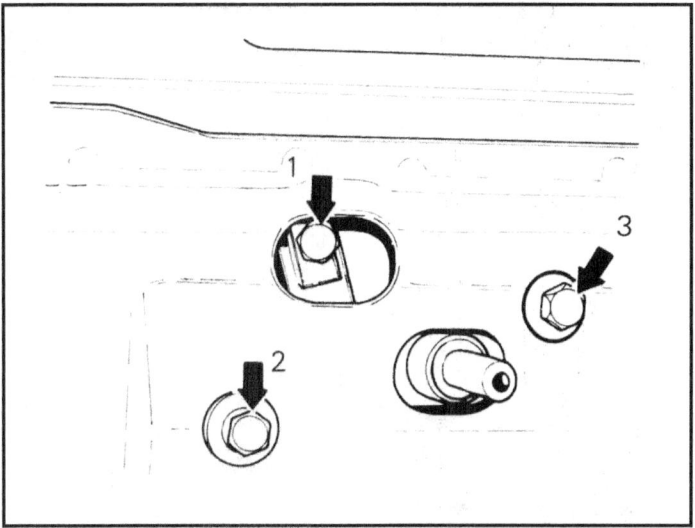

FIG 12:14 Worm gear adjusting and retaining screws

FIG 12:15 Rear door trim clip & retaining screw location

FIG 12:16 Window frame mounting locations

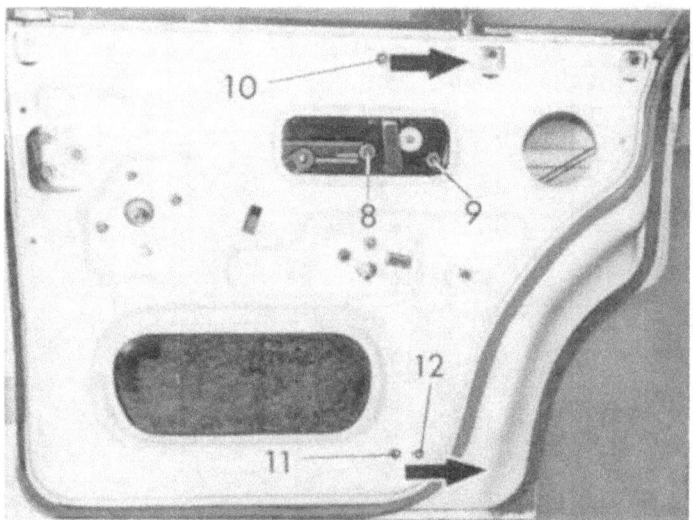

FIG 12:17 Window frame adjustment points

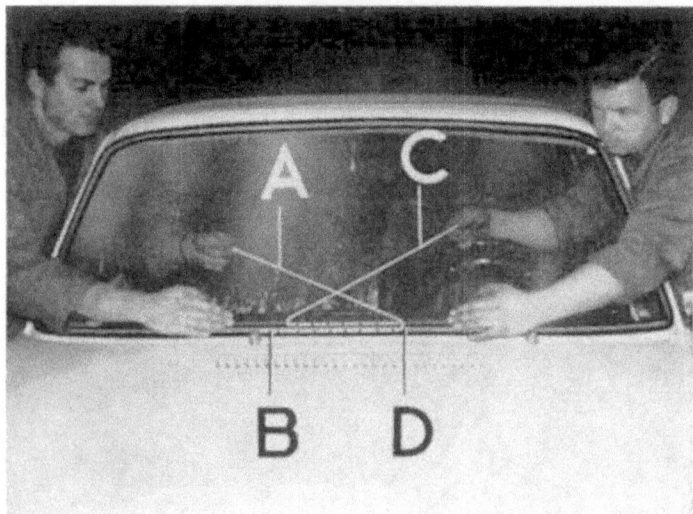

FIG 12:18 Windshield glass replacement

3 With the door closed adjust the window frame clearance relative to the bodywork so that there is an equal space all the way round. Tighten the clamp bolts 1 to 4 and bracket 'W' (see **FIG 12:16**). Ensure that the rubber seal on the window frame is firmly pressed against the body with sufficient force to eliminate any wind noise. Tighten the clamping bolts 5 and 6.

4 Open the window about two inches and loosen the holder clamping bolts 8 and 9 (see **FIG 12:17**). Loosen also the window rail clamping bolts 10 to 12 (see **FIG 12:17**). Carefully push the window rail upwards towards the door lock and tighten the clamping bolt 10. Push the window rail down in the direction of the door lock and tighten the fastening bolts 11 and 12. Finally with the aid of a wide blade screwdriver push the window rail up from the holder and simultaneously tighten down the clamping bolts 8 and 9.

Refitting the dismantled components is the reverse procedure to dismantling.

12 : 4 Front & rear windshield

The procedure for removing and refitting both the front and rear screen glass is identical

Removal :

1 Ease the windscreen wiper arms from their spindles and lift away.
2 Using a windscreen rubber seal lip extractor or a suitably shaped tool detach the rubber window seal carefully from the body.
3 Commencing at one of the two top corners gently push the windscreen, together with the rubber seal and chrome trim away from the body. It is suggested that a second operator be located in front of the windscreen to ensure that when it is finally released from the windscreen aperture, the glass is not damaged.
4 Carefully remove all old sealing compound from the bodywork and the sealing rubber.

Refitting :

1 Place a thick woolen blanket on a flat surface so that the glass may be worked upon as necessary without damage.
2 Offer the glass to the body aperture to ensure that curvature is correct. Place the glass on the thick woolen blanket and starting at one corner gently ease the rubber seal onto the glass. Insert the chrome trim frame into place in the rubber seal and place a length of cord into the lip of the rubber frame with approximately one foot overlap at the bottom.
3 Carefully lay the assembled windscreen into position in the body aperture and hold firmly to prevent movement whilst it is being refitted.
4 Refer to **FIG 12:18** and start with end 'A' of the string and pull the rubber seal lip over the edge of the bodywork until point 'B' is reached. Carefully pull the end 'C' to point 'D'. During this procedure use the flat of the hand or a suitable pad to continuously strike the windscreen at about 6 to 10 inches in front of the point where the string protrudes.
5 Using end 'A' of the string pull the rubber seal lip over the edge of the bodywork until reaching point 'E' (see **FIG 12:19**).

6 Using the string end 'C' carefully pull the other half of the rubber seal over the edge of the windscreen aperture until reaching point 'E' (see **FIG 12:20**). Whilst this is being done continuously strike the windscreen. At any point where the rubber seal lip is not correctly seated in position this may be remedied by using a lip extractor or suitably shaped tool.

12 : 5 Bonnet removing & refitting

2000 models:

Removal:

1 Open the bonnet and using a pencil mark the position of the bonnet hinges on the bonnet lid.
2 Loosen the six bonnet hinge clamp bolts 1 to 6 (see **FIG 12 : 21**), and also the clamp bolts 7 and 8 on the mounting bracket 9. Lift away the mounting bracket.
3 Carefully remove the bonnet sliding the mounting bracket from the main support.

2002 models:

Removal:

1 Mark the position of the hinges on the bonnet.
2 Remove the lower hinge bolts and loosen the third bolt.
3 Disconnect the support arms at the body panel.
4 Remove the upper hinge bolts and lift off the bonnet.

Adjustment:

2000 models:

To adjust the position of the bonnet relative to the engine compartment proceed as follows:

1 Slacken the clamp bolts on both hinges and adjust the position of the bonnet relative to the hinges until the correct location is found. This is made possible by elongated holes in the bonnet and hinges. Slacken the clamp bolts for both bonnet catches and move the catch forwards or backwards until the correct position is found. It should be noted that to prevent the bonnet from being pushed into the passenger compartment of the car in the event of a front collision, the bonnet catches must be adjusted to ensure that the catch plate recedes below the apron when the bonnet is closed. The clearance between the bonnet catch plate and the apron should not exceed $\frac{1}{8}$ inch.
2 Remove the front righthand and lefthand radiator grilles and slacken the righthand and lefthand hinge clamp bolts, 10 to 12 (see **FIG 12 : 22**). To centralize the bonnet in its correct basic setting, insert a centre punch into the bore 'C' and lock the bonnet mounting bracket into place. Gently ease the bonnet back until it rests on the apron. Close the bonnet. Ensure that when the bonnet clearance is being set the chrome beading on the bonnet is correctly aligned with that on the door.
3 Slacken the hinge clamp bolts and adjust the bonnet clearance 'D' (see **FIG 12 : 23**), at the front. The bonnet clearance 'D' at the rear is adjusted by moving the bonnet locks 'S' (see **FIG 12 : 23**). To eliminate excessive bonnet vibration or rattle try fitting rubber cushion pads of appropriate thickness between the wing panel and lower bonnet flange.

FIG 12 : 19 Draw cord movement, stage one

FIG 12 : 20 Draw cord movement, stage two

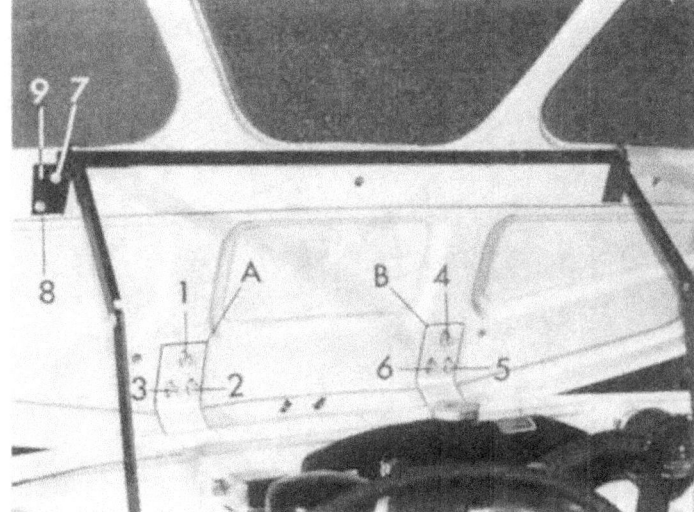

FIG 12 : 21 Bonnet hinge & main support retaining bolts

FIG 12:22 Bonnet to front apron alignment

FIG 12:23 Bonnet lock adjustment

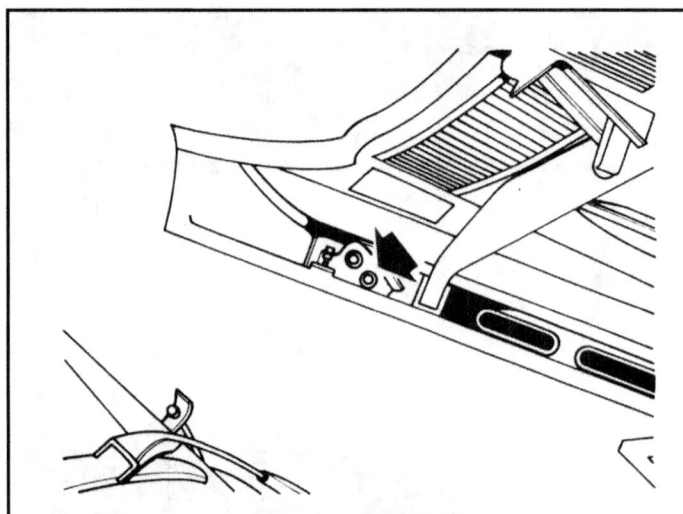

FIG 12:24 Angled catch on bonnet

2002 models:

1. Adjust the bonnet hinges in a similar manner to the 2000 models.
2. The rear gap is correct when the trim strips on bonnet and door are in line. The gap is adjusted by sliding the angled catch (see **FIG 12:24**) to the left or right.
3. Adjust the rubber pads to touch the angled retaining pieces to prevent vibration.
4. Adjust the front rubber stops higher or lower by turning as necessary.

Refitting:

Refitting is the reverse procedure to dismantling. Adjust the location of the bonnet as previously described in this section and lubricate all pivot points using engine grade oil.

Bonnet catch release cable adjustment:

2000 models:

1. Refer to **FIG 12:25** and slacken the retaining bolt 1 for the control cable on the righthand bonnet catch. Also slacken the control cable fastening bolt 2 (see **FIG 12:26**), on the lefthand bonnet catch. Release the cover and pull the control lever back as far as it will go. In this position with the bonnet locks fully open tighten the cable control clamp bolts 1 and 2 as shown in **FIG 12:25** and **FIG 12:26**.

2002 models:

1. Set the lid locking lever against the front stop.
2. Loosen the clamp screw 1 (see **FIG 12:27**) and adjust the wire cable until the locking bar is horizontal and facing the front.

12:6 Boot lid removing & refitting

Removal:

2000 models:

1. Open the boot lid and carefully lift away the top section of the weather strip 1 (see **FIG 12:28**), from the channel. Carefully ease away the plastic lining 2 and bend open the retaining strap 3.
2. Disconnect the licence plate light socket plug 4 and also the clamp nut 5 for the supporting strut 6. Remove the strut 8 clamp nut in **FIG 12:29** and prop open the boot lid using a suitably sized piece of wood.
3. Mark the position of the hinges using a pencil and remove the hinge clamp bolts having first ensured that the boot lid is firmly held by a second operator so that it does not slip, causing damage to the paintwork.

2002 models:

1. Remove the boot lid support arms noting the position of the washers.
2. Remove the support arms from the torsion bar spring.
3. Remove the hinge bolts in a similar manner to the 2000 models.

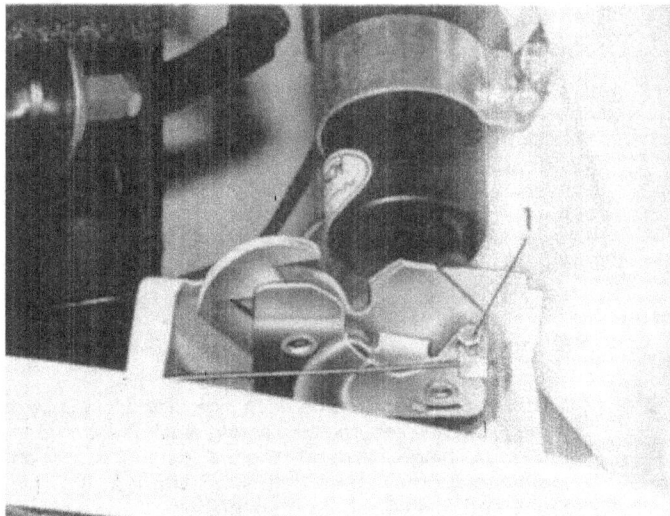

FIG 12:25 Lefthand bonnet release cable adjustment

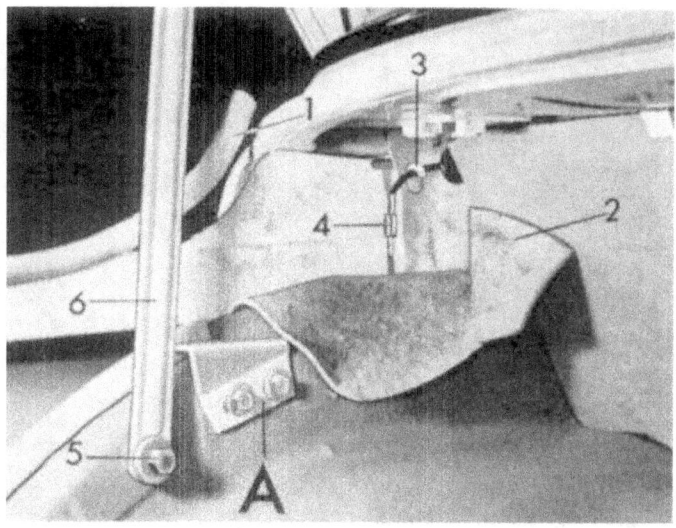

FIG 12:28 Boot lid hinge & support stay mounting points

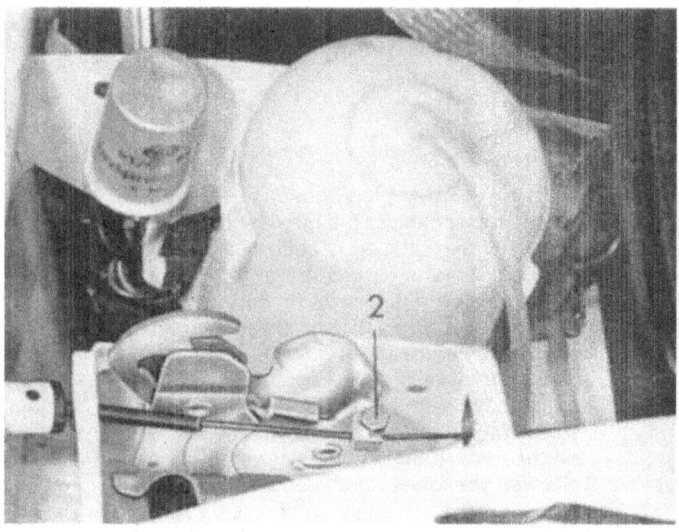

FIG 12:26 Righthand bonnet release cable adjustment

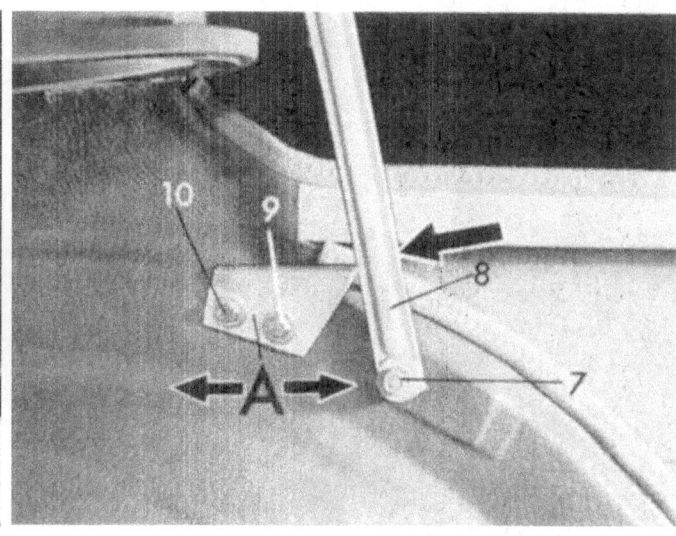

FIG 12:29 Boot lid hinge & support stay mounting points

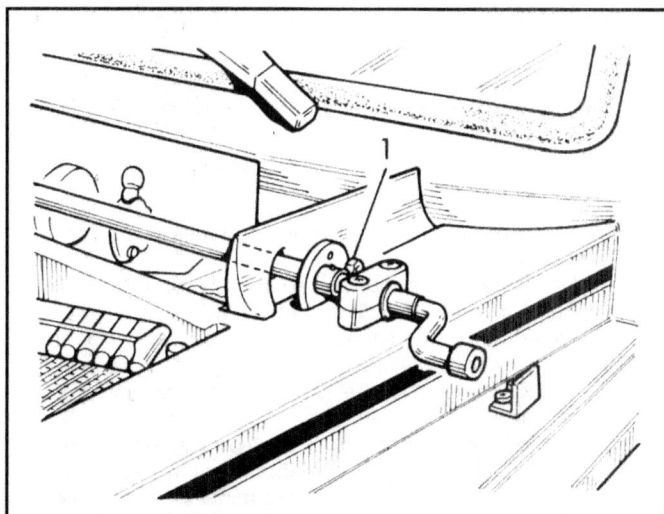

FIG 12:27 Bonnet locking bar

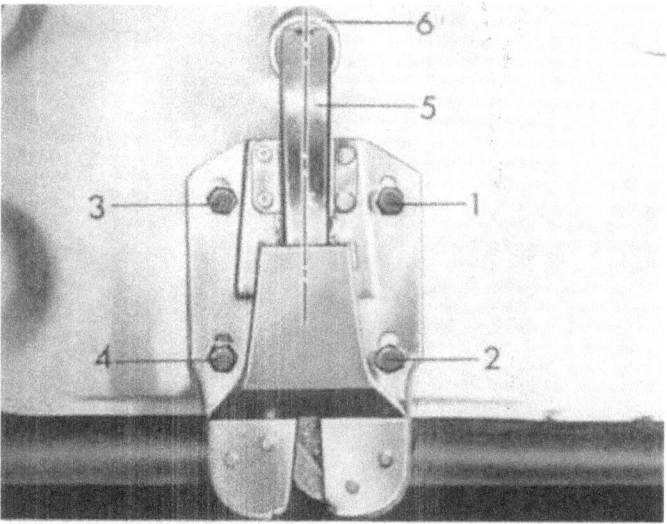

FIG 12:30 Boot lid lock

155

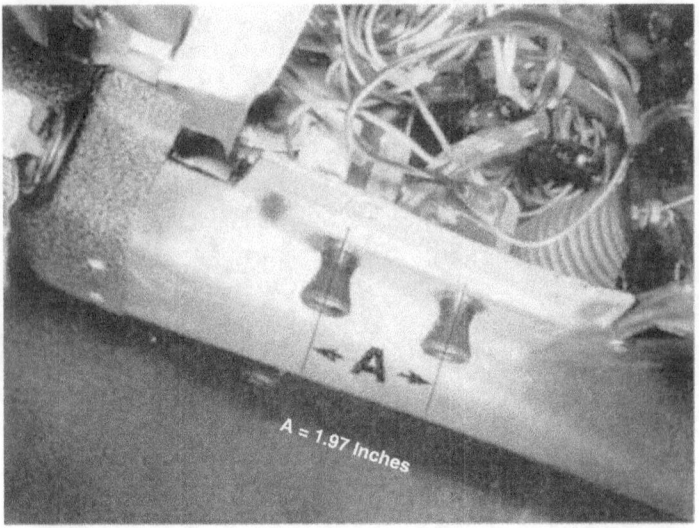

FIG 12:31 Location for the heated rear window switch

FIG 12:32 Guide retaining bolts

FIG 12:33 Locking plate removal

Refitting:

2000 models:

Refitting is the reverse procedure to dismantling but the following points should be noted.

1 Slacken the clamp bolts 9 and 10 (see **FIG 12:29**) and move the limit stop 'A' until the torsion bar spring pressure pushes the strut 8 firmly against the limit stop 'A'.
2 When the boot lid is correctly located in place ensure that its front edge is correctly aligned with that of the rear wing panel.

2002 models:

1 Refit generally in the reverse order of removal.
2 A large washer is fitted on each side of the lid support at the fixing bolt secured by a spring washer and nut.
3 Loosen the hinge bolts and slide the lid panel so that an equal gap is obtained on both sides and that the side panels and lid are flush. Tighten the bolts.
4 Loosen the lid attachment bolts and adjust the height of the lid so that the upper edge of the side panel is aligned with the lid. If necessary correct the gap between the rear window frame and the lid.
5 Adjust the lock if necessary.

Lock adjustment:

2000 models:

1 Slacken the clamping bolts 1 to 4 (see **FIG 12:30**), for the top section of the bonnet catch 5.
2 Correctly align the top section of the bonnet catch 5 with the bonnet lock 6. Push the top section of the bonnet catch 5 upwards in the elongated holes and fasten down firmly. It is important to ensure that the top section of the catch 5 is fitted flush with the lock 6.
3 Should the upper section of the boot catch 5 not lie in full contact with the lock 6 this may be corrected using a soft-faced hammer by gently tapping at the point B on the upper catch until it is correctly aligned.
4 Slacken the lower catch section and push upwards as far as it will go in the elongated holes. To correctly align the lower catch section relative to the upper section push it to the left or right as necessary until the guide bolt centre line is correctly aligned.

12:7 Heated rear windshield

2000 models:

To fit a rear window with a heater element as an accessory proceed as follows:

1 Remove the rear window as detailed in **Section 12:4**.
2 Disconnect the negative lead from the battery.
3 Refer to **FIG 12:31** and fit the push/pull switch as shown in the figure with dimension 'A' being 1.97 inch.
4 Connect the previous unused black/green leads in the wiring harness to the push/pull switch and fuse 6 underneath.
5 Remove the rear seat back cushion and fit the window glass with the heating element incorporated taking very great care that the little terminal on the side of the glass is not in any way damaged. Refer to **Section 12:4** for this procedure.

6 Connect up the loose black/green cable located on the wheel arch to the rear window terminal. Also attach the negative lead to the rear panel and to the rear window. Reconnect the battery terminal and refit the rear seat backrest cushion.

12 : 8 Sun roof removing & refitting

2000 models:

Removal:

1 Open the sliding roof approximately 6 to 8 inches and carefully lever off the head lining frame at the front of the sliding roof.
2 Referring to **FIG 12 : 32** carefully push back the roof bracing and twist off the retaining spring. Remove the two guide plate retaining bolts and slide away the locking plate from the guide (see **FIG 12 : 33**).
3 Close the sliding roof. Using a pencil mark the position of the locking plate and guide and then remove the two retaining screws.
4 Repeat the operations just performed on the other side of the sun-roof. Place an old blanket or protection sheet over the panel work above the windscreen and carefully lift out the sliding roof taking care not to damage any paintwork or lining material.
5 Refitting is the reverse procedure to dismantling.

Roof bracing removal and refitting:

1 Remove the sliding roof assembly as previously detailed in this section.
2 Refer to **FIG 12 : 34**, slacken the corner piece 1, the cover strip 2 and the guide rails 3. Lift the guide rail 3 slightly and lift out the head lining in a forward direction. See **FIG 12 : 35**.
3 Refitting is the reverse procedure to dismantling.

Guide removal and refitting:

1 Remove the sliding roof assembly as previously described in this section.
2 Remove the winder assembly by releasing the three Phillips head screws and remove the winder assembly.
3 Working from the top of the car remove corner piece, cover strip and guide rail by moving sideways and forwards. Pull guides out of rail (see **FIG 12 : 36**). Carefully ease out the guide rail.
4 Reassembly is the reverse procedure to dismantling. It is recommended that the guides be packed with Amblygon grease.

Sliding roof adjustment:

1 After removal of the winder it should be turned back in a clockwise direction up to the stop and then turned back two complete turns.
2 Push the sliding roof evenly onto the front edge of the roof ensuring that the guides line up correctly. Fit the winder and close the sliding roof several times.
3 Close the sliding roof fully and lift away the winder. Turn to the full righthand stop and refit the winder assembly with the knob in the central position in the winder knob recess.

FIG 12 : 34 Roof bracing removal

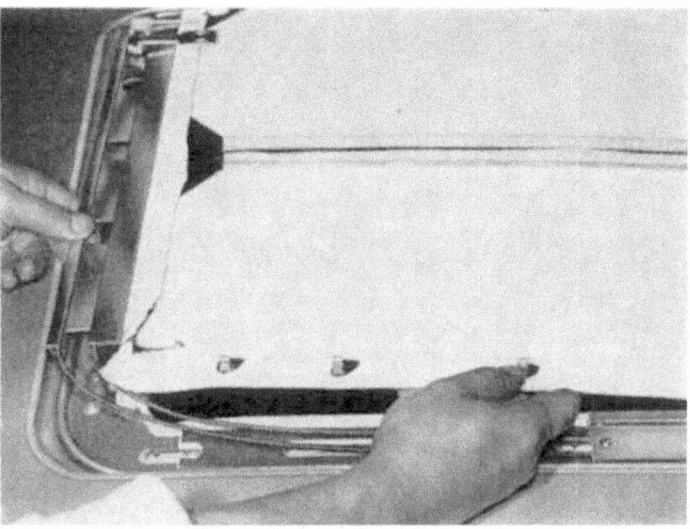

FIG 12 : 35 Head lining removal

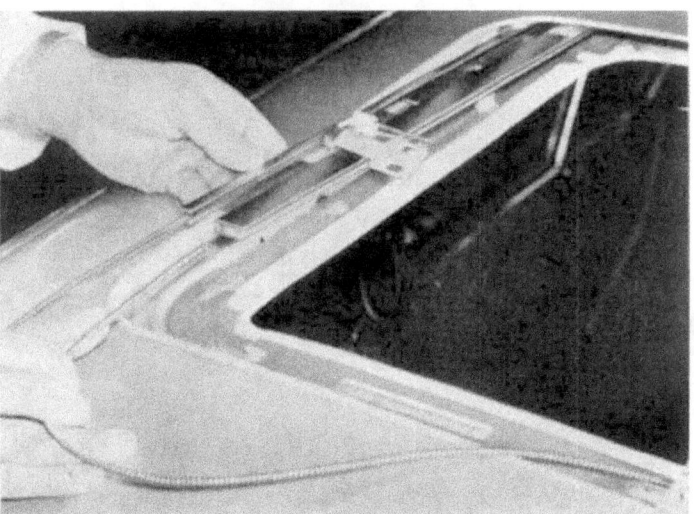

FIG 12 : 36 Guide rail assembly dismantling

FIG 12 : 37 Sliding roof rear end height adjustment

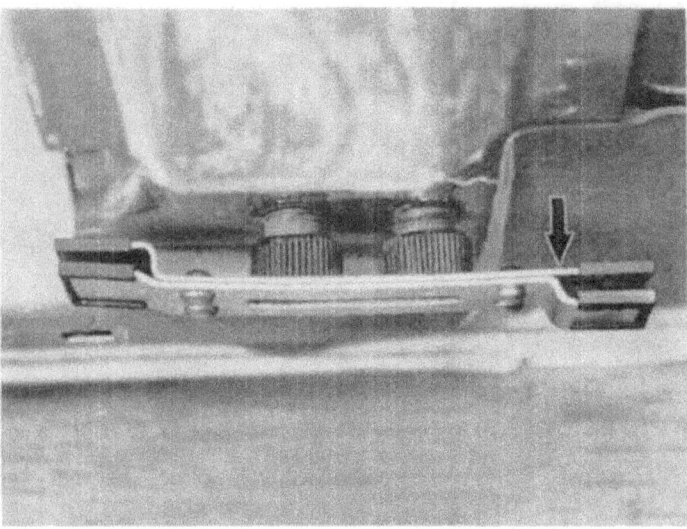

FIG 12 : 38 Sliding roof front end height adjustment

FIG 12 : 39 Additional means of front end height adjustment

4 The sliding roof should be set so that it is .039 inch lower at the front and .039 inch higher at the back than the roof outer skin. To adjust this refer to **FIG 12 : 37** and it will be seen that by slackening the screw 1 the guide may be adjusted using the serrations to lock the adjustment. To adjust the front refer to **FIG 12 : 38** and place the guide with the straight fork side on the guide rail. The milled nuts will rotate for fine adjustment. Should the cranked end of the fork be offered up to the guide rail as shown in **FIG 12 : 39**, the sliding roof will be lower at the front.

12 : 9 Heater removing & refitting

2000, 2000 TI, 2000 TI Lux models:

Removing:

1 Drain coolant (see **Section 4 : 2**).
2 Unscrew retaining screws 1 to 4 (see **FIG 12 : 40**) on intake duct and remove clamp springs (see inset **FIG 12 : 41**).
3 Pull off hoses 5 and 6 from spray nozzles and remove intake.
4 Soften foam rubber seal between bulkhead and upper part of heater casing with petrol.
5 Release control cables from bonnet locks (see **Section 12 : 5**) and pull the cables out of the guide tube.
6 Release cable 1 (see **FIG 12 : 42**) from control lever 2, release cable clamp 3.
7 Disconnect heater hoses at engine end.
8 Remove righthand trim panel 1 (see **FIG 12 : 43**) and console 2.
9 Release cable clamp 1 (see **FIG 12 : 44**) and remove circlip 2 to release cable.
10 Squeeze the coupling union and lift out at the bottom clear of the casing.
11 Disconnect the earth lead 1 (see **FIG 12 : 45**) disconnect lead 2 from the heater blower switch, unscrew screws 3 to 6 and lift heater out upwards.

Refitting:

Refit the heater in the reverse order to removal noting the following point:

Fit the coupling union with the tabs upwards, and insert them into the top of the heater casing, squeeze the bottom into the bottom groove of the casing.

Adjustment (FIG 12 : 46):

1 Push the temperature control lever A to about .2 inch of stop B. The flap C must rest against the stop D.
2 Secure the cable 7 to the operating lever 8 and the outer casing 9 with the clamp 10 on the heater casing 11.
3 Move the distribution lever E as far as it will go to the right.
4 Let the flaps 1 and 2 lie on the casing F.
5 Secure cable 3 to the operating lever 4 with the circlip, and secure the outer casing 5 with the clamp 6.

2000 CA and 2000 CS models:

Removal:

1 Drain the coolant and disconnect battery.
2 Lift out selector plate on 2000 CA (see **Section 6a : 6**) and pull out bulb holders, release screws 2 to 4 (see **FIG 12 : 47**).

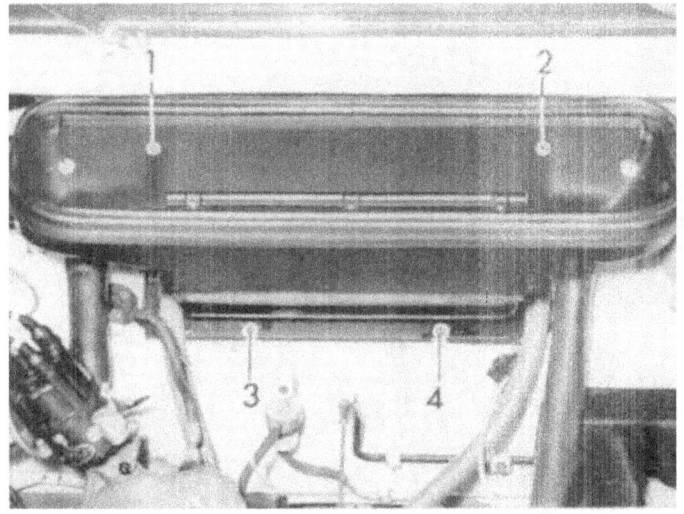

FIG 12:40 Air intake duct securing screws

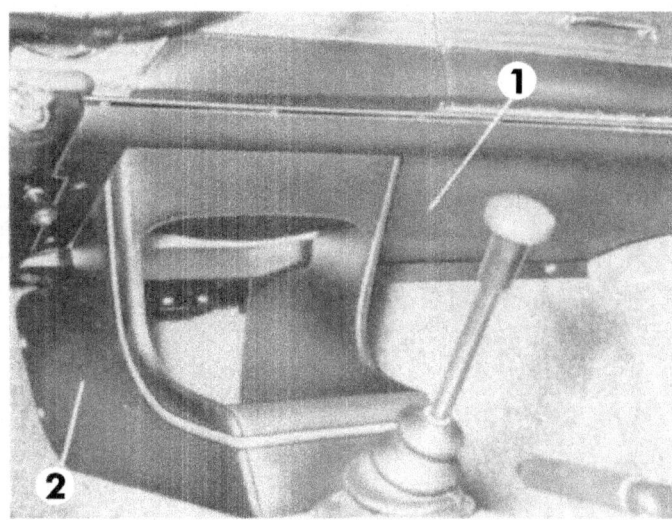

FIG 12:43 Trim panel and console

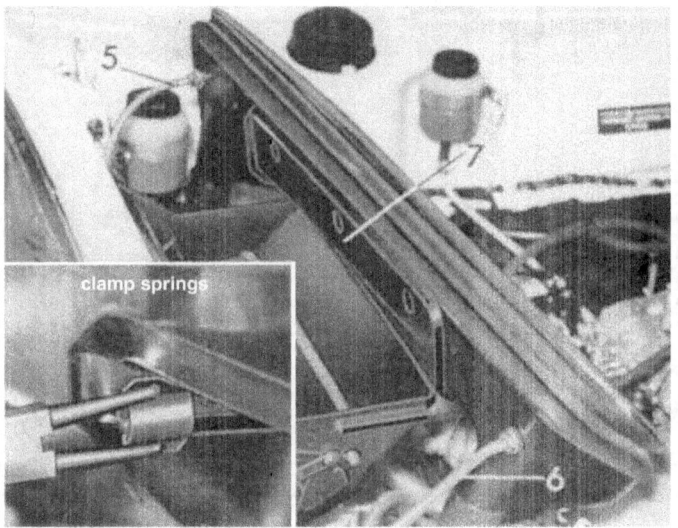

FIG 12:41 Air intake duct clamp springs & spray nozzles

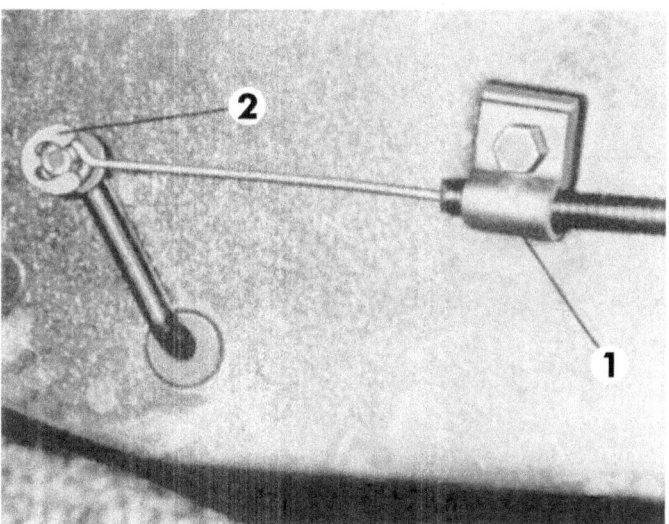

FIG 12:44 Air ducts operating lever

FIG 12:42 Flap and water valve operating lever

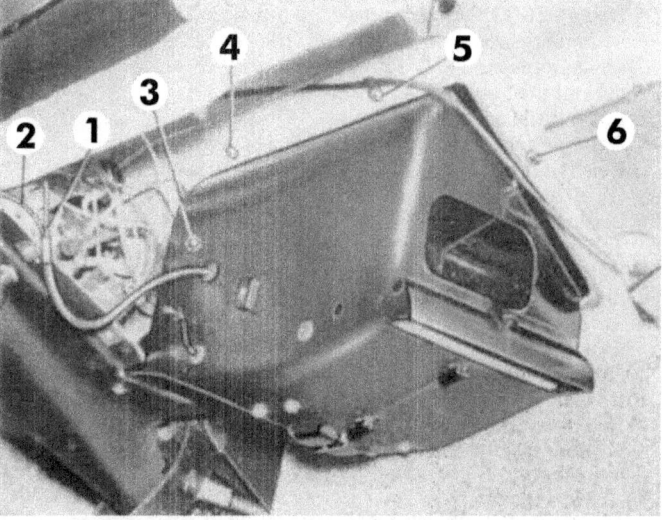

FIG 12:45 Heater leads and retaining screws

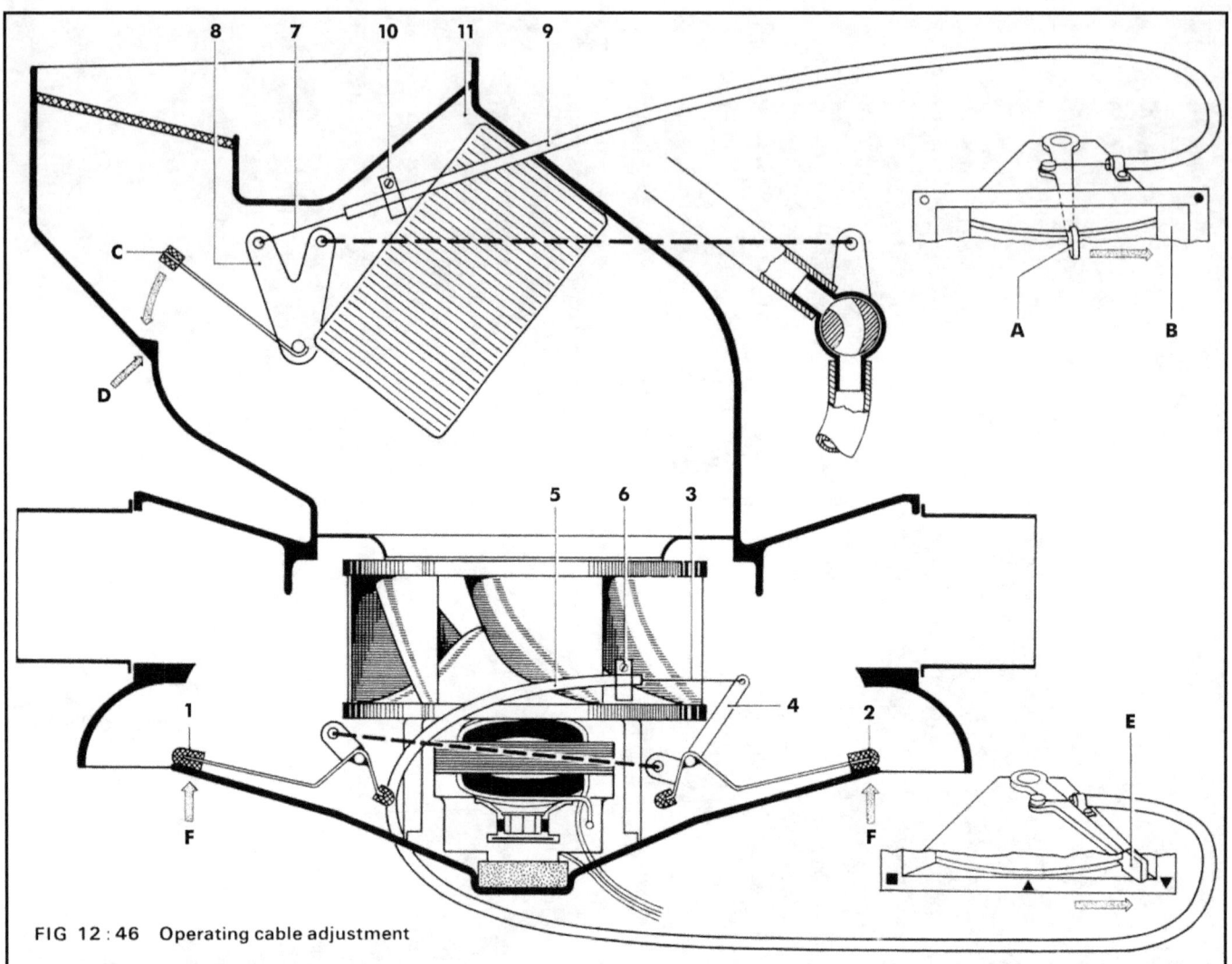

FIG 12 : 46 Operating cable adjustment

3 Lift out the rocker switch plate, 2000 CS, retained by two screws. On the 2000 CA unscrew the Phillips screws on each side of the plate.
4 On the 2000 CA disconnect the leads from the rocker switches, taping and labelling the leads for correct reassembly (see **FIG 12 : 52**).
5 Lift out the floor of the console.
6 Pull out the ashtray.
7 Remove the knobs from the control levers.
8 Release the cover plate and pull out as far as the cables will allow and unscrew the clamp nuts.
9 Unscrew the two Phillips screws (see **FIG 12 : 48**) and pull the control panel from the cover plate.
10 Remove centre section of trim (see **FIG 12 : 49**) and detach the upper joint plate (inset).
11 Remove trim 1 (see **FIG 12 : 50**) and steering column trim 2.
12 Detach the console at the bottom and manoeuvre out.
13 Detach the water hoses at the heater.
14 Disconnect the control cable on the water valve.
15 Disconnect the leads (see **FIG 12 : 51**) and label for reassembly. 1 Blue/red 2 Green/yellow 3 Blue/black 4 Brown/earth
16 Disconnect earth lead and unscrew nut on opposite side.
17 Cut open sealing compound and take out heater in a downward direction together with the windscreen ducts.

Refitting:

Refit generally in the reverse order to removing noting that the earth lead on 2000 CA models is secured under screw 3 (see **FIG 12 : 47**). On 2000 CA models the wiring colours are as shown in **FIG 12 : 51**.

Adjustment:

1 Move the temperature control lever to within .08 inch of its stop.
2 Slacken screw 1 (see **FIG 12 : 53**) push lever A forwards to its stop. Tighten screw 1. The water valve is closed in position B.
3 With the water valve in position A the flap C must be closed. Adjust by slackening screw 2 and moving the cable. Tighten the screw.
4 The fresh air flap is adjusted by use of screw 3 in the same manner. On 2000 CA models the ashtray will have to be removed first.
5 Slacken screw 6 to adjust the windscreen flap cable 4 and footwell flap cable 5.

FIG 12:47 Selector quadrant coverplate screws

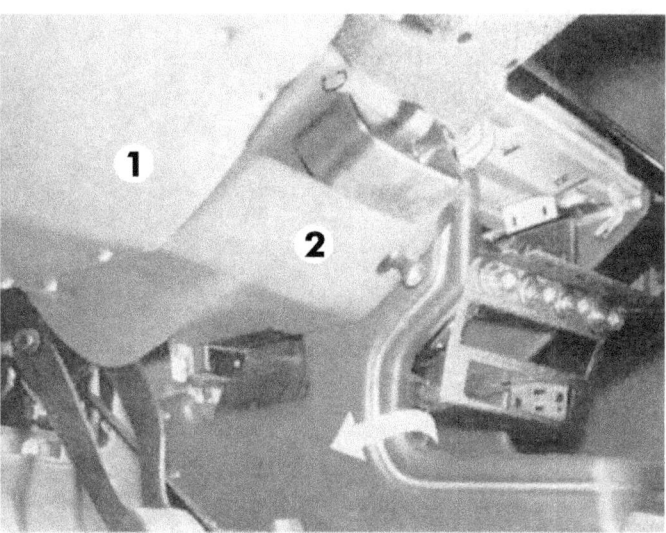

FIG 12:50 Trim and console removal

FIG 12:48 Control panel removal

FIG 12:51 Heater leads and securing nuts

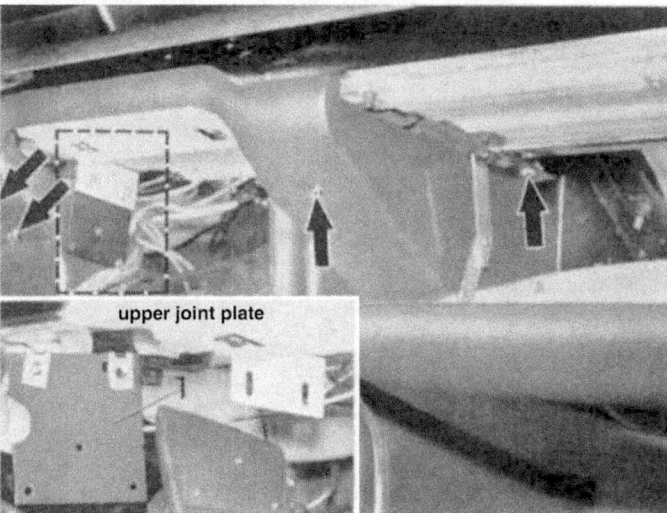

FIG 12:49 Centre section of trim & upper joint plate (inset)

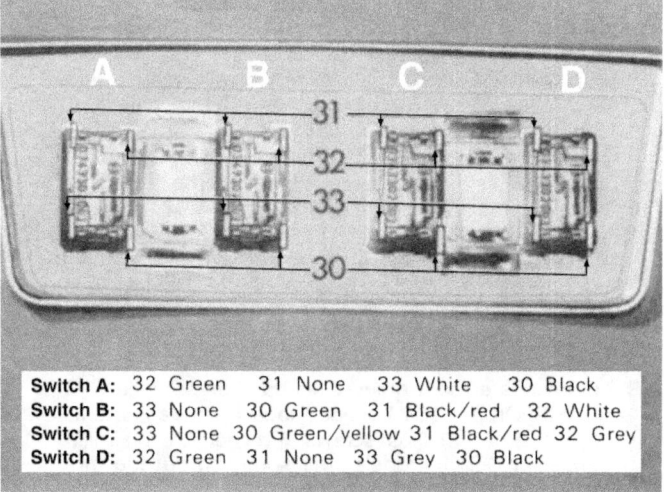

Switch A: 32 Green 31 None 33 White 30 Black
Switch B: 33 None 30 Green 31 Black/red 32 White
Switch C: 33 None 30 Green/yellow 31 Black/red 32 Grey
Switch D: 32 Green 31 None 33 Grey 30 Black

FIG 12:52 Rocker switch connections on 2000 CA models

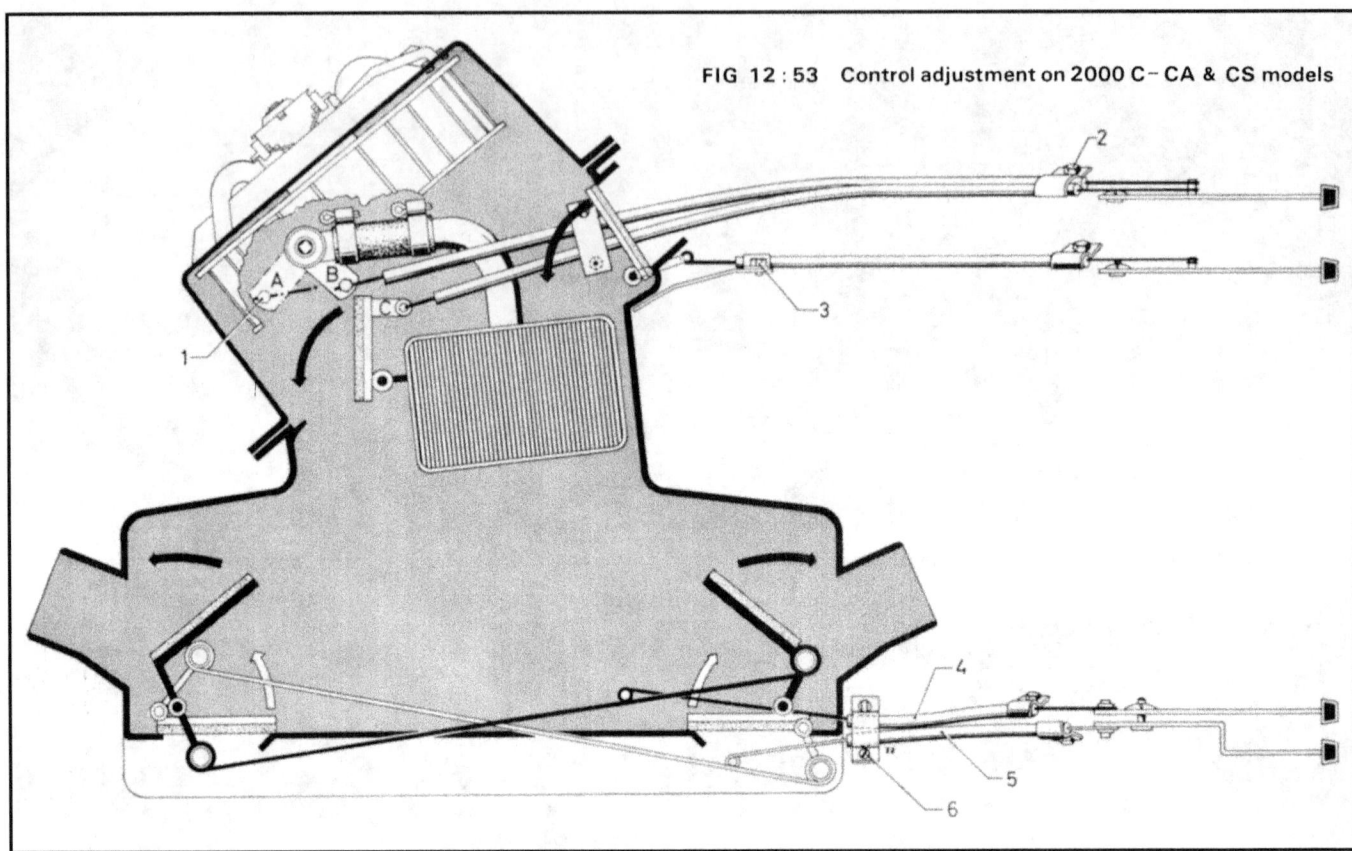

FIG 12:53 Control adjustment on 2000 C – CA & CS models

2002 models:

Removal:

1 Disconnect battery and drain coolant with control lever at 'WARM'.
2 Disconnect the return hose at the heater.
3 Detach feed hose 1 (see **FIG 12:54**) at the water valve 2. 1971 models have an improved valve but the operation is the same.
4 Remove the console on pre-1971 models by removing the screws (see **FIG 12:55**) move console towards rear. On 1971 models unscrew the gearlever knob and pull out the rubber gaiter. Loosen screw 1 (see **FIG 12:56**. Remove screws at each side and take out floor (see **FIG 12:57**). Loosen screw below trim panel. Loosen the retaining bracket screw (see **FIG 12:58**) pull the console back and pull off the hazard warning flasher plug. Remove the console to one side.
5 Dismantle casing for outer tube (see **FIG 12:59**).
6 Remove lower centre trim panel on pre-1971 models (see **FIG 12:60**). On 1971 models refer to **FIG 12:61**).
7 Remove outer trim panel on pre-1971 models (see **FIG 12:62**).
8 Detach steering column fairing by removing the four screws.
9 Pull off heater control lever knobs 1 and 2 (see **FIG 12:63**). On pre-1971 models loosen knurled nuts as well as outer Phillips screws. Proceed in a similar manner on 1971 models after springing out the trim panel.
10 Unscrew Phillips screws at each side of panel.
11 On pre-1971 models pull out ashtray, on all models pull off the knob of the warm air lever, spring out the trim panel on 1971 models, and remove the Phillips screw on each side of the panels.
12 Pull off electrical cable connections (see **FIGS 12:64 and 12:65**).
13 Pull off the righthand warm air hose, unscrew the heater retaining nuts on each side.
14 Pull off the lefthand warm air hose, turn the retaining bracket for the outer tube casing a little for access.
15 On pre-1971 models remove the trim panel beneath the glove compartment.
16 Carefully pull out the heater unit.

Refitting:

Refit generally in the reverse order of removal, check the water valve for unrestricted flow. Ensure that control knobs are fitted correctly. Reconnect the electrical leads for pre-1971 models as shown in **FIG 12:64** where 1 is green/red (1st stage), 2 is green/white (2nd stage) and 3 is brown (earth). Connections on 1971 models are 1 blue/black, 2 green/yellow, 3 blue/red and 4 brown, the earth lead (brown) is secured under the heater retaining nut (arrowed) (**FIG 12:65**).

Adjustment (FIG 12:66):

Adjustment is carried out in a similar manner to that shown in **FIG 12:53**. The heater valve is WARM in position A. The mixing flap C must be closed in this position, adjust at the clamp screw 1. Position B in COLD. Adjust all flaps by moving cables through clamps 2, 3 and 4. Lubricate the flap bearing points.

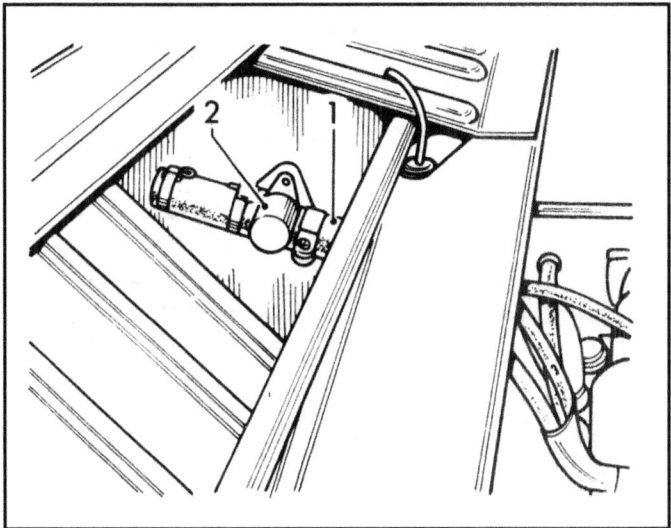

FIG 12:54 Water valve on 2002 models

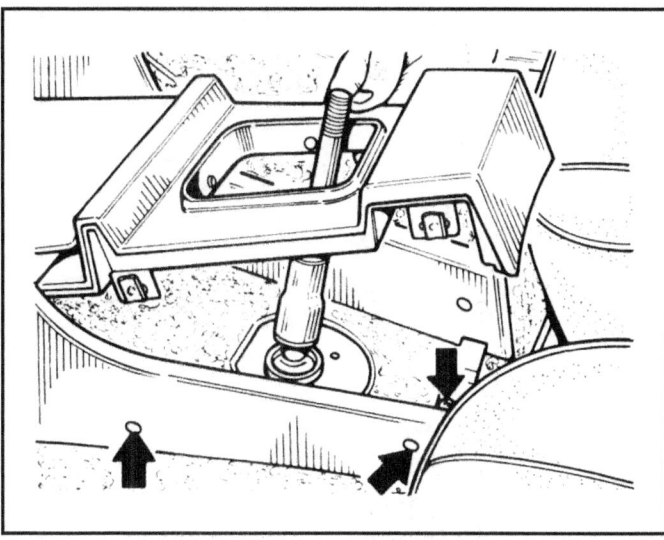

FIG 12:57 Rear console retaining screw on 1971 models

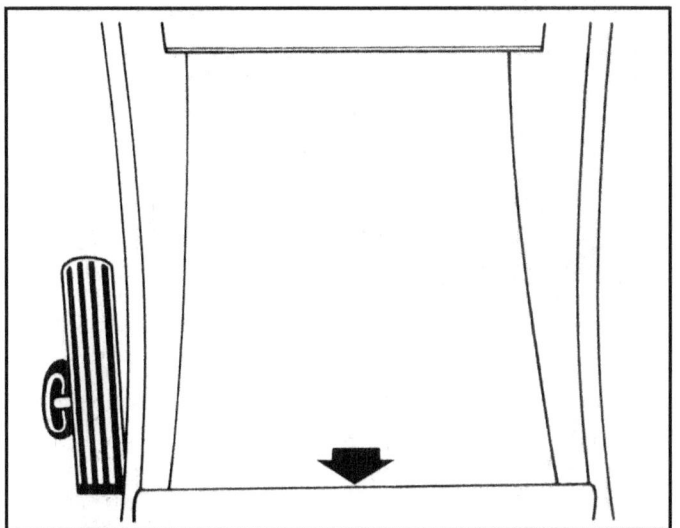

FIG 12:55 Console screw on pre-1971 models

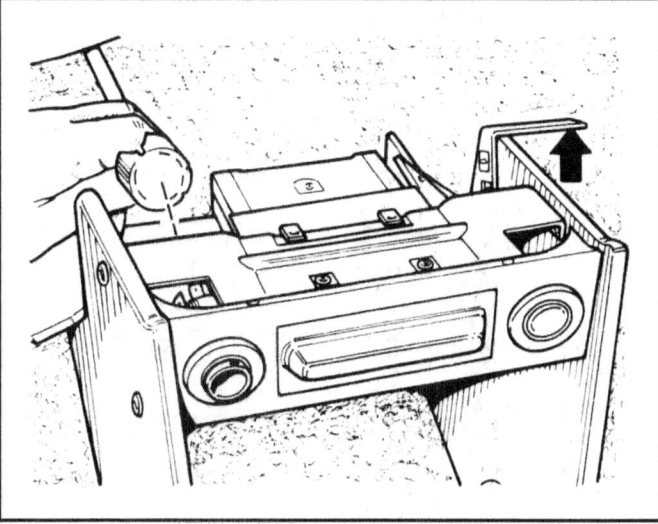

FIG 12:58 Console bracket screw & hazard plug 1971 models

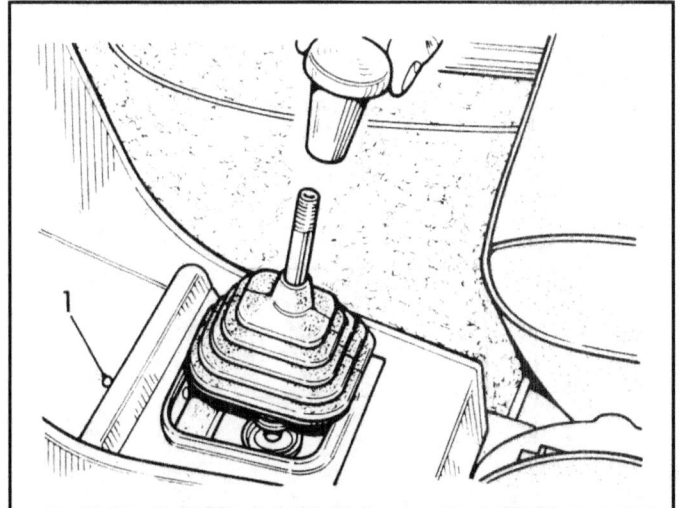

FIG 12:56 Front console retaining screw on 1971 models

FIG 12:59 Casing for outer tube

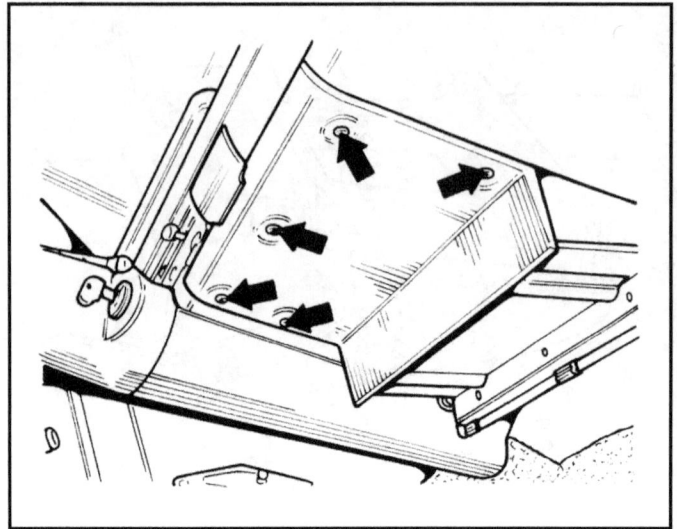

FIG 12:60 Lower centre trim panel on pre-1971 models

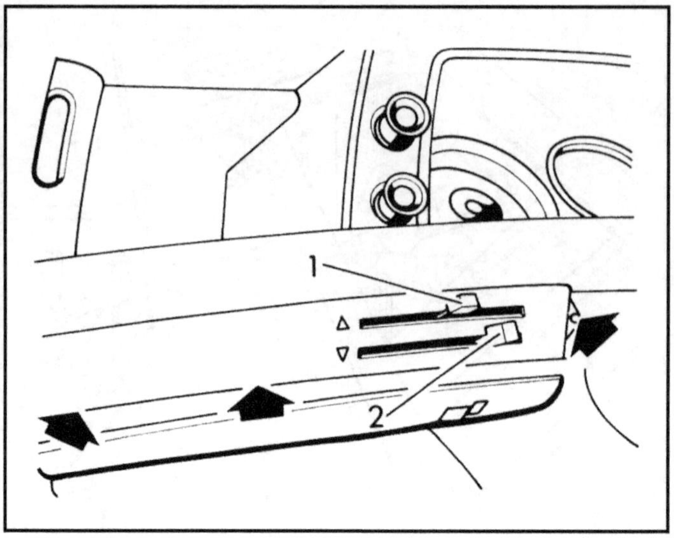

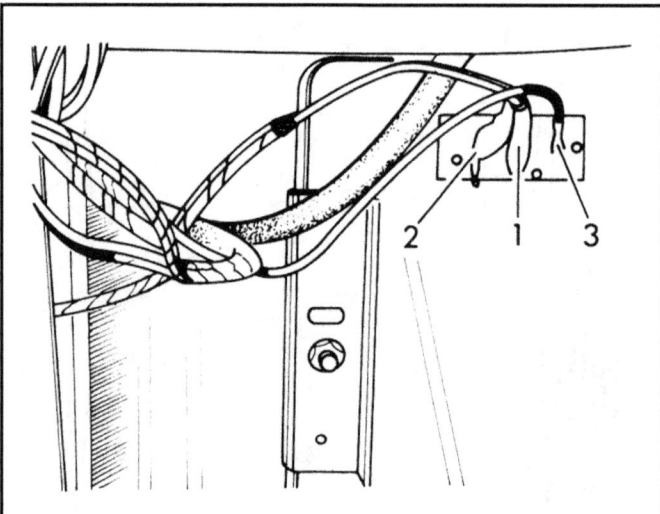

FIG 12:63 Heater control trim panel on pre-1971 models

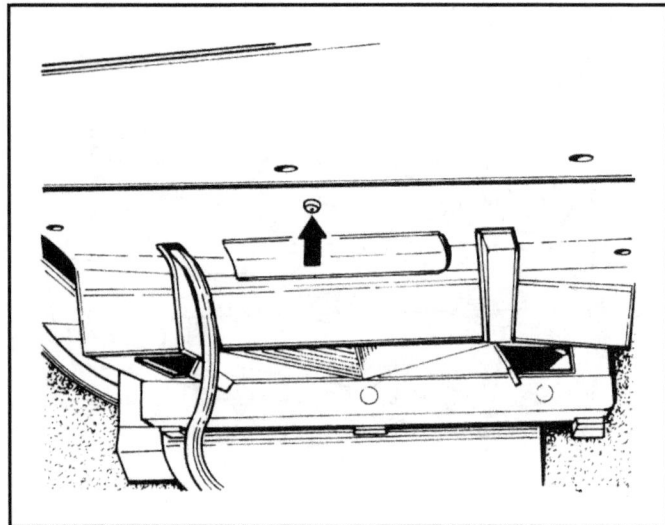

FIG 12:61 Lower centre trim 1971 models

FIG 12:64 Cable connections on pre-1971 models

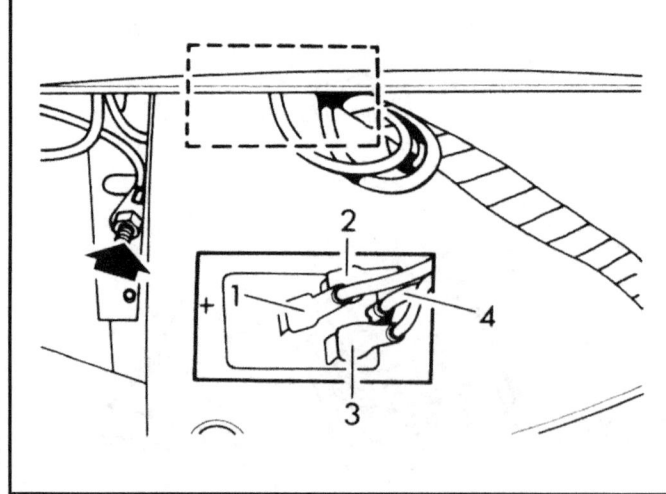

FIG 12:62 Outer trim panel pre-1971 models

FIG 12:65 Cable connections on 1971 models

164

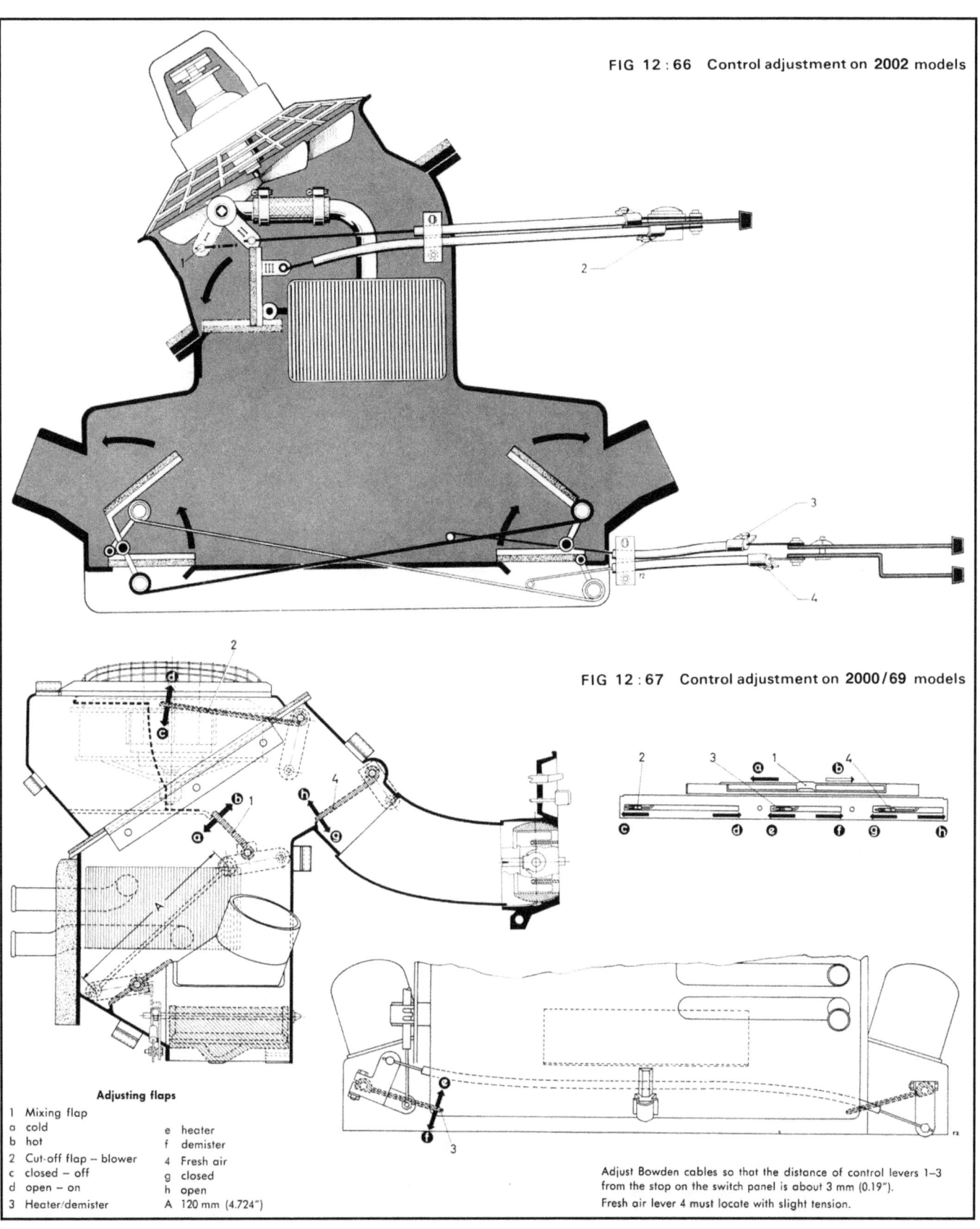

FIG 12:66 Control adjustment on **2002** models

FIG 12:67 Control adjustment on **2000/69** models

Adjusting flaps
1 Mixing flap
  a cold
  b hot
2 Cut-off flap – blower
  c closed – off
  d open – on
3 Heater/demister
  e heater
  f demister
4 Fresh air
  g closed
  h open
A 120 mm (4.724″)

Adjust Bowden cables so that the distance of control levers 1–3 from the stop on the switch panel is about 3 mm (0.19″).
Fresh air lever 4 must locate with slight tension.

NOTES

CHAPTER 13

MAINTENANCE & LUBRICATION

13 : 1 Routine maintenance
13 : 2 Approved lubricants
13 : 3 Weekly maintenance
13 : 4 Initial 600 mile or first month service
13 : 5 5,000 mile or 6 month maintenance schedule
13 : 6 10,000 mile or annual maintenance schedule
13 : 7 Every 2nd & 4th year maintenance schedule

13 : 1 Routine maintenance

Regular inspection and servicing is essential if the vehicle is to be maintained in a satisfactory condition. Whilst it may not always be possible to carry out a service at the exact time specified, no service should be delayed longer than absolutely necessary. The main service intervals are; the standard service every 8000 km (5000 miles) or 6 months, and the major service every 16000 km (10000 miles) or 12 months. However, if the car is operating under abnormal conditions or if a high proportion of short journeys are involved, it may be necessary to shorten these intervals.

For instance, in very dusty conditions the carburetter air filter and servo air filter should be cleaned or renewed more frequently. Similarly, if fuel supplies are suspect the fuel filter should be cleaned more often. Under hard driving or extensive town use, the sparking plugs and brake linings may require attention before the normal service interval has elapsed. If the car is used over unmade roads or rough terrain, tyres, suspension and hydraulic pipes should all receive special attention.

When carrying out any inspection always keep an eye open for any other fault that may be developing. A useful tip is to make a point of inspecting the area over which the car is left standing. This may reveal drip marks which could indicate a loose drain plug, a faulty seal, coolant hose or joint, a leaking brake unit or a fractured hydraulic pipe. Trace the source of the leakage and correct the fault without delay.

13 : 2 Approved lubricants

In order to ensure satisfactory results only oils and fluids of the required standard should be used. If a particular oil is unobtainable, alternative brands of an equivalent specification may be used.

Engine oil :

Any good brand of heavy duty oil with a viscosity of SAE 30, SAE 20W/40 or SAE 20W/50. If temperatures below 10°C are regularly experienced, an SAE 20 or SAE 10W/30 grade oil should be used.

Gearbox, manual :

A good branded gearbox oil of SAE 80 or 90 is preferred. An alternative is a heavy duty engine oil as specified previously. Do not use hypoid oil.

Gearbox, automatic :

Generally any branded ATF Dexron is suitable but where a new or exchange unit is concerned, the initial filling is limited to the following brands: Avia ATF 68, Chevron ATF Dexron, Esso ATF Dexron, Quaker State Dexron Quadromatic, Shell ATF Dexron or Valvoline Valvomatic ATF Type B.

Rear axle :

SAE 90 grade hypoid oil. Check with your local agent for approved brands.

Steering box and idler arm :

Permanently filled; for topping up use a good brand of SAE 90 hypoid gear oil.

Halfshafts :

Sliding joints: SAE 90 hypoid gear oil.
Constant velocity joints: Shell Retinax AM grease.
Universal joints: Molykote BR2 grease.

Wheel bearings :

Shell Darina 1 1 with a high melting point.

Hydraulic fluid :

Castrol Disc brake fluid, Castrol Girling brake fluid green or ATE blue brake fluid S.

Grease, general purpose

Molykote Longterm 2 or suitable equivalent.

Water pump nipple (if fitted) :

High melting point multi-purpose grease.

Coolant/antifreeze :

A suitable brand of antifreeze, as recommended by your local agent, with a corrosion inhibitor added. The correct mixture proportions are given in **Chapter 4**.

13 : 3 Weekly maintenance

Some of the following checks can be carried out when refuelling as the necessary facilities are then readily available.
Check/top up engine oil (engine cold).
Check/top up coolant level (engine cold).
Check/top up brake and clutch fluid reservoirs.
Check/top up battery electrolyte.
Check/top up washer reservoirs.
Check tyre pressures and examine tyres.

When examining tyres look for stones, etc., embedded in the rubber and watch for splits or damage to the tyres. By law the minimum tread depth is 1 mm for at least three-quarters of the tread's width all round the tyre. When topping up the battery, if distilled water is not available, the water obtained when defrosting a refrigerator will be suitable. Also, at least once a week, or before a long journey make a complete check to make sure all lights and the horn are working. Test all controls for correct operation and make sure all glasses are clean.

13:4 Initial 600 mile or first month service

This inspection is only necessary on new or exchange equipment or after a repair or adjustment, when the manufacturer recommends a follow-up check. This then is not a regular service interval and so the items listed will only be attended to if they have been exchanged or repaired.

With the engine at normal operating temperature drain the engine oil, renew the filter and refill with suitable oil.
Check/top up rear axle.
Check/top up gearbox or automatic transmission.
Check valve clearances.
Loosen cylinder head bolts and retighten to the correct torque.
Any other check required after a repair is mentioned in the appropriate chapter.

13:5 5,000 mile or 6 month maintenance schedule

Drain the engine oil, renew the filter and refill with suitable oil.
Check and adjust valve clearances.
Check and adjust sparking plugs.
Check and adjust ignition timing and dwell angle.
Clean the distributor, inside and out, coil and HT leads.
Check the condition of the contact breaker points.
Check and clean air filter element.
Check engine idle speed and exhaust emission.
Check/top up brake and clutch fluid reservoirs.
Check/top up battery electrolyte and clean terminals.
Check/top up cooling system.
Top up washer reservoirs and adjust jets.
Check and adjust drive belt tension.
Check all hoses and pipes for damage or wear.
Check steering box and top up if necessary.
Check steering for excessive play.
Inspect brakes for friction lining wear. Renew if they are unlikely to last until the next service.
Check/top up gearbox or automatic transmission.
Check/top up rear axle.
Oil or grease all lubrication points.
Check handbrake cable.
Inspect all brake pipes and hoses for damage or corrosion.
Check dampers for leakage.
Check tightness of all underbody fixings.
Check tightness of road wheel nuts.
Test all lights and controls.
Oil all hinges and locks.
Check wiper blades and seat belts.

13:6 10,000 mile or annual maintenance schedule

At this service all the items previously listed should be carried out together with the following items.
Renew the sparking plugs
Renew the contact breaker points and lubricate distributor.
Drain brake fluid, fill with new fluid and bleed the system.
Renew the brake servo filter and silencer.
Renew the air cleaner element.
Lubricate water pump shaft at nipple, if fitted.
Lubricate all control linkages.
Check front wheel alignment.
Examine wheel bearings for wear or adjustment.
Examine exhaust system and ensure all connections are tight.
Check propeller shaft joints, bearings and rubber couplings.
Check and adjust clutch.

After each service the car should be thoroughly checked then carefully road tested.

13:7 Every 2nd & 4th year maintenance schedule

Items listed in this section should be attended to at the appropriate service times.

Every two years – drain and renew the coolant in the cooling system. Drain and renew the oil in the gearbox or automatic transmission and in the rear axle. renew the fuel filter and check the clutch for wear, renew driven disc if necessary.

Every four years – completely overhaul the braking system, renewing any pipes or hoses that show signs of deterioration or corrosion. Examine wheel bearings carefully and fit new bearings where necessary. The camshaft drive chain should be renewed at this time.

CHAPTER 14

CAPACITIES, DIMENSIONS & TORQUE SETTINGS

14 : 1 Capacities
14 : 2 Dimensions
14 : 3 Torque settings

14 : 1 Capacities

Engine	7 pints
With filter	7.44 pints
Gearbox :	
Manual, 4-speed	1.8 pints
Manual, 5-speed	2.5 pints
Automatic	8.2 pints
With cooler	9.4 pints
Fluid change approximately	3.1 pints
Final drive :	
Short neck :	
2000	2.8 pints
2002	1.7 pints
Long neck	1.6 pints
Fuel tank :	
2000	12.1 gallons
2002 :	
Early	10.1 gallons
Late	11 gallons
Cooling system, including heater	12.3 pints

14 : 2 Dimensions

Overall length :	
2002	166.5
2000, 2000CA, 2000TI, 2000 TI Lux	177.2
2000CS, 2000CA	179.3
Overall width :	
2002	62.6
2000, 2000A, 2000TI, 2000 TI Lux	67.3
2000CS, 2000CA	65.9
Overall height :	
2002	55.5
2000, 2000A, 2000TI, 2000 TI Lux	55.9
2000CS, 2000CA	53.5
Ground clearance :	
2002	6.3
All other models	5.5
Track :	
Front :	
2000	52.36/53.07
2002	52.76/52.36
Rear :	
2000	52.36/53.07
2002	54.57/54.17
Wheel base :	
2000	100.4
2002	98.43
Permitted trailer load :	
Unbraked	1100 lb
Braked	2645 lb
Automatic transmission	1760 lb
Automatic transmission with oil cooler	2645 lb

14:3 Torque settings in lb ft

Engine:
- Cylinder head (in three stages) .. 1st, 25/33; 2nd, 43/47; 3rd, 49/52
- Big-end bearings .. 38/41
- Main bearings .. 42/46
- Flywheel .. 72/83
- Clutch to flywheel .. 16/17.4
- Crankshaft pulley .. 101/108
- Rocker cover .. 6.5/8
- Timing cover .. 6.5/8
- Sump .. 6.5/8
- Exhaust manifold .. 22/24
- Sparking plugs .. 18/22
- Engine mounting bracket .. 34/37
- Engine mounting .. 18.1/19.5

Gearbox, manual:
- Gearbox to engine .. M8 bolts, 18.1/19.5; M10 bolts, 34/37

Output shaft flange:	2000	2002
Four-speed	159	72.3
Five-speed	72.3	72.3

- Clutch guide sleeve .. 18

Automatic:
- Drive plate to crankshaft .. 72
- Converter to drive plate .. 14
- Output shaft flange .. 86.7

Rear axle:
- Pinion flange/three-arm flange .. 108
- Pinion bearing stop nut (long neck type) .. 289 maximum
- Large housing cover .. 31
- Side cover .. 15
- Crownwheel to differential carrier .. 61
- Halfshaft to axle/rear hub .. 22
- Rear hub nut .. 217; with Tonifer spacer 289

Front suspension:
- Spring/shock absorber unit, top centre .. 52
- Spring/shock absorber unit, support bearing .. 18.1
- Tie rod arm-to-kingpin .. 18.1
- Tie rod arm-to-guide joint .. 43
- Front crossmember to engine crossmember .. 34
- Wishbone-to-front crossmember .. 123/137 (previously 108)
- Tension strut at wishbone/front crossmember .. 43.4

Steering:
- Steering wheel nut:
  - M12 .. 40
  - M14 .. 60
- Joint disc mounting .. 14
- Flange joint mounting .. 18.1
- Drop arm-to-steering box .. 80/94
- Tie rod nuts .. 25.3
- Steering box-to-front crossmember .. 34
- Drop arm bearing .. 18.1
- Track rod clamp bolts .. 8.8/11

Rear suspension:
- Shock absorber upper mounting .. 11
- Shock absorber lower mounting .. 35
- Trailing arms on axle carrier .. 54
- Rear axle carrier rubber mountings .. 21.7
- Rubber couplings .. 32.5
- Compression strut-to-body floor .. 18.1
- Axle carrier-to-body floor .. 86.8
- Final drive-to-axle carrier .. 65.1
- Axle casing-to-body floor .. 65.1

Brakes:
- Brake disc-to-front hub .. 43/48
- Caliper-to-kingpin .. 58/69

Wheels:
- Wheel nuts .. 59/65

AUTOBOOKS WORKSHOP MANUALS

ALFA ROMEO GIULIA 1300, 1600, 1750, 2000 1962-1978 WSM
BMW 1600 1966-1973 WSM
BMW 2500, 2800, 3.0 & 3.3 1968-1977 WSM
BMW 316, 320, 320i 1975-1977 WSM
BMW 518, 520, 520i 1973-1981 WSM
FIAT 1100, 1100D, 1100R & 1200 1957-1969 WSM
FIAT 124 1966-1974 WSM
FIAT 124 SPORT 1966-1975 WSM
FIAT 125 & 125 SPECIAL 1967-1973 WSM
FIAT 126, 126L, 126 DV, 126/650 & 126/650 DV 1972-1982 WSM
FIAT 127 SALOON, SPECIAL & SPORT, 900, 1050 1971-1981 WSM
FIAT 128 1969-1982 WSM
FIAT 1300, 1500 1961-1967 WSM
FIAT 131 MIRAFIORI 1975-1982 WSM
FIAT 132 1972-1982 WSM
FIAT 500 1957-1973 WSM
FIAT 600, 600D & MULTIPLA 1955-1969 WSM
FIAT 850 1964-1972 WSM
JAGUAR MK 1, 2 1955-1969 WSM
JAGUAR S TYPE, 420 1963-1968 WSM
JAGUAR XK 120, 140, 150 MK 7, 8, 9 1948-1961 WSM
LAND ROVER 1, 2 1948-1961 WSM
MERCEDES-BENZ 190 1959-1968 WSM
MERCEDES-BENZ 220/8 1968-1972 WSM
MERCEDES-BENZ 220B 1959-1965 WSM
MERCEDES-BENZ 230 1963-1968 WSM
MERCEDES-BENZ 250 1968-1972 WSM
MERCEDES-BENZ 280 1968-1972 WSM
MINI 1959-1980 WSM
MORRIS MINOR 1952-1971 WSM
PEUGEOT 404 1960-1975 WSM
PORSCHE 911 1964-1973 WSM
PORSCHE 911 1970-1977 WSM
RENAULT 16 1965-1979 WSM
RENAULT 8, 10, 1100 1962-1971 WSM
ROVER 3500, 3500S 1968-1976 WSM
SUNBEAM RAPIER, ALPINE 1955-1965 WSM
TRIUMPH SPITFIRE, GT6, VITESSE 1962-1968 WSM
TRIUMPH TR4, TR4A 1961-1967 WSM
VOLKSWAGEN BEETLE 1968-1977 WSM

VELOCEPRESS AUTOMOBILE BOOKS & MANUALS

ABARTH BUYERS GUIDE
AUSTIN-HEALEY 6-CYLINDER WSM
AUSTIN-HEALEY SPRITE & MG MIDGET 1958-1971 WSM
BMW 600 LIMOUSINE FACTORY WSM
BMW 600 LIMOUSINE OWNERS HAND BOOK & SERVICE MANUAL
BMW 2000 & 2002 1966-1976 WSM
BMW ISETTA FACTORY WSM
BOOK OF THE CARRERA PANAMERICANA - MEXICAN ROAD RACE
COMPLETE CATALOG OF JAPANESE MOTOR VEHICLES
CORVAIR 1960-1969 OWNERS WORKSHOP MANUAL
CORVETTE V8 1955-1962 OWNERS WORKSHOP MANUAL
DIALED IN - THE JAN OPPERMAN STORY
FERRARI 250/GT SERVICE AND MAINTENANCE
FERRARI 308 SERIES BUYER'S AND OWNER'S GUIDE
FERRARI BERLINETTA LUSSO
FERRARI BROCHURES AND SALES LITERATURE 1946-1967
FERRARI BROCHURES AND SALES LITERATURE 1968-1989
FERRARI GUIDE TO PERFORMANCE
FERRARI OPP, MAINTENANCE & SERVICE H/BOOKS 1948-1963
FERRARI OWNER'S HANDBOOK
FERRARI SERIAL NUMBERS PART I - ODD NUMBERS TO 21399
FERRARI SERIAL NUMBERS PART II - EVEN NUMBERS TO 1050
FERRARI SPYDER CALIFORNIA
FERRARI TUNING TIPS & MAINTENANCE TECHNIQUES
HENRY'S FABULOUS MODEL "A" FORD
HOW TO BUILD A FIBERGLASS CAR
HOW TO BUILD A RACING CAR
HOW TO RESTORE THE MODEL 'A' FORD
IF HEMINGWAY HAD WRITTEN A RACING NOVEL
JAGUAR E-TYPE 3.8 & 4.2 WSM
LE MANS 24 (THE BOOK THAT THE FILM WAS BASED ON)
MASERATI BROCHURES AND SALES LITERATURE
MASERATI OWNER'S HANDBOOK
METROPOLITAN FACTORY WSM
MGA & MGB OWNERS HANDBOOK & WSM
MG MIDGET TC, TD, TF & TF1500 WORKSHOP MANUAL
OBERT'S FIAT GUIDE
PERFORMANCE TUNING THE SUNBEAM TIGER
PORSCHE 356 1948-1965 WSM
PORSCHE 912 WSM
SOUPING THE VOLKSWAGEN
SOLEX CARBURETORS (EMPHASIS ON UK & EU AUTOMOBILES)
SU CARBURETORS (EMPHASIS ON UK AUTOMOBILES)
TRIUMPH TR2, TR3, TR4 1953-1965 WSM
TUNING FOR SPEED (P.E. IRVING)
VEDA ORR'S NEW REVISED HOT ROD PICTORIAL
VOLKSWAGEN TRANSPORTER, TRUCKS, STATION WAGONS WSM
VOLVO 1944-1968 ALL MODELS WSM
WEBER CARBURETORS (EMPHASIS ON ALFA & FIAT)

BROOKLANDS BOOKS & ROAD TEST PORTFOLIOS (RTP)

AC CARS 1904-2009
ALFA ROMEO 1920-1933 ROAD TEST PORTFOLIO
ALFA ROMEO 1934-1940 ROAD TEST PORTFOLIO
BRABHAM RALT HONDA THE RON TAURANAC STORY
BUGATTI TYPE 10 TO TYPE 40 ROAD TEST PORTFOLIO
BUGATTI TYPE 10 TO TYPE 251 ROAD TEST PORTFOLIO
BUGATTI TYPE 41 TO TYPE 55 ROAD TEST PORTFOLIO
BUGATTI TYPE 57 TO TYPE 251 ROAD TEST PORTFOLIO
DELAHAYE ROAD TEST PORTFOLIO
FERRARI ROAD CARS 1946-1956 ROAD TEST PORTFOLIO
FIAT 500 1936-1972 ROAD TEST PORTFOLIO
FIAT DINO ROAD TEST PORTFOLIO
HISPANO SUIZA ROAD TEST PORTFOLIO
HONDA ST1100/ST1300 PAN EUROPEAN 1990-2002 RTP
JAGUAR MK1 & MK2 ROAD TEST PORTFOLIO
LOTUS CORTINA ROAD TEST PORTFOLIO
MV AGUSTA F4 750 & 1000 1997-2007 ROAD TEST PORTFOLIO
TATRA CARS ROAD TEST PORTFOLIO

VELOCEPRESS MOTORCYCLE BOOKS & MANUALS

AJS SINGLES & TWINS 250cc THRU 1000cc 1932-1948 (BOOK OF)
AJS SINGLES 1955-65 350cc & 500cc (BOOK OF)
AJS SINGLES 1945-60 350cc & 500cc MODELS 16 & 18 (BOOK OF)
ARIEL 1939-1960 4 STROKE SINGLES (BOOK OF)
ARIEL LEADER & ARROW 1958-1964 (BOOK OF)
ARIEL MOTORCYCLES 1933-1951 WSM
ARIEL PREWAR MODELS 1932-1939 (BOOK OF)
BMW M/CYCLES R26 R27 (1956-1967) FACTORY WSM
BMW M/CYCLES R50 R50S R60 R69S (1955-1969) FACTORY WSM
BSA BANTAM (BOOK OF)
BSA ALL FOUR-STROKE SINGLES & V-TWINS 1936-1952 (BOOK OF)
BSA OHV & SV SINGLES - 250cc 1954-1970 (BOOK OF)
BSA OHV & SV SINGLES 1945-54 250-600cc (BOOK OF)
BSA OHV SINGLES 350 & 500cc 1955-1967 (BOOK OF)
BSA PRE-WAR MODELS TO 1939 (BOOK OF)
BSA TWINS 1948-1962 (BOOK OF)
BSA TWINS 1962-1969 (SECOND BOOK OF)
CATALOG OF BRITISH MOTORCYCLES (1951 MODELS)
DOUGLAS PRE-WAR ALL MODELS 1929-1939 (BOOK OF)
DOUGLAS POST-WAR ALL MODELS 1948-1957 FACTORY WSM
DUCATI 160cc, 250cc & 350cc OHC MODELS FACTORY WSM
HONDA 50 ALL MODELS UP TO 1970 INC MONKEY & TRAIL (BOOK OF)
HONDA 90 ALL MODELS UP TO 1966 (BOOK OF)
HONDA MOTORCYCLES 125-150 TWINS C/CS/CB/CA WSM
HONDA MOTORCYCLES 250-305 TWINS C/CS/CB WSM
HONDA MOTORCYCLES C100 SUPER CUB WSM
HONDA MOTORCYCLES C110 SPORT CUB 1962-1969 WSM
HONDA TWINS & SINGLES 50cc THRU 305cc 1960-1966 (BOOK OF)
HONDA TWINS ALL MODELS 125cc THRU 450cc UP TO 1968 (BOOK OF)
INDIAN PONYBIKE, BOY RACER & PAPOOSE ILL PARTS LIST & SALES LIT
J.A.P. ENGINES 1927-1952 & MOTORCYCLES 1934-1952 (BOOK OF)
LAMBRETTA ALL 125 & 150cc MODELS 1947-1957 (BOOK OF)
LAMBRETTA LI & TV MODELS 1957-1970 (SECOND BOOK OF)
MATCHLESS 350 & 500cc SINGLES 1945-1956 (BOOK OF)
MATCHLESS 350 & 500cc SINGLES 1955-1966 (BOOK OF)
MOTORCYCLE ENGINEERING (P. E. IRVING)
NORTON 1932-1947 (BOOK OF)
NORTON 1938-1956 (BOOK OF)
NORTON DOMINATOR TWINS 1955-1965 (BOOK OF)
NORTON MODELS 19, 50 & ES2 1955-1963 (BOOK OF)
NORTON MOTORCYCLES 1957-1970 FACTORY WSM
NORTON PREWAR MODELS 1932-1939 (BOOK OF)
NSU PRIMA ALL MODELS 1956-1964 (BOOK OF)
NSU QUICKLY ALL MODELS 1953-1963 (BOOK OF)
RALEIGH MOPEDS 1960-1969 (BOOK OF)
ROYAL ENFIELD SINGLES & V TWINS 1934-1946 (BOOK OF)
ROYAL ENFIELD SINGLES & V TWINS 1937-1953 (BOOK OF)
ROYAL ENFIELD SINGLES 1946-1962 (BOOK OF)
ROYAL ENFIELD 736cc INTERCEPTOR FACTORY WSM
ROYAL ENFIELD 250cc & 350cc SINGLES 1958-1966 (SECOND BOOK OF)
SPEED AND HOW TO OBTAIN IT
SUNBEAM MOTORCYCLES 1928-1939 (BOOK OF)
SUNBEAM S7 & S8 1946-1957 (BOOK OF)
SUZUKI 50cc & 80cc UP TO 1966 (BOOK OF)
SUZUKI T10 1963-1967 FACTORY WSM
SUZUKI T20 & T200 1965-1969 FACTORY WSM
TRIUMPH PRE-WAR MOTORCYCLE 1935-1939 (BOOK OF)
TRIUMPH MOTORCYCLES 1935-1949 (BOOK OF)
TRIUMPH MOTORCYCLES 1937-1951 WSM
TRIUMPH MOTORCYCLES 1945-1955 FACTORY WSM
TRIUMPH TWINS 1945-1958 (BOOK OF)
TRIUMPH TWINS 1956-1969 (BOOK OF)
VELOCETTE ALL SINGLES & TWINS 1925-1970 (BOOK OF)
VESPA 1951-1961 (BOOK OF)
VESPA 125 & 150cc & GS MODELS 1955-1963 (SECOND BOOK OF)
VESPA 90, 125 & 150cc 1963-1972 (THIRD BOOK OF)
VESPA GS & SS 1955-1968 (BOOK OF)
VILLIERS ENGINE (BOOK OF)
VINCENT MOTORCYCLES 1935-1955 WSM

PLEASE VISIT OUR WEBSITE
www.VelocePress.com
**FOR A DETAILED DESCRIPTION
OF ANY OF THESE TITLES**

Please check our website:

www.VelocePress.com

for a complete
up-to-date list of
available titles

www.ingramcontent.com/pod-product-compliance
Lightning Source LLC
Chambersburg PA
CBHW060253240426
43673CB00047B/1916